Slow Boat to Panamá: México to the Galápagos Islands and Panamá

Book 4 of the *Naked Canadian Cruising Series*

©Copyright 2018, Andrew W. Gunson

Published by Andrew W. Gunson

Globe & Sextant Publishing
a division of AJ'S Industries
Nanaimo B.C. Canada

This book is available in print and eBook format.

ISBN-13:978-1720956181

ISBN-10:1720956189

Other titles by this author.

Voyage of the *Maiatla* with the Naked Canadian:
One Family's Mexican Odyssey
COPYRIGHT 2004, Second Edition 2012 Andrew W. Gunson.

The Tahiti Syndrome Hawaiian Style.
First Edition COPYRIGHT 2012 Andrew W. Gunson

A Slow Boat to Panamá.
Canada to Costa Rica.
First Edition COPYRIGHT 2018 Andrew W. Gunson

Dedication

For Janet, my mate and love of my life who without her support and love this great adventure would not have been possible. This book is also dedicated to Thomas and Melissa, our childern and crew. With a special dedication to Damien, Savannah and Allyssa, our granchildern and next generation of adventurers.

Photography credits.   Special thanks to all that contributed photographs for this volume. Janet Gunson, Marina Sacht, Nick Longo, Melissa Gunson, Thomas Gunson, Mark Taylor, Teri Taylor, Kara Erickson, Ashley Skender.

Slow Boat to Panamá:

*México to the Galápagos Islands
and Panamá*

ANDREW W. GUNSON

Table of Contents

Prologue

Voyaging around the world has long been a dream, or as some who know me well would say, a passion of mine. Fortunately, my life's partner of over 30 years has shared my cruising aspiration for all of our time together. Perhaps not as enthusiastic as I, Janet has been at my side the entire time nonetheless—if not literally, spiritually. As a result, we have been cruising and living aboard on and off for the better part of our lives together.

In 2012, the netherworld—urban civilized life and a grueling work schedule—had me worn down and wound so tight I felt as if I could snap. It had been a full five years since our return from our four-month voyage through the Hawaiian archipelago, and I desperately needed to bust free and cast off our mooring lines, to head for the high seas once again. I had enough of the twisted whirling netherworld, and it was time to get off the dock and go.

Our most recent voyage commenced in October of 2012, which saw us departing Vancouver, Canada, bound southward along the Washington, Oregon and California coasts. Over the subsequent three years, we ventured further south on a quest, visiting México, Guatemala, El Salvador, Nicaragua and then Costa Rica. After a disastrous run-in with corrupt customs officials, my arm in a sling and a damaged boat with faulty steering, we fled Costa Rica during a gale to run 805 kilometres (500 miles) north up the coast, reaching the safety of Chiapas, México.

Marina Chiapas, on the Méxican-Guatemalan border, was familiar to us, so it was a great place to lick our wounds and refit, but only after a visit home for the summer. *Maiatla* waited patiently for our return, to take up where we left off, to continue onward to Panamá and then hopefully the Caribbean Sea. The following is the tale of the continuation of this voyage, our fourth season exploring Central America and book number four of the Naked Canadian Cruising Series—*Slow Boat to Panamá: México to the Galápagos Islands and Panamá*, a journey which would prove our most thrilling voyage to date.

Andrew W. Gunson, SV *Maiatla II*

Voyage of the Maiatla II

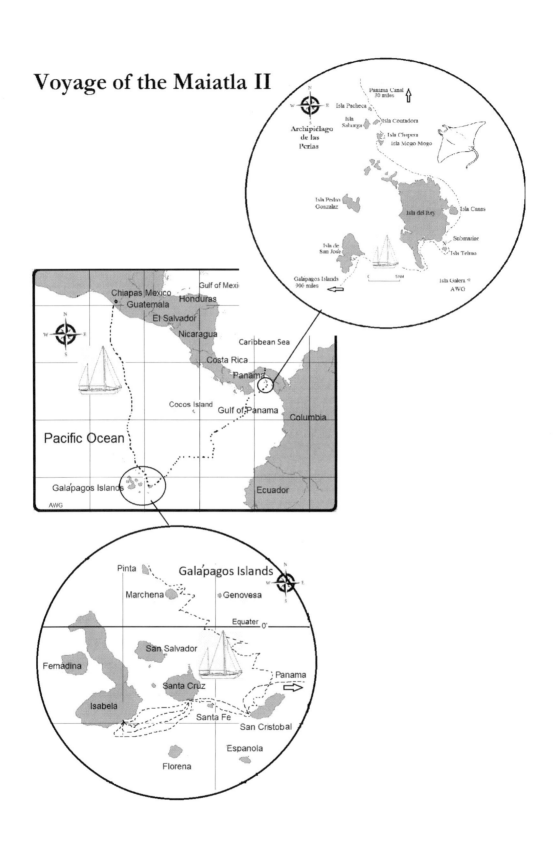

Chapter 1

Preparation for Departure and the Crew Conundrum

*"The use of travelling is to regulate imagination with reality, and instead
of thinking of how things may be, see them as they are."*
—Samuel Johnson

December the 3rd, I found myself and Mark Taylor winging our way back to Chiapas, México to clean up *Maiatla* and prepare her for another offshore voyage. Mark is an old friend and veteran sailor, who has voyaged with me before, once from Vancouver to San Francisco and again from México all the way back to Canada via the old clipper ship route—an epic voyage for the crew of the *Maiatla,* entailing 34 days at sea, 12 of which we were pummelled by hurricane Alma. I was glad to have Mark along for our latest expedition that, just six short months ago, was a far off wish. A "someday" thought that may never happen. "Someday we will sail to the Never Never Land of honey and endless beers." However, here we were preparing to sail to, of all places, the enchanted Galápagos Islands of Ecuador.

The Galápagos is an island archipelago straddling the equator some 965 kilometres (600 miles) west of the coast of mainland Ecuador. The Islands are famous for smoking volcanoes, giant marine iguanas, penguins, precocious sea lions, massive tortoises and, of course, boobies (the winged variety not the ones often found in bikini tops).

I was numb at the thought, as it was a diversion from our original plan of sailing south along the coast all the way to Panamá. It would mean we would be taking a 1609-kilometre (1000-mile) detour out to sea to reach the islands and then sail east-northeast another 1609 kilometres (1000 miles) to sail back to the continent and the Panamá Canal. It was by far the most aggressive winter cruise we had planned since departing Canada some three years previous. I was nervous, not that I had any reservations regarding the offshore voyage itself, but for Janet having issues with back and hip pain, which the motion of the boat continually irritated.

The decision to sail to the Galápagos Islands was born out of Janet's demands and emphatic statement that she, or we, was never going back to see Costa Rica, their customs agents or those nasty Papagayo winds ever again. After being threatened with jail and having our boat seized in Costa Rica, who could blame her. As a result, I was desperately searching for ways to sail to Panamá that didn't include hitting that place that should remain nameless, and the answer lay with going offshore, far offshore, to keep us well beyond the reach of corrupt customs officials and out of the grip of the fierce Papagayo winds that plague the coast. Going offshore was a win-win.

When plotting our offshore course to Panamá, I found myself passing enticingly close to the isolated Isla Cocos, which is renowned for its pristine beauty and hammerhead shark population. I would have given anything to stop and dive, except there were two problems. One, you needed a special permit to visit, as there were park rangers that made sure you had one, and second, the only place you could get a permit was in Costa Rica, as the islands belonged to them. So I had to scrap that idea. Cocos Island has long been a stopping and resting spot for cruisers bound for the South Pacific, but recent changes to Costa Rica's customs practices have made the islands more difficult to reach and enjoy. Aside from the hefty park permit fee that was now demanded, a vessel could not clear into or out of Costa Rica from Cocos. So if you want to visit the islands, you first must stop on the mainland, which lies some 563 kilometres (350 miles) to the east, clear into the country, pay for your permit and then sail out to the islands. This in itself is not the problem; the problem arises when it's time to move on, because that requires a vessel to sail back to the mainland to clear customs to leave the country. A massive backtrack if you want to go anywhere other than Costa Rica.

While I was scanning the charts, hoping to find some other nearby islands with similar attributes as the Cocos, I spied a group of islands some 644 kilometres (400 miles) further southwest, the Galápagos Islands—not exactly in the neighbourhood, but still close enough to give them a harder look. After formulating a plan, I pitched the idea to Janet, and surprisingly, she agreed. I believe she would have agreed to any routing that did not include Costa Rica. Janet was happy we would bypass our infamous customs agent; however, she wasn't looking forward to a two-week passage to the islands, so I suggested she hang back and fly once we arrived there. Janet considered her back and reluctantly agreed it would be the best option for her. I also convinced Mark this could be a good trip to get his wife, Teri, some offshore experience and suggested that she could fly down with Janet, keeping her company and, for a month, explore the islands with us.

Teri also agreed, but not without a measurable amount of resistance at first. It was settled. The voyage from México to the Galápagos Islands and then to Panamá was now on, and the crew was rapidly filling out. Mark and I began to ready the boat to sail to perhaps the world's most famous of archipelagos.

The previous year, I had hired a local tour operator, Arturo of Macaw Tours, to take care of *Maiatla* while she was in Chiapas. Aside from having a couple of new rope chafe marks on the hull, she fared well. Arturo had hired a cleaning lady in an effort to keep ahead of any mould that had been such a problem for us the previous year.

Mark and I were loaded down with five heavy bags of gear and new boat parts, which I was eager to get at installing—most of all, a new radar system. It was a cramped, although short, taxi ride from Tapachula International Airport to the marina where we poured ourselves out of the car, and I do mean pour, as the scorching heat was already taking its toll on these two Canadian boys. We were eager to get out of our blue jeans and into t-shirts and shorts. Sliding the hatch back on *Maiatla*'s cabin top, I stuck my head inside the boat and gave a deep sniff.

"What are you doing?" Mark asked as he tossed the bags from the dock into the cockpit.

"Mould, bud, just checking for mould!"

I was also checking to see if the boat still stunk like rotting meat. As Mark and I unloaded the bags, I told him the pork chop story.

The previous month, I had flown down to the boat by myself to check on the old girl and to work on the hydraulic steering, which I needed to fix if we ever hoped to go anywhere. Well, on that trip, I pushed the hatch back and not only did the musty stank of mould waft by my nose, but the unmistakable stench of a rotting corpse smacked me square between the eyes. Taking shallow breaths, I ventured below to investigate while fully expecting to find some homeless fellow or crocodile that crawled into a bunk and died.

My rebelling nose led me into the port side walk-through cabin, the one my son, Thomas, occupied as a child. With eyes watering from the stench and sweat tricking down my forehead, I found myself halting at the closed freezer door, which occupied the space under the single berth. This was the epicentre of the stench and the sight of the suspected putrefaction. Hesitantly, I reached for the silver handle and gave it a sharp jerk. As the door flew open, aside from releasing a bacterium-laced haze that, with little effort, could have easily been weaponized, the swinging door initiated a mass exodus of what must have been a prime collection of México's insect population. If it walked, crawled, slithered, slimed or had antenna and flew, it was represented here. It was the icky underside of Central America, and I had disturbed it, err or them. Thousands of them!

Well, mystery solved. Apparently when we cleaned the boat to leave her the previous season, someone, who shall remain nameless, forgot to give away the five kilograms of pork chops left in the freezer. One can only imagine the transformation flesh undergoes when left in a nearly airtight container in 40 degrees Celsius (104 degrees Fahrenheit) heat for six months.

Choking back the dry heaves, I bolted topside for some fresh air and to regroup. Once the retching stopped and my testicles dropped back down to where they belonged, I wiped the saliva streamers from my lips and tears from my eyes, then ventured back down below. The cleaning was about as hideous of an operation as one could imagine. I stripped off naked, retrieved an elbow-length rubber glove and garbage bag from under the galley sink and grabbed a tea towel from a drawer. I went to the head where I splashed puddles of aftershave onto the towel, wrapped it around my face and braved the tight corridor once more. Kneeling in front of the tiny door, I reached in to rake out the gelatin mass that quivered with a life of its own. To make matters worse the wingless variety of the insect hoard panicked and fled for the freedom provided by the open door. Unfortunately, most of the spooked critters with legs discovered a convenient path provided by my outstretched arm. As I raked, bugs crawled up my arm in search of a new hiding place, which they found close by, my armpit and head hair being a particularly enticing to them.

After a few long minutes, I couldn't stand it anymore. The creepy crawlers had by then invaded my person, every crack and crevice, so in response I shot out of the room to the head where I jumped into the shower and turned on the water.

"Ah crap! No water!" I forgot to turn on the pump. Three hours and perhaps four showers later, I had the freezer gutted and ready for a new liner, which was required because the stench had penetrated all the surfaces of the freezer. The following day the boat was fumigated, and the day after that, the liner reinstalled.

Mark and I only had six days to make the boat ready before the crew and my friend, Marina, and brand new crew member Nick arrived, and I wanted to leave port as soon as possible, hopefully hours after their arrival. Marina's tight schedule had delayed us, so we would only have 11 days to get *Maiatla* to the Galápagos, as that's when Janet and Mark's wife, Teri, were due to fly in. If all went well, the voyage should only take us seven or eight days. As time will tell, we would not be that fortunate.

On top of our tight schedule, the weather wasn't looking to help us; a calm stretched from Chiapas, south for over 644 kilometres (400 miles). It was beginning to look more like a motoring trip. Not the best prospect, as we would burn a sizeable portion of our fuel, but at least we would be able to clock off some fast miles.

Our short week at the marina in Chiapas flew by as we worked long days inside and out of the boat, whipping her back into shape. Mounting the radar, along with the rebuilt hydraulic ram for the steering, was a highlight for me. We also hauled the boat out of the water and painted the bottom—a requirement for us to visit the Galápagos Islands.

The battery charger had gone berserk the previous year and fried the almost brand new and expensive gel cell batteries. I couldn't find replacement gel cells in the city of Tapachula, and there wasn't time to order them, so three large 8D batteries would have to do for the house-bank. The house-bank is located down in the 1-metre (3.2-feet) deep pit and 2 metres (6.5 feet) forward and on the opposite side of the new air-conditioning unit. A spot as deep in the bowels of the boat and inaccessible as you can imagine. While lying on my side, with great care, I was able to drag the old 150 pound batteries, one at a time, out past the AC unit and then over top of the delicate, copper water and fuel lines with associated valves. Using a block and tackle secured to the boom above the open companionway, I managed to lift the batteries out of the boat. Sounds like it was easy, right? To make matters worse, while walking on deck, I stubbed my shoeless right foot on a deck cleat. After cursing the air blue through clenched teeth, I hobbled back to the aft deck to show it to my paramedic crewmate; Mark had a look at it.

"Mark, I think I broke my little toe! Stubbed the crap out of it on a cleat."

Mark took one look at the appendage that was already turning black and blue while throbbing so hard I thought it would explode at any moment, like a melon in a microwave.

"Yep, it looks broke!" he said.

"Well, it hurts like hell. Can you do something for it?" I asked while sitting cross-legged on the cabin top, with both hands clamped around my foot and sucking air through clenched teeth.

"Nope. Just put some ice on it and stay off of it," he said apathetically.

"That's it! You're practically a doctor, and that's all you got for me? Stay off of it!"

"I could tell you not to do that again, but I figured you knew that already!" he offered, with a smile.

I would spend the next few weeks limping about, and that toe would constantly remind me of its presence by catching itself on sail tracks and legs of salon chairs, me again cursing the air blue each time.

Perhaps the most frustrating moment of the week was when I installed the brand new Simrad apparent wind indicator at the top of the mast. It didn't work! I emailed the company, and after running diagnostic tests, they concluded it was the dial or gauge located in the cockpit that was malfunctioning. They sold me a new one, and I had Marina pick it up and bring it with her, along with an assortment of other forgotten parts. If all of the above wasn't enough, the freezer packed it in.

Apparently all my manhandling of the freezer holding plates created a refrigerant leak, so I purchased a 25mm-thick sheet of Styrofoam (1 inch) and used it to divide the top loading fridge in the galley in half. With the cold holding plates trapped on one side of the Styrofoam and the thermostat on the other and turned way down, I created a makeshift freezer compartment. Not big but large enough to keep our steaks frozen for the duration of the voyage. Just another breakdown in paradise.

By the time the rest of the crew arrived, we were almost ready to go. All we needed to tackle was the provisioning, both food and liquid refreshments. Late one night, I reinstalled the new Simrad wind indicator, the one Marina had brought with her, and too my horror, it too failed to work. This instrument, aside from telling us how hard the wind is blowing, displays the angle of the wind as it flows over the boat. The "apparent wind angle" aids us when setting the sails, maximizing the efficiency of the wind as it flows over the sleek sails. In truth, the boat can operate fine without this instrument, but it sure comes in handy at night when the mast and sails are invisible.

For me, the instrument is nice to have, but for the crew, it's critical. Over the years of sailing *Maiatla*, I've learned to "sense" the wind as it flows over the boat, and I can trim the sails by "feel" and sound alone, without having to see them day or night. My crew, and Marina in particular, were not so in tune with the boat and wind. I swear the best way for Marina to tell from which direction the wind was coming was to soak her with a pail of water and then have her stand on deck. Many times while chasing the wind, Marina had us going in complete circles. I knew that if she still had difficulty finding the wind after years of sailing on my boat and on her own parent's boat, Nick did not stand a chance. We were going to miss this instrument on this voyage.

Figure 1. *Maiatla* at Marina Chiapas getting her bottom painted in preparation for departure to the Galápagos Islands.

Marina once again was joining the crew, and as always, I was happy to have her along, as her unbridled exuberance always made things fun. Marina was also bringing Nick, her love interest of the past several years. I had reservations about Nick. This would be Marina's fourth voyage with Janet and I, and Nick had never shown any real interest in coming along before, so I wasn't sure what had changed for him to want to venture to sea now. What was his motivation? I did not know him well, and at first, I thought he was a bit pretentious, and as couples, Janet and I only spent a few evening together playing dominoes and shared a bottle of wine in the hot tub once. Nick was over 2-metres tall (6.5 feet), in his early sixties and, by all accounts, good looking and educated, as he was confident to speak on a variety of subjects. He was by profession a waiter at an upscale "Hideaway" restaurant called the Mahle House, in our hometown of Nanaimo, and an aspiring actor and talented musician. Not much to offer when sailing, survival skills and blind obedience are required. We do observe cocktail hour and sundowners, but it won't be brandy in a snifter. Instead, beverages are served in aluminum cans full of sudsing Tecate beer. I was content to make this passage with only the three of us. However, Marina pleaded her case to me one evening at my home, weeks before.

"Andy, Nick and I seem to be growing apart, and if Nick can come along on this voyage, I know it will make or break us as a couple."

After some thought, I agreed, but with the understanding that they would do their watches together and that I had no expectations of Nick. He was along for the ride, as far as I was concerned, and if he became troublesome, she was to handle it. I hoped I hadn't brought aboard trouble. What if they had a knock down drag fight out at sea? Things could become ugly fast, ruining the trip for the rest of us.

So for better or worse, we had a full crew, and it was time to set sail, leave México behind, and hopefully, the next time we enter Mexican waters, it will be far from the Pacific Ocean and on the Caribbean side.

Chapter 2

A Not So Congenial Cruiser! And Our Imminent Departure

"Every time I stand before a beautiful beach, its waves seem to whisper to me: If you choose the simple things and find joy in nature's simple treasures, life and living need not be so hard."
—Psyche Roxas-Mendoza

One of the things I enjoy when cruising is all the great and like-minded people we meet along the way—not only cruisers, but often marina staff and locals. At Marina Chiapas, the managers, Enrique and Memo, were terrific and helpful on so many levels. Rides into town and arranging propane or boat repairs were above and beyond. Memo drove us to all the locations required for our check-out: customs, immigration and then the Port Captain's office. That said, not all we meet along the way are so, let's say, agreeable. A few days before the crew arrived, I was out on the bowsprit changing a navigation light bulb when an older-looking gent walked down the dock past me.

"Good morning," I said. He stopped to give me a good once-over before replying.

"Morning. Just got back, eh?"

Well I was surprised to learn he was a fellow Canadian and a retired Royal Canadian Mounted Police or "horseman," as we affectionately call them back home, and this RCMP officer was from our stomping grounds of Vancouver. Mike was his name, and he informed me he and his wife had been cruising for 20 years and have sailed all over the world on their boat, *St. Badger*.

"Nice," I said.

He was eager to talk about his voyages. I was suitably impressed and thought I could get together with him and, over a beer, pick his brains a little and perhaps hear a good story or two. However, before I could suggest anything, he asked, "Where are you going?"

Without hesitation, I told him with some pride, "The Galápagos Islands." I think my chest actually puffed out with the words.

"What the hell you want to go there for?" It must have been a rhetorical question, because before I had a chance to answer, he again blurted out, "Too many rules and expensive as hell!"

His statement took me aback. Now with a clenched jaw, Mike stared back at me expectantly.

"Ah well, I've always wanted to visit there ever since I was a kid. I had read of Darwin and the *Voyage of the Beagle,* and the wildlife is supposed to be incredible," I offered confidently, as if that was all the justification I required.

"Total waste of money," he barked back. "You're crazy, there are better islands in the Indian Ocean in the Seychelles, and they are free to go to. But it's your money. I wouldn't do it," he added as he stepped to the edge of the dock, closing the gap between us.

Feeling like I was being challenged and needing to further justify the expense of our travels, I informed him of my book writing endeavors, which produced tax write-offs as well as some royalties. Then I added, "My crew arrives tomorrow, and one of them owns a magazine back in Canada. She has been writing a series of articles about our travels. The magazine is called *TAKE 5* from Vancouver Island. Ever hear of it?"

"Nope, can't say I have," Mike answered, with a look of derision on his face. "Must be a tiny local rag," he deduced.

I told him of Marina contacting the Ecuadorian tourist bureau to look for some of the perks they usually offer journalists in exchange for free advertising and publicity.

"Perks and tax write offs," Mike snorted while backing up, as if suddenly smelling something foul. "Asking for freebies is an insult to the country you're visiting, and if you have to get tax write offs and free shit to be out here, then perhaps you can't afford your boat and sailing. Best stay at home and pay your fair share."

I'm not so easily flustered, but this fellow was commencing to burrow under my skin. I could feel myself flush even under the hot morning sun as my skin began to tingle. Our present conversation was obviously a sore spot for him, so it was time to stop poking it and change the topic.

"Have you ever been to Costa Rica?" I asked, with some reluctance. The new subject compelled Mike to compose himself a little while again closing the gap between us.

"Yes, I have several times, and I hated it. I sail by as fast as I can whenever I'm on that coast."

Finally, common ground! I smiled as I explained about the troubles we had in Costa Rica the previous year while assuming he could relate. Well, I was dead wrong.

"Look here," Mike said as he pointed his wrinkled little finger at me. "You people need to understand that it is their country, and if a government official tells you to wait an hour or two while they watch soccer or eat breakfast, you just shut up and do it. You have no rights or privileges down here. People sail here demanding things and looking for deals and wanting to barter and Jew down the price of goods and marina docks. It's not right. And if they don't like it, they should stay home."

By the end of his latest tirade, Mike was now red in the face and vibrating with plumbs of froth forming in the corners of his mouth. I was relieved we were still separated by a metre of open water. By now I realized no matter what I said or did, in Mike's eyes I was wrong. I couldn't win any argument here, so I kept my mouth shut while I tried to find a polite way of leaving the vicinity.

However, I didn't have too. Mike took one long look back, with disgust in his eyes, while flapping his hands my way, as if to say he was through with me.

"This is upsetting me. I can't talk to you anymore," Mike spewed back before falling silent. I suspect his mounting frustrations caused his thoughts to blank, effectively ending our conversation. With that, he turned to march down the dock—the way that he had come.

Wow! I thought and I wished that I had pulled out my cell phone to record the event because I didn't think anyone would believe it.

Over the next couple of days, I attempted to mend the proverbial fence by greeting him with a friendly hello, which seldom triggered a response. I couldn't help wonder if I was the only one that set this guy off? Was he having a bad day or was he naturally an absolute opinionated asshole?

On our last morning at the marina, Marina and I were sitting in the air-conditioned office waiting for Memo to take us to see the Port Captain. As we talked, Mike walked in to sit between us at the round table and began scrolling through his phone. Not wanting to get into it while still appearing friendly with about as much cheer as I could muster, I enquired, "So how are you today, Mike?"

Mike sharply looked up from his phone, thought for a moment and then with a pinched expression and a tone oozing with sarcasm, he finally said, "Same as yesterday."

He then stared at me. I assume he was waiting for a reply he could jump on, but I didn't bite. Instead, I introduced him to Marina, who was sitting opposite him at the table. There was some small talk between them at first, and then Mike suddenly became alive, as his mind finally made a connection.

Reproachfully, Mike snapped, "Hey, you're that reporter that was looking for free stuff when you go to the Galápagos."

I could see Marina was suddenly taken aback by the fervour and abruptness of the statement, but she quickly corrected him. Marina retorted, with some authority, "I wasn't looking, as you say, for 'free stuff,' but some assistance from the tourist bureau of Ecuador so that I can write some articles."

I can usually hear a bus that is about to back over me, except this time I didn't hear the beeping. Mike pointed an accusing finger at me. "He said you want free crap."

Marina turned to shoot me a questioning look. I quickly excused myself, as I decided it would be much more pleasant to wait outside in the tropical sun and have my skin seared. So out the door I shot without as much as an "excuse me."

Watching through the window, I could see Marina and Mike going at it. What was being said I could well imagine. Not 10 minutes later, Marina emerged. She spit out the words, "What an asshole!"

I laughed. "I guess it's not just me who sets him off after all." For some strange reason, Mike irritated me, not unlike a nasty rash in a delicate place. Perhaps the first reason he bothered me was, in part, because I had trouble accepting that any cruiser could act in such a manner, as most are so easy-going and in love with life. Secondly, he was Canadian and a West Coaster, and I was ashamed we would have to claim him as one of our own.

I said to Marina, "I wonder if he was such a cynical S.O.B before he sailed away from home, or was it his experiences out here that made him this way?" I suspected the former, and it was most likely a huge factor in his early retirement from the RCMP.

"His poor wife!" Marina exclaimed. "Can you imagine living with that?"

I thought for a moment. "You know, I've never seen her. Maybe he's delusional and doesn't actually have one," I offered half-jokingly.

"Maybe she's chained up below. Who knows?" Marina suggested.

"Yes, maybe." I agreed it could be a real possibility. I will have to walk by his boat later to see if I can hear the manacles rattling.

By 2 p.m., we were standing outside of the Port Captain's office, which is located on the northern side of the harbour in the town of Madero. While waiting for the Port Captain to stamp our papers, Memo, spotting the pretty secretary, placed a hand over his heart, softened his expression and commenced flirting, a national pastime for bravado males in Latin America. Here, rampant machismo is a blight woman battle daily. The rest of us migrated outside to wait.

The captain's office is an impressive-looking block and whitewash building next to a red and white-striped light house that overlooks the huge breakwater to the west and the harbour to the east. The captain took his duties of watching over the port seriously, and from here, he could see all boat movements. No one moved in or out without his express and written permission. Marina noted dozens of 10-metre pangas of various descriptions in line upon the lawn. When Memo finally abandoned his flirtatious advances, he came out to give us our papers. Marina took the opportunity to query about the boats.

"Ah, these are boats that have been intercepted by the navy or found floating offshore," he said. "These are drug running boats that come from Colombia, running cocaine mostly."

"Oh?" Marina remarked. "And what do they do with the boats?"

"Ah, well, they are auctioned off every year. Often to other drug runners who take them further north!"

Dozens of boats sat there, some riddled with bullet holes. These were only a small part of the drug trade caught along this shore. As I looked upon the rows upon rows of boats, I was reminded that we would need to be extra cautious from here on, because we would be cutting straight through this high sea's drug smuggling highway, and assuming that any boat approaching us is simply an honest fisherman wanting to sell his catch could be deadly.

Back at the marina, we took the *Maiatla* over to the fuel dock, took on diesel and purchased a few kilos of prawns from the nearby fisherman's wharf. Then it was back to our own dock. Later that evening, taking the "*colectivo*" bus into town, we made one last provisions run to Wal-Mart, topping up on frozen meat and rum, then took a cab home.

It was 10 p.m. by the time we arrived back at the boat and midnight by the time we managed to stow everything. We were all exhausted, Mark and I in particular, as the heat and long week had been most gruelling. Still the crew was energized for the prospect of our imminent departure at first light, but unfortunately, I still had so much to do to make the boat ready for sea. It was well after 1 a.m. before I gave up and turned in.

I was awake and up even before the first rays of light streaked the eastern sky. I needed to complete a chore before the arrival of the navy and Port Captain. I needed to hide the shotgun and ammo in case the navy brought the gun-sniffing dog aboard. My concealment protocol had been effective in the past, defying visual detection as well as canine noses. Still, knowing we were going to be searched was always nerve racking.

The crew was still sound asleep, and I let them stay that way, at least for now. After making a cup of tea, I moved to sit in the cockpit for a few moments to collect my thoughts. It was a cool morning by local standards, mid 20 degrees Celsius (68 F), and a heavy dampness hung in the air. The nearby mangroves were abuzz with chirping frogs, and next to the boat, illuminated by the dock lights, schools of stinky mullets circled. Finishing my cup, I made a trip to the marina's office, taking my laptop with me to make one last post on Facebook and to send Janet a message saying we were about to get underway. No sooner had I finished a post than a car drove up and parked under a street lamp. Out stepped the Port Captain and his lieutenant, looking all dapper in their neatly pressed russet uniforms. It wasn't even 6 a.m. yet and still dark.

"Oh crap, he's early!" I said aloud. Quickly I made my way back to *Maiatla* and jumped aboard to roust the still sleeping crew. "Hey, everybody, Port Captain is here. Let's move. It's time to go!"

No one needed a second prodding. I knew we still had a bit of time because the captain would wait for the soldiers to show before he boarded us. Fifteen minutes later, we were all sitting around *Maiatla's* salon table as the captain and his assistant checked our passports one more time. Comparing the pictures to each of our faces, they wanted to make sure we left the country with all the people we claimed we had.

While the captain scanned my crew, a pair of baby-faced *marineros* stood a vigilant watch outside while shouldering some pretty impressive fire power, just in case we tried to make a run for it, I guess. Thankfully they left their dogs back at the base. I could only assume they were not worried about people who smuggle guns or drugs out of the country.

With the formalities over, the captain saluted me and shook my hand. I escorted him off the boat and breathed a sigh of relief. We were free to go, which in third world countries isn't always the case. The captain marched down the dock to another departing boat, shook the cruisers hand, then disappeared below.

"Okay, everybody, I will fire the engine up. Get the spring-lines aboard and make ready to cast off the bow and stern lines when I give the command," I ordered.

A chorus of cheers and hurrahs came from the crew as they hopped to it. A few minutes later, we were off the dock and headed down the narrow channel leading to the harbour.

It was a beautiful morning. The clouds in the east were a blood red from the rising sun, and the crimson sky nicely back-lit the crown of a distant volcano. Lined up along the water's edge, like honour guards saluting our departure, white egrets and herons stood poised, taking advantage of the morning light to go fishing. *Maiatla's* bow parted a school of juvenile bat rays as we overtook them. We weren't the only vessel out and about this early. Up ahead, ghosting across the tranquil waters, was a roughly hewn dugout canoe with two shirtless fishermen. One of the boatmen was standing erect in the bow, hurling a net, while the other sat in the stern, with paddle in hand, dipping it into the still waters. It was a grand morning indeed, and just when I thought we were clear of México, an agitated sounding voice, speaking Spanish, burst from the radio. I missed most of the call, but I clearly heard our boat name, and I recognized the word "*retorno!*" Return!

I suddenly had a flash back to Acapulco when the Port Captain ordered us back to the dock for what he believed was an unpaid bill. Quickly I did a mental check. I was sure I had covered all the bases—we were legal (shotgun not withstanding). I turned to look behind us, and there on the dock was the captain flanked with soldiers waving their arms at us to turn around.

"They want us back, guys. Coming about!" I said. The crew was still on deck, clearing away the dock lines and bumpers. "You better put those bumpers back over the side and rerun the fore and aft dock lines, please."

Marina, who was standing next to the cockpit coiling a line, turned and, looking concerned, asked, "What do they want? Did we forget something?"

"I don't know," I offered. "Maybe I misunderstood him, and I was supposed to wait."

For whatever the reason, they wanted us back and I suspected it couldn't be good. Not often is it when people with machine guns are yelling at you and ordering you to come to them. I again flashed back to the Nicaragua incident we had the previous year. As we approached the dock, the captain called through cupped hands, but I was not yet close enough, or my Spanish good enough, to understand. At that moment, a marina worker on an adjacent dock yelled in English, "He lost his radio!"

"Ah, I think I understand now," I said aloud, breathing a sigh of relief. "Marina, go below and see if the Port Captain left his hand-held radio on the table!" I ordered. Seconds later, Marina emerged holding in her hand the captain's radio. I slowed the boat only enough to hand off the radio to a grateful captain, who smiled and waved. Turning around, we headed back out to sea for the second time that morning. Finally,

we were free to go and carry on with the voyage we had commenced back in 2012—
a time that felt like a lifetime ago.

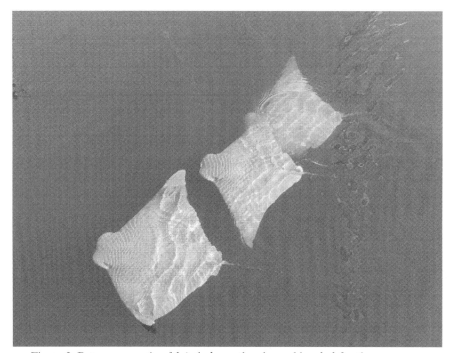

Figure 2. Bat rays escorting *Maiatla* down the channel headed for the open sea.

Chapter 3

Adios México

*"When anxious, uneasy and bad thoughts come, I go to the sea, and the sea drowns them
out with its great wide sounds, cleanses me with its noise, and imposes
a rhythm upon everything in me that is bewildered and confused."*
—Rainer Maria Rilke

As we motored out the breakwater past the lighthouse, it was a bitter sweet moment for me. I was thrilled to be heading back to sea with friends (more thrilled if Janet were at my side). However, also saddened by the realization it may be years, if ever, I sail back with *Maiatla* to México on the Pacific side. For *Maiatla,* who was built to live where the water meets the wind, it was like a homecoming, heading back to where she belonged on the high seas. Our departure marked the end of our fourth season cruising México: three seasons since leaving Canada back in 2012 and one previous seasons back in 2001 and 2002. I was comfortable here in México and with its wonderful people.

Motoring towards the harbour mouth, I spotted ahead of us the harbour dredge at work, deepening the channel. It had floating pipes strung out on pontoons. A couple of small tugs buzzed about like busy bees about a hive. A giant metal monster was in the way. It was going to be tight. I switched on the radar to have a better look, but when I did, the screen wasn't right. The screen showed a solid rock wall dead ahead and open water and the dredge to my right—no! Now the dredge is behind me! No, wait. It's to the left now!

"Oh, shit!" I called out.

"What's the matter, Andy?" Mark asked.

"The dammed radar is screwed. The targets are clocking all around the dial!" I replied. "Nick, can you grab the radar guide and see if you can figure out what's up with this thing? It's probably just a setting."

Nick had a knack for all things electronic, so I thought he could have a crack at it while I got us out of here.

"Sure, Andy, no problem."

Nick went below, grabbed the manual and got right at it. I weaved our way past the dredger with little difficulty, and beyond the breakwater, I altered course to the south to parallel the sandy coast. Heavy surf pounded on beautiful Playa Linda, an exceptional beach that stretches for 32 kilometres (20 miles) to the south. A single road lay behind it, lined with micro cantinas and colourful hotels, with wading pools set back from the surf line. Playa Linda is the last of the Mexican beachfronts resorts the locals frequent. A few miles further south, the buildings dwindle, leaving nothing except a pristine shore backed by jungle mangroves teeming with crocs and iguanas. Less than two hours out and we were off the mouth of a swollen river.

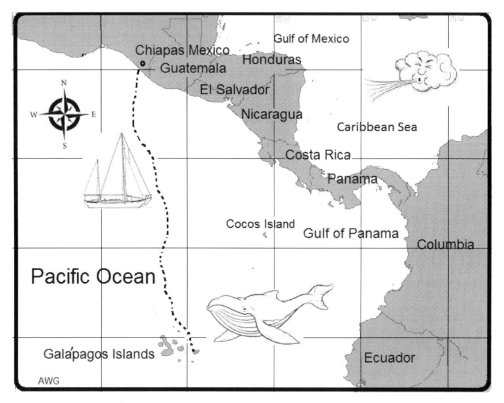

Figure 3. *Maiatla's* route from Chiapas Mexico to the Galápagos Islands.

The Suchiate is a river that marks the south westernmost part of the border between México and Guatemala. The headwaters of the river are in the southern slopes of the Tacaná volcano in the Sierra Madre range of Guatemala and it flows in a south-southwesterly direction. The river's name comes from an Indian word meaning "flower-water," or so the guide book says. But for us, the river meant we had ventured across a new border, sailing into the territorial waters of a new country, signalling our travels had truly begun.

As I feared, despite having a massive gale blowing to the north of us somewhere in the notorious Gulf of Tehuantepec, we had a near flat calm, with the wind blowing only 4 knots out of the northwest. We attempted to sail the first couple of days, but travelling at 1 to 3 knots when you have almost 1609 kilometres (1000 miles) to go and little time didn't cut it. So we motored for almost four days, day and night. As the self-steering was working well, the crew had little to do. Time was spent sitting in the cockpit and watching, which was a good break-in period for Nick. The last thing he needed was a full-blown gale his first few days at sea. In truth, a gale on any point aft of the beam would have been cheerfully welcomed by me, as it would mean for a fast passage, and after being landlocked for the last eight months, a blow would have been a welcome challenge by the crew, stirring the true Bluewater sailors within them once again. However, as fate would have it, we would have opportunity to pitch our mettle and sailing skills against the sea soon enough.

The sea was mirror smooth most of the time, with hardly a wind ripple, but there still was a sizable groundswell running. Waves set in motion by the storm in the Tehuantepec were coming in under our starboard stern quarter and set us to rolling. Not uncomfortable for us, but I was worried for Nick although he was faring well at the moment. Unfortunately, his time would come later.

I set us a course to take us further offshore, as the weather GRIB showed more wind, not much but still more than here. We had also encountered a strong head current, northbound along the shore, so I also hoped going offshore would free us from its grip. Therefore, with nothing to do but babysit the boat, we fished.

Our first day at sea we hooked not one, but two swordfish in the 2-metre (6.5-feet) range. We caught both fish within a few minutes of each other and one on each side of the boat. Nick snagged his first, and when the fish hit, it stripped the line from the reel so fast that it was looking like it would empty the spool before Nick had the rod out of the holder. Applying some drag, Nick slowed the fish's flight down some, but not for long.

We all were watching in hopes of getting a glimpse of whatever he had, and when the beast broke the surface, performed a tail walk while thrashing his head, we all now knew we had a magnificent swordfish. Unfortunately, a look was all we were going to catch, because on the fishes' second jump, it shook its head wildly throwing the hook out. The fish was gone.

However, the excitement wasn't over yet, while Nick was still reeling in his empty line, the other rod took off. This time Mark jumped to it and set the drag. Mark's fish was eating line at a furious pace as well, and we all cheered when the fish, out alongside the boat, leapt to perform its own tail walk. However, like its fellow, it too threw the hook and was gone before we knew what was happening. I have since wondered if we hooked two different fish or the same one twice as they looked suspiciously alike in size and colour.

That day we also hooked and fought a total of seven tuna. We threw all back, except the one yellow fin tuna that we invited for dinner. Nick and I cleaned the fish on the cabin top, a messy proposition, one that required both him and I to take a shower afterwards, but not together.

In between reeling in fish, we were visited at various times during the day by dolphins, some black and white common, as well as spotted and the more easily recognizable bottlenose dolphins, which appeared to receive great joy in gambolling and slashing about the boat.

In the calm water, we easily spotted sea turtles, especially when they had boobies or terns resting upon their backs. From a distance, the roosting birds looked as though they were standing atop of the water. Over the four-day calm, we sighted a great many green sea turtles, which derive their name from the colour of their fat, not their shell, as commonly believed. We also spotted some hawksbill turtles with their bird like beaks, and on our third day, I was treated to a glimpse of what looked like a rare Leatherback turtle.

Leatherbacks are the largest of all sea turtles, and one of the largest reptiles on Earth. The leatherback turtle ranges in size from 1.2 to 2.4 metres (4 to 7.8 feet) in length and weighs between 225 to 900 kilograms (500 to 2,000 pounds). Leatherbacks have a few other claims to fame, like they can consume twice their own body weight in prey per day, feeding exclusively on soft-bodied invertebrates like jellyfish. Due to the nature of their diet, plastic bags pose a real threat to them, as when eaten, can block the digestive track of the animal, causing an agonizing death.

Unlike all other sea turtles, these giants do not possess a carapace or shell covered with hard scales. They possess a smooth, leathery skin that covers a flexible matrix of bone. This specialized flexibility allows them to dive to great depths, unlike other species. In all my time at sea, this was the only Leatherback that I have ever seen, and unfortunately, it was only for a fleeting moment off to starboard. Apparently, he took exception to the boat and quickly dived out of sight.

Since the sea was so quiet, Marina prepared some awesome meals. On our second night out, we dined on a green salad and the prawns that we had purchased the night before our departure, and with the fresh tuna, she made ceviche. The way things were looking, we were all going to gain a few pounds on this trip. Early on, Mark started an exercise routine up on the foredeck. He taped together two lacrosse balls he had brought along to make a portable massage, which he'd place on the deck, lie upon and roll about. We all tried them and it was great for working out those knots. However, because of the heat, the tape started to unravel, so the standing joke often referred to "Mark's sticky balls."

Once clear of the harbour, we hadn't seen any other vessels, not a freighter or even a fishing vessel. It was as if the rest of the world's population had dropped off the face of the earth, which is how I like it. Twenty-four hours after departing Marina Chiapas and Puerto Madero, we had covered 246 kilometres (133 nautical miles) and we were 190 kilometres (118 miles) off of the southern tip of Guatemala. The moon set with the sun, so it was a dark a night as you can imagine. The stars were brilliant, and we lucked out, as we were treated to a meteor shower that kept us looking heavenward most of the night.

I divided the night watches, with Mark starting off with the 6 to 9 p.m. watch. I claimed the 9 to midnight, and Marina and Nick shared the midnight to 6 a.m. watch. I didn't see any other vessels on my watch, but Marina called me on deck at 2 a.m.

when she sighted a ship, a fishing boat all alight hauling otter boards and nets. It safely passed a couple of miles to our port before disappearing in our wake. Mark also called me topside as he spotted a large, northbound containership. Again, it passed a couple miles behind us. I tried to track him on the radar, but the effort was too frustrating, as the ship on the screen circled us at a dizzying pace. Despite both Nick's and my best efforts, we could not make the radar function properly. I sure missed the radar at times like this. We would have to rely more on our senses.

In Central America, it was common for smaller vessels to fish without a single light giving it away, and of course, there were the smugglers and drug runners who also like to skulk about in the dark without lights or radar. Radar waves can be easily tracked back to its source, and if you spot a target travelling at a high rate of speed offshore, you must conclude it is either the military or a smuggler. The idea of being rammed in the middle of the night by a 12-metre (39.3-feet) boat driven by 800 horsepower is frightening to say the least.

Over the next few days, Nick and I continued to take turns trying to sort out the radar, but failed miserably. Well, the radar wasn't entirely useless, as it would tell us that something was out there, but in which direction God only knew. Not a comforting thought when crossing the messy cat's cradle of sea lanes entangling the Galápagos Islands. Not to mention all those islands in the way when we do arrive there. Daytime would not be a problem, but at night or in a gale, it would be a colon twister.

The night before, using the ham radio, I sent an email to the tech guy who sold me the radar unit, and his response wasn't helpful. My tech said the problem most likely lay with a wiring connection somewhere in the dome—the dome that was two thirds the way up the mizzen mast—and he instructed me to go up the mast, open the top of the dome and check each wire, many of which were small and delicate. When I read that, I looked at the dome some 6 metres (19.6 feet) above *Maiatla's* rolling deck and said to myself, "That ain't going to happen anytime soon."

I have been up the mast many times while at sea, mostly in dead calm seas, and if there is even a hint of a swell, I usually come down battered and bruised. I couldn't imagine trying to work on fine wiring with one hand while being whipped about and holding on with the other.

In the wee hours of the morning, I awoke to hear Marina talking and squeaking at the dolphins as she usually does. She was most likely sitting on her perch on top of the propane box, overlooking the dodger top where there is clear view of whatever swims alongside. I laughed to myself, then listened to the other sounds of the boat—the steady thrum of the diesel, the churning of the propeller and the rush of water as it passed the rudder. Satisfied all was well, I decided it was time to roll over and go back to sleep.

Marina would write in her journal this night: *Things look different during night watch. Mars amazes us at midnight. It rises fire red and almost looks like the port light of a ship. I rub my eyes, check the radar and peer with the binoculars just to make sure. As the night wears on stars and ships morph into each other, my mind is free-associating. Is this an adaptation? The land and sea makes us and shapes us. . . . I ponder the mysterious of the universe then wham—I hit the "wall." It's 4:30 a.m., and the chocolate wasn't enough.*

A shadow streaks alongside the Maiatla, followed by another and another, soon a glowing net of bioluminescence criss-crosses the path of the boat. It's a small pod of porpoise, and they have come to play. Now I am wide awake, jabbering dolphin talk, making little squeals, squeaks, telling them my life story in a sing-song voice. "My long lost cousins, so good you came by for a visit!" I fantasize what my life would be like as a porpoise, rubbing up against ships passing in the night . . .welcome to night watch. It's a twilight place where your mind and eyes can't be trusted, and things could get very, very weird.

Our third day at sea brought much of the same weather as a light wind would come and go, so we motored throughout the day. However, by late afternoon, the wind filled in from the stern. We killed the engine, dropped the mainsail, poled the big jenny out to port and hoisted the asymmetrical cruising spinnaker to fill the hole on our starboard.

The colourful red and white spinnaker filled nicely and the boat's spirits picked up measurably as we clipped along at a descent 3 to 4 knots. It was glorious to be a sailboat once again. At this time, I decided to pull the 12-gauge shotgun out of its hiding spot and give it a cleaning. Once satisfied the firearm was in good working order, I fired a few rounds to confirm its readiness in case it's ever needed. For fun, I gave the crew an impromptu lesson on the shotgun's handling and operation. I would never expect any of the crew to use the gun if we were ever boarded by armed drug dealers or pirates (pirates are simply sea born robbers). I assumed the crew would be more comfortable having it around if they were familiar with and understood that the gun itself could not turn on us. Nick in particular got a kick, both literally and figuratively, from pumping a few high-powered rounds into a distant swell, as if it were a charging panga.

We watched the sun set, which permitted the stars to appear, so we gazed aloft. For a few hours, it was pleasant to enjoy the quiet of the high seas and the relative cool of the night. At 9 p.m., I attempted to contact the Pacific Seafarers Net to report our position, but I failed to reach the net controller or a relay. I may have heard them, but I wasn't sure. I, however, did manage to send my daily email off to Janet.

Sending emails via ham radio isn't as easy or reliable as using satellites for sending messages although the principal is much the same. If a boat has a transceiver, you can send a signal upwards to be received by a satellite, which retransmits it back to a ground station. The boat can receive messages just by reversing the process. Ham or shortwave works much the same way, but instead of sending your signal to a satellite, you bounce the signal off the ionosphere (an electrically charged layer of the upper atmosphere), which redirects your signal back towards the Earth where a ground station, again, receives the signal. Simple—but there is one problem and that is the altitude of the ionosphere is constantly changing from between 80 and 650 kilometres (50 and 400 miles) above the Earth. The altitude of this magnetically charged layer affects the angle or bounce of your radio signal, not unlike playing pool where the angle at which you bank the cue ball off the side determines whether it connects with a ball or pocket on the opposite end of the table.

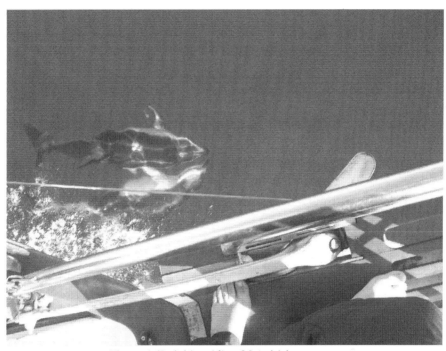

Figure 4. Dolphins riding *Maiatla's* bow wave.

Radio operators use a complex set of tables and computers to help predict the altitude of the ionosphere combined with the location of a known target receiver. For our own location, we choose a frequency and time of day that gives us our best chance of connecting with a transceiver, which then makes a connection to the internet. Despite all the science that is involved, there is still a great many variables that can affect your ability to send and receive signals. Solar and cosmic radiation can distort or nullify your signal; atmospheric conditions that can last from hours to months. When you take into consideration all of this, it is a wonder that we can get messages out at all, but it does work and, most of the time, quite well. But not tonight.

The wind soon shifted to a light headwind, so after the net we were back to motoring. All was good aboard and the crew content—that is except for Mark, who for some reason had developed a slight case of the trots. I thought it funny that on each of my previous voyages with Mark, he would go through a time where he would have something exploding out one end or the other. However, despite his malady, he always managed to come up smiling.

An excerpt from my log reads: *December 13th. Uneventful rest of the day. We again set the spinnaker and poled out our big Jenny to run dead downwind for the rest of the afternoon. Wind was light, 5–7 knots on our stern, making us bounce between 2 and 4 knots of speed. Slow go, but I needed to work in the engine room, so we let it cool down before I crawled in. Got the watermaker running. I'm betting the crew will celebrate with showers all around. Tore a batten pocket in the mainsail as the boat was rolling heavily at one point, so I had a small sail repair to do. Listened to music and cat napped most of the day. Fresh tuna steaks and salad for dinner. Should be a calm night again, but looks like rain on the horizon as the sun set, maybe it will bring some wind.*

Our life had settled into a comfortable routine of lazing about and watch keeping. The crew was getting along well. However, our life of ease would change, along with the weather pattern. By Day 4 at sea, we were only 595 kilometres (370 miles) from Darwin Island, at the northern extreme of the chain of the Galápagos Islands. Northern Panamá lay 1149 kilometres (714 miles) away, due east.

As I was writing my morning log at 10 a.m., I noticed that it was 27 degrees Celsius, (80.6F) with 90 per cent humidity, in the cabin. Puddles of sweat were forming under my elbows as I typed. We had 5 knots of wind steady out of the south. The sky was 80 per cent cloud covered, which was a change from the normal pale blue from horizon to horizon. The rest of the crew was sleeping, a blessing for them, as they apparently had a rough night and didn't sleep much.

Early the previous night, about midway through my 9 p.m. to midnight watch, we crossed a strong current that ran contrary to the light wind out of the south. It created some steep standing waves, cresting waves that *Maiatla* drove headlong into under the power of the motor. We were hobby-horsing, bouncing a bit, with *Maiatla's* head snapping up and back.

Nevertheless, I was thankful for the current because it was giving us a push, and according to the GPS, we were racing along at 10 knots and not the 6.5 knots the boat's speed indicated. This night at sea grew dark with a heavy cloud cover, and to add to the tension (that some felt), for most of the night, we were surrounded by rain squalls and lighting strikes, but little wind, none in fact. I slept fine! The rest of the crew, not so much.

It was nice to have the rain wash the salt off of the boat. However, as I would later discover, most of our port holes were leaking and soaking all of the clothes in Janet's drawers and cupboards.

Mark had woken me some time after 6 a.m. to have a look at a ship that was on the horizon, which he had been visually tracking for a while. When I went topside, I was surprise to find everyone huddled in the early morning light, munching on soda crackers and sucking back anti-nausea meds. Their watch was over, but Marina and Nick found the boat's motion below a bit much and decided to stay in the cockpit instead of going to bed. The sea was confused, setting the boat moving in a chaotic dance that Marina's and Nick's feet could not follow.

Nick was looking the worst, and I could tell by his pallor he was suffering and looking like he was about to engage in a bout of projectile vomiting. Thankfully he mange to choke the urge back.

Mercifully, the rough patch of water ended a couple of hours earlier, but its affects were still resonating within the crew. However, I didn't have time for my crew's pain. We had a ship close by, way too close, and I was upset that Mark had not awoken me sooner. The vessel was a big containership, and it was moving fast. With his decks piled high with cargo and the ship's bridge all the way aft, they would have great difficulty spotting a small vessel close under the ship's bow.

As he approached, I could clearly see without the aid of binoculars both of its running lights. Not a good sign. The red and green-eyed monster was about 5 kilometres (3 miles) away and coming right at us, closing the gap at a rate of better than 0.8 kilometres (half a mile) per minute. At that speed, he would run us down in another five minutes if we didn't do something and fast. We held our current course until I figured out what our best next course of action would be.

We could change our heading and try to run to one side of the ship, but that would be our Plan B. Instead, I went straight to Plan A—picked up the radio microphone and placed a call directed at the oncoming freighter. In a few seconds, a voice with a thick Asian accent acknowledged my call.

"This is the sailing vessel *Maiatla,* and I am approximately 3 miles off your bow. We appear to be on a collision course. Do you see me, Captain?"

"Sailing vessel standby" was the reply.

It was an agonizing minute before the ship came back to me. However, by then, its great bow was looming over us.

"We see you, sailing vessel. Hold your course, and we will go around your sten."

Even before the captain finished stating his intentions, we could see the bow of the ship commence to turn until only its red navigation light was visible, indicating that he would miss us, but not by much. Once they were clear, the captain asked where we were from and where our next port of call was.

"The Galápagos Islands," I reported. Thanking him, I wished them a good morning.

In hindsight, our close encounter was of my own making. Mark was capable of taking evasive action to manoeuvre the boat out of harm's way on his own, but it was my insistence that I be called topside before any action was taken. My captinitis could have cost all of our lives. I went back to bed leaving the boat in the capable hands of the crew, despite their exhausted state of nausea. I slept like the dead for another two hours before my watch, which commenced at 9 a.m. when everyone finally went to their berths.

An excerpt from Marina's journal reads: *Sleeping arrangements. Although it's the rockiest, I always claim the V-berth because it's private. It has a door that closes and a hatch that allows for natural light and fresh air when it's calm—an essential ingredient in preventing seasickness for me. But this trip was different. Andy slept in the luxurious Captain's aft cabin, Mark claimed the roomy amidships berth and I was back in the V-berth, but this time, I was not alone. Alas I was sharing it with the long-limbed Nick. Because he is bigger than me, I forfeited my usual port-side bunk for the starboard one, which was located several feel higher above a series of drawers. This bunk is normally used for stowing gear. A child might be comfortable in it, but I am 5'8" and have generous proportions. . . . When I clambered up, I would have to slide into it. Sitting up was out of the question. If I rolled on my side, my hip would graze the cabin ceiling . . . something I put to use on bumpy days as a way to lodge myself in. Normally, though, I slept on my back, with four inches of space above my face.*

If you have read Edgar Allen Poe, you will be familiar with the premature burial story . . . and now I had a firsthand taste of that. I managed to make myself comfortable the first few days, but once the squalls started to hit and the hatch was battened down, there was no more fresh air; instead hot, rank air, smelling like feet and farts, would collect in that small space, making sleep impossible.

Getting off the bunk presented its own challenge. Not being able to sit up, I would half climb out the hatch, then align my lower body before attempting to climb back down from the bunk. That worked reasonably well until the hatch was shut. What would follow then was a Benny Hill comedy act. I would roll onto my stomach, inch myself out passed the edge of the bunk, then launch myself out to drop down on my hands and knees—Spider-Man-style—onto the bunk below, straddling Nick and trying to not awake him. This maneuver was not only performed with no clothes on because of the heat, but had to be executed with a surgeon's precision, because one wrong move and I'd be landing on some of Nick's more sensitive parts.

Alone on watch while my crew slept, I made eggs, bacon and burnt toast on the open flame of the stove. In the cockpit, I ate while watching schools of flying fish take flight as the onrush of the boat spooked them. Or perhaps the presence of some predator lurking in *Maiatla's* ghosting shadow spurred the fish into flight? It was not unusual to see dorado, dolphins or even sharks clinging to the boat's dark underbelly in an effort to conceal themselves while they planned to spring upon a school of tiny fish that otherwise saw no menace in *Maiatla's* approach. These were first flying fish that we had seen on this voyage. I had forgotten how beautiful they were when they take flight upon gossamer wings.

While watching the fish, I spotted my first whale spout of the voyage. The telltale waterspout of a surfacing whale can be seen for a long way, and this one was some distance off, but it was exciting to see and it appeared to be heading our way. I suspected that we should soon see more whales as we continued to head south, crossing their migration routes.

As predicted, as we approached the 5 degrees south mark, the wind solidly changed to the south and increased to 10 to 15 knots. The wind change permitted us to proceed under full sail close-hauled, and *Maiatla* and the crew loved every minute of it.

We had also noticed the cooling effects of one of the cold-water currents that surround the Galápagos Islands, as there was a decided temperature drop, most noticeable at night when, for the first time, a light sheet was required for sleeping. With the current change, our luck at fishing ended. Being skunked now became the daily norm. It was just as well because Marina had a revelation for us after retrieving the night's dinner out of the refrigerator.

"Hey, guys, if you catch any more fish, there won't be enough room in the fridge. But if you'd like, I can remove some of the beer to make room for it?"

The vote was cast without saying a word, and it was cold beer 3, fish 0. We would abstain from fishing, for a little while, or until at least the beer supplies ran low.

We were five days out of México, and for the most part, the trip had been a benign one. No mechanical breakdowns, all the boat's systems were functioning normally and the boat was sailing well. She was balanced and in the groove. It will be showers all around for the crew tonight, as the captain insisted—some of us were becoming a little whiffy, despite showering the day before.

Figure 5. Crew relaxing after the wind filled in and we were finally able to sail.

Hot showers on board are a real treat, and because everything on a boat is based on economy of movements and conservation, when we shower, we often do laundry in the same water. You round up your dirty laundry, plug the shower drain, and throw clothes in the bottom, shower and stomp on clothes vigorously with your feet. Rinse, wring and towel dry, then hang clothes out on the lifeline to dry. We should be so efficient at home!

The boat had taken on a decided jerky motion, and I assume the confined quarters of our shower stall and the boat's new motion got to Nick. No sooner had Nick finished his shower than he went ominously quiet. It was then we all noticed he was as pale as a ghost.

"You okay?" Marina asked in a sympathetic tone as Nick slowly ventured back into the cockpit while clutching an empty ice-cream bucket.

I couldn't help but find it funny, as being sea sick on your first offshore voyage is a rite of passage into the Bluewater club. Nick settled into the corner of the cockpit, and we all expected the worse.

"Nick, if you're going to be sick, don't do what Mark did last time," I insisted.

Some many years ago, Mark, while seasick off the coast of Oregon, had sat in the exact same spot when his stomach decided to jettison its cargo of eggs and bacon. However, instead of leaning outside the cockpit and being sick over the side (even on deck would have been better than what happened), Mark decided to bolt back below and lunge for the toilet bowl. Unfortunately his innards couldn't wait that long. His projectile vomiting made deposits from the galley table all the way into the head. Hardly a surface was spared the onslaught.

As I told this story to a nauseated Nick, Mark gave me a sheepish grin as he now sat in the opposite corner. Nick's ailment would continue for the next few days, making him utterly useless as far as his watch was concerned. Fortunately, Marina picked up the slack. Nick, however, complained little, and other than having to step over his apparent lifeless body, his sea sickness hardly affected me at all.

This was also an emotional day for Marina as it was the sixth anniversary of her father's death. Although not unexpected, Mark lost his father just weeks before the start of this voyage, and Nick lost his dad just the year before. My father had passed seventeen years previous, and I still miss him dearly. So for a short while we all talked of the profound influences that our fathers had upon us, sharing good memories and stories. Then in tribute, we broke out the wine and made a toast.

Darwin Island was 497 kilometres (309 miles) directly ahead, so we were hoping the wind continued to hold, and if it did, we should sight the island in two and a half days, seven full days after departing México. Once arriving at Darwin, it would take a couple of more days to get to San Cristóbal. We were well on track to complete the voyage in my estimated nine days.

I and the crew were happy, but I did have one concern. The further south we travelled, the harder I found it to contact a relay station to receive and send out our daily emails. I included in the latest email to Janet that if we were to lose contact, not to worry.

In Janet's latest email, she asked if her friend, Brent, could house sit for us all while we were gone this winter. He had fallen on hard times after an automobile accident, and while waiting for a financial settlement from the insurance company, he needed a place to stay. Janet met this fellow through an online study course a few years back. She was given an opportunity to get know him when one of the other students suggested that all the people living on Vancouver Island meet for a study group.

I had never met Brent, but he had already been to the house a few times, so Janet's suggestion for him to house sit was a logical one. Normally while we were away, our daughter, Melissa, who lives a couple of hours away, dropped by to check on the place and two of my good neighbours collected our mail while keeping an eye on things. However, having a full-time live-in would be better for the four months the house would be empty. I agreed, as it was a win-win for both Brent and us. Gore Vidal, a celebrated writer and senator from Oklahoma, was once quoted as saying, "a good deed never goes unpunished." Neither Janet nor I could have imagined how our generosity could turn on us and bite us in the butt.

Chapter 4

The Galápagos Islands—the Hard Way!

*"Broad, wholesome, charitable views of men and things cannot be acquired by
vegetating in one little corner of the earth all of one's lifetime."*
—Mark Twain

Minutes before midnight and on my watch, our sixth day at sea, the wind died, so we fired up the engine. However, by 1 a.m., the wind returned out of the same quadrant, developing into a brisk south by southwest breeze. Marina and Nick killed the engine, returning us to sailing hard on the wind, but it wasn't long before the fresh new wind became more erratic by shifting back and forth, gusting up to 20 knots in great puffs and pants. Nick was still clutching his bucket while dying the proverbial thousand deaths with his sea sickness, but he was now at least able to lend a hand once in a while. The increase in the wind woke me, and when I ventured topside to check on things, the crew was already furling the big headsail, leaving us to continue under mizzen, single reefed main and the staysail. A comfortable sail plan that still had us clipping along at 6 knots through most of the night until the wind expired again right before dawn.

The parting wind left us a gift in the form of a two-metre swell, and a nasty wind chop, which we now had to beat into. With the lack of wind, a mere baby's breath of a breeze, the boat pound into the waves, and each time she nosed deep into a sea, she would stall and almost come to a dead stop. Again we fired up the motor and continued to pound into the waves under the thrust of the churning propeller. Not the best situation, but at least we were making headway. However, not for long.

Everything that goes wrong seemed to happen on Marina's and Nick's watch. This was not an indictment of these members' sailing skills, or a suggestion that dark shadows hang above them—no! They were not stalked by *Maiatla's* notorious little gremlins. It was just an observation, and worth noting here.

In the early hours of the morning, when it was still dark, I crawled out of my cabin to check the computer charts. When taking a seat at the galley table in front of the computer, I noticed that the laptop was partially closed. Not an unusual condition as the night watch would often close the lid to douse the light from the screen. However, when I opened the lid, I found a pair of my reading glasses had been crushed between the screen and the keyboard. It wasn't the state of the glasses that made me ill; it was the jagged broken line that cut diagonally across the laptop's screen, severing the chart in half and leaving the lower portion blank. The navigation computer was screwed!

Figure 6. *Maiatla* with a bone in her teeth.

When I asked the crew if anyone knew what had happened, all were ignorant as to how the screen happened to become destroyed. After some consideration, I came to the conclusion that sometime during the night, someone came down the companion steps and perhaps lost their footing as the boat rolled, causing them to inadvertently extend a hand to arrest their fall. The lid was pressed shut, trapping my reading glasses and breaking the screen. Perhaps due to the darkness, the accident went unnoticed. Despite the monetary issue that would arise, I wasn't too worried about the busted computer as the life expectancy of one on board *Maiatla* was usually short anyway due to the, at times, violent motion and extremely salty air. Fortunately, I had two spare backup computers on board for such an occasion. I went aft to my cabin closet and pulled out the first of my spare navigational computers and tried to boot it up, but nothing happened. The battery was dead, so I plugged it into the inverter and still nothing! I cussed a bit while fiddling with the battery and connections, but still nothing.

"Screw this," I said aloud. I went and dug out the backup computer for my backup computer. Thankfully, the old Dell started without a hitch. That is until I tried to have the laptop interface with the GPS, which it refused to do. I managed to pull up the correct chart, but the computer could not place the boat upon that chart. I would have to take a latitude and longitude reading from the GPS in the cockpit and manually transfer it to the chart. A bit of a pain in the ass, but doable and would have worked nicely if the Nobeltec navigational program didn't keep crashing. UGH! I gave up and went back to bed. I can only assume that the noise from the breaking of the screen had woken *Maiatla's* sleeping gremlins, and as we were all about to find out, they were not happy.

Our venerable old Perkins had been functioning flawlessly since our departure; however, on the night following our computer crash, near the middle of Marina's and Nick's watch, the engine sputtered, then died, as if it had the life choked out of it. We resorted back to sailing, and I immediately crawled into the sweltering engine room to see what was up. Checking the fuel filters, I discovered that they were clogged with water. I had checked the filters earlier that day and drained a tiny bit of water and muck from them, so I was surprise to view their condition now. I cursed aloud, as I knew from past experience what that could mean. I drained and changed the filters and then tried to fill the filters with new fuel using an auxiliary fuel pump that was installed for this purpose. However, as the pump ran, it thumped and rattled, but nothing happened. I couldn't draw fuel from the main tanks. I now had a dreadful feeling that we had run out of fuel. If we had drained the fuel tanks, the engine would have sucked in the last drops of precious oil from the tanks until all that remained was water and crap, the last soiled dregs, a witch's brew of toxic ooze, overwhelming the filters.

After flipping the valve to draw clean fuel from the 30-gallon reserve tank, fuel flowed to the filters, then lastly to the engine. And after bleeding the fuel injector pump, I attempted to restart the engine, but it was no use. Like a man with his head held beneath the water, the Perkins had most assuredly drowned. Too much water had passed through the filters, which in turn destroyed the fuel injector pump. The engine was lifeless, and since I don't carry a spare fuel pump, our Perkins was dead weight and utterly useless.

We were over 1609 kilometres (1000 miles) from the Central American coast and still 270 from Darwin Island, but Darwin was nothing more than an isolated, guano-covered rock ruled by boobies and Albatrosses. There was no help there to be had. After Darwin, it was still another 407 kilometres (220 nautical miles) to San Cristóbal Island where I assumed I could have the pump fixed, even if it meant putting the pump in a backpack and catching a flight to mainland Ecuador to have it rebuilt. However, until then, we had a real problem. In the morning, we all sat in the cockpit where I went over our troubles and formulated a game plan. Without a doubt, our best bet was to carry on to our original destination. We had to. Janet and Teri were flying there in a few days and we needed to be there when they arrived. Also it was the closest port with repair facilities, so we would remain Galápagos bound and perhaps salvage our plans to cruise the famous islands.

"So, guys, here is what we do," I said while bracing myself as I stood on the companion steps. "We carry on, but we need to be extra sharp on our navigation and sailing. We need to stay hard on the wind and the boat moving as best we can if we want to arrive at San Cristóbal on time, okay?"

Everyone eagerly agreed, but the reality of it was that they had no choice. We were now a full-time sailboat regardless, as if time had rolled back a couple of centuries, thrusting us back into the great days of tall ships and sail power. We were truly at the mercy of the wind and ocean currents. Fortunately, the loss of the engine would not affect the boat's other systems. The solar power and the gas genset could keep up the electrical systems; lights and radios would function as normal. I had no doubt that we would arrive at our destination someday, but would we be in time to meet the girls when they landed? I was now thankful that I had reserved a room for the ladies for the entire week of their arrival, in case something like this happened. Janet and Teri would not be happy to be alone in a foreign country, nervously waiting to see when and if the sea was going to spit us out. At least they would have a safe place to stay as they waited for *Maiatla* and her crew to show.

"Andy, how could we have run out of fuel? You said we had enough diesel to motor all the way to the Galápagos if we had too," Mark said as he sat next to the helm seat at the back of the cockpit. I paused a moment to try and fathom why also.

Running my hands through my hair, I searched for a reason. "I don't know, Mark. It's a mystery. We took on enough to top off the tanks in Chiapas. I've checked the engine hours, and we have only run the motor enough to burn less than half of the main tanks, and then I have the reserve." I paused to consider. "We lost or misplaced 80 or 90 gallons," I concluded.

"How?" Mark asked. "If we had a fuel leak, we would have smelt it, as diesel stinks!"

"Yes, I know," I replied. "That much fuel would have filled our bilge right up. The smell would damn near knock us out, and if the bilge pump dumped it overboard, we would have been leaving an oil slick like the Deepwater Horizon in the Gulf of México. So I don't know!"

With the tranquil seas, the crew reverted back to fishing, despite the peril it presented to the cold beer supply. With all of us spending so much time on the aft deck fishing, you would have thought that someone would have spotted an oil slick trailing behind the boat. No! We did not lose the fuel overboard, which was seemingly impossible.

Still I was at a loss. How do you lose that much fuel, or be short changed at the pump and not know it? Well, at this point, even if I found out what happened to the missing fuel, we would still be dead in the water. Fuel pumps hate water, and when the tanks ran dry, we force-fed it a bucket load of scummy, silt-laden water. I had been checking the fuel filters daily, but if I had checked them more diligently, perhaps I might have seen what was happening before the damage was done. The enigma that surrounded the fuel and self-recrimination would haunt me. Eventually, weeks later, as I squeezed deep into *Maiatla's* bowels while attempting to resolve one of *Maiatla's* other mechanical woes, the riddle of the missing fuel would reveal itself.

As if to signal that the conversation was over, a blue-footed booby that had been circling overhead decided to take a dump, scoring a direct hit onto Mark's head. Mark was indignant. The rest of us just laughed—a release, a moment I believe we all needed. Mark? Well, not so much!

"That's supposed to be good luck. Mark, perhaps you need to make a wish," Marina suggested while chuckling and zooming her camera in for a close-up.

I heard Mark mumble something, a wish that I'm sure wasn't in the bird's best interest. For now the boat was sailing well, and we were clipping off the miles. At this rate, we would still meet our deadline, but I also knew that the winds can and would be fickle and we were entering the zone known as the doldrums. I decided to break up Marina and Nick. Now Mark would watch with Nick and Marina, with me. This would ensure that we made the most of the wind that did blow our way.

The doldrums is a zone in the Atlantic and Pacific Oceans affected by a low-pressure area around the equator where the prevailing winds are calm or nonexistent, which can trap sail-powered boats for periods of days or even weeks. Since this zone is the meeting place of two trade winds, the northeast and southeast trade winds, it is also called Intertropical Convergence Zone, or the ITZ for short. In maritime usage, the low pressure characteristics of the doldrums is caused by the expanding atmosphere due to heating at the equator, which makes the air rise and travel north and south, high in the atmosphere, until it subsides again in the horse latitudes at or above 30 degrees latitude, north and south of the equator. Some of that air returns to the doldrums through the trade winds. This process can lead to light or variable winds and more severe weather, in the form of squalls, thunderstorms and, at times, hurricanes. The weather in the ITZ can best be described as eccentric.

If all of the above isn't enough, to make matters worse, no less than six separate and powerful ocean currents were waiting for us. The Panamá current flows from east to west into the islands, and the South Equatorial Current, north of the islands, is also westerly setting, but has a complex array of ever-changing back eddies. The South Equatorial countercurrent lies a little further south and it is east bound. And if that isn't enough, the Humboldt Current skirts Peru to veer out to the islands, the Peru Coastal Current splits into a south countercurrent, and the Peru Oceanic Current is an express train to the west. At the confluence or hub of all these ocean rivers is the Galápagos Islands, which block and deflect the currents, creating maniacal upwelling, spiraling eddies and pinch points to accelerate the waters that can flow up to 5 knots or more. These currents are largely unpredictable and are constantly varying as the tidal forces of the moon exerts its own influences.

Figure 7. Mark and Andrew surveying a calm sea 700 miles offshore of Costa Rica.

I had a tough decision to make and soon. Do we head east? Swing wide of the islands and circle around? Such a course could add days to our voyage. Or do we cut close to or right though the islands and hope we can manage to sail faster than the currents can carry us?

Without a functioning radar, a night-time passage between the islands would be perilous. There are numerous dangerous reefs and islets surrounding the main islands, as well as islands that are deserted and unlit, so if we were to run into trouble, help would be a long time coming. I knew what I should do, play it safe. Nevertheless, my inner adventurer was telling me something else. I believed that I still had time to decide. Perhaps a day or so, but no more than that. However, I would have to decide while wrestling with the knowledge that our very survival may depend on a good decision. But as fate would have it, the conspiring elements would make the decision for me.

It was now well past dawn, and I had given up any hope of going back to bed. I turned my attention to the troublesome computer. After spending the better half of the morning fighting the navigational laptop that refused to keep running, I gave up and packed it not so carefully away while fighting the urge to "deep six it," tossing over the side for a burial at sea.

Reluctantly, I went forward to dig the paper charts out from under the salon sofa where they had been neatly stored in tubes, wrapped in plastic. Many of these charts had not seen the light of day since 2001 when I first stowed them there in preparation for our voyage to México. Computers have been our frontline navigational system going back to the year 2000, and it's amazing just how much I was now missing the ease of navigating while using one. I wasn't looking forward to reverting to paper charts, but I was glad to have them nonetheless. At least the GPS was still functioning and I wouldn't have to drag out my sextant and attempt to remember how to use it.

The last time I dusted off the sextant was way back in 2007, on our 23-day voyage from Hawaii to Vancouver. We had perfect sailing conditions for almost two weeks running, so with little else to do, I used the sextant to shoot the North Star, which I compared to my GPS reading. At the time, I was pleased with the accuracy, as my calculations usually put us within 9 to 18 kilometres (5 to 10 nautical miles) of where the GPS stated we were—perfectly good accuracy for open ocean navigation and finding your way home. However, these circumstances were different. We were fast approaching a dangerous archipelago with notorious currents and light winds. We were engine-less and radar-less, so to lose the use of the GPS at this point would complete the hat-trick of debilitating breakdowns.

While down in the salon, getting ready to pull the drawers out from under the sofa where, like the Dead Seas Scrolls covered in dust, the chart rolls lay, I saw it. There it was. The solution to the problem was staring me in the face while hanging on the bulkhead (wall). I bolted, from lower salon to the port-side cabin, to dig out of the tool drawer the appropriate screw driver. Then back in the salon, I unscrewed from the bulkhead the 22-inch flat screen TV and DVD player.

Using a c-clamp, I secured it to the galley table next to the ham radio station. Running a HDMI cord from my broken laptop computer instantly turned the TV into a functioning monitor. Navigation wise, we were back in business.

Chapter 5

Land Ho! Oh, No!

*"There is nothing more enticing, disenchanting,
and enslaving than the life at sea."*
—Joseph Conrad

Day 7 proved to be a maddening one. After breaking the computer screen and losing the engine, *Maiatla's* bilge skulking gremlins formed an alliances with the wind, which was now taking every opportunity to torment us. By early morning, the brisk headwind dwindled to only a couple of knots. Then it began to clock around the compass, shifting direction almost hourly until fading entirely by early in the afternoon. *Maiatla* is not what you would call a "light air boat," so at times, we had some difficulty keeping her moving. Like a child's toy on a great pond, we drifted along making frequent pirouettes, complete, slow-motion circles at the whim of the breeze, which had decided that we needed to visit all 360 points of the compass—and often. At one stage, we lost steerage and were headed northwest, away from the Galápagos. What was more disturbing was the 2-knot westerly current that now had us on track to make our next landfall in the Marshall Islands in the western Pacific. If there was any positive point to the calm, Nick's sea sickness left him, for now at least.

We all noticed that Nick was undergoing a transformation as his fastidious nature was slowly but surely waning. Nick was de-evolving as he was now barefooted, his shirt unbuttoned and his chin sported the start of a scruffy beard. Marina would later say that Nick was re-discovering his wild side and that we would make a pirate out of him yet. Nick's dishevelled appearance was par for the course as far as cruisers were concerned and totally acceptable. However, it would be on the second to last day of our voyage when it caught me off guard. One morning, as I ventured into the cockpit, I saw Nick all splayed out, and there, as if requiring a breath of fresh air, oozing out of a tear in his tattered cut-off blue-jeans, was Nick's left testicle. At that moment, I believe that Nick's transformation into cruiser was complete.

When we did get the boat straightened out and moving, I was telling myself that I would be happy to be ghosting along, content with the knowledge that we were making progress in the right direction. However, our lack of any movement whatsoever through the water was poignantly pointed out by our twin sets of fishing gear, now hung uselessly straight down beneath the boat. The sun was hot, accentuating the breathless atmosphere that surrounded the boat on a sea eerily still and surprisingly devoid of life.

We had seen little in the way of sea life this morning, no dolphins, fish or birds. Typically, when we stared into the depths, we would see an assortment of gelatin bulbs and spiral slugs drifting or wafting by. The sea is usually a primordial soup, bubbling with wriggling life—bulbous pustules with tentacles or barbs, blindly thrusting at their surroundings. However this morning, nothing, adding, as Marina first noted, to the eeriness of the moment. It was as though all life on Earth had deserted us on our aquatic plain. An extinction of all the world's species, save us aboard *Maiatla*. This notion left me with mixed feelings. Maybe good! . . . Maybe not!

When becalmed and helplessly drifting like this, you pray for a gale or a storm, just to get you moving, giving you back a sense of control. There were high stratocumulus clouds, which usually indicate that a change in weather was on the way, so I was hopeful that some wind may be in the offing. As I stood on the stern deck, under a scorching sun, scanning the horizon for any indications of wind, the surrealism of the image before me brought to mind the poem *The Rime of the Ancient Mariner,* by Samuel Taylor Coleridge, which reads in part,

> *All in a hot and copper sky,*
> *The bloody Sun, at noon,*
> *Right up above the mast did stand,*
> *No bigger than the Moon.*
> *Day after day, day after day,*
> *We stuck, nor breath nor motion;*
> *As idle as a painted ship*
> *Upon a painted ocean.*

It was frustrating for all of us to be losing ground and not be able to do anything about it. Eventually the clouds above thickened as a tickling zephyr from the east slowly filled in, permitting us enough forward motion to regain steerage and eventually our heading. However, we were still losing ground, sailing 1 knot forward while being pushed 2 knots sideways by the unwavering South Equatorial Current, which had us firmly in its grasp. Once again, I decided that "discretion is the better part of valour" and played it cautious by sailing more to the east and giving the Galápagos Islands a wide berth. My original plans to sail right past Darwin Island and perhaps dive with the resident whale sharks were evaporating along with our hopes of a quick passage from México.

The west setting current and lack of boat speed flouted all our efforts to make any easting. The option of an easterly passage had been taken from me. I also feared that if we altered course to round the islands on the western side, we would not be able to sail back due east against the strong Peru Oceanic Current. So at best, I was determined to try and skirt the eastern shore of the Galápagos Islands or, at worst, cut between them and hope for the best.

Figure 8. Mark, Andrew and Nick sharing a watch while relaxing in the cockpit.

With the change of wind, the clouds, now a thick mat of dark cotton, appeared as though they would yield some rain, and rain it did. A couple of hours after the wind returned, the sky opened up and it poured a rain that can only be witnessed in the tropics. I was hopeful the deluge would bring with it some significant wind, but it didn't do anything of the sort. We were forced to close all the hatches and portholes, which, in the tropical heat, created a sauna below, preventing the off watch from acquiring any meaningful sleep.

For a couple of hours, the downpour pounded the boat and the crew huddled within the closed dodger. Water dripped from overhead zipper seams and splashed up under the corners of the canvas, soaking everything. The cockpit cushion became soggy and made a squishing sound as we sat upon them. The only positive note was that *Maiatla* would at least have all the salt washed off of her back. When the rain stopped, the light breeze shifted to the north, so we hoisted the spinnaker and were able to carry on sailing. But more importantly, we were headed south at a steady clip. We had a grand sail for the rest of the afternoon until dusk.

Marina called me away from the computer where I had been updating our position and trying to work out some navigational problems brought on by the west-setting current. I went topside to see what was going on.

"Hey, Andy," Marina said as she sat on the starboard side of the cockpit, pointing to a distant spot off of the bow, "check out the clouds over there."

When I looked, I could see thick cumulus and stratocumulus clouds above the horizon a few miles off and below that a white haze where strong winds stirred up the ocean's surface, casting spray before it. I went on deck for a better look. Mark followed.

"What'd ya think, Andy? Looks like we may have some wind coming. You wanna get the chute down?" he asked, with some concern in his voice.

Mark had every reason to be nervous, as what I believe we were looking at was a line squall in the making. Line squalls are notoriously unpredictable. They may come with stiff breezes or hurricane force winds as a heavy cold front drives a series of thunderstorms forward. Often sea spray is driven before it, which can reflect sunlight, making it appear as a bright line above the water.

A line squall is not the same as a white squall, which is rare, often born out of clear skies and thought to be caused by something called a micro burst—a phenomenon that occurs as air in the upper atmosphere collapses and dense winds fall onto the sea. At sea level, the violent winds spread out while whipping the surrounding ocean into frenzy, creating the characteristic white line streak.

"Yep, bud, looks like a line squall to me, but it don't look like it's coming our way none too fast. Think it's paralleling us?"

I looked back at the big spinnaker and our full mainsail, which, combined, had us ripping along at 5 knots—a speed we desperately needed to keep up. Turning back to the bright streak on the horizon, I said, "Let's wait a bit. See what happens, but let's check to make sure all the sheets and halyards are ready to let loose so that we can get this sail down in a hurry, okay?"

Scanning the horizon once more, I turned aft. "Nick, you want to go below and close all the port holes and hatches, please? And dog them tight!" I ordered. I turned back to Mark and said, "There is definitely more rain in there, but I'm more concerned about a knock down with this much sail up, and we don't want all the ports open if we are driven over onto our beams end. We also better make sure everything is secured on deck."

As we went about our business of making certain everything was secure, I couldn't help but remember the fate of the tall ship *Albatross,* a Brigantine school ship that sunk in 1961. Two crew and five students were lost off of the Dry Tortugas in the Caribbean. As well, the *Pride of Baltimore*, a topsail schooner and a sailing ambassador for the state of Maryland, was lost off of Puerto Rico in 1986, taking the lives of four of its twelve crew. Both ships were believed to have been victims of white squalls. Back in 1977, I had the opportunity to walk the decks of the *Pride of Baltimore,* as it made a visit to Halifax, Nova Scotia, during a tall ship festival. I remember, vividly, standing at the massive ships wheel, clinging to the spokes, looking aloft at the tall rig, as the helmsman most assuredly would do some nine years later when the white squall struck. The hurricane force winds struck *Pride of Baltimore* with little warning, knocking the ship over until her decks were awash, permitting the sea to pour into the open hatches and port holes, sealing the ship's and crew's fate. At the time of her loss, I had a framed picture of the *Pride of Baltimore* on the wall of my home office—a photograph that I had taken as she lay alongside the quay in Halifax all those years before.

Marina and Nick were in the cockpit, and after inspecting the lashings on the spare gas cans and sail bags, Mark and I stayed on the foredeck for the following half hour as we intently watched the slow-motion approach of the squall until we could see the wind whipping the water's surface a half mile to our port. With nose in the air, raindrops speckled my face and I became mindful of a new wind on my cheek.

"Okay, Mark, let's get her down. Now!"

Figure 9. *Maiatla* sailing wing and wing with the asymmetrical cruising spinnaker.

No sooner had Marina and Nick released the guy, the line that controls the clue of the spinnaker, in the cockpit than a great gust took hold of the sail, whipping it violently in an increasing wind. With the new wind came another great deluge of rain that was so thick it nearly took my breath away as I stared aloft at the billowing sail. I already had the line in hand that controlled the snuffer sock, the sheath at the top of the mast that when pulled downward, encapsulates the spinnaker in a long sock-like tube. With a few swift pulls, the sock came down, taming the wildly flailing spinnaker as it went. As soon as the sail was under control, Mark released the halyard and I pulled the spinnaker filled sock to the deck.

Despite the squall's menacing appearance and a few initial gusts of wind over 25 knots, the wind quickly settled out at 15 knots, so we unfurled the headsail, allowing *Maiatla* to charge happily forward. Satisfied that we weren't in any real danger from the storm, I asked Marina to pass us some beers and then we sat on deck in the warm, pouring rain. It was amusing to watch the extremely large drops pound the deck with such a force that they bounced back into the air a metre or more. Mark was sitting cross-legged on the cabin top, and I was cradled in a sail bag as if it were a beanbag chair, a comfy spot to admire and study the weather elements at work. It was an odd sight to be sure, us two sitting out in the rain and drinking Tecates. We had to keep a palm overtop of our beer cans, umbrella-like, to keep our suds from being watered down.

"Andy!" Marina called from behind us as she peeked under a corner of the dodger. "How about I bring the soap and shampoo on deck so we can have a shower? It will save us from running the watermaker. What ya think?"

Well, I was already naked as I had slipped out of my wet shorts during the last down pour earlier that day and hadn't bothered to dress again, so Marina's suggestion made perfect sense. If the sight of Mark and I drinking beer in the rain looked odd, I guess the sight of what followed looked stranger still (if there was anyone around to witness it).

As the sun set, the entire crew got naked and began dancing and showering on the foredeck, lathering up, then allowing the rain to do the rinsing off. It proved to be a stress-relieving moment, one we sorely needed. I might suggest that if you haven't showered with four of your closet friends on the deck of a sailboat in mid ocean, then perhaps you just haven't lived.

Later that evening, after sending out our daily email to Janet and another failed attempt to raise the Pacific Seafarers Net, I retreated to my cabin to have a nap before my watch. As I entered the cabin, the soles of my feet were suddenly wet. A moment of panic shot through me. I believed that we were taking on sea water—that we were sinking! Quickly I reached for the handle in the floor boards and lifted it up, half expecting to see the subfloor full of salt water. However, when I looked, I could see that the space was dry, or was until the water on top of the floor poured in. Considering for a moment, I pressed my palm into the water and licked my fingers.

"Hum, fresh water," I said aloud.

It was then I noticed that directly below some of the portholes, there was a steady stream of water trickling down the cupboards on both sides of the boat. After further investigation, I discovered that inside the cupboards where Janet had her clothes were full of water. Despite having the ports dogged down tight, they were leaking into the liner, the gap between the outside cabin top and the inside walls. What a mess! And what upset me more was that I had sent all of Janet's clothes away for laundering before departing México so that they would be fresh when she arrived. UGH!

I would later conclude that all the caulking around the portholes had dried out over the previous three years in the tropics and would require replacing. Nevertheless, for now, there was nothing I could do. When it rained, it came in and, in turn, soaked either end of my bed as well. It didn't take long before a musty, wet-dog and mildew odour took over, which eventually permeated the entire boat.

For the following two days, we were treated to a barrage of weather conditions: calms followed by heavy rains and short-lived gales energized by, often fierce, lighting storms. We were driving the boat hard, mustering as much sail as the boat would carry at all times while trying to sail as sharp as possible to eliminate covering any extra miles. We needed to keep a close eye on the boat's trim and to be at hand if the wind suddenly blew up. Sleeping in the cockpit on my off watches was now my new routine, something I would continue to do for the remainder of the voyage.

The doldrums were living up to its reputation, and the conditions were taking its toll on the crew, especially Nick, who reverted to being deathly ill. With the cycling weather conditions, the sea's waves became confused, so Nick, who had also attempted to sleep in the cockpit, was, as he would described it, "a washing machine." Even the cockpit was extremely uncomfortable for him, and his gangly length took up most of the room, making it difficult for the watch crew to trim sail or even make themselves comfortable. There was no room for two of us to sleep out there at the same time! Nick had to go! So I made a suggestion.

"Nick, why don't you go down below and jump into my bed. It's a good sea berth in these conditions. I have a fan right above, and the hatch is open a crack, so you can get some fresh air."

All the other hatches and ports were closed due to the rain and spray coming over the deck at times. My hatch over the bed was the only one that could be left open without having all that weather coming inside the boat and I wasn't using the bed at this point anyway. Nick groaned at first, then declined.

"Marina, you need to help," I said "You need to get him into my bed. He will feel better. I insist!"

I don't know if it was because Nick didn't want to impose on me by accepting the offer or perhaps he believed he would die if he attempted to move, but he still continued to refuse until Marina and I badgered him enough to get him in there. Marina stripped the wet sheets off the bed and made him a dry bunk, and while she was doing that, Mark disappeared below and came back with a strip of pills.

"Here, Nick. Take these," he said as he passed the tablets to him. Nick had been taking Gravol TM to combat his seasickness, but they failed miserably to relieve his symptoms. After Marina dragged Nick below and put him in my bed, Mark looked at me.

"Those are the Stugeron that I was saving for emergencies, but I guess Nick qualifies. I couldn't watch him suffer any longer," Mark said, with a chuckle.

Before we departed México, Mark and I went to the pharmacy where he purchased Stugeron tablets. They contain cinnarizine, an antihistamine medicine that works in the brain. It prevents an area of the brain called the vomiting centre from receiving nerve messages sent from the vestibular apparatus in the inner ear. Stugeron is not available in Canada or the United States; it's expensive, but is one of the best anti-nausea meds around. With Nick properly drugged and out of the way, we settled in for another unsettled night of more lightning and baby gales, necessitating a great deal of sail handling. Mark and I were up and down most of the night. By morning, the sky cleared and the sea conditions had improved and, fortunately, so had Nick. A good night's sleep and Mark's pills had done the trick, and Nick was back to his usual self.

We had a relaxing day for the most part and were able to keep *Maiatla* moving between 3 to 5 knots in a northerly wind. But by sunset, the conditions deteriorated, and it was getting ugly again. The winds first shifted back to the south, then veer to the west and back again to the south, bringing with it more rain, which only seemed to fall during the calms between wind shifts. It was a dark night, dark as any that I have known, and unnerving. We were only 112 kilometres (70 miles) from Isla Pinta, the northeastern most island and guardian of the gateway to the Galápagos.

Under normal circumstances, this would have been an exciting time as we approached land and nearing our destination, but we were fighting the current, trying to stay on the eastern side of Isla Pinta and not be pushed down, which would carry us deep into the island chain and all of its reefs and wicked currents. Slightly before sun up, I awoke crumpled up on the port side of the cockpit where I had spent the night wrapped in a blanket. It had turned surprisingly chilly in the wee hours of the morning. I wanted to check on our progress, so slipping below, I put the kettle on for a cup of tea and then checked the chart. We were within 8 kilometres (5 miles) of Isla Pinta. On our present heading, which was south by east, we would miss her by only a couple of miles. A little too close for comfort, but I had little choice. I wasn't happy, but at least we would pass the island on her eastern shore during daylight.

"Morning, Andy," Mark greeted me as he exited the head and made his way back to the cockpit to sit next to the radar screen. "I have the island on radar about 5 miles out. I think it's off our starboard bow a little bit, but it's hard to tell with the screen spinning about as it does."

By the light of the dim flashlight Mark was holding, I could see Marina sitting upright in the back of the cockpit opposite Mark. I'm not sure when our watches became so mixed up, but with the constant sail changes and trimming, we all found ourselves on deck often during our off watch. Nick, who would normally be on watch at this time of the morning, was back in my cabin and more than likely out of it, fast asleep. However, like the rest of us, he was up at all hours as *Maiatla* required constant attention, and we all found it easier to sleep when the opportunity presented itself.

"Yes, I know the island is near. I had a look at the chart, and it is right out there," I said as I pointed forward into the dark. It was pre-dawn, and I had to strain my vision to see the faint loom of the distant sunrise. We all nervously waited, wondering what sight the daylight would bring. We knew the island was there, and I was hoping that the thick cloud cover would permit us to at least a glimpse of our foe. At about 5 kilometres (3 miles) out, there was enough light to make out an island if it was there, but the low clouds and what looked like a mist or tropical haze blurred the horizon. Isla Pinta was a fleeting ghost on our confused radar, but I knew she was there and close now. As if Poseidon had heard our most inner thoughts and prayers, a break in the clouds to the south opened up. Like fiery lances, the sun's streaks backlit a rounded peak that rose out of a broken sea as black as ink.

"There it is," I called out as I pointed. "Land Ho!" I called half-heartedly. I was thrilled to finally see the Galápagos Islands, to have finally have made it here, but the joy was tempered with the reality that I could not welcome the sight as if it were a friendly one. In fact, I wished that we were passing too far to the east to even see this island. For us, the island was an unwanted apparition and over the next few hours we watched as Isla Pinta grew large and more menacing. As if one island wasn't trouble enough, Isla Pinta's bigger sister, Isla Marchena, a place already known for shipwrecks and tragedy, appeared in the distance.

While ghosting along under full sail, the advancing day brightened, the wind began to falter and the currents increased as we approached these volcanic peaks. The looming islands sent an involuntary shudder through me as I feared that we would be soon fighting for the boat's survival as well as our own.

Figure 10. A frigate birds circles our mast looking for a place to roost.

Chapter 6

Paradise's Hostile Lands

"The future is in the hands of those who explore . . . and from all the beauty they discover while crossing perpetually receding frontiers, they develop for nature and for humankind an infinite love."
—Jacques-Yves Cousteau, oceanographer

The Galápagos were discovered in 1535 by Fray Tomás de Berlanga, the Bishop of Panamá. This was the epic time of Spanish exploration and discovery. However, de Berlanga was no explorer, and his discovery was by pure chance. He had been sailing to Peru when his ship became becalmed and was carried west by strong currents, driving his ship in amongst the islands. Tomás de Berlanga saw little value in his newly-discovered land. He wrote that it was inhabited only by birds, seals and reptiles, and was *"dross, worthless, because it [had] not the power of raising a little grass, but only some thistles."*

When de Berlanga and his shipmates sighted the first of the islands, his ship had only a two-day supply of water remaining. The island he sighted was most likely Genovesa, which lies a score of miles southeast of Isla Marchena, apparently unseen by de Berlanga. They found no fresh water on the first island they landed on, so they carried on to a second (one with high peaks, possibly Santa Cruz), but ran out of water by the time they reached it. After several days, they succeeded in finding water *"in a ravine among rocks."* (Later visitors learned to find water by following tortoise paths into the highlands.) In the meantime, de Berlanga's men were reduced to squeezing water from prickly pear cactus pads. De Berlanga reported sighting two more large islands, possibly Santiago and Isabela, and landed on the smaller of the two. The archipelago, consisting of 18 main islands, three smaller islands, and 107 rocks and islets and submerged reefs, would eventually be labelled on the world map at that time as "Insulae de los Galopegos," named for the saddleback giant tortoises de Berlanga found thriving upon this otherwise unforgiving land.

On the morning of our ninth day at sea, Isla Pinta grew more defined as the morning light intensified and the clouds parted, as if directed to do so. The excitement of our first sighting of the Galápagos Islands and witnessing the beauty of the uninhabited, green and black volcanic isle was lost to us, because even from 3.2 kilometres (2 miles) out, we could see the surf breaking with an incredible force upon the inhospitable shore. White breakers stood out in sharp contrast against the black bolder beach. The sea dashed upon the island's fringes. Its foaming plumes emerged like the teeth of a great beast, ready to chew upon the bones of any unwary ship that dare venture too close. Such were the sights and thoughts that swept through the minds of the weary crew of the *Maiatla*.

Isla Pinta is a small, elongated island that has an area of 60 square kilometres (23 square miles) and the peak of its still active shield volcano rises out of the sea to a height of 777 metres (2,549 feet). Isla Pinta last erupted in 1991. However, she appears to be asleep. Isla Pinta has been uninhibited by humans since its birth, some three-quarters of a million years ago, only moments ago in geological time, making Isla Pinta a mere infant when compared to Espanola, the oldest of the Galápagos Islands. Espanola is believed to be almost four million years old, approximately the same age as the island of Kauai in Hawaii, which lies some 6437 kilometres (4000 miles) of desolate ocean to the northeast. Today, Isla Pinta is parched under the equatorial sun, boasting no water of its own, with sparse vegetation that relies on tropical showers and the settling morning dew for hydration.

From the foredeck of *Maiatla,* we could see the paths of the most recent lava flows, a moonscape of pillowing lava slashed by deep crevices, all surrounded by patches of low-lying scrub brush and reaching cacti. Despite the alien and unforgiving environment, the island is still home to a healthy population of swallow-tailed gulls, marine iguanas, sparrow hawks, fur seals and a number of other birds and mammals.

Isla Pinta was also the most northern major island in the Galápagos that supported a thriving tortoise population. However, that all changed with the intentional introduction of feral goats. Left behind by explorers, merchants, whalers and pirates, goats arrived in the Galápagos in the 16th and 17th centuries. The animals were intended to provide a source of meat for passing ships. The slow moving tortoises proved much easier to catch and would survive for months in the dark holds of a sailing ship. The goats, with no natural predators, flourished over time. By the 1990s, it was estimated that as many as 250,000 goats were bleating and ravaging with impunity across the Galápagos. They ate everything, stripping the islands of their foliage and competing with the islands endemic creatures. The islands' tortoises, those ancient standard-bearers of biodiversity, began to die out as their food source was decimated when the landscape changed due to the erosion of the soils once anchoring vegetation.

Today, on Isla Pinta, the giant tortoises are now all gone. Its last surviving member, a celebrity by the name of Lonesome George, was rescued and taken to the island of Santa Cruz where he would spend 40 years of his life under the watchful eyes of caretakers. While living at the Darwin Interpretation Centre, all efforts to entice George to breed failed. George would not produce any offspring. Lonesome George, the last of the Isla Pinta species of Galápagos tortoises, died on the 24th of June, 2012.

After the formation of the Galápagos National Park in 1959, efforts commenced to rid the islands of any invasive introduced species, with the feral goats at the top of the hit list. It took almost 20 years, but the goats were finally eradicated on Isla Pinta by 1990 when the use of "Judas" goats were employed. Locating the last of the goats proved to be challenging in the rugged terrain, so the park's people employed an ingenious method to hunt them down.

Feral goats are gregarious in nature and like to live and travel with others. The hunters took advantage of this nature by radio tagging goats, then releasing them onto the island. The "Judas" goats would seek out their own kind and, by doing what comes naturally, betrayed the herd's location. Using helicopters as shooting platforms, the park's hunters would use radio tracking devices to locate herds, and then they would cull them until the goats were all eventually eradicated. While today the vegetation and natural wildlife on Isla Pinta has mostly recovered, the likes of Lonesome George will never again graze upon her volcanic slopes.

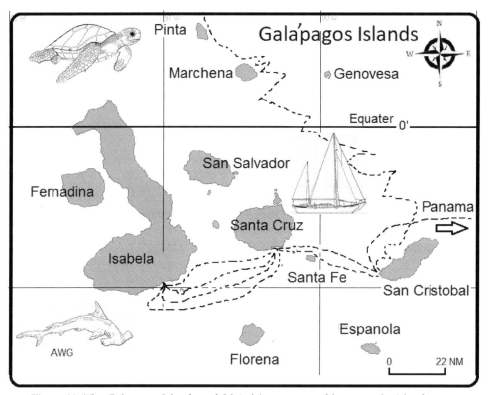

Figure 11. The Galapagos Islands and *Maiatla's* route to and between the islands over the following months.

The volcanic eruption, the demise of Lonesome George and the goat genocide capper were not the only recent events of note to have occurred upon this bastion of lizards and finches.

Isla Marchena is also entwined in the 1930s Mystery of Floreana Island, involving politics, feuding clans, love triangles and the mysterious disappearances and deaths (suspected to be murder) of local settlers. One of the prominent figures of the day vanished in transit to the mainland. However, many months later, his dismembered body, along with his ship's captain, was found mummified on the slopes of Isla Marchena.

Despite fighting the westerly-setting current, by late morning, we had successfully left Isla Pinta behind in our wake and were fast approaching its nearest neighbour. The light wind had again switched to the south, and the sky had cleared—by all accounts, it was a beautiful day. Under full sail, we were hard on the wind, sailing at 3 to 4 knots. The fine weather brought with it a relaxing mood that seeped into the souls of the crew, soothing nerves and temperaments, or at least for the time being.

Isla Marchena was named after Spanish Monk Fray Antonio de Marchena, who was among the first to visit the island. The seventh largest island in the Galápagos, at 130 square kilometres (50 square miles) in size, Isla Marchena is two times larger than its neighbour, Isla Pinta. However, despite its much larger size, Isla Marchena's volcano only raises to 343 metres (1125 feet) or half the height of Isla Pinta. However, like any sibling, the pair of islands shares geographical features, a similar terrain, and flora and fauna habitat.

"Andy, looks like we are getting pushed over towards the island," Mark said, with some concern.

"The wind is shifting as we get closer to land, so I can head more easterly, but I don't think we are going to clear the island on this tack."

All the crew had been relaxing in the cockpit for most of the morning, taking turns steering and sail trimming. We had opened the top, unzipped the dodge, to let the sun in and to hopefully dry out some of the cushions. We had all been watching with a keen interest our approach to Isla Marchena, and the closer we got to the island, the more obvious it became that we were being sucked between the two islands as the current accelerated between them. We were still about 5 to 6 kilometres (3 or 4 miles) offshore, and despite having the bow of the boat pointing away from land at a good 45-degree angle, it was obvious that we were on a collision course with the shore. "Let's hold our course for a little bit. Maybe the current will weaken as we approach the point," I said.

It would prove to be wishful thinking on my part, because as we closed on the southernmost point of the island, the stronger the current became. Before I realized it, we were within a mile of the beach and closing fast. To make matters worse, the wind was slowly dropping and so was our speed.

"Okay, let's tack and head back offshore and get away from this island, guys," I ordered.

Marina took the helm as Mark and Nick handled the sheets for the main and head sail. *Maiatla's* head slowly swung across the wind. As Marina found our new tack and heading, we quickly sheeted the sails home.

"I didn't think we had enough headway to make the tack," Mark said while sounding both surprised and relieved.

Often when we tack in light air, the boat would stall as she comes head to wind, leaving us dead in the water. Under normal circumstances, if this were to happen, we would fire up the engine and give ourselves a little push to drive the head of the boat out of "irons," as it is called. But we were engine-less and didn't have that option. So, in this case, we would have to wait until we drifted backward, driven by the wind until the rudder grabbed, swinging the head one way or another. Stalling head to wind in light wind is a common trait shared by most heavy displaced vessels; still, I was reasonably sure that *Maiatla* would make it around this time, so I attempted it. However, if I had any doubt about completing the tack, I would have employed a trick used by the tall ships of the great days of sail—a trick called "to ware ship."

To ware ship is to haul about to an opposite tack by jibing or having the wind cross the stern instead of the bow. Using this technique, the sails remain full of wind and don't flutter and lose their drive. You will spin almost in a complete circle, but at least you will end up pointing and sailing in the direction that you intend to go.

On our new heading, Isla Marchena was now directly astern, and thankfully, we were making good on our escape, albeit slowly. We spent the better part of the rest of the day tacking offshore, then making another run for the headland in an effort to round the island. Several times we tacked and tacked back, at times coming perilously close to the shore. By the late afternoon, as we were headed back in shore and it began to look like we would make it this time, but Isla Marchena was not about to give in and let us pass.

The crew was tensely quiet until Mark broke the silence. He cast a gauging look towards a shore that was now closer than it had been all day. "Shit, Andy, I think the wind is dropping again, and at this rate, we won't make it past that point."

I had noticed that some time earlier, Mark had fallen silent. He was now looking a bit sullen, assuming a brooding posture and air. The frustration of tacking back and forth, trying to clear the headland with nothing more than incremental gains was taking its toll not only on Mark, but the rest of the crew as well. Mark was right, within a few minutes, the wind had all but vanished, and if we didn't do something and fast, we would be at best drawn closer to shore and then shot through the pass or, worse, driven onto the beach. To be drawn between the islands would mean that we would lose all hope of getting any wind as we drifted in the wind shadow of the island's volcano. Dead in the water without the ability to manoeuvre—who knows where we would drift too or how long it would take to sail or drift back into some usable wind? We desperately needed to stay on the windward side of the islands.

"Okay, I've had enough of this shit!" I said aloud as I stood and left the cockpit, heading to the aft deck. "I'm going to launch the dinghy and put the 15 horse outboard on her and pull us back offshore and around this stupid Island! Mark, Nick, come back here and give me a hand!" I ordered.

Within 15 minutes, I had the inflatable dinghy in the water, strapped tight alongside the boat, and while I was getting ready to start the engine, I discovered a stowaway in the bottom of the dink.

"Marina, you wanna grab this?" I said as I stood up in the dinghy with arms stretched out and cupped hands. Marina came to the rail and took hold of the tiny black and white bird. The bird appeared to be almost dead, as it didn't have the strength or desire to struggle.

"Ah, poor thing. Must be exhausted," Marina said as she took the critter into the cockpit. While I carried on firing up the outboard, Marina made a temporary hospital bed out of a plastic cat litter box and a piece of non-skid matting. We have rescued exhausted birds at sea before with rarely a positive outcome. I suspected that this little bird's situation was also hopeless, but it would not hurt to let Marina try and nurse it back to health. Fortunately, in the morning, Marina would cast the tiny bird aloft where it would take to wings and fly off, and hopefully in the right direction.

With the dink's mercury revved fully, it managed to drive *Maiatla* up to a swift 3 knots.

"Okay, Mark, show our ass to the island and let's get out of here!" I ordered.

I remained in the bottom of the dinghy, keeping my hand on the throttle, while Mark spun *Maiatla's* spoke wheel to turn us onto the desired course. There was still a considerable swell that had *Maiatla* rolling hard, and when it did, the dink was nearly jerked clear of the water. Then, as *Maiatla* rolled back the other way, the dink was in danger of being dunked beneath the water. Waves exploded between the two boats, sending sheets of water over me on a regular basis. Thank goodness the water was warm, as I was soon drenched and sitting in several inches of sloshing water. The whole experience was not unlike sitting in a tubful of water while riding a rollercoaster.

It was a rough ride, but it was working. Mark steered a course that took us away from the dangerous shore, and after only half an hour, the wind filled back in from a favourable direction. Aloft went the sails, and we made ready to lift the dinghy back aboard, casting off, then manoeuvring the dinghy aft to where I was able to hook on the davit falls. Once secured, I decided that it would be a good time for a swim.

"Marina, go in the handhold on the port side of the cockpit and get my face mask will you, please? I wanna have a look at the bottom," I said.

We were required to arrive in the Galápagos with a perfectly clean bottom. Even a hand full of barnacles could get us turned away, so this was a good a time as any to have a look.

Donning the mask, I rolled out of the dinghy while making sure to hang onto a hand rope. The boat was still only drifting, but in the rising breeze, she was still moving through the water at better than half a knot. I did not want to get left behind. For a few moments, I dunked my head to peer beneath the boat. It was astounding. The water was as warm as any bath tub and clear as a pool. Looking down, the bottom wasn't visible, but that was not surprising, as it was over 300 metres (985 feet) deep here. Nevertheless, I'm sure that I could easily see over 50 metres (164 feet) down.

Maiatla appeared as suspended in air as she wallowed between swells. Equally above and below the water, it was a lonely looking place, a placid sea, with little in the way of marine life. Even the few birds that we did see were as lazy as the wind and sea. They would causally glide by or bob effortlessly upon the swell while looking thoroughly bored with life and disinterested in us. I pushed off the dinghy while reaching for the rudder under the boat. If we had any marine growth, it would be on the boat propeller because it is the only part of the underside of the boat without antifouling paint, which inhibits marine growth. Again, pushing off the trailing edge of the rudder, I shot down and quickly latched onto the four-blade bronze propeller. Nope, nothing—she was clean. It was surprising not to find at least some growth on the propeller. After having the bottom painted, the boat had been back in the water for a good 15 days, time enough to give barnacles a foot hold on any unprotected surface. Things can and do grow fast, but it was looking good. Satisfied that the hull was clean, we hauled the dink back aboard and got underway.

With the slight change of wind direction, we finally sailed past the southernmost point of Isla Marchena, but barely. It was a tense time as we nipped by the land by the width of a seal's whisker, so to speak. A sense of relief flooded across the faces of the crew when we realized that we had finally made it around, even Mark returned to his customary cheery self. Mark would later confide in me that the long day of being beaten about by Isla Marchena, the island that wouldn't let us pass, was his darkest moment of the voyage. Marina, later hearing this, concurred and said that she had become concerned enough to check the items in her "ditch" bag—just in case.

With the relatively calm seas and Nick back to his old self, it was time for dinner, and we were all eagerly anticipating him to cook up something grand. Marina went below to see what we could have, but when she opened the lid of the refrigerator, her nose told her that something wasn't right. Apparently due to all the rough weather, we had not been able to run the generator as much as hoped. This left the ship's batteries depleted to a point where the refrigerator was not functioning properly.

After digging around, Marina located a rancid chicken, which was immediately and unceremoniously buried at sea. After sniffing the pack of pork chops, they were deemed salvageable and became dinner. Nick made a killer meal of mashed potatoes, the last of the carrots with butter sauce, sautéed cabbage, garlic and onions, with soy sauce and pork chops. If the chops did smell a bit funky, the reams of garlic Nick used did the trick. Yummy, but everyone was still too stressed out to truly enjoy it.

Later that night, I sent on our usual email update, without too much difficulty, to the family and friends. Then I addressed an email to Bolívar, my Galápagos agent on San Cristóbal Island, informing him that we had broken down, but were not in danger and still on track to arrive on the 19th of December. I also asked him that if required, could he arrange for a tow into the harbour when we arrived. Under normal circumstances, I would not have hesitated to tack right into the bay and drop the anchor while under sail. It was a manoeuvre we have had done on other occasions and always with success. However, Puerto Baquerizo Moreno is surrounded by reefs, with large breaking waves pounding upon them if the swell has a westerly component.

When I Google Earthed the harbour, the satellite photograph clearly showed great white and menacing breakers flanking the anchored boats. It was obvious why the north shore was reported to be a popular surfing spot. That and the 3 to 5 knot current running paralleling the shore gave me reason to pause. On English charts, Puerto Baquerizo Moreno is called "Wreck Bay" and for good reason. The last victim to suffer the wrath of the anchorage was as recent as May of 2014 when the island's supply vessel, *Galapaface,* ran aground, causing the release of thousands of litres of fuel oil into the otherwise pristine waters. Asking for a tow into the harbour was the prudent thing to do.

Isla Marchena, with its lonesome ghosts, both human and tortoise alike, fell astern. The wind remained solid after increasing to 12 to 15 knots, so we continued to tack up wind, clawing our way south with nothing in front of us but our final destination on San Cristóbal, some 137 kilometres (85 miles) away—less than a day away if we could sail straight there. However, in reality, we would have to cover almost twice that distance, as our long tacks off to either side of our rhumb line would add precious miles and another day to our voyage. Also ahead, lay in waiting, was a less tangible obstacle—a dark line etched upon the chart, an imagined line of epic notoriety and of great importance to me, in particular—the equator.

Zero degrees of latitude, the division between the northern and southern hemispheres, was a short 42 kilometres (26 miles) to the south of us now. The equator, the line that people often refer too when they talk of friends and family as being "a world away." After some 15 years of cruising *Maiatla* to distant shores, I would finally sail *Maiatla* cross the equator and enter the legendary South Pacific, the sub-equatorial Oceania and the dominion of Darwin, Cook and Melville, along with so many other cruisers and explores that I have been reading about and living vicariously through since my early childhood. I was personally excited with the prospect.

The equator is the only place on Earth where water runs straight down when you pull the plug on the sink, and it is also where you weigh 5 pounds less. We did not have a scale to prove this assertion, but Marina claimed she could feel the difference as she felt lighter on her feet.

Looking to windward, I could see the clouds filling in and an apparent thunderstorm on the horizon. It was looking like we were in for another long night of gales and sail changes, which would mean another night of catching catnaps in the cockpit. However, in truth, I was happy to have wind, even if it would prove to be too much wind. When conditions were rough, I did not like to let Nick or Marina on deck, but at least, I had Mark. Mark loved to do the foredeck work in foul weather. On the foredeck, Mark was in his glory. The rougher and wetter it was up there, the better he liked it. Me on the other hand, not so much.

Marina's journal from the following morning read: *The wind has been building steady. I have not seen any whales, but during the morning, I saw a cloud shaped like a whale. Was this some kind of sign? The wind had been building nicely, and when the boat was making 7 knots steady, I had orders to wake up Andy. He and Mark harnessed up and went out to reef some of the sail.*

This time it isn't a squall, but a gale blowing 30 plus. The guys love being out there in the wind, with the boat bucking. As I write this, I watch from the helm, waiting for orders, keeping an eye on them should one fall overboard. Their balance is amazing. I'd have a hard time crawling at this point. When they come back, their faces are flushed and spirits are high. Mark's leg is bleeding. Our joke is that it wasn't good unless he bled. There are cuts and bruises on both of them. Visibly, we have all gotten leaner, fitter. We joke that we should start a fitness sailing program. Just walking on a boat and keeping balance is a workout. Now imagine doing it 24/7. Back in the cockpit, Andy stares out to the confused sea. Pointing at the waves, Andy says, "There is something strong out there. It's going to blow all day. There will be little cooking."

Chapter 7

Shellbacks Are Made, Not Born!

"I have sea foam in my veins, I understand the language of waves."
—Jean Cocteau

Many contemporary nautical traditions date well back to the time of the square sail, but with more vessels cruising the high sea than ever before, and not to mention the advent of the small cruising vessels, nautical traditions are as prevalent as ever.

No one is sure when or how the "line-crossing ceremony," or the "Order of Neptune" as it is called, first came about. The nautical ritual dates back at least 400 years in western seafaring. The ceremony observes a mariner's transformation from slimy Pollywog, a seaman who hasn't crossed the equator, to trusty Shellback, also called a Son or Daughter of Neptune. It was originally a way for sailors to be tested for their seaworthiness. Normally, crossing the equator is a big event for sailors and is often celebrated with grog and pranks set upon the crew.

When a ship crosses the equator, King Neptune comes aboard to exercise authority over his domain and to sit in judgment of the charges brought against any Pollywogs who are only posing as sailors and haven't paid proper homage to the god of the sea. High ranking members of the crew and those who have been Shellbacks the longest dress up in elaborate costume and each play the part of King Neptune's court. Often the ship's captain might play the part of King Neptune himself.

What follows is a day of festivities and revelry, which builds camaraderie among the seafaring crew, and often later, the event is commemorated by an ear piercing or a tattoo. (My crew discussed getting a Southern Cross tattoo.)

As for the crew of the *Maiatla*, neither Mark nor Nick nor Marina had ever sailed over the equator before, and they were looking forward to it. As for myself, I too was energized despite having crossed before on other vessels. I had planned some challenges and pranks to play upon the crew, but my shipmates were becoming exhausted and may not be in the mood to don a wig made of fish entrails accented with flying fish earrings. We would have to wait and see when the time comes.

Our tenth night at sea proved to be our most challenging. It was a difficult night of sailing close hauled on a wind that kept clocking and backing 15 or 20 degrees (shifting clockwise, then counter-clockwise). The wind died to an almost calm and then quickly built to a gale as another squall charged in. I did not believe it possible, but it rained harder than at any another time. A deluge of biblical proportions that I was sure would cause the ocean to rise while engulfing the very islands that we were seeking. Then when the rain stopped, the gales screamed in.

Figure 12. Mark and Andrew preparing to put a reef in the main sail as a squall approaches.

Another batten ripped out of the mainsail, and to make matters worse, before midnight, while attempting to furl the big headsail in advance of the next blow, the furling gear jammed. *Maiatla* was dangerously overpowered, and now she was constantly on her ear. We needed to reduce sail and quickly!

"I'm going to go onto the foredeck to see what's up with the furling gear," I said to Mark and Nick. "Give me some slack on the line when I tell you. Then you guys can try rolling the sail up when I give you the word, okay?"

Maiatla was charging headlong into a 3-metre (9.8-feet) swells, with her port rail buried in the sea and the water hissing and foaming as it rushed close by like a raging river. First donning a head lamp, I harnessed up and clipped onto the jack line that ran the length of the deck. Exiting the cockpit on the high side and with a spray blowing over me each time the bow took the plunge, I crawled on all fours to the bow pulpit. Seawater washed along the length of deck. Then with a gurgle and urgency, it shot out of the scupper on the leeward side to escape back into the sea.

I wedged myself into the pulpit and looked forward. The night was black, and the headlamp was useless for illuminating anything beyond a few metres. I could hear and sense the waves coming from up ahead as they crested, then collapsed. Most rolled harmlessly under the bow, but others slapped *Maiatla's* starboard cheek, causing her to shudder under the blow as spray was launched high into the air.

"Okay, Mark, get Marina to let the sheet go, and you guys haul in the headsail," I shouted over my shoulder.

As Marina let lose the sheet, the line that was under tremendous strain hissed as it was pulled off of the winch drum, causing the big sail to dump all the wind it contained. Flapping and snapping wildly, the big sail shuddered in the still building wind. With losing the drive from the genoa, *Maiatla* slowed right down as she no longer had the power she needed to overpower the head swells, decelerating the boat from 7 knots down to 2 knots in a matter of seconds. Grabbing the roller drum where the furling line was attached, I tried to give it a twist while calling back to the cockpit. "Okay, guys, give me some slack!"

I attempted to furl the sail by hand, but only managed to spin the drum a quarter turn. I worked the drum backwards and forwards, hoping to make a complete revolution, but could not. Twisting the drum this way and that, in hopes of freeing whatever was stuck, but while doing so, I could feel a grinding in the lower bearings.

"Shit!" I said to myself. "The bearings are going!"

I glanced upward, towards the top of the mast, but I couldn't see the upper drum. If the problem was there, a fouled line around the head stay perhaps, there was nothing I could do about it now. However, we had too much sail out, and we needed to reduce sail or risk damming the rigging or tearing the big sail. While wiping the rain from my eyes, I shifted position so that I could plant my feet on the pulpit while gripping the furling line with both hands.

"Okay, now, guys, pull!" I ordered while leaning back to heave on the line. My hands were soaked and wrinkled, causing the taught line to cut into my hands, tearing flesh. It would have been smarter to have worn gloves. Despite the three of us pulling with all of our might, the furling gear refused to budge at first, but then it slowly spun once, then twice. With each turn and heaving grunt from the three of us, it became easier as the sail continued to roll up. Once three quarters of the sail had vanished, I called aft.

"Okay, that's good. Cleat it off there, and, Marina, sheet it back in and get us driving!"

Marina wrapped the now limp sheet around the winch and began pulling. Once under tension, she inserted the winch handle in the drum and cranked until the now much smaller sail was taught as a board and filling with wind. As the sail took hold of the wind, the boat accelerated until we were back driving into the waves at a respectable 6 knots. More importantly, we were no longer heeled hard over.

This process would be repeated several times during the night by either Mark or myself going forward. For the most part, *Maiatla* was doing well, allowing us to flog her like she was a rented mule. We were sailing her hard so that she could drive into the big swells while fighting the strong cross current. So far, this voyage had been hard on her, and the furling gear wasn't the only boat system that was showing signs of failing.

If the bearing in the furling gear was starting to go, not only was I in for an expensive and difficult repair, but any work done on the furling gear would have to wait until we arrived in Panamá, some three months later. The loss of the furling gear would mean that the big sail would have to be manually put up and taken down and one size would have to fit all wind conditions, as there would be no way of reducing the size of the sail once set. I have a smaller number two headsail that we could use, but with either sail, the manual handling of sail from now on would mean much more work.

It had been almost four years since we departed our home port of Ladysmith, on Vancouver Island, and we had driven the boat hard, mostly in the tropical heat and humidity, which plays havoc with a boat's systems. *Maiatla* was in need of some TLC. Unfortunately, that too will have to wait till we arrive in Panamá.

Aside from the freezer packing it in, the electric bilge pump had also mutinied, so we were forced to hand pump. There still was an enormous amount of rain water finding its way into the bilge, and the hydraulic steering pump had also developed a nasty habit of spitting oil out of one of its orifices. A viscous trickle streamed down the back of the engine instrument panel, finding its way into the towel drawer in the head below. What oil that wasn't caught by a bath towel seeped down through the engine room, coating the transmission before completing its downward migration to finally collect in the bilge along with the rain water. Aside from the resulting greasy mess it was creating, the steering was working fine as long as we kept the fluid in the reservoir topped up.

Marina woke me with a nudge early in the morning as I slept on the low side of the boat. "Andy, we are nearing the equator, and I know you want to be up for that!"

I hadn't been out long. We had thrown another reef in the main only half an hour earlier. Mark and Marina were already fixated on the GPS coordinates when the countdown commenced. Taking the captain's chair, I studied the readings; we were only half a mile from leaving the northern hemisphere and entering the legendary South Pacific.

"I'm going to go down below and get my dad's hat," Marina said. "Do you think I should wake Nick for this?" she asked while pausing at the top of the companion steps.

I looked at Mark for a moment. "I don't know. Not much to see, just some numbers counting down, but if you want to go ahead," I suggested.

Marina returned to the cockpit a few minutes later wearing a white Gilligan-style hat, the hat her father wore when he and Marina's mother departed Vancouver and sailed to Hawaii on their way to the South Pacific. Unfortunately, they would never cross the equator, and Oahu is as far as they would ever sail.

Nick stumbled up to the cockpit, shortly after her, with bleary bloodshot eyes. Sweet sleep would be sacrificed for this once-in-a-lifetime occasion.

In the wee hours of the morning, soggy misery was haunting the cockpit, yet the crew sat in quiet expectation. We were catching our breaths after having just finished reefing the main as another gale crashed upon us. No one was in the celebrating mood. We watched the GPS count down the last few seconds. When the GPS kicked over to display all zeros in the line indicating latitude, and the big "N" switched to an "S," we furnished a weak cheer. Nick and I broke out into the song "Rawhide" and gave ourselves a verbal pat on the back. Not sure how we decided on "Rawhide," but somehow the situation seemed to demand we sing something rough and manly, and since nothing nautical came to mind, the old cowpoke song would have to do. All in all, it was an anticlimactic moment as exhaustion had taken its toll. This was my third crossing of the equator by boat and by far the hardest won.

Not surprisingly, the Order of Crossing the Line is not the only nautical tradition that involves a vessel and crew passing or reaching a geographical position on this blue marble of ours. Below is a list of "Orders" recognized and often celebrated by the nautical set.

- The Order of Shellbacks is for sailors who have crossed the equator.
- The Order of Golden Shellback is for sailors who have crossed the point where the equator crosses the International Date Line.
- The Order of Emerald Shellback or Royal Diamond Shellback is for sailors who cross at 0 degrees off the coast of West Africa (where the equator crosses the prime meridian).
- The Order of the Blue Nose is for sailors who have crossed the Arctic Circle.
- The Order of the Red Nose is for sailors who have crossed the Antarctic Circle.
- The Order Imperial Order of the Golden Dragon is for sailors and marines who have crossed the International Date Line.
- The Order of the Ditch is for sailors who have passed through the Panamá Canal.
- The Order of the Rock is for sailors who have transited the Strait of Gibraltar.
- The Order of the Safari to Suez is for sailors who have passed through the Suez Canal.

- The Order Realm of the Czars is for sailors who have crossed into the Black Sea.
- The Order of Magellan is for sailors who have circumnavigated the Earth.
- The Order of the Lakes is for sailors who have sailed on all five Great Lakes.
- The Order of the Spanish Main is for sailors who have sailed in the Caribbean.
- The Order of the Sparrow is for sailors who have sailed on all seven seas (North Atlantic, South Atlantic, North Pacific, South Pacific, Indian, Arctic, and Antarctic Oceans).
- The Order of the Ebony Shellback is for sailors who have crossed the equator on Lake Victoria.
- The Royal Order of Purple Porpoises is for sailors who have crossed the junction of the equator and the International Date Line at the Sacred Hour of the Vernal Equinox.

Despite spending the better part of my life mucking about in boats, I can only claim three orders from the above list. The Order of Shellbacks—I have crossed the equator by boat on three separate occasions: once back in 1968, returning from Australia to Canada by ship; again in 2009, sailing a motor launch from Nuka Hiva, Marquises, to México; and of course, *Maiatla's* most recent crossing as described in this book. The Order of the Blue Nose—I achieved this in the early 1980s when I spent three seasons in the high Canadian Arctic working as a commercial diver on drill ships and salvage vessels in the Beaufort Sea. The Imperial Order of the Golden Dragon—I also achieved this in 1968, on our voyage from Australia to Fort Lauderdale, Florida.

Nevertheless, before this year's voyage is over, I will be able to add the Order of the Ditch—a long anticipated event for me, which would enable me to place a big checkmark on my life's bucket list.

For the first time in four days, we spotted the lights of not one but two other vessels: one approaching from our stern; the other, from the bow. Since they weren't large vessels, we assumed that they were charter boats travelling between the islands. We had heard that the charter boats like to travel at night, after departing their last anchorage and after sunset, so that the guests could sleep while they travelled to their next destination—a good practice, as it allowed for maximum shore time at that location. The lights passed within a couple of miles, only to disappear. We had finally altered our course from a due south heading to a westerly course. We were paralleling the island of San Cristóbal, now some 8 kilometres (5 miles) on our port beam. It was looking as though we were going to make it to our destination a full day ahead of the girls, but our struggle wasn't over yet—not by a long shot.

Chapter 8

Landfall and Encounter with an Ecuadorian Patrol Boat!

"The sea does not reward those who are too anxious, too greedy, or too impatient. One should lie empty, open, choiceless as a beach—waiting for a gift from the sea."
—Anne Morrow Lindbergh

It is a long and rugged island, with sharp black spires protruding from fields of congealed lava. The crown of the island, the volcano Cerro Mundo, is often concealed in the dusky clouds, and its verdant cape, shoulders draped in lush vegetation streaked with veins of black rock, cascades down to adorn the haunches of the sleeping mountain.

A couple miles from shore, surrounded by deep clear water, stands an ancient volcanic plug, Roca Pateadora, as it is marked upon the chart, but called León Dormido by the islanders and Kicker Rock by the gringos. No matter what you call it, the rock reaches over 100 metres (328 feet) into the sky. As if cleaved in two by the gods, the plug is split from its guano-covered brow down to the coral-carpeted seabed, creating a natural passage that the sea surges through, a fissure wide enough for herds of sea lions, manta rays and smalls ships to navigate. The rock appeared as I envisioned the 'The Pillars of Hercules" in Homer's legend and Greek mythology.

A thick mist drifted along on the breeze, partially masking the shore that was home to primordial looking creatures. Strange and massive fowl floated effortlessly aloft. Fleet amphibians played in the surf while armoured reptilians patrolled the island's hinterlands. As viewed from the deck, the island's appearance, its very nature, suggested the existence of lurking dragons.

It is the easternmost island in the Galápagos Archipelago, as well as one of the oldest islands geologically. The island is approximately 40 kilometres (25 miles) long by 16 kilometres (10 miles) wide or 640 square kilometres (250 square miles). Its Spanish and official Ecuadorian name is "San Cristóbal," which comes from the patron saint of seafarers, St. Christopher—a dude I can relate too and whose medal my parents had gifted me as a young man venturing off to sea. I assume it brought them some level of comfort to imagine that I had a saint along for the ride, as their young son had a habit of disappearing for most of the day exploring Lake Ontario, often all on his lonesome.

San Cristóbal Island is composed of three or four fused volcanoes, all are believed to be extinct. The island is home to the oldest permanent settlement of all the Galápagos Islands. San Cristóbal is also where the crew of the English surveying-vessel the *Beagle* first went ashore in the Galápagos in 1835. On board the *Beagle* and keen to explore was a young English clergyman and aspiring naturalist by the name of Charles Darwin (1809–1882). Darwin was astonished by the islands' creatures, and it was here, after studying the islands' diversified finch population, that an idea first germinated in his mind that would eventually flower into the Theory of Evolution. Darwin's finches would prove to be the root of his controversial theories that would ultimately change, for some, how people viewed the natural world and, for others, their understanding of God.

After flunking out of medical school in Edinburgh, Scotland, Darwin attended Cambridge University in England to pursue a Divinity degree. A 22-year-old Darwin graduated, but barely. Still, it was while at Cambridge that he had a chance encounter with a group of scholars calling themselves the Northern Light Society. Their goal was to advance the fledgling science of naturalism and to have it recognized as a true profession. It would prove to be a fortuitous encounter for the young Darwin, who, at the time, was struggling to find his own place in the world. I found it interesting to note that, in Darwin's time, amateur naturalists were often members of the clergy and people of deep religious conviction.

It was believed since God had created all of the natural world and its creatures, the close study of the world's flora and fauna would indisputably prove the existence of God. Evidence of the divine that skeptics and atheists alike could ill refute. This informal pursuit to be naturalists was tailored made for the men of the cloth and, in particular, to a young Charles, who had an eye for detail, along with a deep fascination for beetles and other things that crawled, slithered or flew.

When the Cambridge Dons were approached by the British Admiralty to supply a naturalist for an upcoming voyage to the bottom of the world, to the notorious Cape Horn, members of the Northern Lights were approached. Since such an arduous voyage of an indeterminate length of time was the realm of young men, Darwin's name was presented as a likely candidate, a choice that would change science forever.

Darwinism, as it would later be referred too, is a theory of biological evolution developed by Darwin and refined by others, stating that the survival of all species, their ability to compete and reproduce, is determined by natural selection—a radical concept for the day and one that was hotly disputed by the church at the time, igniting a theological and secular conflagration that still to this day burns as hot as ever.

However, what Darwin and other naturalist of the day eventually concluded was that instead of proving God's existence by studying His creations, the exact opposite happened. The Northern Light Society at the time saw this trend developing, but did not want to rush to any judgment, upsetting the powerful religious sector, and thus make it difficult for the Society to achieve their goal of having naturalism recognized as a valid profession. The young, impressionable Darwin, who didn't have a scientific reputation to protect, may have been a good choice for the Northern Lights to help advance their own agenda.

Over the following 30 years and after Darwin's and other scholars' theories came to light, the church and clergymen distanced themselves from this science that ran contrary to their beliefs. It had become painfully obvious that the more they studied nature, the less connected to God the natural world appeared to be. God's natural world was full of contradictions that Biblical scholars were at a loss to explain or even accept.

For many years after his insightful voyage, Darwin kept his opinions and conclusions to himself, fearing ridicule from the church and his colleagues. Darwin even kept this secret from his own wife due to her own fierce religious beliefs. If Darwin could not find the courage to present his findings to his own spouse, how could he possibly approach the church and tell them that what they believed was wrong? Darwin had no doubt that his theory would shake English piety to the core, creating a firestorm of debate. Darwin was fully aware of the fate of others in the scientific community that had suffered for challenging the doctrine of organized religion. Death for heresy had all been too common in the not too distant past. Fortunately for Darwin, the mid-1800s were more enlightened, and he did not need to fear being burned at the stake for his views. However, that the religious and scientific community alike would ostracize him was extremely probable.

Eventually, through ongoing scientific research, the connection, the tie, between the natural world and God was strained enough that it finally snapped. The days of pastors romping through green fields with butterfly nets were over. The church decided that it best distance itself from natural sciences and rely on their belief system to prove God's existence. They knew it, so therefore, it must be so.

On San Cristóbal's volcano Cerro Mundo, there is a small lake, which is the only large source of fresh water in all the islands. The availability of fresh water is what led to the early settlement of San Cristóbal and the development of a penal colony built on the island in 1880 for prisoners from mainland Ecuador. The colony later turned into a military base for Ecuador, and then, some years later, the export centre for the island's products, including sugar, coffee, cattle, fish, lime and cassava (the starchy tuberous root of a tropical tree used as food in tropical countries).

On our eleventh morning at sea, we closed in on San Cristóbal's western shore where the harbour Puerto Baquerizo Moreno is located. The wind was fresh out of the southeast, at 15 to 20 knots, as we sailed fast to the west while being pushed by a 1 knot westerly setting current. Still in the predawn, we tacked back towards shore to cover the remaining 16 kilometres (10 miles) to the harbour, but as luck would have it, as dawn broke, the wind died, leaving us to wallow in a deep swell with 12.8 kilometres (8 miles) to go. Although frustrating, I knew the wind leaving us at this stage wouldn't last long. The wind customarily dropped at this time of the morning, but then usually returned within an hour or so. Normally, I would have had no problem waiting for the wind to return, but the strong west setting current had me worried. It was already dragging us back offshore while threatening to drive us right past the harbour mouth.

If the wind remained light throughout the day, we may not be able to sail back, forcing us to alter course and head to Isla Santa Cruz, some 74 kilometres (40 nautical miles) to the west. Aside from not having a permit to visit there yet and that my agent was on San Cristóbal, my biggest worry was that we would miss the girls' landing. We needed to make our intended landfall on San Cristóbal today and by whatever means possible. I decided that if we could manoeuvre closer into shore and anchor until the wind returned, that would be our best option. Quickly I checked the depth sounder, and I was not surprised to find the water right where we were still 50 fathoms (150 metres or 300 feet) deep. Anchoring in 25 fathoms was possible, but 50 fathoms was far too deep. The contour line on the chart showed deep water almost all the way into beach, so we were too far out.

Figure 13. Kicker Rock comes into view as we approach San Cristóbal Island.

Still, from this vantage point, so close and yet too far from shore, we could see what we would later learn was Kicker Rock, a popular snorkelling spot. After an hour of bobbing about without a breath of wind, I decided to again launch the dinghy and attempt to tow *Maiatla* the remaining miles to the harbour.

Once we had the dink in the water, rather than tying it alongside and pushing us along, as we did off of Isla Marchena, I decided to pull *Maiatla* along. Nick ran a line over the bow which I took and secured to the stern of the dinghy. I throttled up with the intent to taking my girl in tow, but she would have none of it. She was like a stubborn horse that refused to be led out of the barn. With each passing of a swell, *Maiatla* reared her head, jerking the dink back with such force that on the very first wave, I fell off the seat to land abruptly in the bow, legs and arms flailing. No matter how hard I tried and despite the engine at full throttle, *Maiatla* refused to be lead, and twice I was jerked backwards with such violence that the sea rushed over the stern while I, fearing the transom would be ripped right out of the boat.

I have towed *Maiatla* in this manner a few times over the years, but never in such a swell. Apparently this was not a good idea and right up there with sticking a wet finger in a light socket. After a few minutes of losing this battle, I decided to revert to my old tactic and strap the dink back alongside. In frustration, I dropped the tow line to motor around to the far side of *Maiatla*. However, when I moved clear of the bow, I noticed a large vessel, with a great bone in her teeth, off in the distance, and she was coming our way and fast.

Quickly, I jumped back aboard, took up the binoculars and studied the craft for a few moments. It was blue in colour with a helicopter pad on a raised platform at its amidships. The pad was likely a later addition, as the structure appeared flimsy. The little ship had the lines of an ocean tug, and from the speed at which it was headed, they were apparently on a mission. My crew had taken up station along either side of me as we all watched.

"Well, guys, looks like we are going to get a visit from an Ecuadorian patrol boat!" I said, with some trepidation in my voice.

The patrol boat manoeuvred to within a 100 metres (328 feet), reversing its engines to come to a complete stop paralleling us. We could see uniformed crew milling around the deck while looking us over.

A call came blaring over the VHF radio, and I knew it was directed at us. Dropping into the companion way, I snatched up the microphone. Using rudimentary Spanish, I manage to explain to the ship's captain who we were and what our intent was. I asked them if they could call my Galápagos agent to see if he could give us some assistance. It was obvious they recognized my agent's name, Bolívar, and I informed them that he was aware of our engine-less condition.

I had sent Bolívar an email over the ham radio a few days previous, so I was hopeful that he was ready for us. The patrol boat had in tow—a large skiff which was drawn up alongside. Three sailors quickly boarded the skiff then raced over to quickly come alongside *Maiatla*. One of the crew, who we later learned was the pilot of the helicopter, spoke some English. Javier informed me that his captain would request permission from the Port Captain for the patrol boat to tow us in.

After a few minutes of friendly talk, the three returned to their vessel, so we had no option but to hoist the dink back aboard and wait while drifting about. However, after an hour of waiting, the patrol boat suddenly launched its helicopter. We could see Javier waving to us as he raced towards shore. We were still watching the helicopter approach the island when we heard the Patrol boat re-engage its engines and motor off to the east in pursuit of Javier, leaving us to wonder what was going on.

While standing on the foredeck, watching our supposed help motor off, I felt a puff of wind from the south and it quickly built to a breeze. Not wanting to waste such a good wind, Mark and I hoisted the mainsail and, with much difficulty, unfurled the jib. I put *Maiatla* on a heading that would take us back offshore a few miles where I would then see if we could lay the harbour. We were happy to back underway.

Figure 14. *Maiatla* gets a visit from an Ecuadorian patrol boat.

Maiatla was sailing well at 5 knots, and as long as the west setting current didn't suck us past the point, I was confident that we would make it into the harbour. While the crew was tidying the lines, a burst of staccato Spanish came over the radio.

The voice was a bit garbled with static, as if transmitted from a long way off or from a weak radio, but I heard our boat name in there. Taking the binoculars, I scanned the shoreline, and sure enough, a couple of miles back, I spotted a small fishing boat, with two people in it, which appeared to be in hot pursuit of us.

"Hey, guys, I think our tow has arrived!" I said.

"Do we need it now, Andy?" Marina asked.

"We should be able to sail in. right?"

"Yes, I think so, but if they came all the way out here just for us, I guess we better take their help," I said, with some reservation.

I did not want to end the voyage this way, but it would at least ensure that we got into the harbour in time to meet the Janet and Teri.

"Let's tack back, and Nick, you wanna get that tow line ready again, please?"

We quickly spun the boat around and closed in on the fishing panga. Bolívar, our Galápagos agent, a bull of a man, and his lanky friend, Nacho, came alongside, and with a single 150 horsepower Evinrude, it was packing, easily taking us in tow. Upon first sight, it occurred to me that this pair could pass for a reasonable, but Latino, version of the Skipper and Gilligan from the TV sitcom Gilligan's Island.

So there we were, 11 days after departing México, making our landfall at the end of a long tow rope behind an 8-metre (26.2-feet) sports fishing boat. Perhaps not the most dignified way to conclude our (1609-kilometre) 1000-mile voyage to the islands, but we were all were exhausted and grateful for the assistance. As we entered the harbour I couldn't help but notice the massive surf breaks that bordered the channel that was less than half a mile wide. To enter under sail power alone would have been doable as long as the wind held out, but what if it didn't?

Nacho towed us in among some anchored charter boats and next to what looked like an 11-metre (37–foot) racing sloop. Bolívar called to me while gesturing that I should drop our anchor here, so in eight fathoms of water, we set our hook. It was a relief to finally get the anchor down in the tranquil waters of the bay.

The dropping of the anchor officially signalled the successful competing of the voyage to the Galápagos Islands. We still needed to clear in with customs, immigration, the Port Captain and the park's people. However, when Bolívar and Nacho pulled alongside, Bolívar let us know that clearing in would happen later that afternoon so until then, there was no going ashore. But no one was disappointed. Looking a little battered and dishevelled, the boat and crew were in desperate need of some TLC.

As our tow was made ready to cast off and head for shore, Bolívar discreetly pointed at Nacho when he wasn't looking while whispering to me in Spanish that I should tip Nacho for the tow. I was careful not to be overheard.

Figure 15. Rigging for a tow.

"How much do you recommend?" I queried Bolívar.

After a moment of thought, he said, "*Doscientos dólares de los Estados Unidos deberían hacerlo!*" (Two hundred United States dollars should do it!")

Nacho genuinely looked surprised when I handed him a wad of bills and thanked him for his services. I guess it was money well spent, but now that we were in the islands, the bloodletting had now commenced and the hemorrhaging that my wallet endured continued for several months.

Our rescuers motored off, leaving us to reflect on where we were and what to do now. We were in a full day ahead of the girls, which was a great relief for us as well as Janet and Teri, who were already in transit from Canada to Ecuador. The shore side celebrations would have to come later. For now, we would all settle for cracking a bottle and a stiff rum drink, then a nap.

Chapter 9

San Cristóbal Island, the Galápagos

" . . . by far the most remarkable feature in the natural history of this archipelago . . . is that the different islands to a considerable extent are inhabited by a different set of beings. . . . I never dreamed that islands, about 50 or 60 miles apart, and most of them in sight of each other, formed of precisely the same rocks, placed under a similar climate, rising to a nearly equal height, would have been differently tenanted. . . . Extreme tameness . . . is common to all the terrestrial species . . . A gun is here superfluous; for with the muzzle I pushed a hawk off the branch of a tree."
—Charles Darwin, The Voyage of the Beagle

We had only been napping for a couple of hours before I heard a nearby voice calling in Spanish over the whine of an outboard engine. Feeling worse for having a short and interrupted sleep, I reluctantly leaped out of my berth to make my way topside. The fresh breeze helped to waken me as I spied a panga, a water taxi, approaching and loaded with several people dressed in pressed, tan-coloured uniforms. I found it odd the panga was flying a large skull and crossbones, the Jolly Roger pirate flag, and along the side at the stern, painted in bold script, was the name "*La Perla Negra,*" *The Black Pearl.*

Standing in the stern with the outboard's tiller in hand was a dashing middle-age Latino male, sporting a Led Zeppelin t-shirt, blue jeans and a red bandanna on his head. Apparently Johnny Depp and his swashbuckling character, Captain Jack Sparrow, had even invaded this faraway outpost. Danny, the owner and operator of this particular water taxi, would soon befriend us. Next to Danny was what looked to be a diver in a wet suit, mask and snorkel, and in front, waving with a welcoming grin, was our agent, Bolívar.

It was time for our visit from the islands' officialdom—our inspection and check in process was about to commence. I wasn't worried as I thought I had all the bases covered and my paperwork was in order. I had my Mexican fumigation certificate, my Mexican international zarpe (permission to leave México) and crews' passports. All of which had to be photocopied in triplicate. I had "Do Not Dump Overboard" signs in English as well as Spanish posted next to the bilge pump, head (toilet) and garbage can.

Once the delegation was aboard and the inspectors accepted the cold bottled water that I had offered, the interrogation began with the scrutiny of my ship's papers and passports. There were many questions asked of me by the Port Captain, a lanky fellow whose uniform looked to be a size or two too large for him. I attempted to answer the Port Captain's questions, but Bolívar gave me little opportunity to respond, as he quickly cut me off. I didn't mind. He was ready with all the right answers. I said little the whole time, which I decided was a good thing, as the process to receive permission and the procedures to visit here were long and complicated and I believe it could have been easy to say or do the wrong thing. The Port Captain passed our paperwork to a pair of Immigration officers, who followed with more questions that Bolívar fielded.

While we were all occupied, the young diver with jet black hair and brown eyes, a strapping lad barley out of his teens, gently slipped over the side to perform the bottom inspection. However, I was startled when he resurfaced and clambered back aboard in less than a couple of minutes. This, I thought, could be either a good or bad sign.

I had been told that if the diver finds so as much as a single barnacle, we would be sent back to sea, over 64 kilometres (40 miles) out, beyond the islands' territorial waters and have to clean the bottom. They may even send divers with us to make sure that we complied and charge us some great sum of money for the privilege. Since we were still engine-less, heading back to sea was out of the question, and under international shipping law, a state cannot force an non-seaworthy vessel out of a safe harbour. So if the diver did locate some growth, we may be in for some legal problems.

However, when I went under the boat a few days ago, I didn't see anything, but I had forgotten to check inside the thru-hulls that lead to the engine and toilet. In the calm and security of these holes, sea critters often like to make their home, and I was fully aware how fast marine life can take hold and grow. Back in 2007, when we departed Hawaii, I cleaned the bottom the day before our departure. When we arrived in Nanaimo 23 days later, I found on the transom above the rudder at the waterline a clump of white goose-neck barnacles, with stems almost 25 millimetres (1 inch) thick and 200 millimetres (8 inches) long. After a vigorous steaming, the barnacles would have been suitable for the galley table if they hadn't been growing on supposed toxic paint.

Here in the Galápagos, we would later see an American boat ordered out of the harbour under such circumstances. The yacht's captain claimed that he had the boat hauled and cleaned 10 days previously before leaving Panamá and he "had the paperwork to prove it!" I heard him declare over the radio. However, it was no use; all his bitter complaining and ranting fell on deaf ears. The yacht had to go and now! The unnecessary members of the crew were given permission to land and check into a hotel. The captain and mate, ordered to leave, hauled anchor before sunset and reluctantly headed back to sea. It was entertaining to listen to the events unfold over the radio, and I'm sure that we weren't the only ones in town listening in.

I thought it funny when the captain claimed to have supporting paperwork from the boat yard in Panamá. I already knew that paperwork doesn't prove anything. When I had the boat fumigated back in Chiapas, after repairing my buggy freezer, another cruiser approach me at dockside while I watched great clouds of fumigation dust waft out of *Maiatla*. Sounding a bit confused the fellow asked me what was going on.

"Got some bugs that I need to get rid of because I'm heading to the Galápagos next month and I need a certificate," I said. I wasn't in the mood to dive into the bugs-in-the-freezer story, so I left that part out.

"Funny," he said while still sounding a bit confused, "I saw a lot of boats heading to the Galápagos from Panamá, and they all got their fumigation certificate without getting sprayed. The cruisers just pay their $100 and a guy delivers the papers! In my six months there, I never saw once a boat gone through like this!" He pointed at *Maiatla,* now looking as if she were on fire as dust billowed out of the cockpit in a mushroom like cloud.

I guess in Panamá money talks, and as I later found out, it also spoke loudly in México. My fumigation job was done far ahead of schedule. I was still six weeks away from departing for the Galápagos and fully expected to have it performed a second time, not only to ensure that the pests were all dead, but to have a certificate dated a day before departing for the islands. However, I did not have to worry. Enrique, from the marina office, later came to me and asked, "So what date do you want on your certificate? Perhaps you want it for the day of your departure next month? Yes?" He suggested this with a knowing smile.

Back aboard *Maiatla* in the Galápagos, for me, receiving the third degree from all these officials was a tense few moments. The diver stood close by, obviously waiting for a break in the conversation to make his report. I breathed a sigh of relief when the Port Captain finally looked over to the diver, and the young man gave a smile and a thumbs up. Lastly the Port Captain asked to see the placement of the "No Dump" signs and to have a look in the bilge, a request that suddenly put a lump into my throat.

Leading the way below, I pointed out the signs, then opened the engine room door and stood back. The Port Captain stuck his head inside the room, and with a flashlight in hand, he peered under the engine. Below the engine, for all to see, were several gallons of black oily water, sloshing about—the result of my attempt to repair the fuel injector pump and the repeated bleeding of the fuel lines when I unsuccessfully attempted to restart the engine. In hindsight, I regretted not flushing the bilge water and oil out while still far at sea, but I assume now that, in my exhausted state, the thought never had occurred to me. This was a big problem and may even lead to our expulsion from the islands until we were able to deal with it. However, after explaining where the oil had come from, the Port Captain warned me not to dump it here. Eagerly I agreed to comply.

With the Port Captain satisfied, the agricultural agents had their turn and asked about fresh fruits and vegetables, but after being at sea for almost a week and a half, there wasn't anything fresh remaining. With our voyage taking longer than anticipated, our provisions were running low, and Marina had started rationing the food. Breakfast was oatmeal; the eggs were being saved for dinners. Our last package of meat had turned and been tossed overboard. Marina had also dumped the last of the fruit overboard that very morning. Whatever scraps were left found their way into a magnificent omelette Nick had made as we were being towed into port.

Nonetheless, to make sure, they requested to go below and check the refrigerator. After finding nothing of concern inside and closing the fridge door, the inspector suddenly noticed a small leafy plant that clung to a stick, a piece of driftwood that Janet had tied to the swinging basket hung atop of the galley sink. This basket usually held apples, bananas and other fruit, but it was now empty. The inspector pointed out the plant to his aid, who asked me in Spanish what it was. I did my best to explain, and with the help of Bolívar, whose English wasn't much better than my Spanish, we told them that it was an "air plant" that my wife had collected last year in Costa Rica.

The plant was an epiphyte, a shrub that grows harmlessly upon another plant and derives its moisture and nutrients from the air, rain and sometimes from debris accumulating around it. It was the only living organism we had on the boat (excluding us, mould and possibly some hard to kill cockroaches), and I had forgotten about it. I fully expected to have the plant confiscated, but after some animated conversation between the pair of agricultural agents, they decided that we could keep the plant, so long as I placed it into a Ziploc bag until after we had departed the Galápagos.

Next it was the park's representatives turn to ask questions and to present to me a folder of the do's and don'ts while on the islands. Again we agreed to abide by the rules, of which there were oh so many.

In our original conversations, via emails months ago, Bolívar recommended that I apply for a 60-day visa with the right to visit, one time only, three different islands—San Cristóbal, Santa Cruz and Isabela. I was told that we would not be permitted to back track, so we had to choose wisely how we would visit the islands and how long we would want to stay on each. When Bolívar handed me our visa and I read it, I was delighted to see that our permit was for 90 days, not 60. An unexpected surprise and one that would come in handy if my boat problems continued.

After almost two hours of paper-shuffling and rubber-stamping, we were officially in—well, we were as soon as I handed the thick envelope stuffed with American $100 bills over to Bolívar, who would handle the disbursement of cash. The Galápagos would prove to be an expensive trip. Now we were free to go ashore and explore, and all were eager to do so.

It was by now late in the afternoon, so we quickly hailed over the radio a taxi *acuático*. The crew of *Maiatla* was soon headed for a large concrete quay where we would step ashore onto dry land for the first time in 11 days. The harbour was a busy one, with what must have been over 20 inter-island charter boats and dozens of local fishing vessels scattered around the bay. The fishing boats all looked as if they had been driven hard, as many were in obvious states of disrepair, in total contrast to the various prosperous-looking charter vessels. Obviously, filleting the wallets of rich tourists was much more lucrative than filleting fish.

Figure 16. The happy crew set foot on dry land for the first time in 11 days.

The tour or charter boats often arrived late in the afternoon, at which time they disgorged their passengers into waiting inflatable boats to ferry them ashore for an evening of sightseeing. The mother ships were usually large power vessels, with only a few sporting sail. The vessels could accommodate anywhere from 20 to 60 guests. Often these boats would depart late at night, bound for their next destination, making room for the next wave of tour boats. The barrage of small boats heading in and out never ended, as there was a constant flow of people heading to and from shore all through the daylight hours and late into the night. The economic prosperity of the island ebbed and flowed with the tide of tourists.

The quay is the centre of town and the hub of all the boating activity. We had to wait our turn to unload onto the small floating dock next to the concrete quay, as one of the inter-island ferries was unloading passengers. Boisterous tourists and locals alike, with reams of baggage, clambered up the sloping ramp and crumbling concrete steps. These ferry boats are not what we are used to back home. These island ferries are nothing more than 10 or 12 metres (32 to 39 feet), converted sports fishing boats with three enormous engines (600 horsepower or more) and seating for as many people as humanly possible. I'm sure Noah's Ark was never so crowed. At least the passengers are offered life jackets, and the boats travel in packs in case one of them got into difficulty transiting the 80-odd kilometres (50-odd miles) of open ocean between most of the islands.

At the head of the dock, there was what appeared to be some kind of customs inspection. Four uniformed officers sat behind table tops, waiting to inspect the ferries passengers—an inspection station not unlike one found at an international airport. As we were about to learn, these inspectors were in place to scrutinize all new arrivals to this island, making sure they do not intentionally or accidentally bring other insects, animal or plant species from any of the neighbouring islands. Even transporting beach sand or seashells from one island to the next was strictly forbidden. Fortunately, we were now exempt, as we had already undergone our inspection out on *Maiatla* earlier that day when our air plant was quarantined, so we would not be required to stand in line here.

Figure 17. A majestic marine iguana greets us.

While we drifted around for a few minutes, waiting for our turn at the dock, I was surprised to see dozens of resting sea lions lounging on some unused concrete steps and even under the ramp of the floating loading dock. The giant Galápagos sea lions napped while paying little attention to all the people passing by. These seemingly lazy creatures, some 3000 or so, call the harbour home and can be seen almost anywhere around the town's waterfront. That is a disproportionate amount animals, considering that the town's human population is slightly ahead at 4500 souls.

At first glance, the site of all these apparently fearless animals, many with adorable-looking pups idling or squawking to be fed, appeared charming. We also spotted large black marine iguanas sunning themselves upon the rocks while ignoring the red Sally Lightfoot crabs that scurried about. With all the wildlife and people, it was magnificent spectacle of organized chaos and all under the indifferent gaze of dozens of blue-footed boobies, roosting upon handrails and signs. This wild menagerie of animals cohabitating and interwoven with human urbanites is a shining example of how man and critter could live in relative harmony, and exactly how Darwin had described it, with the animals having no reason or history of fearing man.

However, upon closer scrutiny, I could see that the symbiotic relationship between man and beast was not as harmonious as it had first appeared.

The creatures, often the size of a sofa, would layabout on sidewalks, forcing pedestrians to walk around, or they would decide to have a nap in street gutters, at times dozens in a row, as if parked cars. Vehicle traffic was often halted as sea lions took it upon themselves to cross the roads without regard for normal pedestrian-crossing protocols.

Figure 18. Fearless the marine iguana stands its ground.

A coveted spot that the animals often fought over was atop of the many park benches. Snot-filled growls and barks were the noisy sign of a territorial dispute over some coveted resting place. The dispute that may be with another sea lion or, as often, a human wanting a seat, or with a picture-taking tourist approaching too close.

No place was safe from the creatures, as any open or unattended boat became a choice spot for a nap. Thankfully, *Maiatla* had enough freeboard, so the sea lions could not get aboard. Other boats were not so fortunate. Even the bed of a pickup truck, whose owner carelessly left the tailgate down, was a clear invitation to sea weary beast to rest and holiday. I had intended to bring *Maiatla's* inflatable ashore, but I was told that left at the dock, or even in the water alongside *Maiatla,* it would soon be filled with noisy smelling creatures. Not only that, but aside from the possibility that they may use the soft rubber sides as a teething ring, they would fill the dink with the worst smelling, fishy excrement possibly known to man.

The pinnipeds weren't the only culprits when it came to importing sights and smells better left at sea. The marine iguanas were constantly leaving thumb-sized poop bombs upon the sidewalks, and handrails often appeared to have been whitewashed from all the seabird droppings. In an effort to combat the unsightly and nose-offending by-product of nature close at hand, the town employs a special cleaning squad that, commencing at daybreak, works to shovel the crap and hose the urine-stained streets and paths. It's an ongoing battle (principally for the benefit of the tourist) for the town's people, one that the wildlife is oblivious to. Still the locals accept that it as part of everyday life here in the Galápagos Islands, with the understanding that it's the animal's presence that attracts the dollars that the town's residents rely on.

Danny gunned the panga's engine to shoot for a spot as soon as the ferry moved out of the way. It was a bit like bumper boats because a couple of the tourist inflatables also made a run for the same spot. Never to be outdone, the captain of the *La Perla Negra* was quicker and, with practised efficiency, brought us alongside the dock, but not without enduring a salvo of rude comments from one of the boats that Danny had cut off. It may have been in Spanish, but the curse and hand gesture transcended all languages, making it self-evident.

I noticed, as we started up the ramp, a massive head protruding from under the steps. The big bull never lifted his head. He only opened one eye, which suspiciously watched us slip by at a distance within easy nipping range, if the animal made a short lunge. At the top of the ramp, there was a sign welcoming all to San Cristóbal Island, so we stopped long enough to have another tourist take our picture. It was an emotional time for us all. We had successfully crossed 1609 kilometres (1000 miles) of hostile open ocean, overcame mechanical breakdowns, exhaustion and sleep deprivation to finally make landfall on not just any tropical South Sea island—we had made it to the enchanted Galápagos Islands.

I had first read about the Galápagos Islands in Robin Lee Grahams's book, *Dove*, first published in 1972. *Dove* was the true story of an American teen who set out in 1965 to sail solo around the world.

On his final leg of his five-year odyssey, in 1970, Graham landed on San Cristóbal and sat on anchor not far from where *Maiatla* was now moored. As a teen, I had dreamed of following in Graham's wake, and to be standing here now, where that young man had once stood, was a bittersweet moment for me. Gazing around the harbour, I felt myself commence to tear up. I had completed one of my lifelong dreams, and that filled me with great joy and satisfaction. But, in another way, the bell tolling our success rung hollow, as I wasn't able to share this moment with my soul mate. I missed Janet terribly. I wiped my eyes as the crew gave each other a round of high fives and hugs. Then we were off to find a restaurant for dinner, celebratory drinks and to talk about what we would all do after Janet and Teri arrived the following day.

Chapter 10

Foreigners in a Foreign Land

"A man who dares to waste one hour of time
has not discovered the value of life."
—Charles Darwin

The island of San Cristóbal is the only island in the Galápagos with an abundance of fresh water. The source of the water is mainly due to the extinct volcano, Cerro Mundo, which has a crater lake, with a larger perimeter lake, sitting in a valley in its northern wind shadow. The town of Puerto Baquerizo Moreno on San Cristóbal is the capital for all of the Galápagos province. The island is home to many of the government offices, as well as an Ecuadorian Navy facility, and an airport with daily flights to the mainland. There are approximately 5,400 residents on the entire island, making it home to the second largest human population in Galápagos, after Santa Cruz. The majority of inhabitants make their living in government, tourism and artisanal fishing. Artisanal fisheries are small-scale fisheries set up for subsistence or local markets, such as restaurants. Generally the fishermen use traditional fishing techniques and small boats, which was what we found moored around *Maiatla*.

This port town is also home to the Galápagos Academic Institute for the Arts and Sciences (GAIAS) of the Universidad San Francisco de Quito. This institution serves as a base of operation for local university students to carry out thesis work and for international students to participate in semester abroad programs. Many of the students could be seen after class laying about or playing at the nearby beaches. The GNPS Interpretation Centre is located near town, and we were told that it is an excellent source of information for visitors.

A short drive inland is the only other community upon the island. El Progreso, which was established in 1869, is the oldest surviving settlement in the Galápagos. Approximately 500 people live in this small farming community located on the side of an extinct volcano approximately 8 kilometres (5 miles) from Puerto Baquerizo Moreno. In the mid-1800s, a penal colony was established there for prisoners from Ecuador. Later the area was taken over by a business man named Manuel Julián

Cobos. He was a cruel despot of a man, who founded a sugar cane plantation and constructed a sugar refinery around 1870. Cobos built a fortune selling sugar to the mainland while using the prisoners as slave labour, but as typically happens to such tyrants, his workers revolted and killed him. Today the sugar plant is gone, and the area has reverted to a peaceful farming community.

There is an unusual phenomenon associated with walking on land for the first time after spending some time at sea. It can be unsettling and involves the same mechanism that causes seasickness with the motion of the ocean. The sensation of still being at sea once you again trod upon land is a common one that most people experience. People often describe it as feeling the boat rocking despite having both feet planted firmly on the ground. This phenomenon can have real consequences, which can cause a person to stagger while walking (the common sailor swaggering), lose balance and, in some extreme cases, fall over.

When I was a mere child of eight years, my family and I crossed the Pacific Ocean on a cruise ship. We spent some weeks at sea crossing from Sydney, Australia, to Acapulco, México, with only a brief stop in Suva Fiji along the way. When we visited shore for the first time in Acapulco and I found my footing on the concrete dock, the lack of movement caused what I call "land sickness." There, in front of all, I threw up "my heart," a condition that wouldn't stop until my parents acquiesced to my pleas to take me back to the ship. No sooner had I returned aboard than my vomiting ceased, and I felt fine. Fortunately, the condition only lasted until the next day when, reluctantly, I attempted to become a landsman once again.

This time in the Galápagos, it was funny to see everyone weaving their way down the dock.

"My feet are too heavy! Who tied the weights to my feet?" Marina asked, with the others looking on and obviously feeling the same way. Fortunately, none of us succumb to "land sickness" here in the Galápagos, which in hindsight would have surely be a cruel blow for poor Nick (but funny as hell to be sure!).

Our planned ripsnorter of a night on the town to celebrate our successful (mostly) landing in Ecuador was a bust, but it wasn't due to the lack of entertainment opportunities or cantinas. Once we found our land legs on shore, we made our way along the *malecón,* snapping pictures of sea lions and iguanas. Curiosity led us inland as we turned onto José de Villamil, a cobbled brick side street that has concrete block buildings, one or two stories tall, painted in bright colours, with perhaps the intention to clash. Tiny shops, tucked in alleyways next to tour offices and souvenir shops, dominate this part of town while, in the adjacent block, restaurants and tiny grocery and hardware stores rule. And still a block further, on the main thoroughfare, Avenida *Alsacio Northia*, street venders sell hibachi roasted, glazed chicken on a stick and barbequed corn painted with butter and dipped in grated cheddar cheese. All served curb side el fresco, or in Spanish, *el aire libre* (outdoor) dining, under a street light, usually by the city park and grade school.

This feasting experience would soon become one of Janet's and my favourites. We'd sit by the beach Playa Mann while watching the sunset over the harbour and a contently anchored *Maiatla*.

Figure 19. Marina shares a park bench with a sea lion.

There were many places to eat, some of which were nothing more than a doorway that provided a scrap of shelter from the hot sun, a pair of tables or battered wooden stools against a hastily fashioned counter. These family run, tiny alcoves restaurants offer surprisingly tasty dishes and inexpensive meals. Perfect for a cheap cruiser who loves to eat while watching interesting locals, and with my big white Tilley hat and San Diego t-shirt, I blended right in.

We also discovered that most restaurants offered a "set" lunch during certain hours. For $3 to $4, you would be served a glass of fresh juice and a big bowl of delicious soup—Ecuador is well known for its soups—followed by the main entrée of rice, salad and your choice of fish, beef or pork. Most would indeed be fortunate to eat this well. These micro restaurants were popular with the locals and became our favourite haunts. We would often eat out twice a day.

With Bolívar's help, we found the farmers' market, which was located several streets inland from the harbour in a dirty alleyway. Stalls, constructed from corrugated metal sheeting and old shipping pallets, lined one side of the road and were usually well stocked with fresh eggs, meats, fish, prawns and yellow-skinned chickens. All produce goods were locally grown and fresh.

Pineapples, papaya and lemons were abundant, and most of the goods were at a reasonable cost. We purchased whole large chickens, ready for the *Maiatla's* barbeque, for $10. Around the corner from the farmers' market was the island's only large grocery store—a co-op where all the goods were imported from the mainland at great expense, which would explain why we had to pay $15 USD for a small jar of peanut butter. If it was not caught, harvested or grown on the islands, it was expensive. Rum and other spirits were no exception. The previous year, we had stopped in Costa Rica to see an old cruising buddy, Travis of the sailing vessel *Mystery Tramp*. Travis had swallowed the anchor and married a Costa Rican *chica* and opened a waterfront bar. I asked Travis if he needed anything. Well we ended up purchasing a case of Tequila in Mexico and smuggling it in *Maiatla's* bilge into Costa Rica. I was now sorry that I had turned over all of the case to him to sell at his bar or had the forethought of purchasing one for myself.

At this time of the day, in late afternoon, most of the restaurants were surprisingly empty of customers, so finding a good eating place based on the size of the crowd did not work. We made our way to an intersection where an open-sided restaurant called Rosita's sat. All hungry, we decided to take a table there, as it looked much safer or perhaps more "normal" than the alley diners. I guess we weren't that adventurous yet, but that would come. Because it was still hot enough to scorch the hide off a desert rattler, we decided to take a table in the near corner where the two open walls met and where a breeze entered the building. The meal was great; some had roast chicken, others fish or prawns and, of course, all washed down by the local Pilsner beer. Not surprising because of the heat, we were all sweating a deluge, so the cold-bottled water went down as often as the beer. By the time the meal was done the sun was setting and so were we.

Instead of finding a Latin salsa club to gyrate and drink the night away in celebration, we all voted to return to the boat to sleep. It wasn't until then that I appreciated how exhausted we all were and how much of a toll the voyage had demanded from us all.

It would be several days of taking it easy and napping at the drop of a hat before any one of us began to feel truly normal again. We could not locate our new friend Danny down on the dock, so we took an alternate water taxi back to our boat.

Back aboard, it was more beers while one another took a shower before bed. While waiting my turn, I stripped off and dived headlong into the ocean for a swim alongside. The water was gloriously warm. Floating on my back, I gazed aloft into the rapidly advancing night to watch for the stars and constellations as one by one they appeared.

For an hour, I was content to drift around while being rocked gently by the swell that reached deep into the bay. It was a magical moment for me. After countless years of dreaming about sailing to the legendary South Pacific on my own boat, I was here, basking in its warm sea, bathing in the golden light of the moon as it rose over the top of an ancient volcano. We had made it, and I could not stop the smile from invading my face.

I was sorry I did not have Janet floating by my side, but I was happy with the knowledge that she would soon be. While lying there, I even had several sea lions swim over to check me out, first circling at arm's reach, then diving under to further check me out from below. One of the beasts, while below, blew a set of large bubbles that rose up under me to tickle my back. I hoped that the air came out of the head end.

I don't know if it was from the meal, the beer or the relaxation, or from being satiated, but I began to drift, not only away from the boat, but into sleep. With my head immersed in the water, I could hear the waves as they crashed upon the nearby beach, the clicking of tiny pebbles as they tumbled in the surf, and the muted barking of sea lions—a symphony of natural sounds that succeeded in numbing all senses. I was at peace.

Listening carefully, I noticed a faint and distant whine, an unnatural sound, hardly noticeable at first, but it quickly grew in intensity, more distinct with each passing moment, until the sound eclipsed all other noise. When the sound finally registered in my numb brain, I snapped my head up to find myself staring at the bow wave of a racing inflatable poised to run me down. Quickly I waved my arms in the air, catching the attention of several people riding in the bow, who instantly called to the driver to stop.

The Zodiac, with perhaps 20 or more tourists on their way to shore, came to a halt directly next to me. I grabbed the side of their boat to keep from sliding under the hull and perhaps getting entangled in the propeller, which would have been a nasty business to be sure. I was asked in English by the tourists, who were largely geriatric, if I was okay. (I think I detected a southern U.S. drawl in the group.) I responded that I was fine and that my boat was over there. Next came a barrage of questions— "where are you from?" and "how long did it take you to sail here?"

I did my best to give them the short version, and many were surprised to learn that we were Canadian, which lead to more questions. Some of those questions could leave a person to ponder. I was asked, "Do we sleep on the boat?" "Where do we anchor at night on the high seas?" "Has our boat ever sunk?" "Have we ever been attacked by pirates?"

This reminded me of my favourite question that came not from this group, but from a gentleman on the dock in México. When the man spotted the wind generator at the top of the mizzen mast, he asked, "What is the fan for?"

I said, "It's a wind generator." He smiled and replied, "That would come in handy when there wasn't any wind. Ah, just how much wind can it make?"

I did my best to answer all the questions thrown at me by this group in the inflatable dinghy. Satisfied that I was okay, the driver, obviously annoyed and anxious to get moving, indicated that I should swim away.

When I complied, a new wave of aghast elderly voices rose as the group suddenly realized that the person they had almost run over and had been causally chatting with was butt naked. Janet has always said that I have wonderful swimmer's butt and legs, so I believe I showed my finest side as I breast stroked back home.

Chapter 11

The Admirals Arrive

"There is nothing more admirable than when two people who see eye to eye keep house as man and wife, confounding their enemies and delighting their friends."
—Homer, *The Odyssey*

J anet and Teri arrived without a hitch in the afternoon of the following day. It had been a long two days of travelling, and they were tired. A sense of relief filled them both when their aircraft circled San Cristóbal harbour and they saw out the window *Maiatla* at anchor below, surrounded by crystalline blue water. They had arrived and they knew now for sure that we were waiting for them. The four of us checked into our hostel, Casa de Nelly, located two blocks from the water. Our hostel, as they are called locally, was a three-story white stucco building that surrounded an open courtyard. It boasted meandering cobblestone paths between buildings, and cozy-looking hammocks were suspended between shade trees.

Our hostel had 10 rooms in all, each with a sparsely furnished décor. In our deluxe room, there were three double beds, a desk, a couple of uncomfortable wooden chairs and a small flat screen TV. The room was lit by two anemic, curlicue florescent light bulbs that hung naked from the ceiling. We had a small but private toilet and shower. I'm not sure why you would want too, but you couldn't open the bathroom door while sitting on the toilet. It wasn't the Ritz, but it was clean and, most important of all, it had a luxurious air-conditioner poised in the window—a godsend in the heat of the day. Mark and I had been sweating it out in the tropical heat for over a month now, and for the most part, we had adjusted to the often stifling heat and humidity. However, the girls had just walked off an air-conditioned aircraft and were smacked direct in the face by the steel-withering heat that exists in the most torrid regions of the tropics. As Janet and Teri passed though the sliding glass doors of the airport to tread upon the sunny sidewalk, uncharacteristically Janet blurted out, "Fuck, it's hot!" Janet is not prone to using such profanity, but under the circumstances, no other word was worthy.

Janet and I, with Mark and Teri, would share a single room on the second floor of Casa de Nelly, which would become our shore-side home for the next five days. Nick and Marina, decided to stay aboard and enjoy being alone on the boat, sans captain. A decision that I welcomed since *Maiatla* didn't have a working engine—keeping a good anchor watch was critical. I offered them the use of the master cabin while we were ashore, assuming that it would be nice for them to be able to share a bed for a change. However, Marina quickly declined the offer, sighting that they didn't want to take over Janet's and my room out of respect.

Okay, I can accept that, and it was good to see that the "help" knew their place! All joking aside, respecting personal space on a cramped yacht at sea is critical for the general happiness and disposition of the crew. Marina had also grown fond of sleeping outside in the cockpit, and that is where Marina slept for the remainder of her and Nick's time aboard. She was not eager to climb back up into the V-Berth.

Putting others first and being aware of difficulties a fellow crew member may be experiencing and making allowances are earmarks of a good crew member and an attribute that I look for when choosing and mixing crew members. A selfish crew member can ruin the whole voyage for all, as well as force me to make unpopular decisions. Such an incident arose on our first night ashore in the hotel with the girls— an incident that I feared may put in jeopardy the serenity of the voyage for the following month.

We had dined out and returned to our hostel room by 10 p.m. It had cooled down some after sunset, so we decided to shut off the air conditioner and open the two large windows that were on opposite sides of the room, permitting a relatively cool breeze to blow through. It was still warm but bearable. Jan was still having trouble with the heat, but she decided not to say anything. After taking turns showering, we all went to bed. During the night, the curtains continued to billow inward; the open windows permitted the street noises to filter into the room. Music could be heard from down the street.

Cars frequently drove by and revellers wandered home after the restaurants and bars closed. Somewhere around midnight, the palm trees began to rustle in earnest as a torrential rain fell. The sounds of massive rain drops pounded off the exterior walls and the red tile roof, followed by a waterfall-like rush of rain sluicing off of the building. Not the most conducive atmosphere for sleeping, but we were all managing.

Jan and I attempted to spoon under a single light sheet, but Jan quickly pushed me away, saying that I felt like a heater. So much for midnight passion in a tropical paradise.

By 2 a.m., the skies cleared, revealing a waning gibbous-half moon that illuminated the harbour. The wind fell away, leaving a new wave of humidity to invade the room, as if a boiler room steam pipe had ruptured. Jan nudged me awake from my tenuous sleep.

"Holy crap is it ever hot, and I think I'm having a hot flash. Can you close the window and turn on the air conditioning, Andy?"

I placed a hand on Jan's shoulder. She was drenched in sweat despite sleeping in a light nightshirt, which now clung to her soaked body, as if she had been caught out in the earlier down pour.

"Ya, sure, babe. No problem," I said as I jumped out of bed and went on a search for the remote control for the air conditioner.

"What's up, Andy?" I heard Mark's voice coming from the far side of the dark room.

"Jan is having a hot flash, so I'm going to close the window and fire up the air conditioner."

"Ya, ok," was Mark's response. Mark sounded ambivalent regarding cooling the room, but Teri was a different story.

"No, you can't turn on the air conditioner!' she stated in no uncertain terms. "I want the window open to let the breeze blow through."

Before I knew it the lights were on, and we were involved in a heated debate over the AC. "There was no breeze," I stated, to which Teri rebutted with, "The AC is too noisy and will keep me awake."

The debate raged on for several minutes, with both Teri and Janet becoming visibly distraught. Finally, I had to put an end to this.

"Look, Teri. Jan is suffering terribly, and the AC will give her some relief, so I'm turning it on!" With that, I closed the windows and hit the high cool switch on the remote.

"Andy, it's too noisy, and I won't be able to sleep!" she said in a last ditch effort to have her way.

"Well, I don't think this air conditioner is any noisier than any other you have experienced, and you can't tell me you have never slept in a room with one running, so I think you can manage for tonight."

With that I killed the lights and went back to bed. If I had any delusions that the fight was over, I was wrong. In the dark, I could hear Teri tear a strip out of Mark for not taking her side and standing up for her. I heard Mark make a comment that supported Jan and me, which sent Teri into a tizzy. With Mark's apparent inaction, Teri decided to remove herself from the conflict. She grabbed a sheet and pillow, then stormed out into the night, slamming the door behind her. I heard Mark curse aloud. Reluctantly, he crawled out of bed to follow his wife out the door. To say that neither Jan nor I could believe what just happened would be a gross understatement. By this time, we were both so worked up that sleep was not possible, but after an hour or so the AC did its job and Jan's hot flash had passed. From our bed, I could hear our friends outside the door, muted voices that were unintelligible, but the angry and placating tones were evident.

Finally, I had to go and see what was going on. When I opened the door, I found Teri on the tile floor curled in the fetal position wrapped in a sheet. Mark was leaning against the wall, with his arms draped around his drawn-up knees. It was obvious that he was still trying to talk some sense into his otherwise irrational wife.

"Hey, why don't you guys come back inside? I don't think it's safe to be out here," I offered. I couldn't believe this—here we were in a third world tropical country, one we knew next to nothing about, and Teri took it into her mind to sleep out in the hotel hallway, exposing herself to any number of people who may wander the streets at night, not to mention all that slithers, slimes, crawls or blood sucks during the night. Nevertheless, my pleas fell on deaf ears, so I returned to my bed. Moments later, Mark came back inside.

"Hey, bud, what ya doing?" I asked.

"I need a pillow and a sheet. The tile floor out there is cold," he said, with more than some reluctance in his voice.

"Hey, sorry about this, Mark, but I don't think we were being unreasonable about the AC," I said.

"No, I don't think so either. I'm not sure why Teri took it the way she has, but if I don't go back out there and seem to support her, there will be hell to pay later."

With that, Mark slipped back out the door where he made a bed next to his wife.

"This is nuts!" Jan exclaimed as she lay atop of our bed. "Turn off the air conditioner and open the windows and get them back in here!"

I looked at Jan, who still appeared to be overheated.

"You sure, babe? If Teri wants to camp outside, then let her," I said.

"No, I'm better now. Turn it off."

Reluctantly, I did as she asked and then went to the door, but before I opened it, I paused and turned to Jan. "You know if that were you out there acting like this, you'd be sleeping alone. You know that right."

Jan smiled, "Yes, hun, I know, and I love you too. Now get them in here."

In the morning, no one made any mention of want transpired during the night, and surprisingly Teri acted as if nothing had happened at all. Later that morning, I took a private moment to speak to Mark.

"So what the hell happened last night, Mark? Why was Teri being so unreasonable regarding Jan needing the AC for a bit last night?"

Mark looked genuinely concerned; I would later learn that he had the same fears as I. "I don't know. Maybe she was overtired after spending close to 40 hours travelling down here, and she just snapped," Mark offered. "It could have been like two queen bees butting heads," he added as he considered the situation further.

"Well, I hope it was her being exhausted that fuelled this because I hate to say it, but if this keeps happening and if Teri needs to continually challenge Jan, we have a real problem," I said, pausing for a moment so that Mark could fully appreciate what I was saying. "I think you know what I mean, Mark. Jan has been having a rough time medically, and I need her to have the best trip possible. This is Jan's boat, our home and her life, and if Teri feels the need to challenge Jan, right or wrong, Teri will lose because Teri will be put off the boat!" I said while trying to be as clear as possible without offending my long-time buddy.

What had gone on had surprised us both. The girls had been friends for years and socialized regularly without Mark or I being present, so why the clash now? In preparation for a worst-case scenario, Mark looked online for flights home for him and Teri, but neither of us wanted it to come to that. Nevertheless, there was a dense shadow of doubt looming bold on the horizon, as if a black gale was poised to strike.

Figure 20. Janet, Teri and Marina at the public market.

Marina and Nick had a blissful week aboard *Maiatla* with only one seemingly minor incident occurring on their second day. It was early in the morning when I ventured up to the rooftop to see if my boat was where it was supposed to be, and I was relieved to see that it was. Just to make sure all was well I used the hand held radio to call and was surprised to hear Marina respond almost immediately.

"Hi, Andy, I'm glad you called, as I've been trying to reach you," she said while sounding a bit frantic. My first fear was that the anchor had started to drag, and then I quickly imagined that the boat had somehow sprung a leak. Fearing the worst, I waited for the news.

"I'm not sure just how it happened, but the toilet is plugged and I can't flush it," Marina stammered with frustration. Relieved that the crisis was not a major one, I chuckled to myself mainly because I was not aboard and would not be for at least a couple of days. The crew would have to take care of the problem—that is, if they didn't want to revert to using an ice-cream bucket. *Maiatla* has only one head on board, which at times can be an issue with a full crew, especially because it is easily plugged and clearing it is perhaps one of the worst domestic tasks on board.

The problematic head has always been an issue, so much so that it has earned a place in the governing *Maiatla Articles,* which states:

Use of the Head

The vessel's head (toilet) is connected directly to the ocean, and improper use can result in the flooding of the vessel. Each crew member will be instructed in its operation prior to its use. Printed instructions are also placed upon the bulkhead as a reminder. Only the provided toilet paper shall be placed in the bowl, along with what comes naturally. No foreign object, such as Q tips, paper towels or feminine hygiene products, shall be flushed. Anyone who plugs the toilet will be required to dismantle the unit to clear any obstruction. The captain will be happy to coach you through the operation as he has done it far too many times.

Marina would later passionately protest that she had been very careful not to overtax the head, insisting that someone else had set her up for failure, as far as flushing the head was concerned. Fortunately, with a little cajoling, Nick was able to evacuate the bowel without having to dismantle the entire unit.

From the rooftop patio of Casa de Nelly, we had a clear view of the busy harbour and all the comings and goings of mostly charter boats. And there in amongst the bedlam was *Maiatla,* peacefully suspended between two anchors. To make the boat as comfortable as possible, I laid a stern anchor, which kept *Maiatla's* transom pointed out to sea, so regardless of the wind's direction, her butt was always pointed into the near constant ocean swell, limiting her roll.

One of Janet's greatest pet-peeves is trying to sleep when the boat in rolling in the swell while at anchor, so I had devised a solution for that. Using the topping lift, I set the spinnaker pole up so that it hung at 90 degrees to one side of the boat. I then ran the spinnaker halyard down to run through a snatch block attached to the end of the pole. I extended the halyard with a 5-metre line while suspending a pair of 10-gallon canvas pails on the end. To make sure the pails sank when placed in the water, I weighted them down with a few diving lead weights. Hanging approximately 3 metres (9.8 feet) below the boat, the pails would create drag as they were pulled upward when the boat rolled one way, and then rapidly re-sink when the boat rolled the other. This makeshift flopper stopper served well to dampen *Maiatla's* roll while at anchor.

For the final finishing touches, in an effort to make our home as comfortable as possible, I installed a pair of wind socks to channel the breeze below, one located in the forward hatch and the other in the aft hatch in our great cabin. Lastly, we suspended three shade tarpaulins: one over the bow; the second, amidships; and the third, over the aft deck to protect the boat from any direct sunlight. *Maiatla,* with her large Canadian Maple Leaf flag fluttering off of her backstay, looked proud, content and appeared as if she was right where she belonged.

This was Ecuador, and over the past 15 years under my and Janet's command, *Maiatla* had sailed close to 48,280 kilometres (30,000 miles). This was her ninth country or international territory that she had visited. It was a proud moment for me as I gazed down upon her, but I had little time to relax, as there was so much to do.

The reality was that I had a ship in distress, and not being able to manoeuvre her out of harm's way if required did not sit well with me. My first priority was not to play tourist, but to get the boat and engine repairs underway as soon as possible. I needed her fit for sea in case we had to leave in a hurry. There were many reasons for vacating the harbour with short notice: political strife or corruption (Costa Rica was still in the forefront of my mind), storms, an approaching tsunami or we may simply hate the place and want to leave, to name a few. Being able to sail away would at least give us, or the boat, a fighting chance if our position became untenable.

Our week of hostel living went by fast, I was sorry to leave the air-conditioned room behind, but the AC was all I would miss. I was glad to be back aboard *Maiatla*. We settled back aboard with Nick and Marina, making for a cramped but happy crew.

Despite Christmas only three days away, Bolívar sent a mechanic out to the boat to remove the fuel injector pump, and it was soon on a flight to the mainland Ecuador for a rebuild. Likewise, a refrigeration mechanic came aboard and discovered that corrosion had weakened the holding plates of the freezer, and when I had moved them to rebuild the walls of the freezer, holes had opened up. Believing that all was lost when it came to the freezer, Manuel, the mechanic, said he would custom make new plates out of stainless steel in a few days. At first I hesitated while dreading the potential cost, but I told him to go ahead anyway without asking how much. After all, it was Christmas and showing a bit of faith in humanity was the custom of the season. Besides, how could we possibly spend the next four months in the tropics without a freezer to keep cubed ice for my rum and cokes?

The day before New Year's Eve, Manuel was back with bright and shiny freezer holding plates. In less than two hours, the freezer commenced to frost up, and it only cost $400 USD. Not cheap, but a third of the cost of a new unit, and most importantly, we had ice for drinks. We were elated. The rest of the repairs—the furling gear, ripped sails and more—would be addressed in order of importance, as Mark and I dedicated a part of each day to these chores that seemed to never end. No sooner had we completed one task than two more revealed themselves.

One day I had made a trip to the top of the mainmast to check the bearings in the upper part of the furling gear, and on the way down, I noticed what looked like a crack in the wire shroud jumpers. These wooden jumpers are designed to support the upper portion of the mast. The pair of wooden arms, which are 460 millimetres by 25 millimetres (18 inches by 1 inch) thick and form a V shape, with the junction of the V secured to the mast, support the wire shrouds in notches at the ends. Well, it was at the junction of the V where there was a crack.

"Stop!" I called down to the deck to Mark and Teri. They were controlling the electric windless and the halyard that was now lowering me. I was stunned when I poked a finger into the crack and found the wood crumbling away. It was dry rot, a product of fungi and moisture that penetrates the wood causing it to rapidly decay and crumble away. It was looking like *Maiatla* was now paying for being so long in the damp tropics. These jumpers, although small, are critical in supporting the mainmast—without them, it would not be safe to return to sea. After the engine, they became the priority. Fortunately, Danny, our water taxi friend, told me that there was a good carpenter, a furniture maker, in town who would be able to repair the jumpers. So off came the jumpers, and I went in search of the furniture shop on the far side of town where the paved road disappears into the surrounding jungle.

Figure 21. *Maiatla* at anchor at Puerto Baquerizo Moreno with spinnaker pole out and flopper stoppers set to reduce the boat's roll.

Along the main road leading out of town, the tiny wood shop was easy to find. There were great piles of roughly cut planks stacked haphazardly about and several crudely constructed shelters without walls, revealing several band and table saws, most surrounded by great heaps of sawdust. On the far side was what appeared to be the painting area. Several wooden chairs were hung from hooks and a dark fellow, wearing a handkerchief for a mask, was spray painting the wooden chairs white. There were a half dozen young men working on various projects, but all came to a halt as I entered through the yard's open gate. I stopped just inside, and while searching for someone who looked to be in charge, I said, "*¿Está el jefe aquí?*" ("Is the boss here?")

I waited as the young men shot questioning looks at each other. After a moment, one young man stepped forward to ask me in Spanish what I wanted. As I learned later that the fellow's name was Sebastián. He was an apprentice carpenter and his uncle owned the shop, but the uncle was not there right now. Using rudimentary Spanish and a flurry of hand signals, I showed him the rotting jumpers and explained that I wanted them repaired while stressing that they needed to be made "*muy fuerte*" ("very strong"). Sebastián appeared to comprehend and instructed me to come back the next day. We shook hands and I was off, heading back to the boat confident that the repair would be completed well.

As I headed back down the road to the harbour, the sky opened up, and for the third time this morning, it rain and rained hard. Within seconds, I was soaked to the skin—perhaps I should have heeded Janet's advice and brought an umbrella. The rain was irksome, but at least it was a warm rain.

Figure 22. View from the mast of Puerto Baquerizo harbour, San Cristóbal Island.

I returned the following day as instructed by Sebastian to retrieve the set of jumpers and was pleasantly surprised to find that they were ready and already repainted. Back aboard *Maiatla*, Mark once again hauled me back up the mast, with jumpers in hand. Once on top, I commenced to reinstall them, which would have normally been an easy task, but this was not normal circumstances. A mast is an inverted pendulum, so any amount of rolling or movement of the boat's deck is magnified tenfold at the top of a 17-metre (55.7 feet) mast. Even when petite Teri walked from one side of the boat to the other, I would shift almost a metre (3.2 feet) either way while near the top.

The harbour this day, like all others, was busy with boats of all sizes scooting about, leaving tsunami-size wakes to challenge *Maiatla's* disposition, which in turn had me hurling around like a rag doll on the end of a long stick. The challenge was to keep my butt in a bosun's chair and hang on with one hand while the other attempted to thread a 6-millimetre (1/4-inch) nut onto a bolt. By the time the operation was done and jumpers reinstalled, I had dropped four nuts, two bolts and one screwdriver, which all missed the deck to land in the water, and to top it all off, I had a nasty set of bruises on my forearms and on the inside of my thighs from having my legs tightly wrapped around the mast. I was putting the finishing touches on the jumper by using a crescent wrench to tighten the wire shrouds when I heard a loud crack. At first, I was scared to look, but when I did, to my horror the jumpers had split once again. Apparently the glue Sebastián had used was either the wrong type of glue, or it simply failed to cure. In any case, off came the jumpers for a second time, and later that afternoon, it was back to the carpenter's workshop.

Needless to say Sebastián was upset to see his work in shambles. We renegotiated a new deal whereby he would construct a new set of jumpers out of local wood. Again I stressed that they must be strong. He shook his head in agreement and told me to come back in two days. This I would do.

While waiting for the jumpers, I made a trip up the mizzen mast to check out the radar, as instructed by my tech guy back in Canada. The mizzen was shorter than the mainmast, but not much less treacherous. Though, like its brethren, it whipped me around whenever a vessel passed, and if I had not been sterile when I ventured up, I most assuredly had been by the time I was safely back on deck. Disassembling the radar dome proved to be a challenge, and it was nothing short of a phenomenon that I had not dropped the top half of the dome, or one of the many nuts and bolts that required removing during the inspection. As the tech suspected, I managed to locate a tiny wire and connector that was loose, and it was a quick fix.

While still up the mast and ducking, as not to have the intense beam of radar waves cook my eye balls and have them explode like a pair of eggs in a microwave oven, I had Mark turn the radar on and give it a try. I could not see Mark since he was under the tarps in the cockpit, and anxious as to the outcome, I called down, "Is it working? If so, I need to get it all put back together before the next ferry roars by and flings me half way to the beach!"

"Hang on a minute. It's still warming up!" an unseen voice shouted back. Seconds later, I got the word. "Yeah, looks like it. You fixed it!"

Well, nothing short of a miracle, the radar was now working, but it still wasn't without a problem. Apparently in our effort to fix the rotation image issue earlier, we had pushed and tweaked the button on the screen, which affected the picture alignment. After measuring the angle between us and the boats anchored ahead, we determined that the radar's orientation was approximately 15 degrees off. This meant a boat that lay directly ahead was shown on the radar to be off to the right of the bow. Not a good arrangement if you want to avoid a collision with a freighter in the dark. However, at least we had radar that worked; I would have to take the time later to figure out how to adjust the unit, perhaps when I had nothing else to do? Yeah right!

As promised and $250 later, the jumpers were ready. It was time for a third trip up the sadistic mainmast to reinstall Sebastián's new jumpers. Fortunately, the reinstallation went well, with the minimum amount of tool and nut dropping and pain or maiming of body parts. The job was complete, and the jumpers looked good. I had my doubts to their structural integrity nonetheless. But, as time would ultimately prove, San Cristóbal's apprentice carpenter got it right the second time. Three days after Christmas, the fuel injector pump was back, and without delay, the mechanic had it reinstalled. I breathed a deep sigh of relief when the engine fired up, exhaling a great black puff of smoke. The price, which I happily paid, was twice what I would have paid in Canada.

Figure 23. The wooden jumpers with the junction of the V rotted away. Several of the island charter boats can be seen in the background.

I was surprised to find the climate of the Galápagos, or in this case San Cristóbal, was as hot and humid, and apparently unsettled, as it was, with plus 30 degrees Celsius (90 degrees Fahrenheit) temperature reached during the day and the night time only cooling off a little. The dry season began in December, or so I read. However, when I mentioned this to Janet, she claimed to have read it was the beginning of the wet season. Surprisingly, we were both correct, with two of our local guide books stating as such. But as our first week rolled into our second, Janet's book hit closer to the mark than mine. Ever since our arrival, aside from our first day when it was partially clear and sunny, it had been cloudy 80 per cent of the time and rained often—not just the "oh, I may need an umbrella" type of rain, but rather the "where did I put the scuba gear?" type. It rained hard and came on fast, often after avalanching down the side of the volcano.

Whenever it rained, the boat's hatches and port holes had to be closed, making the sleeping conditions below almost unbearable. At night, it would shower every two hours, so we were constantly getting up to close the boat, and then when it stopped, we would open her up again to get a breath of life back inside. We did not sleep well for the first while, but we were becoming acclimatized and soon found life on the hook bearable and then, at times, pleasant. What also helped was that we made friends with some locals and another cruiser.

Surprisingly, there was only one other foreign flagged boat in all the harbour, and it flew the tri-colours of France. The boat was called *Oiseau Noir* (Black Bird) and its captain was a lean 70-year-old university professor by the name of Eric. Eric was three years and two thirds of the way from achieving his dream of sailing from France, around Cape Horn and then returning to Europe via Peru, the Galápagos Islands and the Panamá Canal. However, he was not alone as he had a volunteer crew of up to three young people from various parts of the world that changed frequently.

Later, over a glass of wine and Mexican train, a game played with dominoes, one night aboard *Maiatla*, Eric confessed he had planned that once he had reached Cape Horn, he would sail across Drake Passage to visit Antarctica. But when he had reached the Horn, local sailors advised him against it because they believed his boat was too lightly built and would not survive a collision with an ice flow—a valid point considering what an iceberg did to the Titanic.

Encountering mountain-sized icebergs or ice bits the size of a football stadium is a real possibility at that latitude and an ever-present danger, especially at night. The boat's radar would help, but may not be able to detect low-lying pack ice in a big sea. *Oiseau Noir* was custom built by Eric for the express purpose of challenging Cape Horn. Speed and ease of handling, as well as the ability to shed water if a wave were to climb aboard, were the boat's best attributes. However, as all compromises do, the desire for speed came with a price, and in the case of this sleek 11-metre (37-feet) racing cutter, the trade-off was a thinly constructed plywood hull. The boat was never intended to be an ice breaker, perhaps an oversight on its builder's part. The *Oiseau Noir* was the black boat that we had spotted and anchored next to when we first arrived on San Cristóbal. We would become fast friends with Eric and share some interesting adventures together while on San Cristóbal.

Chapter 12

Captain Mark's Admiral and the Cape Horner

"The sweet-smelling aroma of the island spices still hung in the air. It filled his nostrils and titillated his appetite all over again. His appetite drove him mad for something much more than food."
—Luke A.M. Brown

In many ways, it was fortuitous for us to make the acquaintance of Eric, the Cape Horner. Sailing around the bottom end of South America has been a lifelong dream of Mark, and for both I and Mark, it was like meeting our favourite rock star. Mark first spoke of his dream to me over beers one summer back in the late 90s, and it has been a reoccurring topic whenever sailing stories were told, usually over sundowners. Over time, Mark's enthusiasm had infected me, and before long, I was looking at Southern Ocean current and seasonal wind charts, the pilot charts plotting all possible routes and destinations. I read, with much revere, the tales of many who sought to challenge one of the great capes at the bottom of the world. Men like Charles Darwin (1809–1882), Captain James Cook (1728–1779), Sir Francis Drake (1540–1596) and, of course, Ferdinand Magellan (1480–1521), who, in 1520, first discovered the strait, which now bears his name, by passing the dreaded Horn. In actuality, Magellan, who was seeking a passage into the South Pacific Ocean, never saw or even knew of the Horn's existence. In many ways, he was the fortunate one.

Today, Cape Horn is to sailors as Mount Everest is to climbers and would be a truly epic story, worthy of Homer, and an adventure to rival that of Sinbad the Sailor and Jason and the Argonauts—well, almost, as I doubt we would be encountering any one-eyed cyclops or doing battle with the Seven Heads of the Hydra. Nonetheless, it would still be a monumental challenge.

A voyage to Cape Horn entailed visiting such wildly exotic destinations as Rio de Janeiro, Patagonia, Peru, Easter Island and, of course, the great uninhabited fjords of Chile, with its ancient glaciers and notorious katabatic winds or williwaws as they are known. In the Fuegian Archipelago (Tierra del Fuego) in South America, a williwaw wind is a particular dangerous condition that has its origins in the snow and ice fields of the coastal mountains. It is caused by dense, unstable air cascading off the mountain tops to strike the sea with winds that can exceed 120 knots—a terrific force and not a pleasant condition for any vessel that may be traversing the coast or at anchor in a fjord.

It is in Chilean Territory, in Tierra del Fuego, at the bottom of the world that Isla Hornos, with its southernmost cape, Cape Horn, resides. From Vancouver, Canada, a round trip would entail a 19,000 nautical mile voyage navigating both the tropics and the sub-Antarctic during the southern hemisphere's summer solstice in December. I do not recall precisely when, but one day (perhaps after too many rums), I said, "Okay, buddy, I will do this Cape Horn voyage with you."

It was agreed. We were going to become Cape Horners together. (Later talks would include Marina and another friend and former crew member Al, aka, also known as Raúl.

When this would happen wasn't discussed much, but soon! Soon, I proposed, before either of us got too old for such nonsense. Mark and I even went as far as to discuss whose boat would be better suited for tackling the infamous Roaring Forties and Screaming Fifties, which refers to the stormy latitudes that the Horn inhabits. The island that claims Cape Horn is just shy of 56 degrees south latitude, in a tumultuous zone where the South Atlantic and South Pacific Oceans and their currents clash in the relatively narrow gap, called Drake Passage, between South American and the Antarctic continent. Uniquely, it is at this latitude that the west to east southern ocean winds can blow around the globe without being encumbered by any significant land mass. These winds have effectively unlimited fetch, or the unimpeded ability to build waves, great waves that can travel for thousands of miles circling the globe before encountering their only obstacle—the land funnel that is the Drake Passage at Cape Horn.

Kristi's Joy, Mark's custom-built ferro-cement Samson C-Witch 63 ketch, is tough and fast. She was constructed as a centre cockpit ketch by Harold Tribe, who made sure she had all the bells and whistles. *Kristi's Joy* boasts an inside steering station, with a viewing bubble to keep the helmsman safe and dry during the ugliest of weather. Below decks, he managed to cram in a diesel generator and a watermaker, both of which were large enough to supply utilities to a small town. The boat was innovative for her time, back in 1975, and can provide comfort for a large crew, necessary for extended offshore voyages.

I could not help to compare boats one day when *Maiatla* and *Kristi's Joy* were moored alongside of one another one weekend back home in the Gulf Islands. Despite being only 3 metres (9.8 feet) longer than *Maiatla*, *Kristi's Joy* carried over four times *Maiatla's* sail area. Mark's mizzen mast is approximately the same size as *Maiatla's* mainmast and *Kristi's Joy's* number one headsail consisted of more square footage than all of *Maiatla's* sail area combined. *Kristi's Joy* was built and equipped for speed, and I believe her designer and builder had the wild Cape in mind when he conceived of her.

Maiatla is a good seaworthy boat and has proven her capabilities time and time again. She has safely brought my family and I through gales and a hurricane

(Hurricane Alma, México, 2002), and I would not hesitate to take her on such a voyage as rounding the Horn. Still, in reality, *Kristi's Joy* would be better suited, and with her greater waterline and speed and more crew accommodation (we would need a camera crew for this expedition), she could take us down and around perhaps faster and with more comfort.

Although both boats possess thickly constructed hulls that are capable of surviving a severe blow from an impact with southern ice, *Kristi's Joy* would be the better boat for this job. Besides, if we broke Mark's boat or were clobbered by a big sea, I wouldn't be the one who would have to pay to repair it!

That said, deciding to take *Kristi's Joy* around the Horn was not that simple because as storms or land masses dictate the courses we must follow, so do spouses. After discussions with my admiral, Janet, on this particular voyage, she was emphatic that under no circumstances was she going to sail down there and around the Horn, but if I wanted to do it, she suggested that I do it without her and do it sooner as opposed to later.

Receiving Janet's support for this voyage accomplished two things. It removed the first big hurdle and that was to receive consent from my admiral to do it. (I would not say "attempt it" because the word "attempt" brings with it an element of doubt as to the outcome). The second thing it accomplished was to force me to get on with it or slide off the proverbial pot! That is, to do it or "shut up about it!" Janet, the love of my life was on board, or at least figuratively, if not literally. She confessed to have had every confidence in me in pulling off such an endeavor, but at the end of the discussion, she asked, "You are going to keep your life and boat insurances up aren't you?"

Likewise, Mark's new wife, Teri, was similarly empathic, but not in the way we both had hoped. After explaining what we wanted to do, Mark's admiral let him in no uncertain terms that not only was "our boat not ever going offshore, but you are not sailing around the Horn with Andy!" So no! Mark cannot come out to play! I was heartbroken.

When Mark questioned his resolute wife, she said it was just too dangerous and that she did not want to be left alone after he got himself killed on the far side of the world! She even went as far as threaten to leave him if he ever attempted to do such a thing. The decree was passed and subject closed.

Ah, okay, a new hurdle. On some levels I could well appreciate Teri's stance on the matter. It was true, such a voyage held some level of risk, but manageable risks. There would be a great deal within our control, namely the condition of the boat, skill level of the crew (we planned to take others), choice of course and weather windows. In actuality, we possessed a great deal of control, and with advanced weather forecasting capabilities these days, there is no reason to ever be caught in any truly fierce weather. However, that did not matter to Teri.

At this time, Teri surprisingly had no sailing experience whatsoever. She knew nothing of boats, did not sail, she had never been to sea and had no desire to learn how to swim. Later, she admitted to me that she was effectively afraid of the water and she had no intentions of ever living on *Kristi's Joy.*

I argued to Mark that he had been married to *Kristi's Joy* for over 15 years and wed to Teri only three, so the boat had seniority. Mark contemplated my assertion for a moment before saying, "No, I don't think I want to go there." He followed that with an uneasy chuckle.

At the time, I thought their union a strange one, considering Mark had been living and raising two children aboard his sailboat in Nanaimo with his second wife. The kids were mostly gone, and so was his second wife, and at the time, even before I had met Teri, I questioned his sanity when he told me he was thinking about moving ashore to live with his new girlfriend. Nevertheless, I'm a strong believer in love, and later, I could see why Mark fell for this beautiful woman. I know life can be a lonely one if you are all by yourself. However, to swallow the anchor to give up life on the water? That was serious business.

Figure 24. Mark and Teri aboard *Kristi's Joy*, Gulf Islands, B.C., Canada, 2017.

It wasn't until after a few years of marriage that Mark spoke of the Cape Horn voyage to Teri for the first time—and last time for a while anyway. I must give Teri her due; she has since made every effort to learn how to sail and now genially loves her *Kristi's Joy.* I have encouraged Mark to make sure she gets out on the boat as often as possible so that she feels comfortable on her and has an opportunity to experience the life we love.

When I first proposed to Mark that he sail with me from México to the Galápagos, Teri was dead set against it while reciting similar objections she exuded regarding the Cape Horn venture.

"Look, Mark," I said over the phone one day while attempting to finalize my plans. "Sailing from México to the Galápagos is about as safe and benign a passage as you can get. If you can't get Teri to agree to let you go on this short voyage, you might as well sell *Kristi's Joy* because you are never going anywhere on her, least of all Cape Horn!"

On the phone Mark sounded as if he had been struck broadside by a pair of torpedoes. What I said obviously hurt, but I felt it was the truth.

"Yes, I know, and I'll work on her!" Mark replied while sounding as dejected as one could be.

It wasn't until I suggested that Teri could fly to the Galápagos with Janet to meet us, cruise the islands and then sail to Panamá did Teri start to come around. Now, here we all were in the Galápagos, sitting at a restaurant table, chatting with Eric, our new friend and a 70-year-old Cape Horner. New hope for our voyage filled both Mark and I, as the charming Eric recounted his tale to all while Teri listened intently. Likewise, one night aboard *Maiatla,* Eric showed us a slide of *Oiseau Noir* sailing the fjords of Chile and it gripped Teri; she was wide-eyed with wonder. Neither Mark nor I dared to mention the proposed voyage at this time. We both thought it better to let Teri mull over the prospect all on her own. (It's always better to let the admiral believe that it was her idea in the first place.)

I decided to once again revisit our proposed course around the Horn, and in doing so, an idea occurred to me, which I brought to the Mark's attention. Janet and Teri were below preparing dinner as Mark and I nursed a couple of Pilsner beers, the local brew, while sitting in the cockpit, watching the sunset over San Cristóbal Island.

"Mark, after meeting Eric, do you think Teri will change her mind about the Horn?" I asked in a hushed tone so that the girls could not hear.

Mark gave a slight chuckle while peering below to make sure Teri was still out of earshot. "Maybe. I think she was surprised how old he was and how tiny and frail his boat looks. Who knows, if this voyage goes well, she might just come around." Mark took a long draw from his can.

"That's great," I said "You know, I've been looking at the charts, and Cape Horn is only 833 kilometres (450 nautical miles) from Greenwich Island at the tip of the great subcontinent. You know, I would hate to go that far and not sail across Drake Passage and spend a couple of weeks photographing penguins in Antarctica." I paused as Mark seemed to have found a bone in the bottom of his beer can. "So what ya think, bud?"

Eric would not be the only interesting cruiser we would meet here on San Cristóbal. One day, after spending the morning ashore at the internet café updating my blog, I was motoring our dinghy back out to *Maiatla* when I noticed a new cruising boat anchored out in the bay. Despite having what appeared to be a freshly painted hull, the topsides of the Formosa Peterson 46, named *Tainui,* looked to be weatherworn. Her decks were cluttered with the usual array of fuel jugs and other debris, typical of a veteran cruiser. I altered course to have a better look and to perhaps welcome the new arrivals to our bay. As I came alongside the boat, a jovial grey-haired man, sporting several days' worth of chin growth, popped out of the companionway. Upon seeing my approach, he broke into a big smile and waved me over to the opposite side of the boat where a boarding ladder was secured.

It was already well past 10 a.m., so I offered little resistance in accepting a tall rum and coke from the ship's master, Big John Vallentine. After settling into the cockpit with a tall warm one (no refrigeration, no ice), I quickly learned, John was a retired doctor, a surgeon in fact from Australia, a lifelong sailor, cruising author and an acclaimed Bluewater sailor, all according to the Coastal Cruising Club of Australia. At 79 years of age, the tall charismatic John looked remarkably like a gaunt Ernest Hemingway and was apparently into his tenth year of sailing around the world. John being the adventurer chose the less travelled routes that took him to both the boundaries of the Arctic and Antarctic seas, Cape Horn, Patagonia and the Mediterranean Sea.

As recently as 2012, *Tainui,* under John's command, completed an epic 4828-kilometre (3000-mile) journey down the Volga River, exploring Russia—something no other cruising yacht has done to date. He was now in the Galápagos with his daughter Rosie and on his voyage back home to Australia. As most experienced cruisers I have encountered through the years, John was eager to share his stories. I was eager to listen.

I would make it a habit to swing by *Tainui* whenever I was passing, for a quick drink and a new story. John was easy to talk to and spoke in a laidback, no nonsense way, without the breast-beating bluster or egotistical chest puffing that often comes with people who have accomplished great things. However, I did have to listen closely as John's voice was laden with a sort of muddiness. Despite John's formal education, his thick Australian accent and lazy diction, a common trait for people from the land "down under," was at times a bit hard to follow, especially if he got excited or when he became animated after having one too many. Anyone who has spent time with an Australian would appreciate what I am saying, as the accent, although English based, sounds coarser to our ear, less posh or refined. It's kind of a lethargic language that is weak on pronunciation. Instead of saying, "river," they would pronounce it as "rivah," or saying "master," they pronounce it as "mastah."

Regardless of any linguistic challenges that we may have had (I have been told that I have a thick Canadian accent, but I don't think so), John was living an incredible life, and I loved hearing all the details. As casual as anyone else from the netherworld (dirt dwellers) may perhaps tell their neighbour that their cat had gone missing, John told the story of how, on the voyage across the Atlantic, a long-time friend and crewmember had died. After trussing him in a sleeping bag and weighting it down with some rusty anchor chain, he said a prayer over his friend before rolling him over the side, completing the burial at sea.

"I knew there was the possibility that he could pass away along the way, so I was prepared," John said matter-of-factly as he refilled my still half-filled tumbler of rum and coke. "You see, my friend had been fighting terminal cancer, so it wasn't of great surprise to find him dead one morning in his bunk." John said this with a tone of reverence and tipped his glass in a causal salute.

Unfortunately, we were due to set sail from San Cristóbal in a day or two, bound for Santa Cruz. Our wakes would cross again, first on Santa Cruz, then on Isabela, but neither occasion would permit time enough to sit with Big John and, with a sundowner, share further adventures.

Chapter 13

The Crew Takes to the Road

*"The heart of man is much like the sea, it has its storms, it has its tides
and in its depths it has its pearls too."*
—Vincent van Gogh

Our time spent on Isla San Cristóbal had been busy and exciting. The whole crew, consisting of Mark, Teri, Nick, Marina, Janet and I, along with our new friend, Eric, the French Cape Horner, decided a road trip was in order. Through our agent, Bolívar, we hired a taxi to take us on an island-wide tour. We arose early and were waiting on the concrete dock for our ride, which arrived on time, but when our transportation pulled up, I was taken aback. I had my doubts that all of us could fit inside. I had told Bolívar that we had seven people and that we would need a big van. He assured me that seven people would not be a problem. So now, here we were, staring at our taxi, which was a small Toyota 4-door pickup truck. Apparently, all the taxis on the island are these Toyota's, so this was it. I expressed my concern to the driver who said, "*No problema.*" Our driver had it all figured out. One could sit in the front with him, three in the back seat and the rest could sit outside in the box.

"*Ver más fácil,*" ("See easy,") he said, with a great smile!

I looked at Janet and the rest of the crew, then suggested we hail another taxi to take two vehicles instead of one. Marina, with her usually joviralness chirped in, "Naw, come on, Andy. It will be fine. Nick and I will sit in the back. It will be fun."

With that, Teri also volunteered to be cargo as well, so it was settled.

"Besides, it's a nice warm day, and it would be easier to see the sites from the open back of the truck," Marina further declared.

I have sat in the back of a pickup truck many times, and I remember that the novelty of flying down the open road wares off after a few short miles, especially if any off-roading is to be done. But who was I to discourage my friends from having this experience.

"Okay, let's get moving," I said as I opened the back door of the truck for Eric and Janet to climb in with Mark riding shotgun.

Figure 25. Teri and Marina loaded in the taxi for our road trip inland.

It was sunny and warm, too warm, when we left the port of Baquerizo, but as we departed the city limits, it quickly clouded over and cooled off. Then it started to rain, and hard!

The downpour for us in the cab of the taxi was unpleasant. It obscured our view out of the windows while steaming up the glass, making it hard to take pictures of the jungle as it shot by at 80 kilometres per hour (50 miles per hour). For the crew in the back, the ride was a bit more unpleasant. Teri and Marina leaned against the cab of the truck, which protected them from wind and rain. Nick, however, had decided to face forward while leaning against the tailgate, which in hindsight may not have been a good idea. When I looked over my shoulder and elbowed the condensation off of the glass, I could see Nick with his head down, holding his hat in place with both hands, while being whipped by the near hurricane-force wind-driven rain. By the time we made our first stop, 30 minutes later, Nick was soaked through and through, and despite the tropical heat, he was chilled to the bone.

This day, we trekked to the top of Cerro Mundo, but saw little, as the clouds were still hugging the hillside. Then we were off again, treated to a scenic tour of the island's inland jungle until we reached the southern shore of the San Cristóbal. We stopped briefly at a banana plantation that doubled as a restaurant where the driver suggested we pre-order a meal and return later. After meeting the family that would be doing the cooking and a necessary bathroom break, we were off to visit the Galápagos Islands tortoise breeding centre.

The breeding centre consisted of several stucco-clad buildings and an interpretation centre. Apparently, we had arrived in time for the noon feeding, as a worker was throwing what looked to be some type of rhubarb at a group of veracious tortoises milling about next to the path. We were told the group of perhaps 10 animals were all males and were merely juveniles, all approximately 20 years old. Since they can live to be well over 100 years old, I guess they were still kids.

The tortoises were all approximately the size of a car tire, and when food or sex was involved, it was surprising how fast they could move. We fell in behind another group of six people from mainland Ecuador and a pair of habit-wearing nuns, who were taking a guided walking tour of the centre. Fortunately for us, one fellow spoke good English and translated the guide's spiel.

The centre is a sprawling complex of dozens of acres where hundreds of adult tortoises roam freely, either scattering around or wallowing in muddy ponds. The centre has pens where they raise the young tortoises until they are big enough not to be carried away by a local hawk species. Apparently, the hawks will pick up a young tortoise, carry it high into the air, then drop it to break the shell. Dinnertime! Once too big to go airborne, the park keepers release the young tortoises into the wild.

Figure 26. A juvenile tortoise (40 years old) comes in to check us out.

It was interesting to note that each island, due to its isolation, has developed different distinct species of tortoises. Like Darwin's finches, no two island tortoises are the same, and when viewed side by side, it is easy to see the differences. Despite the obvious variances between the islands' tortoises, Darwin never included the Galápagos tortoises in his theory of evolution. The reptiles were relegated to nothing more than an amusing footnote, not to mention fresh meat for the officer's dinner table.

Captain Fitzroy, R.N., the commander of the *Beagle* and of Darwin's expedition, informed Darwin that the tortoises looked like the animals he had seen on the Seychelles Islands in the Indian Ocean, north of Madagascar. He suspected that passing whalers had brought the tortoises here to use as a source of meat. Accepting this assertion at face value, Darwin assumed the Galápagos tortoises were not native to the islands; thus, today's most noted icons of the Galápagos Islands were ignored.

Deep in the breezeless scrub brush of the centre, the heat was almost intolerable, so our progress along the kilometre-long trail was slow, with near constant stops for water breaks. It wasn't until we returned to the parking lot after an hour tour that we were once again treated to the cooling effects of the sea breeze. We could see the ocean, and it was beckoning us. The tortoise breeding centre was impressive, but both Janet and I were lightheaded from the heat, so we were glad to get moving again. After loading back into the Toyota, we left the breeding centre to head along the paved road to what is perhaps the most beautiful beach on all of the islands—Playa Chino. With its turquoise waters, flour-fine white sand, Playa Chino is home to lounging sea lions and marine iguanas, basking on the black volcanic rocks. Not to mention, we were told that only a small handful of tourists would be there.

The taxi driver dropped us off at a trailhead and said the beach was that way, approximately a mile, and he would be back in an hour. With that, he drove off, leaving us to fend for ourselves. I popped open our umbrella, donned my backpack loaded with beach towels and water, then followed the rest of the crew down the paved path. Once back in the bush, the wind died and it was just as hot as it was at the tortoise centre.

Janet halted a mere handful of steps down the path. "Andy, I can't do this," she said as she looked back towards the parking lot while perhaps wishing our cabbie would sense her withering and return with the air-conditioned truck. I took a long look at Janet, then turned back to watch Marina and the crew disappear around a clump of sprawling cactus trees. The terrain looked parched and windless, and with the black volcanic rock and soil absorbing the afternoon sun, the air shimmered, creating wavering mirages off in the distance. Or perhaps it was heat stroke.

As much as I desired to see the beach and swim in the surf, I knew Janet would not make it, so we opted out of the 20-minute walk through the noonday heat. A trek that I imagined was not unlike like the fiery tombs of the sixth circle of hell depicted in Dante's Inferno. No, we would pass on this beach today.

The rest of the crew slugged through the heat and humidity to spend 30 minutes on the beach. While the crew made their beach march, Janet and I had flagged down a passing taxi to take us back to the cantina and banana plantation for a few cold beers while we waited for the others arrival. That is if they survived.

At least Nick was given a chance to thoroughly dry out on his long hike through a field of black lava rock and cacti. I imagined it was like strolling through a giant hibachi. Once the crew made their way back to the cantina, it was lunch and more beers at a hillside cabana, which sported a spectacular view of the coast, with the sea breeze keeping the afternoon heat in check. Janet dined on fresh lobster, and I had a roast chicken that was to die for. In addition, for dessert, the restaurant owner said we could go outside and pick some bananas off the trees, of which there were several varieties, bordering the building. It was all organic too!

Back on the road, it was a quick trip to the interior where we stopped to look at a funky tree house built on and inside a giant ceiba tree. Access to the tree is gained by a dubious-looking suspension bridge, with missing planks under your feet—a picture right out of *Indiana Jones and the Temple of Doom*. All that was missing was a raging river below, and natives taking pot-shots at us with blow guns.

The tree house has a living area, tiny kitchen with a balcony big enough for two, and a single bedroom-loft, which you can rent for the night. If living in the branches wasn't to your liking, you can sleep in the basement, which is accessed through a hole in the tree trunk and down a steep ladder. If you ever want to live like the Swiss Family Robinson or Tarzan, this is your chance.

It was interesting and well worth the $1 price of admission, and I would have stayed longer, but the mosquito swarms quickly convinced us to move on. We might have endured the onslaught better if we hadn't forgotten to bring the bug spray. Who would have thought the tropical jungle might have had biting insects?

It was a long and tiring day, but well worth the meagre cost of $100 USD, split seven ways.

Mark and I were making great headway on the boat chores and we even managed to solve the jammed furling gear issue by disassembling the unit and greasing the bearings. A couple of days after the road trip, I called Bolívar regarding another excursion that he had booked with Nacho, the fellow who had towed us into the harbour upon our arrival on San Cristóbal.

Early one morning, we met Nacho on the town quay where he loaded us into a 7.6-metre (25-feet) speedboat for a snorkelling tour out to "Kicker Rock." (The great volcanic plug that first greeted us when we arrived.) The ride along the coast was fast, wet and surprisingly cool, as the sun had disappeared behind a dense bank of clouds. There were the six of us, and we shared the boat with four others: a couple from the mainland Ecuador and their two teenage daughters—nice people who spoke passable English. Nacho manoeuvred the boat close to the steep 100-metre (328-foot) cliff of Kicker Rock, and it wasn't until that moment that I could truly appreciate the grand scale of this massive volcanic spire. Once in the wind shadow of the rock, we dressed in our snorkelling gear and jumped overboard, all except for Teri, who was the only non-swimmer of the group. She stayed aboard and took pictures of the rest of us.

The visibility within the water wasn't great, but we did encounter a school of 1.2-metre (4-feet) long blacktip sharks, a pair of sea turtles and spotted eagle rays, and we even had the opportunity to play with sea lions. The vertical rock wall was mostly barren of marine growth, with some barnacles and strands of seaweed here or there, as the constant swell kept walls scoured clean. Nevertheless, there were many colourful parrot and angel fish schooling about. We even swam through the tunnel that passes through the width of the island. All in the water had a good time, and even Nacho and his crew had an opportunity for a chuckle at Marina's expense.

At the end of our snorkel, Marina swam over to the short boarding ladder at the side of the boat. I watched from a handful of metres away as Marina struggled to get one of her legs on the first rung of the ladder. Despite all her effort, she could not. It did not help that there was a large swell running and the boat was constantly rocking, causing the ladder to first plunge under the surface, then rise clear out of the water. I was about to swim over to lend a hand, but Nacho and his deck hand beat me to it. The two men reached down to take hold of Marina by each arm, and when the ladder took a dive on the next roll, the men pulled. It worked, but as Marina was jerked from the water, the receding wave filled Marina's bathing suit top. The weight of the water ripped away part of her suit clear off her body, permitting Marina's ample left boob to escape and cavort about with carefree abandon.

With both of her arms fully engaged in holding on, there wasn't anything for Marina or the men to do, but to carry on and get her out of the water. On deck with Nacho and his deckhand grinning from ear to ear, Marina nervously asked if they had seen anything, to which they assured her that they most certainly had, and plenty. Marina laughed it off as she attempted to shove the girl back where she belonged before anyone with a camera could take advantage of the photo op.

Leaving Kicker Rock behind, we motored further along the coast to a beautiful beach called Puerto Grande. We beached the boat and, once ashore, were told we could do some exploring inland. It was a stunning, jaw-dropping landscape to behold, one as you would imagine you'd find on the surface of Mars—burnt, rutted, furrowed and shattered volcanic rubble interspersed with cacti, and all undercut by magma tunnels. Well, no cacti on Mars, I suspect. Again, Janet and I, along with Marina, decided not to venture too far from the cooling effects of the sea, so we stayed back at the beach while the guide took the rest further inland to explore.

Back at the beach, Janet and I cavorted in tidal pools full of brilliantly red Sally Lightfoot crabs and snapped pictures of blue-footed boobies and marine iguanas. We all snorkeled in the bay, but we were less than impressed with the lack of marine life on the rocks, again a function of local waves and currents. We spent the better part of the afternoon ashore, and while we did, the tide receded, forcing Nacho to haul the boat off the beach and anchor beyond a rocky reef 30 metres (98 feet) or so offshore.

Figure 27. Blue-footed boobies at Puerto Grande.

"Oh, crap," I said to Janet as we returned to the beach from our little snorkelling trip.

Figure 28. Nick exploring inland at Puerto Grande.

"What's the matter?" Janet asked as she followed my gaze out to the boat.

"I would say that Nacho is expecting all of us to swim out to the boat because it's too shallow and rocky for him to come back in here," I said.

"So what?" Janet replied, sounding a bit confused about the concern in my voice. "So we swim!"

"Well, I don't think that will fly with Teri, will it?"

"Oh my God, you're right. She'll freak!"

When the group arrived back at the beach, I took Mark aside to tell him that Teri was going to have to swim out to the boat. Mark's response was as expected. He was not happy, and we knew that Teri wouldn't be either when we told her, but there was no alternative, short of leaving her behind. After some discussion with Nacho, we devised a plan, which we laid out for Teri. Surprisingly, Teri took the news well, and without much fuss, she agreed to do as instructed. However, in reality, she had little choice.

We placed all our gear in waterproof bags, and the guide and I took turns ferrying the equipment out to the boat. While we were doing this, the rest of the guests swam for the boat. When it was Teri's turn, we had her don a life jacket and sit butt first in a life ring.

Then, ever so carefully, the guide and I floated a white-faced-looking Teri out to the boat. Once alongside, Nacho hauled her aboard. Considering how afraid of the water she was, she proved to be remarkably brave. However, I also know if I happened to have dumped her, neither Mark nor I would have ever heard the end of it. While sharing a couple bottles of wine, we found our ride along the coast back to the harbour fast and quick, though it was late by the time Nacho pulled alongside *Maiatla* to drop us all off.

After another great day in the South Pacific, we were all exhausted, but I could not relax, not yet. I fired up the portable gas generator on the stern to charge the batteries, then started the watermaker to top up the water tanks. When we first arrive on San Cristóbal, I was surprised to find no fresh water to be had, neither on the public dock nor at the naval facilities. If we wanted water, we would have to purchase it at the local grocery store and tote it out to the boat in 10-gallon jugs. Thankfully, our watermaker was working fine, which proved to be a great luxury. Producing 200 gallons per day, we had plenty of water for showers and cooking. Every time anyone went for a swim, a fresh water shower was mandatory. It was not permitted to lay about the boat, inside or out while covered in sea salt. With my chores well in hand, generator running and fresh water flowing, it was time for me to relax. But, just when I found a comfy spot in the cockpit to have a beer, the clouds let loose, the rain came and we all bolted around sealing the boat.

Six full days after our arrival on San Cristóbal, it was now New Year's Eve, and Nick and Marina had decided to move on by catching the ferry to their next island, which would be Santa Cruz. Our friends' time with us had run out. They would fly out in four days and wanted to have some time exploring Santa Cruz before departing.

But their departure would not be that easy. The *La Perla Negra* taxi *acuático* was enjoying the New Year's Eve holiday. The replacement taxi operator was having a nap and could not be reached despite us hailing repeatedly over the VHF. Eric had spent the night aboard the *Maiatla*, but had left his dink with his young crew to use. We could see it hanging off the end of their stern, but the guys were not monitoring the radio. Time was ticking, and Marina started to panic.

"Don't worry," I reassured her. "I'll drop the dink, and fire up the motor, and we will get you to the ferry dock in no time." We had not dropped our dink while anchored because of the strong likelihood that the sea lions had been using it as their personal waterbed and bathroom.

After we dropped the dink, the outboard sputtered and stalled. Oh, crap! They were going to miss their afternoon ferry, and there would not be another one until tomorrow.

Just as it seemed that they were going to be staying another night, Raphael's blonde head poked out of the *Oiseau Noir's* cockpit. He was one of the crew members intending to continue to cruise with Eric.

"Over here!" Marina beckoned wildly, her arms flailing in desperation. "Come over here!"

Her call was heard, and while waiting for Raphael, we all exchanged hugs and said our goodbyes in *Maiatla's* cockpit. I told Nick that he had done an incredible job on this voyage, and I would be happy to have him crew for me again, anytime, and I meant it. Any doubts I may have had initially regarding Nick had long since vanished. Somewhere out there on the high seas, perhaps during one of the many gales that we encountered, Nick had won the right to call himself a Bluewater sailor and Shellback. I would miss him and Marina both. It was with great reluctance and sadness that I watched them leave.

They were a sight to see—three people, luggage, backpacks and purses piled haphazardly into the tiny inflatable, roaring away to the dock.

They would make it with seconds to spare before the ferry left. Consequently, for the next two and a half hours, they would endure an extremely bumpy ride in the worst seats on the 30-passenger boat.

Marina would later publish some articles chronicling our voyage in her Magazine, *TAKE 5*, a couple of which were penned by her captain. Marina would also produce and publish on YouTube a 12-part video mini-series of our Galápagos adventure.

I watched the pair go. Then as the ferry departed carrying our friends, the boat past right next to *Maiatla,* and when it did, I broke out into a big smile.

"Hey, get a load of that ferry's name," I said to Janet as she was standing at the galley sink. "Quick, look out the window," I ordered as I waved to all the passengers seated around the stern. Many waved back, but I did not see our crew. It did not matter—I knew that they were there somewhere looking back at *Maiatla.* I took some photographs as the "*Andy*" throttled up to head for the open sea.

By now, I had *Maiatla's* engine up and running and most of the other necessary boat repairs completed. Bolivar even arranged to have my Laptop computer's screen repaired, but it wouldn't be ready for weeks, but I was assured that it would find its way to me. True to his word, six weeks later, Bolivar flew my now functioning laptop to Isabela Island where I was able to retrieve it. The final bill was $100 USD. I was ecstatic.   So with the boat now up and running, we were preparing to move on to Isla Santa Cruz. For now, it was Janet and I and Mark and Teri, just the four of us.

We stayed on San Cristóbal for New Year's Eve and went ashore to watch the festivities. The waterfront *malecón* was busy, mainly with locals all dressed to the nines, in their best or sexiest outfits. Not sure why, but stuffed mannequins with papier-mâché heads were placed about, some with photos of real people glued to their heads. Perhaps the mannequins represented friends or family members who were not here or who had perhaps died in the previous year. I wasn't sure, but vowed to dig into this ritual a bit more to find out.

What I learned was the heads, most with fully-clothed bodies, were part of a tradition that involved the burning of these effigies—also known as *Ano Viejos,* which was believed to get rid of the bad from the old year and bring good luck to the new year. The dummies are generally made to look like human beings. People take clothing and stuff it with waste paper, cardboard or straw to fill it out. Legs and sleeves are sewn shut to keep the stuffing inside. Many of the effigies masks were of well-known people, such as the president, the devil, Hillary Clinton or Obama, whereas others might simply represent a woman or a man. Some were life size while others were as small as a metre (3.2 feet) tall.

Live and recorded music played ashore at several outdoor venues, with hordes of children running around. Despite the amount of beer flowing, it was a family affair. By 10 a.m., we were all pooped out, so we caught a ride with our friend Eric, who dropped us back off on *Maiatla*.

Figure 29. The boat that rounded Cape Horn with Captain Eric at the helm. *Oiseau Noir* (Black Bird) and the interisland ferry "Andy" departing Puerto Baquerizo.

I invited Eric aboard for a glass of wine or two and a rousing game of Mexican Train dominoes, which he eagerly accepted. At midnight on New Year's Eve, an anemic fireworks display took to the sky, followed by the raucous chiming of the church bell, as if the hunchback of Notre-Dame himself, Quasimodo, was on crack and swinging through the belfry. That was enough for us, so it was off to bed. However, not for the hordes ashore. Apparently, things were just getting started on the beach, and we would miss the best part of New Year's Eve on San Cristóbal. The noisy party ashore lasted until dawn, and the music never stopped all night.

After dominoes, I assisted the now wobbly Captain Eric into our cockpit, then again helped him chase a reluctant and sleepy sea lion out of his dinghy so that he could head back to his own boat. Eric's boat owned a low transom (back end) where the sea lions were able to easily board. Once onboard they would find a comfortable spot for a nap. There were days when his boat was covered in sleeping beasts, from bow to stern. Eric even found one large female sound asleep on his galley floor one day after he forgot to close the hatch before going to shore. Eric kept a big bumper on a rope that he would swing to clear the squatters whenever he arrived back home. However, apparently the unruly sea lions were not Eric's only problem.

Over dinner, one evening, Eric confided in us that he had been having issues with a couple of his young crewmembers, which included impromptu and unauthorized parties aboard his boat. It was common for Eric to arrive home to find half a dozen strange young people binge drinking, often lasting into the wee hours of the morning. We also found Eric stranded on the beach after the crew commandeered the dinghy to go back to the boat and then to bed, leaving the captain to fend for himself ashore. The water taxis were all done by 7 p.m., so unless you had a dinghy or wanted to swim out to your boat, you were stuck until morning. Once while we were here, Eric spent the whole night on the beach because the crew deserted him to have a party on his boat. I was stunned when he told me this.

Figure 30. Teri, Mark and Janet on a water taxi headed for shore.

"Eric, that sucks," I said. "Why don't you just lay down the law with them? If that ever happened to me, I would kick their asses off the boat so fast their heads would spin."

Eric sounded dejected when he responded. "I wanted to, but my wife, who is a lawyer back home in France, warned me not to. She thinks we could face legal action that may stop me from completing my voyage."

My heart went out to Eric; he had my respect and admiration. He had accomplished so much, but it was becoming obvious he may have lacked strong command skills and was subjected to "captain abuse."

Crew can be like children at times and need controlling and direction. If you cannot command your vessel while anchored within a tranquil harbour, I would suspect that at sea during a crisis, the survival of the boat and crew could be at risk. Long before anyone sets foot on *Maiatla's* decks, I have them read and sign the *Maiatla Articles* that state, in no uncertain terms, what is expected of the crew and who is in charge.

Section 9 of the articles reads as follows:

The captain reserves the right to expel any crewmember from the vessel for whatever reason he deems fit. If a crewmember exhibits socially unacceptable, physically violent behaviour or is uncooperative in regard to the agreed common goals of the ship, they will be put ashore at the nearest port to be repatriated to a place of their choosing, at their own expense. If asked to leave under the above circumstances, you agree by signing this agreement not to seek redress or sue for any real or imagined damages.

In truth, the captain of the vessel is responsible for the actions of his or her crew, and if you bring a person into a country and they do not have the funds to keep themselves or possess airfare home, the owners of the vessel are responsible to get them back to their home country. Needless to say, all cruisers must choose their crew carefully before departing. (See the complete set of *Maiatla Articles* in the back of this book.)

Chapter 14

Cruising Plans Are Written on the Wind, and the Winds of Change Were Gale Force

"A good traveler has no fixed plans and is not intent on arriving."
—Lao Tzu

During all of our time sightseeing and performing repairs while at San Cristóbal, I had a sense of dread festering inside of me, and the longer we were here, the worse it became. A tight knot slowly developed in my stomach, and I knew sooner or later I would have to deal with it. Our original plan was to spend one week on each island and another week to travel between the islands, giving us approximately a month to explore the Galápagos Islands. We would spend an additional 10 days sailing to the Pearl Islands, then the remaining 48 kilometres (30 miles) onto Panamá where Mark and Teri had flights booked home. Six weeks all inclusive. It was a good plan, but it was rapidly becoming obvious that all of my planning was going by the wayside. We had already burned up over two weeks here on San Cristóbal alone, so if we stuck to our schedule, that would leave only ten days to visit Isla Santa Cruz, then Isla Isabela—that is if we departed Puerto Baquerizo Moreno in the morning.

With a full day's sail between islands that would not leave us much time ashore, perhaps five days per island. My carefully planned timeline was shot all to hell, but I knew what we had to do. However, I wasn't looking forward to explaining it to the crew. I had informed both Mark and Teri before they signed on that all cruising plans were written on the wind and subject to change. Well the winds of change were now blowing at gale force, and I needed to deal with it and now. After conferring with the admiral, I received my orders to broach the subject with the crew and let them know what we had decided. It was after breakfast when I called both Mark and Teri to the cockpit to discuss something important.

"Guys, I need to talk to you about something," I said while no doubt sounding deathly serious. My crew looked a bit perplexed as they waited for me to spill the beans, so to speak. "It's like this, guys. What with the repairs that we had to do, we have spent far too much time here in San Cristóbal. If we stick to our original timetable, we won't have much time to explore. So, Janet and I have decided that we are going to spend the next couple of months here in the Galápagos."

I paused for a second to try and gauge their reaction. Both looked stoned faced as the reality of what I was trying to say sunk in.

"We didn't come this far just to blow through the place. We may never be here again, and since we have a 90-day permit, I think we need to take advantage of it."

Again I paused to give them a moment. Then ever so slowly, while shooting glances between each other, Teri spoke, "Okay . . . so what does that mean for us? Do you want us to leave now?"

"Oh, no! No!" I replied. "Not at all. The way I look at it you have a couple of options. One is to cruise the islands with us until your time is up, and you guys fly home from here. I'm sure you can switch your tickets or book a flight from here to Panamá, maybe stay and visit there for a few days, then fly home as planned." I suggested while trying to sound positive. Maybe I could convince them that this was a good thing. However, I didn't believe so.

Either way, it was out there now, and I must admit I was expecting some heartbroken resistances, not so much from Mark, as he has been sailing with me for years and understands how cruising timetables work. However, Teri was another matter. I expected some quarrel if not a downright melt down; thankfully, I was wrong on both accounts.

"Well, yes," Teri began all so calmly, "we had been counting the days, and we figured something like this was coming. We had already talked some about it, and we thought we would fly home from here, if that's okay?"

Well, that was easy, and I was so relieved we would not have to disappoint our dear friends. Mark gave Teri a reassuring look.

"Actually, Andy, I had already looked for flights home from here after Teri's meltdown in the hotel, and it will work," Mark said while not realizing that he had just put his foot in it.

"What meltdown at the hotel?" Teri asked while looking both puzzled and concerned.

"Oh shit!" I thought to myself, "just drop it Mark don't go there!"

For a second, Mark had the old "deer caught in the headlights" look as his mind raced to conjure up some damage control.

"Ah, it was nothing, hun. My mistake. I was thinking of something else. So anyway, Andy, what was the second option that you were going to mention?"

"Smooth, Mark. Nice change of subject." I thought.

Mark breathed a deep sigh of relief as Teri turned back to me.

So I continued, "I know that you wanted to get Teri some offshore sailing experience, and if you fly home from here that won't happen, so I talked to Eric. He is leaving in a few days for Panamá and would be happy to take you both on as crew and drop you off there. What do you think?"

I could see the possibility racing through Mark's mind. Eric's boat was a cut down racing machine and having a chance to sail with a man with his experience would be awesome. I, in fact, would have jumped at the opportunity if it had presented itself to me. It was instantaneously obvious that Mark was charged by the idea. However, Teri did not share his initial enthusiasm for the endeavour. Eric had difficulty finding new crew after letting go a couple of his trouble makers (he took my advice) and was now down to only 22-year-old Raphael, so when I mentioned my crew may be available, he jumped at the chance to take them on.

"So, it would be just Eric and us?" Teri stated, with ponderous hesitation.

"No, he still has one crew with him. So there would be four of you, but you two can do your watches together," I suggested.

After several minutes of discussion between themselves, it became obvious to me that Mark was all ready to jump ship and sign on with Eric, but his admiral wasn't.

It was all over but the crying when Teri finally said, "I don't want to be stuck for a week on a tiny boat with no privacy and three men peeing over the side!"

Well, that was settled. They would spend their remaining three weeks with us— Admiral's orders.

Eric would spend a few more evenings with us aboard *Maiatla,* playing Mexican Train Dominoes. Then, on a Wednesday, our Cape Horn friend, with only one other crew, departed for Panamá and then back to France. As a farewell gift, I gave him copies of my two books so that he would have something to read along the way. Two days later, it was our turn to haul anchor and head out.

Figure 31. Andrew presenting his own books to the Cape Horner, Captain Eric.

While on San Cristóbal, I had loaded a couple of jerry cans into a taxi and had the driver take me to the only fuel service station in town. The government owned service station had six fuel pumps and an eager attendant for each one. The price of diesel fuel was clearly marked at $1.15 USD per gallon—a real bargain. In most places in

Central America, I was paying over $4 USD. I unloaded the cans, but the attendant refused to fill the jugs. He kept asking for my papers. I could not understand this man, but my cabbie, who spoke some English, attempted to translate. After much discussion, I was finally made aware that all foreigners of yachts must have written permission from a government agent before they could purchase fuel. Well so much for my plan of refueling *Maiatla* with cheap fuel, 20 gallons at a time. The cabby pleaded my case, but to no avail. I was about to leave when the cabby again said something else to the attendant, who took a long look at me and then shot a sideways glance over his shoulder in the direction of his office on the far side of the parking lot. More words were exchanged, and then I watched as the attendant commenced to fill my jugs.

I conferred with my driver for a moment before I realized what was going on. The cabbie was purchasing the fuel for me. I was elated, but when the job was completed, the cabbie took me around the corner where he asked me for the money. I looked at the pump price, then pulled out $25 USD to cover the $23 dollars' worth of fuel, but when I went to hand the driver the money, he shook his head and said, "Oh, no, *señor*. The foreigner's price is $6 USD a gallon."

Left with little choice, I paid. I watched as the pump attendant rung in $23 dollars for the fuel, then with sleight of hand, the remainder of the money disappeared into his pocket.

By the time I paid for the cab ride and a generous tip to the driver, I had paid over $8 a gallon. Well so much for cheap Ecuadorian-subsidized fuel. Later, I learned that Bolívar could deliver as much fuel as I needed directly to the boat out in the harbour with a couple of days' notice, and all for the foreigner's price of $6 USD. Still not cheap, but I wouldn't have to lug it out to the boat either.

After taking on 70 gallons of fuel that was arranged for by our harbour agent, we took delivery and it arrived in 10-gallon jugs carried by a water taxi. The cabbie dropped the jugs onto my deck, then departed after saying he would be back tomorrow to pick up the empty jugs. It was a tricky process transferring the diesel into *Maiatla's* tanks, and it got exciting when the hose I was using to siphon the fuel from jugs to *Maiatla's* tank popped out and dumped a couple of gallons of fuel oil into the harbour. Frantically, I ran below to retrieve a squirt bottle full of soap to spray on the spill, which helped to diffuse the now massive slick. There were several minutes of freaking out on my part as the oil spill first surrounded *Maiatla*, clinging to her like crap to a blanket, then trailed out behind the boat for over 50 metres (164 feet). The shimmering rainbow slick pointed back to *Maiatla*, like an accusing finger. For over an hour, the air stunk of fuel. Fortunately, the outgoing tide slowly began to dilute the mess, taking it harmlessly out to sea.

It was a Godsend that the navy or a passing park guide had not spotted our little ecological disaster. Tragedy and expulsion from the island averted, we were now ready to depart the following morning.

We awoke early at first light. We had removed all the shade tarpaulins the previous evening, so that left us with the flopper stopper to drop, disassemble and spinnaker pole to stow. We had some difficulty retrieving the stern anchor that was fouled in some rocks. Then came the main bow anchor's turn. For the past two weeks, it had been working itself deeper into the sand with each passing gale. Both Mark and I broke out into a sweat, but at least the clouds overhead had decided not to dump any more rain on us.

When we finally got underway, the sun popped over the Cerro Mundo to peek through the gap between the mountain top and the heavy overcast cloud—the same cloud that seemed to have taken permanent residence over the harbour at the time we had first arrive. I would miss San Cristóbal and its people, but not the rain storms that dominated the local weather. We motored out between the channel markers and the breaking surf on either side. It would be a good test of our rebuilt fuel injector pump, and it would be several days before my confidences in it returned.

Once clear of the harbour, the wind filled in to 10 to 12 knots out of the south, with a 2-metre (6.5-feet) deep swell rolling beneath our keel. The crew were all happy and eager to get on with our adventure. We had a great sail on a tight reach for the 48 kilometres (28 miles) over to Isla Santa Fe, the next uninhabited island.

Isla Santa Fe was formally called Barrington Island after Admiral Samuel Barrington (1729–1800), who had never set eyes upon the Galápagos, but he had distinguished himself in 1759 while fighting against the French. Santa Fe Island is 24 square kilometres (9.3 square miles) and lies in the centre of the Galápagos archipelago, to the south east of Santa Cruz Island.

Geologically, it is one of the oldest volcanically produced islands, at approximately four million years of age. The vegetation of the island is characterized by brush, palo santo trees and stands of a large variety of the prickly pear cactus. The island is low lying, so it does not encourage the formation of clouds that can produce the rain that typically falls upon the much taller islands. Still despite the harsh climate, there is an abundance of wildlife, with numerous endemic subspecies, such as the Barrington land iguana, not to mention the Santa Fe rice rat.

We would not stop at Santa Fe, but we did move close inshore for a photo op of its beautifully protected bay on the east end. It would have been the perfect place to anchor and cavort with the abundant marine life, but it was off limits to us, as we did not have a permit. To sail by was painful, and what made it even harder was seeing half a dozen charter boats floating atop the crystal clear lagoon, looking all so peaceful and tranquil.

Maiatla had a 90-day, three-island cruising permit. The only islands we were permitted to stop at were San Cristóbal, Santa Cruz and Isabela. That's it. If we wanted to visit any other island, we had two options. The first was to hire a local charter company to take us there. The cost of visiting the other islands this way ranged from $100 to $1000 USD per day per person, depending on the island and the level of comfort we desired. The other way was to hire a park guide directly to accompany us. This seemed like a reasonable alternative, and I looked into it, but quickly backed off when I found out that the cost of doing so would be $200 per person per day. With four crew that would mean $800 USD per day. Ouch. So that was out.

With blue-footed boobies circling over the island's cliff face, we skirted Santa Fe, dropped the fishing gear into the water, and then altered course to head for Isla Santa Cruz and our next port of call. Puerto Ayora on Santa Cruz is the largest town in the Galápagos Archipelago, boasting over 15,000 people, and is ground zero for the island's massive charter fleet.

Chapter 15

Santa Cruz's Tortoises, Magma Tubes and Interned Cruisers

"Among the scenes which are deeply impressed on my mind, none exceed in sublimity the primeval forests undefaced by the hand of man; whether those of Brazil, where the powers of Life are predominant, or those of Tierra del Fuego, where Death and Decay prevail. Both are temples filled with the varied productions of the God of Nature: no one can stand in these solitudes unmoved, and not feel that there is more in man than the mere breath of his body."
—Charles Darwin

Isla Santa Cruz is the second largest island after Isabela, with an area of 986 square kilometres (381 square miles) and its volcanic peak reaching a maximum altitude of 864 metres (2,835 feet). The island is situated in the centre of the Galápagos archipelago and is the most visited island, with the most populated urban centre of all the islands, its capital, Puerto Ayora.

I was astounded to learn that approximately 250,000 tourists enter the Galápagos annually, and that number appears to be on a steady incline. While Ecuadorians account for 30 per cent of all tourists, approximately 70 per cent are from foreign countries, with American visitors the most prevalent at 26 per cent, followed by British visitors at 6 per cent, German, Canadian and Australian visitors at 4 per cent each, Argentinean visitors at 3 per cent visitors, and the remaining 23 per cent divided among 153 other nationalities. Looking at the above numbers, it was no wonder why we hadn't seen any other Canadian yachts in any of the harbours.

In regard to the forms of tourism on the islands, my research revealed that 35 per cent of travellers visit the islands on cruises lasting approximately seven days, while 65 per cent prefer to stay in the various inhabited towns for a period of around five days. Seventy-five per cent of all tourists arrive at Baltra Airport, here on Santa Cruz, so it was no wonder why we were encountering so many people and tour boats.

In the highlands, away from the sea, nestle some small rustic villages that have schools and churches and whose inhabitants work mostly in agriculture and cattle raising. Isolated family farms and ranches abound, producing food products, growing bananas, papaya, pineapples and an assortment of root vegetables, and of course, raising chickens—lots of chickens—most of which are sold to the hotels that support the flourishing tourist trade.

Geologically, Isla Santa Cruz is essentially one large dormant volcano, with multiple vents and a crater. It has been estimated that the last eruptions here occurred around a million and a half years ago. Like most of the islands, an elaborate array of magma tunnels, created by subterranean magma flows, crisscross Santa Cruz. There is a massive magma tunnel that is over 2000 metres (one nautical mile) long which, according to the guide books, we could walk through. Near the centre of the island, along the two-lane highway that bisects the island on its way to the airport, there are two great craters that were created when massive magma domes collapsed. Los Gemelos, or "The Twins" as they are called today, are surrounded by dense *Scalesia* forest, with large trees covered in epiphytes that hang to blow in the wind.

After seeing these epiphytes, I now understood why, when we first arrived in the Galápagos, the agricultural people didn't become all that excited after discovering Janet's epiphytes or "air plant" hanging above *Maiatla's* galley sink.

Near the town of Puerto Ayora and a short walk, or even shorter water taxi ride away, is one of the best beaches on the entire island. From the beach parking lot, it is still a 2,490 metres (1.55 miles) walk down a scenic path. As this area is considered part of the National Park, all visitors must sign in and out with the Galápagos Park Service office at the head of the path, and they must be out of the area by 6 p.m. Tortuga Bay has a gigantic, perfectly preserved beach, with brilliantly white sand, but it is forbidden to swim here and is preserved for the wildlife. Just walking along the sand, you will see many marine iguanas, Galápagos crabs and oystercatchers as they forage along the shore or volcanic rocks.

However, you can find a separate mangrove-lined cove where it is permissible to swim, a place where it is common to view white tip reef sharks swimming in groups, and we were told on occasions that tiger sharks can be seen lurking about. We all were eager to make the rounds of the island to see all the sights. I was particularly interested in the sunken crater located 2.8 kilometres (1.5 nautical miles) offshore of the north-east corner of the island—a place called "Gordon Rocks."

One of the first things I did after deciding to sail to the Galápagos Islands was to find out where the best scuba diving sites are, and during my research, one location kept popping up. Many of the divers who visited the Galápagos before me all raved about Gordon Rocks. The Rocks are a collection of three little rocky islands, the remnants of the rim of an extinct volcano, which have created an oasis for marine life in the deep open ocean. However, the main attraction for me was that all divers reported encountering great schools of giant hammerhead sharks. These strange-looking creatures, with their hammer-shaped heads, often congregate in the shallows during daylight hours. I could not leave the Galápagos without attempting to swim with these magnificent, but potentially dangerous, beasts. Diving with the hammerheads was on my bucket list.

We arrived at Puerto Ayora, Santa Cruz—our second island on our Galápagos tour—on a Friday afternoon. The sail from Santa Fe was pleasant, but we only caught one small tuna that we threw back. Perhaps part of the reason fishing was so poor was because we had to quickly haul in the lines whenever a charter boat or water taxi passed by, which was disturbingly frequent. Legally, we weren't permitted to fish, as that was the purview of the locals.

Puerto Baquerizo Moreno was busy back on San Cristóbal, but our first glimpse of Puerto Ayora (Academy Bay on British charts) sent a shudder through me. It had been a long time since I had seen that many boats in one place. I laid a course to take us through the mile-wide gap between Coamaño Island and the rugged mainland, but from this angle, it looked as though the entire harbour was choked off by anchored cruise ships and large tour boats. With Janet on the helm and Teri snapping pictures from inside the dodger, Mark and I furled the headsail and dropped the mainsail before we began to visually pick our way through the traffic. We needed to weave our way through this mess to the inner harbour and find a suitable place to anchor. I called back to Janet, "Just slow us down some, babe, and cut between that big blue cruise ship and the big sailing catamaran to the starboard, okay?"

Janet shot back from her seat at the helm, "I can't see well because the sun is glaring up the windows, so you will have to direct me!"

Academy Bay is tiny at best, and I feared there would be no room for us, but once we motored past the Disney and the National Geographic cruise ships and entered the shallow water of the inner harbour, a vacant spot between some occupied mooring balls and shore became visible.

"Look at that, Mark," I said pointing off to the starboard. "Looks like another cruiser who got himself into trouble."

One of our soon-to-be neighbours was a vessel from the Netherlands. A 12.2-metre (40-feet) steel Seahawk ketch, with its mizzen mast canted over on a painful looking angle. Several wire shrouds dangled limp, and apparently the only thing stopping the mast from going over the side was the base that was jammed into the far side of the cockpit.

"God, I hope no one was standing in the cockpit when that happened because that mast would have cut the legs right out from under them," I said to Mark as we cruised by the stricken vessel. Mark and I would later meet the owner and crew of *Chica*—Captain Pieter, Mike and Mark. The male retired teachers were on their way to Australia when, in the middle of the night, the boat's rigging let go. *Chica* in Spanish means "girl," and I though a strange name for a vessel registered in Bergen, Norway. Pieter was in the cockpit when it happened; fortunately, he was sitting in the only safe spot at the time. In almost complete darkness, the mast toppled over with the base, shooting right past and narrowly missing him as he jumped back. Although he didn't realize it at the time, Pieter, in his rush to get out of the way, had broken his shoulder which he did not discover till many months later. Still he was lucky.

Also by good luck, they were only a few hundred miles to the west of Santa Cruz at the time of the dismasting, so they altered course to come here to make repairs. Pieter said, "We had not intended to stop in the Galápagos, but we had no choice. These people have treated us as if we were some kind of criminals because we didn't have a permit to visit."

Pieter sounded hurt and frustrated. "They wanted us to pay for a visitor's permit and pay for the park fees even though we

Figure 32. *Chica* with its broken mast on Santa Cruz.

have no intentions of travelling outside the city limits. They wanted thousands of dollars, and we do not have that kind of money."

Pieter and the crew were ordered to stay aboard *Chica* while it took several days for the Port Captain and immigration officials to make a decision. Under international maritime law, Ecuador was required and expected to provide a safe refuge for the stricken vessels, but the law doesn't say that the refuge has to be free. The *Chica* and her crew were eventually permitted to stay, but only long enough to repair the mast. They could only go ashore to use the phone, seek out provisions and any parts that they required to make the necessary repairs. They were to report to the Port Captain's office each day via radio, and they were not permitted to do any form of sightseeing. No tours or even walking about the town. If they weren't conducting business in an effort to get their boat mended, they were effectively under boat arrest—so much for a friendly port in a storm.

We dropped *Maiatla's* hook in 5 metres (16.4 feet) of water, and I hailed a water taxi to take me ashore to check in with the Port Captain and our agent. Our agent, Loretta, was in partnership with Bolívar, and I was told that she would be waiting for us when we arrived. The water taxi dropped me off at the main dock that had dozens of other taxis jockeying for dock space. It was pandemonium as literally hundreds of passengers were embarking and disembarking in what looked like a choreographed chaos—and all under the watchful eyes of several park guides attempting to control the flood and ebb of passengers.

Over the following two months, we would spend almost three weeks anchored here, and during that time, while being ferried ashore, I would be involved in three separate, high speed collisions and dozens of near misses between my water taxi and another vessel. Fortunately, no one was ever injured and each took no more than a few minutes to resolve. Typically, after a lot of finger pointing, a barrage of foul language and cursing in rapid fire Spanish, fault would be assigned and then all could move on. Interestingly, after involving me in their pileup and altercation, the drivers still expected their tips.

And if all the humanity and waterside drama wasn't enough, in and among the long water taxi cues and milling tourist, there were several portly sea lions that had claimed all the bench seats on the pier. The beasts were napping as if they didn't have a care in the world, and I would guess that they didn't. The noisy tourists to the sea lions were no more a nuisance than the flies buzzing about the smelly beasts. I also noticed six large brown pelicans sitting upon the pier's handrails, looking equally disinterested, though the ambivalent birds took turns pecking at curious tourists who dared to approach too close.

No sooner had I left the dock to stride upon the *malecón* than a pleasant-looking dark-skinned, middle-aged lady waved me over. I could only assume that this was my agent and not a hooker trying to catch the eye of some sea-weary sailor, looking for company. How Loretta picked me out of the crowed, I could only guess. She must have been waiting for us to arrive, and I could only assume that the big Canadian flag gave us away. My agent was pleasant and gave the impression that she was genuinely happy to see us. Loretta did not speak a word of English; still we managed to complete our business without difficulty. Loretta asked how long would we be staying, but I wasn't sure.

"Perhaps a week," I told her. She informed me that she would require at least two days' notice, and if I wanted to leave on the weekend, the fee would be double. With that, I decided we would depart in a week's time, next Friday. She agreed to meet me here at 7 a.m. on Friday, with my paperwork and clearance to depart for Isabela. Once I accepted the papers, I had 24 hours to depart the harbour. What would happen if weather or mechanical breakdown prevented me from leaving, I did not ask. I would cross that bridge when and if the time came. I paid Loretta the $15 USD handling fee for the paperwork. Then she instructed me to go back to the boat and wait, which is what I did, however, not without first taking notice of all the goings on around the *malecón*.

The waterfront *malecón* was awash of not just tourists, but street vendors, hawkers, musicians artisans and raucous school children. At the junction, where the pier merged with the street, a sun shade had been erected were a pair of musicians from Peru, dressed in colourfully embroidered traditional garments, were skillfully playing a haunting tune on pan flutes. The high-pitched tones, aided by the microphone and speakers, could be heard for blocks. Directly behind the flute players, in a recessed amphitheatre, a score of locals were engaged in a friendly but passionate game of volleyball.

On the sidelines, spectators cheered everyone on while vendors sold drinking coconuts, roasted peanuts, empanadas or barbecued chicken. The smells were incredible and made me hungry, but I didn't have time to indulge my stomach. Off to one side of the court, artisans displayed their locally manufactured jewellery of

Peruvian silver, jade and opals or intricate wood carvings of Iguanas or Tortoises upon plain coloured blankets spread out on the ground.

Here, as we have found in most Central American communities, the town's centre in the cool of the evening was the gathering place for young and old, a place where families came out to socialize, to commune with friends and neighbours. This affinity for kinship is ingrained in Latin American countries. There, a tangible sense of community is interwoven into the fabric of their daily lives. The Latinos possess a social conscience and genuine care and love for family and neighbours—a trait I believe we once possessed in North American yet sadly, have lost. North America's humanity, our humanity and ability to care for others, has become a casualty of our netherworld bustle, drive for perceived success and deep-seated narcissism—a trait that is omnipresent today in most North-American youth.

That Friday evening, Puerto Ayora was promising to be an exciting place after dark, if you are into that kind of thing. As I pushed my way through the masses to hail a water taxi, I noticed that the land wasn't the only thing abuzz with life. To the left, or on the north side of the pier, a black rocky reef protruded from the water. The air was thick with the aroma of the salt brine. It was now low tide, which exposed barnacles and bright orange starfish. Schools of tiny fish darted between the rocks as several marine iguanas remained motionless on their exposed perches atop of the reef. From where I stood, I could see a pair of spotted eagle rays cruise along the shallows adjacent to the shore. Several young boys pushed by me, racing along the pier to dog a pair of metre-long (3.3-feet) nurse sharks paralleling the pier.

An hour after our arrival, I had the Port Captain, looking all dapper in his dress white uniform, sitting in *Maiatla's* cockpit, going over my ship's papers. Finding them in order, he requested to see the ship's flares, life jackets and then quizzed me on my life raft and radio equipment. It was a complete vetting to be sure. After instructing me to discard some outdated flares that I possessed, he stamped my papers and hailed a taxi. We were in! I received permission to move to the only unoccupied mooring buoy, which happened to be a little deeper in the harbour and directly off of the two-story Port Captain's office. Whether by coincidence or by design, the Port Captain could keep a close eye on us, which may force me to limit my skinny dipping off the boat to night time endeavours. Or maybe not! We quickly moved the boat to the buoy, then launched the dinghy to set the stern anchor to keep the bow pointed out of the harbour. We needed to keep the boat's nose pointed into the sizable and constant swell rolling into the bay. It was now almost 7 p.m., and everyone was tired, so we decided to wait until the next day before heading to shore to see the sights.

That night, as the sun set, we were pleased to witness marine iguanas swimming by the boat, and just as thrilling was spotting a giant manta ray scoot by. A few minutes later, the dorsal fin of what I believed to be a large tiger shark leisurely cruised between the boats. Despite what may be lurking below, after a few sun downers, I went for a long swim, but I was forced to stay close to the boat, what with all the harbour traffic that only died out after 9 p.m. At that time, I assume all the other boats' guests were aboard and getting ready for bed, as most charter boats would depart right after midnight. It was a pleasant night—the air was warm, warm as the water, and the sky was filled with stars and constellations that we don't normally see further north, the Southern Cross being the most prominent celestial body sitting low on the horizon.

Mark and I would swim most days off the boat, and on our first day, we were pleased to see that a large school of sergeant major fish had taken residency under *Maiatla*—the fish claiming the underside of the boat as if it were a new extension of the reef below. The palm-sized fish were yellow and silver with vertical black stripes, and as if in support of their military moniker, the sergeant major fish were surprisingly aggressive in protecting their new turf.

Entering the water, the fish schooled about, darting this way and that, in apparent aggravation. But it was Mark who received the full brunt of the assaults, because not only did they dart around him in a frenzy, but they commenced to bite his legs and arms. Fortunately, the fish possessed tiny mouths with indiscernible teeth that could do no real harm to a person. However, Mark did a bit of squealing when attacked. Afterwards, he was always reluctant whenever I suggested we go for a swim.

In the morning, we ventured ashore to join the many hundreds moving about. The downtown core and waterfront of Puerto Ayora is well kept and full of the typical tourist shops selling cheap trinkets at exorbitant prices. However, we were pleased to see that most of the souvenirs are produced in Ecuador, unlike in other parts of Central America where the goods are made in China. Most stores are hawking wood carvings of marine iguanas and t-shirts that read, "I Love Boobies," with a picture of a pair of snuggling blue-footed boobies across the chest. This is not the true Galápagos or the Galápagos that we had imagined, but interesting, nonetheless. It is "Disneyland" as Janet called it—an elaborate show designed to separate tourists from the contents of their wallets. Surprisingly, it is mainly an all cash society where tourists seldom use credit cards.

When we first arrived, I tried to use a credit card, but the merchant promptly informed me there would be a 25 per cent service fee added on top of my bill to use the card. Assuming the shopkeeper was trying to fleece me, I reverted to cash. It only took a few inquiries to learn that the massive fee for using a credit card is collected everywhere in the Galápagos. I'm not sure whether it is the government, merchants or the banks who have applied this extraordinary fee, but it is sure a good cause to keep your plastic in your wallet.

As you can imagine, I had not brought enough of the greenbacks to support us in the islands for three months, so I was forced to make frequent trips to the bank, which did accept my debit card in exchange for cash—again for a fee, of course.

Long after I arrived home, my bank statement showed I was charged $6 for each debit transaction, and I had over 30 such bank charges. The reason for so many withdrawals was because the local banks set a limit of $300 per withdrawal, up to $1200 per day. Some days, I hit the machines a maximum of four times to fund our shore-side touring. I could have wallpapered a room with all the ATM receipts I dutifully collected.

We had fun when we came across the open fish market where the morning catch is cleaned and displayed. Buckets of fresh lobster line the front of the counter ($7 per lobster), and sailfish and giant red snapper are displayed next to Mexican hogfish, which are splayed out on the tiled countertops for viewing and purchase. However, the most interesting spectacles are the dozens of pelicans waiting unwearyingly at the ladies' elbows, looking for handouts as the fish are cleaned. And when we were there, under the counter—like an obedient puppy dog—quietly sat a large sea lion, waiting for a handout. I noticed that if the sea lion had to wait too long for a titbit, it would gently nudge one of the ladies in the butt to remind her to feed him, or her.

We negotiated a price with a cabbie to take us on a couple of island tours. (Later I would conclude we paid too much—we needed to bargain harder.)

Figure 33. A Santa Cruise tortoise at the ranch.

First we drove deep into the interior, to a tortoise ranch where free-roaming Galápagos tortoises scamper around like rabbits. We walked the muddy bush in the tropical heat, taking pictures of the giant beasts, lumbering along or wallowing in murky pools. Seeing the ranch, it was easy to imagine tens of thousands of great tortoises roaming this island—that is, before the appearance of man.

The driver took us to a spot within the ranch where we were led to a great gaping hole in the ground. Following his directions, we took our bottles of water and went inside to follow the tunnel.

Figure 34. A friendly tortoise.

He would meet us a kilometre away where the other end of the magma tube emerged into a cattle pasture. A scary-looking string of lights, hanging from a frayed electrical cord, poorly lit the tunnel. Not all the bulbs were working, leaving some sections of the tunnel hard to navigate in the dim light.

The tunnel, with its rutted walls oozing slimy groundwater and muddy floor, was for most of the way over 5 metres (16.4 feet) in diameter. Its pleasantly cool air offered an enjoyable break from the oppressive heat above. Apparently, in the Galápagos, the location of heaven and hell are reversed as hell, the hot place, is overhead.

At the midway point, we were forced to crawl on our hands and knees to squeeze past a recent cave in. Someone had thoughtfully provided a muddy carpet that offered some measure of padding for our knees as we pressed through the narrow slit. Neither Janet nor Teri objected, but as Janet emerged from the far side of the cave in, she stated, "Perhaps long pants instead of my dress may have been a better choice of clothing for spelunking."

I was surprised to find the remains of coral clinging to the rocks. This tunnel had been submerged at some time in its distant past. A strange thought, as the tunnel was now several kilometres from the sea and 400 metres (1312 feet) above sea level. We enjoyed the magma tube and would eventually explore several others over the coming months.

With our first subterranean experience over, we were off to the east side of the island where we walked down a long cobblestone trail to Playa El Garrapatero. I wish I could say it was a pleasant kilometre-long walk down the attractively laid cobble path and through what looked like a cultivated desert garden, but the heat and the thousands of yellow paper wasps that were constantly menacing us took away from the enjoyment of the natural beauty of the trail.

In keeping with the naked brutality of our surroundings, with the lack of breeze, the late afternoon sun was scorching. If the heat was not enough to convince a person to return to the parking lot, like the gauntlet of flying monkeys surrounding the castle of the Wicked Witch of the West, yellow wasps swarmed us. I had read that these wasps are not as aggressive as hornets or the "yellow jackets" back home, but they can still be ornery if you venture too close to their nests. We were all happy to finally break out onto the beach and leave the wasps behind. The yellow paper wasp is an invasive species. First spotted on San Cristóbal Island back in 1988, it has since spread to all the major islands. Playa El Garrapatero is undoubtedly the most picturesque pink sand beach I have ever seen. The beach arches around to form a protective bay, with broken lava rock and crashing waves on its shoulders. It has scores of marine iguanas basking in the sun and long-billed oystercatchers chasing after receding wavelets.

Figure 35. Janet enters one of the many magma tunnels around Santa Cruz.

Brown pelicans were diving for lunch beyond the beach, which is bordered by scrub brush and towering cacti. Interspersed amongst the prickly pear are pretty little apple trees called "*manzanilla de la muerte*" ("little apple of death"). This refers to the fact the manchineel is one of the most poisonous trees in the world. And apparently you don't even have to eat the lime green fruit; sap dripping from a tree branch has the similar effect on your body as being splashed with an Alien's acid blood, not a good place to spread a beach blanket despite the fact it makes for a nice shade tree.

A handful of metres inland, we found a freshwater lagoon surrounded by mangrove swamps. The waters were teeming with long-legged pink flamingos, pintail ducks and black-necked stilts, all searching for crustaceans along the water's frothy edge. The Galápagos flamingos are smaller and pinker than species found elsewhere in the world, but no less impressive. We only spent a couple of hours here, as the afternoon heat, despite the lovely sea breeze, was oppressive. I went for a swim and had an incredibly fun time seeing how close I could get to the iguanas sunning on rocks before they would start to bob their heads, a warning for me not to come any closer. Janet and the rest declined to swim because they didn't want to get back into the taxi in wet cloths. We departed after my dip.

Figure 36. An old magma tunnel that was once under water as evident by the presence of coral inside.

The following day, we took the water taxi out to the point on the south side of the harbour where we landed on a trail between some low-key, yet high-priced hotels. Some of the B&Bs and hotels were reminiscent of old English stone cottages, with rubble rock walls constructed out of volcanic rock. The head height walls were perfect perches for lounging lizards and iguanas to sun themselves.

Figure 37. One of the "low key" expensive restaurants located on the south point of Academy Bay, Santa Cruz Island.

The trail meandered along the coast, then through inland marshlands full of blue herons and white egrets, spending most of their day ambushing fiddler crabs.

After a couple of kilometres, we climbed a brown stone ridge where, when we turned back to look where we had come, we were treated to a panoramic view of Puerto Ayora. From the ridge top, we saw a pretty community surrounded by pale blue water and black volcanic rock splashed white with breaking waves.

A little further along the trail, we came across a deep fissure filled with water. We followed the trail as it ran along the ridge skirting the Grotto until we came across a set of wooden stairs, leading down the cliff side to a small dock. At the top of the stairs, we were stopped by a park ranger, who asked us to sign in while presenting a log book for us to write our names.

The number of visitors to the Grotto is tightly regulated to make sure the environment is not overwhelmed by bodies, but it is also a way to keep a head count. A system designed to ensure all who ventured into the Grotto came back out again. The park guide smiled and thanked us for signing his book, but before he permitted us to descend the stairs, he gestured to a pile of well-used snorkelling equipment on his right. *"¿Necesitas alquilar algo de equipo?"* ("Do you need to rent some gear?") he asked hopefully.

"No, trajimos nuestro propio," ("No we brought our own,") I replied while pointing at the big black fins sticking out of the top of my backpack. Looking a little disappointed, he waved us on. Down the stairs we went into the fracture where we were prepared to go for a snorkel in water as clear as glass.

The Grotto, despite having the appearance of being separated from the sea and landlocked, is tidal and connects to the sea by subterranean caves and fissures, permitting the water to rise and fall as dictated by the cycles of the moon. The Grotto is an old magma tunnel where the ceiling collapsed, leaving a chasm approximately 20 metres (65.6 feet) wide and several 100 metres long, with the water approximately 10 metres (32.8 feet) deep. You can reach a series of interconnected pools by climbing over some great boulders that separate the pools, or as I did, swim underwater through the interconnecting tunnels between the canting boulders. The water is refreshingly cool and filled with large mullets and lime green parrot fish. It is a great place to spend during the heat of the day. The Grotto became my favourite spot on Santa Cruz and we visited and explored it on four separate occasions.

We made several grocery shopping trips into town, with an emphasis on locating cheap beer, which we finally found on main street away from the waterfront. Neither Janet nor I were impressed with the crass commercialism of Puerto Ayora, but we began to feel better about the town once we learned to get off the main streets and explore the back alleys and narrow, cobbled side roads where many of the locals shopped and conducted business. The back alleys are dirty and poorly lit at night. They appear as one might think of the quintessential underbelly of a city—writhing with all manner of peril and underworld lowlifes ready to maim, rape and plunder unsuspecting tourists. However, in reality, this area was the home turf of principally honest, hardworking people. It wasn't long before we were felt comfortable navigating the back streets and bartering with the locals, and at no time did we ever feel threatened or afraid. That said, we also made sure to travel in groups while keeping our guard sharp, as here, and anywhere else in the world we have travelled, there was no sense setting yourself up for trouble.

On one of our shopping trips, we found an awesome local bakery tucked into a tiny storefront. I believe our noses lead us to it, as it had fresh buns and bread that was incredible. The sad part was after that first discovery we were never able to locate that shop again. Were we lost, or did it just close its doors and move? I was also pleased to find there were a couple of good marine stores in town where I managed to purchase some boat parts as well as a repair kit for the inflatable dinghy since it had sprung a duo of air leaks. For the past couple of weeks, we had to keep pumping air into the dink if we didn't want it to sink.

A couple of days after our arrival, we discovered another great location. During the daytime, this was a busy side street with fleeing taxis and scooters, but after dark, a great transformation occurred—the locals closed off the road at each end of the block. Now separated from the traffic, the streets were filled with tables and chairs. Then out came all the barbecues, flame broilers and steaming pots of prawns, lobsters and other seafood. It seemed like out of nowhere every type of restaurant imaginable magically appeared. Every night, it was a city block-long feast, complete with beer to wash down the fresh lobster, grilled grouper, chicken or beef stuffed empanadas.

Janet and I would often eat at street vendors while in town, and our favourite was either corn and chicken on a stick or deep fried Empanadas (which are made by folding dough over a stuffing consisting of meat, cheese, huitlacoche or other ingredients), and all for $1. It was a pleasant and filling treat. I had to ask what huitlacoche was and was surprised to learn that it is a black fungus, like a mushroom, that grows on corn. Although considered a disease, huitlacoche is a great delicacy in México where cooks use it to flavour food.

"I wonder if we can get Guinea pig on a stick here as well as chicken, or Guinea pig empanadas?" I asked Jan as the lady pulled our corn and chicken off the smoking hibachi, rolling the corn first in butter, then grated parmesan cheese.

"What are you talking about? Guinea pig, really?" Janet asked with some amusement as she took her meal and sat on the stone wall next to the street.

"Ya, babe, while sailing over here Marina told us that they eat Guinea Pig in Ecuador. It's some kind of delicacy. She thought we could find some and try it. What you think? Wanna try some Guinea pig pie?"

"Sounds disgusting and how much meat can you get off such a tiny thing?" Janet questioned.

"Don't know, but I heard they were big, like cat size or like footballs down here, not like the type pet stores sell at home."

My statement and question forced me to have a better look at my splayed roast chicken on the stick, re-examining it at different angles. Then noting, "You know, babe, if you roll or bend this chicken around so it's no longer flat, it would look kind of like a Guinea pig. See here's its nose." I pointed.

Janet was enjoying her chicken, but to humour me, she took a moment to look at what I was pointing. She laughed. "That's its butt, you dolt!"

It wasn't until sometime later while doing a bit more research on foods of Ecuador when I learned that Guinea pig is one of the traditional foods served in Ecuador, Bolivia and Peru. It is more commonly known as *cuy* (kew-y) in the indigenous language of Kichwa Indians.

Guinea pigs were the main source of meat before the introduction of cattle into the country. Eating *cuy* became a status symbol because it meant you could afford to eat meat; however, it was never an everyday meal, but instead a luxury to impress guests.

Most days, Janet and I, often accompanied by Mark and Teri, would eat at one of the many open air restaurants by the waterfront (where there was a breeze). As on San Cristóbal, they offered inexpensive lunch specials, which included lemonade, rice or plantain, with a choice of beef, chicken or fish—all for $5.

Our fourth day in port, Mark and Teri ventured off by themselves to explore another grand beach, Tortuga Bay, which again you had to hike to through the baking brush for 2.5 kilometres (1.5 miles) each way to visit. Janet declined to attempt the hike, so we hung around the boat and played at being lazy.

Like a seal, I lay in the sun, swam and drank beer. Well, seals don't drink beer, but if they could, I'm sure they would! I love to watch boats, and it was fun to see all the different types of vessels that were coming and going. Most were typical small cruise ships, yet others were converted private yachts. Instead of having some billionaire's helicopter sitting on the aft flight deck, the helipad now cradled several inflatable boats, and nestled midst the ridged inflatables were scores of bright yellow and orange kayaks, among other floaty toys.

However, what I loved most was the number of sailing vessels engaged in the tourist trade.

There were dozens of sailing ships in the 20- to 30-metre (65.5- to 98.4-feet) range, but there were also a couple of square-rigged tall ships at anchor. I also saw an old steel schooner of 40 metres (131.2 feet) that I was reasonably sure had participated in the Alaskan seal hunting trade in the early 19th century. Of more recent vintage, there was a 66-metre (216.5-feet) barquentine. The tall ship or "windjammer," appeared majestic as she rode gently on her anchor off of *Maiatla's* bow. I would later learn this ship was the *Mary Anne,* and despite her aged design, she had only been constructed in 1997.

The *Mary Anne* was a barquentine with three lofty masts. A barquentine is a ship that has three or more masts: a square-rigged foremast, fore-and-aft rigged main, mizzen and any other masts. The *Mary Anne* was designed to offer complete luxury under sail while exploring the Galápagos Islands.

The ship for hire came with a crew of eight and boasted accommodation for up to 24 passengers, with basic rates starting at $1000 per person per day for either an eight- or 15-day cruise. Cruising here on *Maiatla* was expensive, but in reality, it was a bargain. I would later take our crew for a dinghy ride around the *Mary Anne* to see how the other side lived.

"No, I don't think I would want it," I said to everyone as we passed under the tall ship's towering bowsprit.

"Why not?" Mark asked. "I bet it goes like stink under sail in a good wind," he added.

Figure 38. The barquentine *Mary Anne* anchored near us at Academy Bay, Isla Santa Cruz.

"Yes, but *Maiatla* has only one toilet, and it's bad enough when it plugs up. This girl must have at least 20 toilets, so you would be spending most of your time unplugging heads, which is a nasty business," I countered.

Despite the commercialism, the overcrowded condition and general busyness of the harbour, we did find something (aside from the street food vendors) that we found appealing—the weather. No rain either during the day or the evening—it never rained. Most days started out sunny, but clouded over early in the afternoon and then clear again most nights. We erected the tarps, but here it was for protection against the sun, which was marvelous.

By our fifth day on Santa Cruz, Janet still wanted to lie about and surprisingly so did Mark and Teri. Apparently their visit to Tortuga Bay was a nice, but aside from being all tired out from trekking in the hot sun, Teri received a nasty sunburn, so she decided to hide out for the better part of the day. They talked of maybe walking over to the Darwin Research Centre later in the afternoon when it cooled. On the other hand, I was anxious to do some more serious exploring, so I charged the GoPro camera and made preparations for heading out to Gordon Rocks in the morning in search of some hammerhead sharks.

Chapter 16

Schooling Scalloped Hammerhead Sharks and Is That a BOMB?

"It is a curious situation that the sea, from which life first arose should now be threatened by the activities of one form of that life. But the sea, though changed in a sinister way, will continue to exist; the threat is to life itself."
—Rachel Carson

Most of the dive charter boats working out of Puerto Ayora, departing from right here in the harbour, are high-speed motor vessels in the 12-metre (39.3-feet) range. While at anchor, I watched the daily progress of half a dozen dive boats that departed each morning to various dive spots along the coast, Gordon Rocks included. What I noticed about these operations was they crammed as many bodies on board as humanly possible, and since there was little room for dressing into your wet suit, all the divers were all decked out in their wet and drysuits before boarding the boats. I could well imagine what it would be like to spend an hour or so motoring out to the dive site in a black wetsuit, sitting in the tropical sun while getting your spine jarred as the boat pounded through the waves. Perhaps the only comfort would be knowing that since you were jammed tightly in between a pair of equally uncomfortable divers (strangers most likely), it was unlikely you would be hurled out of the boat while broaching a big wave. No! That did not look like fun to me.

Over the previous days while strolling ashore, I queried all the dive charter companies who were advertising trips out to Gordon Rocks. Finally, I decided to sign on for a two-dive day trip aboard a sailing vessel that accommodated up to 30 divers out to the rock. The *Nautilus* was a weather-worn 25-metre (84-feet) ketch of dubious origin, but she possessed graceful lines and most assuredly had been a beauty in her day. From the pictures the seller of tours showed me, at his booth down on the *malecón*, the old boat had acres of deck space for dressing in, so no crowding, and since it would take almost two hours to get out to the rock, there would be time to lounge (in shorts) in the sun and take in the sites. Besides, the idea of viewing the Galápagos coast was more romantic while done from the deck of a sailing vessel, even if the boat was . . . experienced!

"Oh, yes, and we provide all the drinks and a lunch too," the eager sales clerk said. Well that was it for me. I was sold, as this was a much more appealing adventure than the motor boat option. However, since the *Nautilus* was slower, she did not depart from this harbour; her berth rested on the far side of Santa Cruz, which meant taking a taxi all the way across the island to rendezvous with the boat. So this tour would include a road trip. Again a bonus, I reasoned.

I gave Janet a goodbye kiss as I left our bed at 6 a.m., grabbed my wetsuit bag and other gear, hailed a water taxi, and was quickly whisked ashore. Despite the early hour, the harbour was wide awake and already abuzz. Outside the tour office's booth, a friendly group of mostly young people milling around greeted me. This group would become my dive buddies for the day. (As I'm now past the half century mark, anyone under the age of 40 is a young person.)

After piling dozens of scuba tanks into the back of a threesome of Toyotas, we all piled in and quickly headed out of town on a road that would take us over the top of the volcano, then to the opposite side of the island. Isla Santa Cruz has a small neighbouring island called Baltra where the main airport is located. There is a narrow channel of a couple hundred metres between these two islands called the Itabaca Narrows, and it was here we were to meet our boat.

Baltra is a small flat island that was created by geological uplift. The island, as well as most of the northern portion of Santa Cruz, is arid. Vegetation consists of salt bushes, prickly pear cactus and the aromatic palo santo trees. The spindly-looking trees are often used for incense or decorative carvings. During World War II, the island of Baltra, or south Seymour as the Americans called it, was taken over by the U.S., who established a United States Army Air Force Base. Crews stationed at Baltra readily patrolled the eastern Pacific for enemy submarines while offering air cover and protection to friendly shipping vessels bound to and from the Panamá Canal.

After the war, the facilities were given to the government of Ecuador. Today the island continues as an official Ecuadorian military base. The foundations of buildings and other remains of the U.S. base, including the old airfield, can still be seen on the island.

Until 1986, Seymour Airport was the only airport serving the Galápagos. Now there are two airports that receive flights from mainland Ecuador, the other, of course, located on San Cristóbal Island where Janet and Teri flew into. On arriving into Baltra, all visitors are transported by bus to one of two docks. The first dock is in a small bay where boats cruising the Galápagos await for passengers. The second is a ferry dock that connects Baltra to the island of Santa Cruz via the Itabaca Channel. The new airport is run under a 15-year concession by ECOGAL, a subsidiary of the Argentinian group Corporación América, and has been promoted as "the first ecological airport worldwide" due to its reduced energy consumption for lighting and ventilation, rainwater collecting and waste recycling. There is even a solar-powered electric ferry shuttling people across Itabaca Channel.

I was particularly interested in seeing the airport because Janet and I were expecting a crew change soon and may have to come here to pick them up. However, since we would not be permitted to go to the airport to meet anyone, we would have to find a place to hook up after the crew crossed the channel on the electric boat.

Once our Toyota crested the northern slope of the volcano, a panoramic vista was displayed for us—the sight left me in awe. The landscape was red with low brush, trees and cacti, and peppered with small, bowling ball-sized rocks. For several kilometres, the island slowly descended to merge with the pale blue sea. Off in the distance, across the Itabaca Channel, lay Baltra and the airport. I was surprised to see what must have been 30 or more charter boats, either at anchor or passing through the gap between the islands. It is a beautiful coast, cut deep by numerous tiny bays, perfect for a boat of *Maiatla's* size to hunker in. I was envious of anyone who had free rein of such a place.

Our road, the only road, led to a small concrete ferry dock, sporting a tiny grill making meals and a seating area under a tall tin roof. After some milling about, our driver pointed out into the bay and said that there was our boat. *Nautilus* had been one of the many vessels anchored out that I had seen from the mountain top. Little time was wasted. We were all loaded into a pair of large rigid inflatables and ferried out to our boat that was slowly motoring through the channel. We formed a human chain to quickly hand the dive gear aboard. Unloaded, the inflatables were moved aft to be secured so that they would trail behind the mother ship.

Once aboard, I had a good look around. I was happy to see the *Nautilus* was not much different than *Maiatla*, aside from being perhaps twice her size, with room to play hockey in the salon. Down in the galley, I found cooks already preparing the food—beef, beans and salads—and steaming on the flat-top stove was a big bowl of white rice. It all smelled so good, and since I had only a peanut butter sandwich for breakfast, I was already eager for lunch. However, that would have to wait.

As soon as all the tanks were stored for sea, the captain throttled up the engine getting us underway. Within 10 minutes, we were leaving the protection of the narrows, nosing into a building sea. As typically happens on such adventures, we made introductions all around, and since it was a long ride out to the rock, we all had time to get to know one another. My fellow divers, consisting of 16 in all, included four women, two older ladies and a pair of young ones in bikinis, sporting semi-erotic arm and thigh tattoos. The group was from all over the world, and all were thrilled to be there. Gordon Rocks was considered an advanced dive and not one for the faint of heart. It was a deep (30 metres or 98.4 feet) open water current dive, with the likelihood of encountering dangerous marine life. There were a few couples, but since most of us were strangers, we did not know each other's capabilities. In this case, it would be best to rely on yourself if you got into trouble.

Juan, the dive master who was running the show, was a squat Ecuadorian fellow who spoke decent English. Juan first had us tell everyone a bit about ourselves and our diving experience. It took some time to listen to everyone. Juan paired up divers of similar or complementing experience and identified the people he would have to keep close to him or one of the other dive masters. However, this group of divers was well travelled, and most had hundreds of amateur dives under their belts.

When it was my turn, I briefly explained I had been a professional bell and mixed gas diver, working on the oil rigs in the Arctic, and a former submersible co-pilot, which I thought would have been of more interest than how I came to be here in the Galápagos. My claim to fame amongst this group was not having dived beneath the polar icecaps, but my stories of sailing to the Galápagos on *Maiatla*. Apparently this group chose this vessel for much the same reasons I claimed. The draw and romance of voyaging under sail was a strong one. Throughout the day, I was constantly being asked of our voyage. Some even asked if I needed any new crew.

Before signing on for such a technical dive, I suspected I would be the oldest one in the group, but in fact I was not. In our number was a German couple, well into their sixties. Franz was an experienced diver; his wife, Hilda, was not. Both appeared fit and confident, but this would only be Hilda's fourth dive, so they would be taken aside and dive alone, with their own private dive master to keep an eye on them. Juan, our dive master, showed us a map of the submerged crater where we would enter and exit the water and where the strong currents were located. The northern part of the crater can be quite rough, so it was sometimes referred to as "the washing machine," and for good reason.

The sky was overcast and a light breeze slipped out of the south, which made for a pleasant motor over to the rocks. Gordon Rocks is a small rocky island of a couple of acres, with a pair of smaller rocks breaking the surface a few hundred metres away from its shore. Each rock is the tip of the submerged crater. The water depth within the crater is slightly over 30 metres (98.4 feet) deep. However, the depth diminished as you approached the sides of the crater until reaching the rim, which for most of the site is only 10 metres (32.8 feet) from the surface.

From the deck of the *Nautilus,* it was easy to visualize the rim of the crater as we approached. Since the water around the rocks drops off into the depths, our boat could not anchor. So instead, she would hover around the island while we dived. The captain brought us close into the rocks so that we could have a thorough look at the tiny islands and take photographs of the herd of sea lions basking in the sun, just out of range of the swells that surged by. Circling overhead were blue-footed boobies, terns, pelicans, swifts and shearwaters—a good sign the surrounding waters were teeming with life and food.

I provided all my own diving gear, only using the dive boat's air tanks, buoyancy compensator and regulators. After dressing in, we loaded eight divers per inflatable and set off for the far side of the crater. As we did so, Juan gave us all a couple more pieces of valuable advice.

"Okay, first thing is NO feeding the sharks! Okay? We haven't had a diver eaten yet, and I don't want to start today. And also remember, there is a strong current swirling around the north side of the island, so if you leave the crater, you may get sucked off the seamount and taken out to sea." He said this with an unnatural calmness, as if getting sucked out to sea and telling people not to get eaten was an everyday occurrence. However, in truth for Dive Master Juan, it was.

"If you do get lost," Juan continued, "just re-surface and go for the ride, and don't worry. We will come and get you." Juan cut a smirk while letting out a subtle laugh. "That is, sooner or later."

Not getting eaten or getting lost at sea was a sound piece of advice; I would do my best not to disappoint him on either account. I was buddied with a 30-something-year-old architect from Adelaide, Australia, named Jason. The young man with a "top knot" or "man bun" was on an old-fashioned Australian walkabout, a yearlong sabbatical to see the world. Jason was single, travelling alone and had already spent two months hiking around mainland Ecuador and the Andes Mountains, reaching the headwaters of the Amazon River. After his month long stay in the Galápagos, he was next headed for Peru to visit the 15th-century Inca citadel Machu Picchu, which is located some 2,430 metres (7,970 feet) above sea level.

Being an adventurous lad that had been diving for many years, I suspected I would not have to worry about him. Our group, once in the water, was not required to stay together, but we were required to stay within eye contact of our buddies, and Jason Top Knot was mine. The driver of the inflatable took us out to the approximate centre of the crater, and even before the boat had come to a complete stop, Juan gave the command and all nine of us nearly simultaneously, back flipped into the water. In a flurry of erupting bubbles, I sank like a rock until I was able to pump some air into the buoyancy compensator to stop my rapid decent. At 3 metres (9.8 feet) deep, I leveled off, adjusted my gear and cleared my ears by pinching my nose and blowing.

Once satisfied all was well with me, I glanced back towards the surface to look for Jason, and there he was bobbing on the surface with most of the rest alongside the inflatable, adjusting their gear before descending. I learned the hard way a long time ago that it was far safer to get down a few metres as quickly as possible before playing with the equipment. By doing so, you are less likely to get clobbered by the boat when an unexpected wave drives it overtop of you or, worse, when an anxious boat driver suddenly throws the boat back into gear and catches you with the propeller as he runs over you.

Jason joined me after a couple of minutes, then flashed the "okay" sign, which I answered. Glancing below we saw a large school of tiny silver fish passing by. The fish were in such great numbers they obscured the sea bottom from our view. Without hesitation, I gave a couple of great kicks and dived headlong into the school, which quickly parted, providing me my first glimpse of the crater's floor, still 25 metres (82 feet) or so below. I continued on down until I came to rest on bended knees on the sand. I had high expectation when I booked this dive trip, and it only took a few moments after entering the water to realize I wouldn't be disappointed. Within a few minutes, all the divers were sitting on the bottom, and like me, most had brought their GoPro Cameras and were already busy recording the marvels laid out before us.

The water clarity was remarkable at 25 or 30 metres (82 to 98.4 feet). The course white sandy bottom appeared perfectly flat. Scattered around were boulders of various sizes covered in a dense mat of marine growths and soft corals, resembling a shag carpet and displaying all the brilliant colours of the rainbow. Vibrant reds, purples and oranges were the most prominent colours of this reef.

Many of the rocks strewn about sported yellow-spotted sea cucumbers clinging to their sides between the branches of orange and purple gorgonian sea fans wafting in a gentle current. Schools of plate-sized burrito grunt fish were on patrol, and off to the right was a sloping rock wall, which I assumed was the side of the crater. The wall was likewise decorated in soft corals and swaying fans, and the entire wall appeared to undulate as a massive school of yellow and black surgeonfish swarmed around, picking morsels off of the rocks. From this one spot, there was so much to take in. Jason grabbed my arm to get my attention, and pointed off to our left. There, to my amazement, was a group of seven spotted eagle rays flying in a slow formation, close to the bottom. As I filmed, the rays disturbed a sea turtle that had been resting next to a small bolder. The startled turtle first swam in a circle as if to orientate itself, and then, after taking notice of all the divers, it swam directly towards me. The animal seemed to have had a purpose in mind, as if it wanted to investigate this strange creature. Freezing I continued filming until the turtle finally collided with my outstretched arm and camera. Well that was a close-up.

Figure 39. A sea turtle that came in to bump noses with the camera.

I followed the turtle for several minutes, taking pictures, and when finally done, I realized I was alone. Oops, I let myself get distracted. After spinning about until I spotted some moving shadows off in the distance, I began to swim in that direction. As I did, I found Jason and what I first believed were the other divers, but I was wrong. Instead of the rest of our group of tank suckers, a school of perhaps 3-metre (9.8-feet) long scalloped hammerhead sharks passed directly over a now excited Jason. The sharks were charcoal grey, long and sleek, with coal black eyes at the tips of their oddly-shaped heads. The animals effortlessly moved through the water—a slight undulating of their bodies and tail was all that was required. They were the epitome of grace and power while giving the impression they were capable of great speed. They were magnificent and they didn't appear to be hungry at all. The sharks circled around behind me, disappearing off in the direction of the open sea. To say I was thrilled would have been a gross understatement.

Over the next half hour, Jason, I and some of the other divers continued to explore the crater and its side walls that were thick with both plant and animal life. The sharks thrilled us all by making several more casual passes. After the third or fourth encounter, the hammerheads grew accustomed to our presence, intentionally coming a little closer.

Near the end of our first dive, the school of sharks materialized directly behind me and kept coming. I froze, permitting myself to sink and come to rest on the bottom. While video recording, the school quickly overtook me, and just when I thought I was going to have a repeat of the turtle slamming into my camera lens (but this time by a minivan-sized shark), the hammerheads ever so slightly parted to pass within arm's reach on either side and above me.

It was an incredible encounter. In an effort to conserve some air and to increase our bottom time, I directed Jason to ascend the crater wall where we found a ledge at 10 metres (32.8 feet) deep. On this ledge, we found nesting black damselfish, which are territorial—if we came too close to their dens, they would attack by biting our arms and fins. The hand-size fish are harmless yet persistent and utterly fearless. It was here we also encountered a metre-long grey reef shark, displaying a tear behind its dorsal fin. The recent-looking wound was most likely the result of an unsuccessful attack initiated by another shark.

While I was poking my head in a hole looking for lobster, I felt a tug at my right elbow. It was Jason, who indicted he was almost out of air and needed to surface. I checked my pressure gauge, which showed I still had almost 400 psig in my tank. At this depth, I could remain another 15 or 20 minutes on the bottom. Without waiting for me, Jason began his assent. I looked around in hopes of seeing some of the rest of the group, assuming I could join them until I sucked my tank dry, but there was no one else in sight. I had no qualms about hanging out on the bottom all by myself; in fact, I have usually enjoyed it. However, if everyone else was already out of the water, Dive Master Juan may be doing a head count, and perhaps finding one still missing might initiate Juan to form a search party. I peered towards the surface where I could see Jason treading water a short distance away. The inflatable was approaching him for the pickup. With some reluctance, I slowly kicked my way to the surface to greet the boat when it arrived.

Back aboard the *Nautilus*, I peeled myself out of my wetsuit and towelled off. Some of the group had been back for awhile and had already eaten lunch. They were lounging around the deck, resting from the exertion of the dive. I grabbed a bottle of cold water out of a cooler that was on deck and made my way aft to where there were several trays set out with food. But instead of seeing the beef, baked beans and salad lunch, the food I'd seen in the galley when I first boarded, there was lettuce and tomato sandwiches, with a side dish of cheese and crackers.

"That's it? Hey, where is the rice and beef that I can smell?" I asked Juan as he passed me on his way to the galley where the enticing aroma was originating.

Juan was apparently in a hurry to eat and didn't even slow down when he answered. "Oh, that food is for the crew. The sandwiches are for you guys."

Since I hated tomatoes, I ended up seizing the lion's share of the cheese and crackers, washing it down with cold lemonade. We would make a second dive after a rest following the pitiful excuse for a lunch.

Figure 40. Schooling hammerhead sharks at Gordon Rock, Isla Santa Cruz.

We entered the water on the near side of the crater where it was much shallower, but the marine life was no less intense. On this dive, we all managed to stay together, as there was little reason to wander. All you had to do was sit your ass on a rocky ledge and watch all the fish either school by or come to you out of curiosity.

Again, we were treated to several sea turtles, eagle rays, stingrays, marbled rays, mantas, white-tipped reef sharks, Galápagos' sharks, hieroglyphic hawkfish, flag cabrillas, wrasse in various growth stages, cardinalfish, king angelfish, sea lions, yellowtail surgeonfish and barracudas. Still hungry, I eyed the amber jacks and thought of *Maiatla's* barbeque grill. It was like being inside some giant aquarium, and as if to make an encore appearance, both the hammerheads and our wounded grey reef shark graced our presence several more times.

It was magical, and just when it couldn't get any better, a metallic chattering sound filled the water. I searched the group for the source of the sound. It turned out to be Juan shaking a steel rattle in an effort to draw everyone's attention. Excited, Juan was pointing straight up at a big black shadow above.

My first thought was that it was a boat backlit by the sun. From my vantage point, the shadowy mass was indistinguishable, but as it moved out of the sun's starburst, I recognized it for what it was. And it was marvelous. We had a giant mola circling overhead. I had seen these before when diving many years ago at both the Farallon and Channel Islands, off the coast of California, and more recently at the start of this

Figure 41. Nose to nose with an inquisitive hammerhead shark.

voyage with Marina, 161 kilometres (100 miles) off the coast of Oregon, but I had never seen one this large. Mola are the heaviest of all the bony fish, with the largest specimen reaching 4.2 metres (13.7 feet) vertically and 3.1 metres (10 feet) horizontally and weighing nearly 2,268 kilograms (5,000 pounds).

The fish appear to be all head and tail, and this one was the size of a boat. Perhaps not the largest mola in the sea, still it must have been somebody's granddaddy. Juan, led by his own GoPro camera, shot off after the mola, with the rest of the group quickly following, myself included. Unfortunately, the fish was moving fast, and I was too far away to manage any good video, so I slowed down, allowing myself to sink to the bottom. I was getting tired and in need of a nap, but sleep would have to wait. Reaching the bottom, I came to rest atop an oddly-shaped rock covered in soft coral. The "rock" looked oblong, approximately a metre (3.2 feet) in length and perhaps a third of a metre in diameter.

It oddly looked familiar but out of place. The rock had a smooth surface in total contrast to most of the broken rubble strewn around. I grabbed the rock in an effort

Figure 42. Giant Mola, Ocean Sunfish.

to roll it over, but my attempt was futile, as it was too heavy to move. Taking a moment to further examine the rock, I noticed a hole in one side. After visually checking it for finger-eating creatures, I stuck a hand inside to discover that this rock was hollow.

It was at this time, I recognized what it was. It was likely an old bomb, and as I later confirmed, it was part of the familiar story of how the Americans used offshore islands near their air or military bases for target practice. Fortunately, this was obviously a harmless dud, but I must admit that for a moment when it first dawned on me what it was, I was a little nervous.

We had a pleasant motor back to Itabaca Channel and our awaiting tender and taxi back to Puerto Ayora. It was an incredible diving experience and would rate perhaps as one of my top four recreational diving experiences. I was so happy to have been able to see this wonderful place and share it with some pretty incredible people.

Back in town, over beers at a waterfront canteen, we shared video files and exchanged emails, with vows of getting together for some more great diving, but as often happens, we were all on divergent paths, unlikely to converge again.

Making my way back to the *malecón*, I spotted a tall set of masts alongside the fisherman's dock. It was *Chica* the boat from the Netherlands, and there was Pieter giving directions to a crane operator busy re-stepping the boat's mizzen mast. Pieter had little time to talk, but the repairs were going well and they were hoping to depart for Australia in a couple of days. This would be the last time we would see them.

Back aboard *Matatla* by dinnertime, we barbecued chicken and ate in the cockpit. Placing my laptop on the cabin top the crew ate while watching my "swimming with the hammerhead sharks" videos. After a full seven days on this marvellous island, we prepared to set sail for Isla Isabela where we hoped to encounter perhaps the last wild creature you would expect to see in equatorial tropics—the cute and cuddly Antarctic Penguin.

Chapter 17

Isla Isabela, the Jewel of the Galápagos Islands

"I like animals. I like natural history. The travel bit is not the important bit. The travel bit is what you have to do in order to go and look at animals."
—David Attenborough

I rolled out of bed in our aft cabin, early on Friday morning to make tea and ready the boat for sea. As I do first thing every morning, I ventured topside to check the mooring lines for chaffing and to make sure all on deck was in order. I also like to make sure no other vessels dragged anchor during the night and were threatening us. Surprisingly, this happens more than you would believe. This morning, a heavy dew had settled, and the boat shone in the early twilight, as if freshly painted. We had dropped all the deck tarps the night before, so all I would have to do was retrieve the stern anchor and drop the mooring lines, and we could get underway. I jumped into the dinghy, which was already in the water alongside the boat, and fiddled with the engine. When we arrived here, we had been amazed at how few sea lions were hanging around the harbour of Santa Cruz. Unlike San Cristóbal Island where the harbour and town are overrun with the beasts, here the creatures are few and far between, with most hanging out on the pier and around the fish market. During our whole time in Santa Cruz, our inflatable dinghy had been safe from sea lion invasions, save for only one young pup I had to chase out of the dink, and I felt it safe to leave it hanging alongside.

"Andy, what are you doing up so early for?" Janet asked as she peered down from the cockpit.

"Hi, hun. I thought that since we have a long way to go, perhaps an early start might be smart," I said as I commenced to use the foot pump to re-inflate the soft sides of the dink. Despite three attempts to find all the air leaks in the dink, one leak constantly eluded me.

"It's barely light out, and you told everyone that we wouldn't be leaving early. Mark and Teri are still in bed. Have you told them that you want to leave now?" Janet asked while sounding a bit annoyed.

"No, I haven't woken them yet. And well, I thought about it last night, and if the wind builds from the southwest, as it has been doing later in the morning, we will be hard on the wind. And with the currents between the islands, we may have trouble getting there before dark," I offered in my defence. Besides, I usually do not sleep well the night prior to a planned departure for an offshore voyage. There were usually too many details and probabilities running through my head for meaningful sleep.

The distance from Puerto Ayora to Puerto Villamil on Isla Isabela is only 80 kilometres (43 nautical miles), as the crow flies, and for us, it would be a straight shot, with little in the way. Other than a couple of offshore rocks and a pair of islands to keep an eye on, it should be clear sailing. The winds for the past week had been light, 5 to 10 knots in the morning out of the south-southwest, but usually increased in strength as the day advanced, dying out late in the evening. However, it wasn't the wind that concerned me.

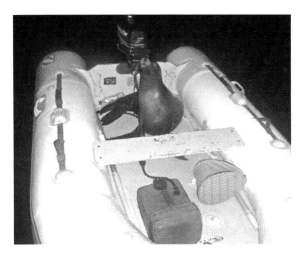

Figure 43. A visitor that did not want to give up its comfy bed in *Maiatla's* dinghy.

Making it into Puerto Villamil and the anchorage before dark was what had me anxious.

The approach to the harbour at Puerto Villamil is a tricky one when attacked from the east, as we were about to do. The port is protected by a group of broken islands and submerged reefs extending several miles offshore of the town and beach. I possessed up-to-date charts of the area, but still the warning "un-surveyed" was printed atop of much of the offshore reefs that become exposed at low tide. We would have to stay well offshore until we could get around the reefs and islands known as Las Tintoreras before turning in towards the notoriously shallow harbour. Las Tintoreras were our first obstacle. Once around the islands, the approach entails sailing directly towards the beach and the enormous breaking surf. Then before the water becomes too shallow and the breaking waves grip your boat to launch you onto the beach, you need to manoeuvre into a hard right turn to pass next to a rocky islet and a navigation buoy. With reefs all around, at times metres away, you had better make sure you are on the right side of the can! To make matters worse, I still had not figured out how to realign the radar. It was still reading approximately 15 degrees to the starboard, so using it to navigate in tight quarters in the dark could prove disastrous.

Needless to say, for your first time, the approach into Puerto Villamil is best done in the light of day and preferably during calm weather.

It was now time to depart Santa Cruz Harbour. I cast the dink off, grabbed the anchor rode where it attached to *Maiatla's* stern and started to pull myself over to where the anchor lay on the bottom. Standing, in an effort to achieve a better angle of attack, I pulled and pulled hard, but it was no use. Our stern anchor stubbornly refused to come up. I cursed aloud, as I knew the anchor must be fouled in the rocks, so off went my shirt, and clad only in shorts, over the side I dived.

The air and sea felt cool, and the water was dense with the colour and viscosity of liquid mercury in the oblique morning light. Grabbing the anchor rode, I tied it to the dink so that it wouldn't drift away. I gave the knot a couple of sharp pulls to test it before I waved back at Janet, who was now watching me with bemused interest from *Maiatla's* aft deck. I didn't need an early morning swim, but I had little choice in the matter. Taking a deep breath, I then pulled myself to the bottom. The rope turned to chain, and while being careful not to impale myself on the spiny sea urchins that were everywhere, I continued to pull myself along on the chain as it rested atop a rubble field. I had not brought with me a facemask, but it didn't matter anyway. Three metres (9.8 feet) down, it was still almost black, and I could barely see the ocean bottom right in front of my face.

As I pulled myself along, scattering schools of tiny fish, I suddenly remembered the big tiger shark we saw cruising the harbour when we had arrived. These sharks normally hunt at night time, and down here in the dark, it was effectively still night. I forced myself to shake the *Jaws* image and melodious music out of my head and concentrate at the task at hand. The chain snaked around a small boulder, and there on the opposite side sat my Danforth anchor, with the flukes hooked under a rock. The anchor was easily removed, and once free, I placed it where it wouldn't get fouled again when I was ready to retrieve it.

Relieved to be back in the dink, I waved to Janet, indicating my success in freeing the anchor while not being eaten. Pulling the ground tackle into the dinghy, I quickly motored home.

It only took me a few minutes to lift the dinghy back into the davits and secure it for sea. Job accomplished, I stripped off my shorts and made my way to the foredeck where a sun shower hung from the mast. The water in the black bag had cooled off even though it had spent the previous day in the tropical sun. By the time I rinsed the salt water from my body, Janet was by my side with a dry towel and a hot cup of tea.

"How was your swim?" she asked as she handed me a steaming cup and began to towel off my back.

"Not bad. Woke me up though," I answered, then took a sip of tea.

"Mark and Teri are still in bed. I don't know if they are awake, but you may want to warn them that we are about to go," Janet suggested as she handed me the towel to finish drying myself off.

"I think they will get the message when the engine starts. I just need to find some clothes and check the engine oil." Despite the warm air, I gave an involuntary shiver as a slight gust of wind whipped by.

Janet laughed. "I felt that shudder. You must be acclimatized to the heat now if you think this is cold," she said as she instinctively began to rub my naked arms in an effort to ward off my chill.

"Yes, it's cold. Here warm me up," I said as I drew her in close for a tight hug, but Janet pushed back.

"Hey, none of that. We got to go now, right?" she asked, with the grin of a temptress.

The day was promising to be a nice one. Boats were waking up, coming to life all around us, and off in the east, the sky was streaked crimson, appearing as a ragged wound in the pale blue tunic of heaven. There were several finger-like clouds stretching out, as if the hands of the sun were attempting to claw their way around the curvature of the Earth. Despite the sky's ominous appearance, I still thought it was looking like it was going to be a fine day. Janet and I again embraced each other, watching in silence the sun broach the horizon, and doing so, it back lit the tall ship *Mary Anne,* setting its tall spars and rigging afire. We instantly felt the welcoming warmth of the sun upon our faces and my naked body.

We returned to the cockpit, and I asked Janet to grab the camera from down below. Quickly, I snapped some pictures of *Mary Anne,* along with a pair of marine iguanas swimming past the boat, heading out to the reef for breakfast. Moments later, the engine roared to life, and as soon it did, Mark arose from the dead to join me in the cockpit.

"Morning, bud. Help me wipe the dew off the windows, then go forward and release the mooring lines and stow them for sea, will ya, please?"

By the time we were motoring past the big barquentine, the whole crew was sitting in the cockpit, sipping tea or coffee, silently watching the ship and the point of the harbour pass by. From the expressions on everybody's faces, all were content this morning. It was looking like it would be an uneventful day, but I suspected our little bilge gremlins resented being woken so early and decided to cause some mischief.

The engine had been running well ever since the fuel injector pump rebuild; however, when I checked the engine instrument panel, I noticed one of the two alternators, the one charging the house bank, was not putting out any current. I didn't say anything to Janet or the crew, as I didn't want them to worry needlessly. It was not a critical issue anyway, but it would have to be addressed later. For now, I turned auto on and went down below to flip the battery switch. With the remaining good alternator doing double duty, it was now charging both the starter battery as well as the house bank. We would be fine as long as the smaller of the two alternators didn't burn itself out.

It was another great day in the tropics. We enjoyed Santa Cruz much more than expected, and we were sorry we would not be permitted to return here again on this voyage. Perhaps we will visit another time, not likely, but we were cruisers free of the constraints and demands of the netherworld, so you never know.

Isabela is the youngest of all the Galápagos Islands and is located at the western most part of the archipelago. The whole of the Galápagos chain owes its existence to the Galápagos hot spot, a hole in the earth's crust, near the junction of the Nazca and Cocos Continental plates. Isabela violently erupted into life approximately one million years ago and was formed by not one volcano, but the merger and overlapping lava flows of six shield volcanoes: Alcedo Volcano, Cerro Azul, Darwin, Ecuador, Wolf and, the giant of them all, Sierra Negra.

Sierra Negra Volcano is one of the most impressive examples of a volcano in the archipelago. Its caldera measures 9.6 kilometres (6 miles) across from north to south and 9 kilometres (5.4 miles) from east to west and is considered to be the second largest caldera in the world. All of these volcanoes, except Ecuador, are still active, making Isla Isabela one of the most volcanically active places on Earth. A good example of how dynamic these islands are can be seen on the northwest coast of Isabela. Urbina Bay is located at the base of Alcedo Volcano between Tagus Cove and Elizabeth Bay. This area experienced a major uplifting in 1954, causing the land to rise over 3 metres (9.8 feet) overnight and expanding the land mass of the island as the coastline moved out to sea a full kilometre (approximately half a mile), leaving marine life, starfish, sea urchins and corals to quickly perish under the tropical sun.

Figure 44. Janet on watch as we sailed from Isla Santa Cruz to Isla Isabela.

Isabela Island is the largest of the Galápagos Islands, with an area of 4,640 square kilometres (1,790 square miles) and length of 100 kilometres (62 miles), and is almost four times larger than Santa Cruz, the second largest of the archipelago. From space, Isla Isabela has the decided shape of a Seahorse where its most north tip, or the head of the seahorse, is severed at the neck by 0 degrees latitude, or the imaginary line better known as the equator. In 1684, Isabela Island was originally named Albemarle Island for the Duke of Albemarle by Ambrose Cowley, one of the first men to ever set foot on the islands. However, it was later changed to Isla Isabela after Queen Isabella of Spain (1451–1504). Isabela was the same Spanish Queen who funded the voyage of Christopher Columbus in 1492 when he supposedly "discovered" or found the Americas. I say supposedly discovered or found, because at the time, the local inhabitants of San Salvador or Guanahani, as it was called by the Lucayan Indians, didn't even realize that their home islands of the Bahamas or the Americas for that matter were even missing!

Tagus Cove on the northwestern side of Isabela has, from the time of its first discovery, provided a sheltered anchorage for countless ships commencing with explorers, then pirates, buccaneers, whalers and many others, along with Charles Darwin, who visited Tagus Cove in 1835. The name Tagus comes from an English warship that stopped by the islands in 1814, looking for giant tortoises. Many of these early visitors wrote their names on the cliffs along the shore. The oldest include the Phoenix in 1836 and the Genie in 1846.

In 1893, Antonio Gil, a businessman from Guayaquil, Ecuador, arrived on Isabela with the intent of colonizing the southern part of the island and founded the town of Puerto Villamil. Villamil is reported to be the most beautiful town in all the Galápagos, with its long white-sand, palm-lined beaches and several brackish-water lagoons frequented by pink flamingos, common stilts, whimbrels, white-cheeked pintails and gallinules, not to mention the ubiquitous marine iguanas that are constantly underfoot.

Sometime later, a second town was established in the highland jungles where the community of Santa Tomás now sits. The port of Villamil began as a centre for lime production, which is crucial in the production of cements and concretes. The lime was made by the burning of coral collected in the coastal waters.

Figure 45 Pink flamingos are commonly seen in the lagoons of the Galápagos

The community of Santa Tomás later became the centre for a sulfur mine in the caldera and a nearby coffee plantation. However, due to the lack of fresh water, all of these ventures struggled and would eventually fail. . With the mine closing, the people of Santa Tomás were forced to rely on raising livestock to sustain themselves until the start of the tourist trade, which exploded in the 1990s.

Today, the majority of Isabela's 3000 residents make their living through fishing, farming and tourism. The centre of population is on the southern coast at Puerto Villamil. Unlike the other large islands, the vegetation

152

zones on Isabela do not follow the normal pattern. There are many relatively new lava fields, and the surrounding soils have not developed sufficient nutrients to support the varied life zones typically found on the other islands. In addition, the high elevations of the volcanoes Wolf and Cerro Azul reach above the cloud cover where little rain falls, resulting in an arid zone at the top of the island devoid of flora. Nevertheless, the island's rich fauna is beyond compare.

Isla Isabela is home to more wild tortoises than all the other islands combined, with a separate species living on each volcano. Isabela's large size and difficult topography created barriers for the slow-moving tortoises. Apparently, the creatures were unable to cross rugged lava flows and other obstacles, such as deep fissures, trapping the cumbersome beast, causing several different sub-species of tortoise to evolve. On the west coast of Isabela, where the sea bottom drops away, the upwelling of the nutrient-rich water creates a feeding ground for pelagic fish, whales, dolphins and seabirds. These waters, we had been told, are the best place to see whales in the Galápagos, but due to our permit limitations, I was doubtful we would get to that part of the Galápagos. Apparently, some 16 species of whales have been identified in the area, including humpbacks, sperms, sei, minkes and orcas, some of which we hoped to see while transiting between the islands.

Still, despite all its wonders and resilience, the immense size of Isabela increases the various conservation challenges that are found on the other islands. On Isla Isabela, an eradication program was commenced in an effort to eliminate introduced species on the island, but the sheer size of the island presented new and costly problems. Nonetheless, the eradication project was ultimately successful when the eradication of wild goats and donkeys in northern Isabela was completed. The program is still ongoing as the presence of cats and rats on the island are causing problems for some of the more endangered and vulnerable birds, as well as snakes and other small reptiles. When planning our cruise of the Galápagos, I saved this island, the best island, for last, and the crew of *Maiatla* was excited about this stage of our adventure.

It was a pleasant sail in light winds under a blue sky. Our progress was slow, but we were enjoying the sea time, so I was reluctant to start the engine and increase the speed. However, in hindsight, we were travelling too slowly in the light wind. By the time we arrived off of the Las Tintoreras, it was late in the afternoon, and I began to worry that we wouldn't make it in time. We had been sailing hard on the wind for most of the time, and as we rounded the outer reef of the islands, we gybed the mainsail, putting *Maiatla* on a dead run with the sails set wing and wing. I went forward to see if I could see where we needed to go. Mark followed.

From our vantage point, we could see the long beach stretching for miles, and its pounding surf, the town pier and, to the far right, a group of islets and rocks protecting the small boat anchorage. The pier was constructed as a waterfront centre piece for the town where food concessions would eventually be erected and festivals held. The shallow water around the stone jetty make the structure useless for docking any size of a vessel. However, it does make for a nice protected swimming area for the local children and tourists. The larger ships and tour vessels are forced to anchor out, well offshore and in deep water, with the smaller vessels able to head into the tight and shallow anchorage in the lee of the Las Tintoreras. And that was where we needed to go, if we could find our way in.

After scanning the beach and town with binoculars, I spotted a pair of towers with red lights on top. I suspected these might be range markers, navigational aids used to show an approaching vessel where the preferred channel is located. However, the problem was neither Mark nor I could make senses of the arrangement, something didn't look right. Perhaps they weren't range markers after all; maybe they were simply a pair of unrelated radio towers. We couldn't tell from this angle. We decided to creep into the bay a bit further, in hopes of figuring out the towers or finding the passage into the anchorage ourselves.

I called aft to Janet, who was in the helm seat. The autopilot was engaged, so there was nothing for her to do other than watch up to this point. "Hun, start the engine and put us into gear. Mark and I will get the sails down, okay?"

Janet nodded and fired up the engine. Then I made a request of Teri.

"Teri, what is the water depth now?" I asked while un-cleating the main halyard in preparation for dropping the big sail.

Teri glanced at the instrument gauge before answering, "40 feet, Andy."

"Great, Teri. Let me know when it hits 20 feet, okay?"

Minutes later, all the sails were down and neatly tucked away, and we were motoring at 3 knots towards the beach. Even from a mile out, we could clearly see the humping backs of what must have been the 3-metre (9.8-feet) tall breaking waves assaulting the beach. If we ventured too far in, we would be lucky to escape with our lives, and there would not be any hope of saving *Maiatla* from being torn to pieces in the surf. Nervously, we continued straight on in, with Teri keeping a stern eye on the water depth. As the water shoaled, the swell passed under the boat, and it grew as the water depth decreased.

As we approached the beach, I kept looking to our right for an opening in the reef, the narrow passage into the protected waters of the anchorage. However, all we could see was turbulent water surging around rocks and islets, but I knew there had to be a way in, because there, on the far side, were several small fishing boats peacefully at anchor. That is where we wanted to be. Then I noticed between us and the other boats was what looked like the same type of mooring buoy that we had tied to back in Santa Cruz. We could now see the harbour, but how to get in? I was trying to decide what to do next when a particularly large swell lifted the boat. The swells were growing in height fast as they piled up in the shallows, and I wasn't surprised when Teri called out.

"Andy, I've got 18 feet all of a sudden!"

We were about as far into the bay as I dared to go. The waves were now breaking 100 metres (328 feet) directly off our bow, so I had Janet make a 90 degree turn to the right. I ran aft to check the chart, then looked forward to see if our position on the chart reconciled with what lay before us. The chart and the GPS indicated we were in the channel, but to look ahead, I was not so sure. We only had a few minutes to make up our minds as the rocks were coming up and fast. Again Teri called out, "15 feet, Andy."

"Mark! The charts show a red navigation can, and it should be just off to our right. Can you see it?" I called forward to Mark as he was still on the bow. While Mark searched ahead, I searched the lumpy water to starboard where several groups of rocks were breaking the surface.

I did not feel good about this at all, and then Janet said, in a low voice, "Andy, I don't like this."

With Janet voicing her concern, I decided it would be best if we turned around and regrouped, figure out a Plan B, but just as I was going to tell Janet to turn and head back to open water, Mark excitedly yelled, "I see the can. It's right over there!"

I looked to where Mark was pointing, and sure enough, the can was less than 30 metres (98.4 feet) away, right where the GPS said it was, but due to the waves it was hard to see. I let out a nervous laugh while saying, "Okay, now I know where we are. Janet keep on this heading."

We passed the buoy close on our starboard side, followed by a small rocky point with a small light structure that was not visible from the direction of our approach. As we cautiously motored in behind the low point, the waters stilled. There were a couple of other sailboats in the anchorage, both from the U.S., but there was no sign of life on either. At a snail's pace, we made a circular tour of the anchorage while trying to get as deep in behind the reefs and islands as possible in an effort to get away from the swell.

As we approached the far end of the tiny bay, with some excitement, Teri again yelled, "It just got shallow, Andy. I've only got 9 feet of water!"

I looked at the sounder, then forward at the flat water. There below the surface was a dark shadow—the telltale sign of submerged rocks.

"Put it hard over, Janet, and take us back toward the entrance!" I ordered. Janet made the tight turn, and for a few moments, the water continued to shallow until we had less than a metre (3.2 feet) of water under our keel. As we finished our turn and motored back out, the water depth dropped back to comfortable 10 metres (32.8 feet) of water. Satisfied we were safely back in deep water, I took a moment to have another look around, which was when I spotted a small fishing boat entering the bay. It was a ramshackle old fibreglass boat, with three scraggly-looking young men huddled inside. As we approached each other, one of them waved at us, then suddenly and with great exaggeration began pointing down into the water.

"What are they doing, Andy?" Teri asked as she watched the antics.

After deliberating for a moment, I concluded, "I think they are telling us to anchor right where they are now."

And that was what we did. Local knowledge is priceless. We finally settled where the fishermen indicated, a spot in 10 metres (32.8 feet) of water in the centre of the bay. Once I paid out approximately 30 metres (98.4 feet) of chain, Janet backed the boat up to give a hard pull on the ground tackle, to bight the anchor in. Satisfied we were secure, the engine was shut down, but we were not done yet. I quickly grabbed the boarding ladder and my snorkelling gear and jumped overboard to dive down and physically check the set of the anchor. Under the boat, I found a sandy bottom, and I was pleased to see *Maiatla* was already attracting all kinds of little fish. I followed the chain along the bottom until it finally disappeared beneath the sand. The big CQR anchor was completely buried. We weren't going anywhere.

Back on board, I towelled off, and then got on the radio to try to report our arrival to our new agent, an American expat by the name of Jim Hinkle. However, after repeated calls, Jim, Bolívar's man on this island, did not answer. I knew I had to report to the Port Captain, so I put out another call. This time to the *"El capitán del Puerto Villamil."* On my first try, I reached the Captain, but we were obviously having some language problems. I gave him the name of my vessel, how many people were on board and our last port of call. I also informed him of my agent's name, but he kept asking questions I could not understand or answer. I informed him I would be coming ashore to his office, which I thought he understood. I signed off, grabbed my paperwork, lowered the dinghy and headed to shore. No sooner had I landed on the dock than Janet called me on the radio to report that the Port Captain and immigration people had come out on a water taxi and were waiting to speak to me. It was back out to *Maiatla* to greet the Port Captain and other officials. Despite the initial confusion, our check in process went well. As the sky grew darker, the smartly dressed officials all shook my hand and welcomed us to Isabela, then departed on a water taxi that was waiting for them.

Well, we made it into a difficult anchorage on our third island of our Galápagos cruise. For the first time since our arrival, I was able to take a deep breath and relax a little by cracking open a beer. While standing on deck with Janet and the crew, we had a good look around and what we saw was simply breathtaking.

Chapter 18

Rammed by Humping Turtles and an Encounter with a Park Nazi

"You don't choose the day you enter the world and you don't chose the day you leave. It's what you do in between that makes all the difference."
—Anita Septimus

From the moment of our arrival at Isabela, we instantly knew it was going to be a magical place full of strange but friendly creatures, floral and geological wonders. After the Port Captain's departure, we took advantage of the remaining light to stand on deck and take stock of our new anchorage. Although we didn't know it at the time, this place has a distinct character and an intensity all of its own, and this island would become our home for the following four weeks. A score of metres to *Maiatla*'s south sat the low-laying rocks and islets of Las Tintoreras covered by scraggly brush, the islet breaking the will of the relentless southerly swell. The tranquil millpond that it created was almost half a kilometre in diameter and filled with turquoise water teeming with anchovies, sardines, mullet, and spotted eagle and devil horned manta rays.

The wave-washed black rocks, as well as the air above, harboured a flurry of marine fowl of every description. Terns and lava gulls, brown pelicans, blue- and green-footed boobies, cranes and herons. Above the water, the birds rule here. Lining the rocks, standing as if at attention, each facing the water, were over one hundred Antarctic penguins. The flightless birds looked cute, cuddly and resolute in their formal attire. The tropics is the last place you would expect to see these birds, normally associated with the frigid waters of the Antarctic, which lies some 6482 kilometres (3500 nautical miles) to the south.

The Galápagos penguin is endemic to the islands, and on Isabela, it is the only species of wild penguin living north of the equator—thanks to a small population residing on the north tip of the island. These penguins can survive in the tropics due to the cool waters of the Humboldt Current, which lower the water temperatures, and the cool waters of the Cromwell Current, which lower temperatures at great depths.

The Galápagos penguin is of the banded penguin family, with the other members of its clan living mostly on the coasts of South Africa and mainland South America. No one was able to agree when these birds first arrived in the Galápagos. Some scientist suggests these birds are fairly recent arrivals and first appeared in the islands between 500,000 and 800,000 years ago. However, others disagree and claim the penguins first waddled ashore not long after the islands were formed, perhaps some four million years ago, brought here by the cold Humboldt Current. Regardless when the birds first arrived, one thing was for sure—it was a one-way trip and these birds were destined to stay, never to return south.

It is estimated there are only 1500 Galápagos penguins in existence on all the islands, which makes them an endangered species. Although protected from interference by man, the Galápagos penguin has many predators. On land, the penguins are preyed upon constantly by crabs, snakes, rice rats, cats, hawks and owls. While in the water, they are hunted by sharks, fur seals and sea lions. However, the increasing frequency of a weather phenomenon called El Niño is now proving to be the birds' greatest threat.

In El Niño years, the strong southeast trade winds diminish, allowing warm water from the western Pacific to move east, flooding the eastern Pacific Ocean with surface water as much as 0.8 degrees Celsius (1.4 degrees Fahrenheit) warmer. This warm water holds less oxygen and life-giving nutrients. When this occurs, the great schools of anchovies and sardines, the penguin's principal food source, vanish and the penguins are threatened with starvation, causing a dramatic drop in birth rates. An El Niño year typically occurs irregularly, approximately every two to seven years, but in the past decades, the frequency has been trending upwards, perhaps in connection with climate change.

The reality is, during an El Niño year, it is not only the penguins that are affected, but all life in the Galápagos suffers. Along with the warmer water comes less frequent rains, affecting the islands' vegetation and thus its land-dwelling animals and birds, particularly Darwin's Finches. The worst or hottest El Niño year on record occurred in 1997. And here we were, in the new year of 2016, in the midst of yet another El Niño season. Climatologists were saying that we were on the verge of setting a new all-time record for water surface temperatures. Ultimately, the 1997 record would stand, as this season failed to reach a new high, but it was close. The 2015–2016 El Niño season would go down as the second hottest in recorded history—a distinction, I am sure, not lost on the marine and wildlife of the Galápagos, as they would suffer through another potential species extinction event in the archipelago.

The average Galápagos penguin is 49 centimetres (19 inches) long and 2.5 kilograms (5.5 pounds) in weight and is the second smallest species of penguin after the little penguin found along the coastlines of Australia and New Zealand. Galápagos penguins have a black head with a white border running from behind the eye, around the black ear coverts and chin, to join on the throat. Juveniles differ in having a wholly dark head, greyer on the side and chin, and no breast-band. The female penguins are typically smaller than the males. The Galápagos penguin are found primarily on Fernandina Island and the south and west coasts of Isabela Island, but small populations are scattered on other islands throughout the Galápagos archipelago. We would be seeing a great deal of these wondrous little birds over the next few weeks, and even get to swim with them.

Figure 46. Andrew and Janet (Teri in the background) on a deserted beach at Puerto Villamil, Isabela Island.

As the sun's rays began to vanish for the night, a flight of dozens of boobies flew in formation overhead and then, in perfect unison, nosed down to dive into the water onto an unsuspecting school of sardines passing by *Maiatla*. This example of superb aerobatics would become a daily scene for the crew of *Maiatla* here in the lagoon.

With dinner time approaching, Janet and the rest slipped below, but I remained topside, still spellbound. It was fortunate that I had because I was about to be treated to one more natural spectacle. While looking to the west, towards the remains of the setting sun, I spotted what looked like a short log or perhaps a partially submerged oil drum, drifting in on the rising tide. Not wanting to get bumped, I kept an eye on it for a few minutes. After a while, I realized the object was moving faster than the incoming water. As it grew closer in the dim light, I was able to distinguish not one object but two. Then a head poked up, and with tiny beady eyes and stoic expression, it peered at me. Excitedly I called below.

"Janet, grab the flood light and get up here. You got to see this!"

With everyone back topside, I turned the flashlight on the pair of massive hawksbill sea turtles as they were busy bobbing on the surface while mating. The animals did not mind the spectators nor did they miss a stroke even when they bumped headlong into the side of *Maiatla*. We watched as the bigger male, atop of the female's back, clamped his front flippers around his mate's shell to hold her tight. The female appeared to be struggling to keep her head above the water under the bulk of her lover. Apparently, male turtles can be aggressive during mating season and can stay atop her for many hours, eventually tiring her out to a point where she may drown.

In an area where there is a shortage of receptive females, several males clamped onto a single female is often observed, which was what we witnessed while sailing along the coast of México two seasons ago. The result of this mating behaviour is a tangle of turtle bodies and probing penises in an underwater orgy. The female, with a stack of males atop of her, can be weighed down and driven under where, again, she could drown.

This drive for procreation is so strong in male turtles that, lacking a partner, a male will climb aboard almost any object. The indiscriminate humping of anything that even resembles a mate has not gone unnoticed by fishermen. Man has learned to exploit this instinctive trait of turtles by employing crude decoys, as male turtles are harvested in several locations around the world. Brazilian fishermen use a wooden disc attached to a rope. The fisherman reel in the disc after a male turtle mounts it, secure in the knowledge the turtle will not release the decoy. Likewise, Caribbean fishermen also use wooden decoys, and Polynesian fishermen use floating taro leaves to attract male turtles for spearing. Surprisingly, this drive to mate is so strong male sea turtles occasionally attempt copulation with human swimmers, snorkelers or scuba divers.

The loggerhead turtle mating population in Southeast Florida lies adjacent to one of the most densely populated coastlines in the world, and every year a few people are approached or (more rarely) mounted by male loggerheads. When there are aggressive sharks in Florida's water, warning signs are posted to "swim at your own risk," but they do not post signs warning swimmers that being gang raped by 400-pound horny turtles is also possible.

After several minutes, the pair of turtles near our boat moved off to carry on, so we retreated below for dinner and an early night. It was a calm and peaceful night at anchor, and all slept well. Fortunately, it did not rain and we were able to leave the hatches and portholes open, permitting the cooler night air to circulate throughout the boat.

In the morning, we had a few chores to do. First order of business after breakfast, as instructed by my admiral, was to install all the sun awnings. It was heavily overcast this morning, but we knew from experience when the cloud cover final did break, the sun would burn through with a vengeance. With the tarps in place, we lowered the dinghy and set the stern anchor to keep us parallel to the rocks and in line with the flood and ebb of the tide. This taken care of, I went for another swim to check the stern hook and to see if we had acquired any more fish under the boat. Indeed, we had. Aside from the usual sergeant fish, thousands of yellow, black and neon blue pilot fish, the size of a dime, had adopted us and had decided the propeller, rudder and boat overhead offered great protection from the diving birds above.

Many times while anchored here, Janet or I would be scared out of our skins. Often while we were sitting quietly in the cockpit, reading or staring off into oblivion, deep in contemplative thought, one or more birds, the size of turkeys, would suddenly appear from overhead to dive into the water right next to us, raising a great splash. The attraction and intent for both boobies and pelicans was to make a meal out of some poor hapless fish that happened to have ventured too far out of *Maiatla's* protective shadow. No matter how often it happened, we never got use to this unexpected, kamikaze-like dive-bombing raid, which once brought the birds so close that I could hear the tip of the bird's drawn back wing clip the side of the boat as it dived past.

By noon, it was time to head to shore. I needed to locate my agent, James Hinkle, who I was told owned a restaurant on the far end of town by the name of the Booby Trap. We all loaded into the dink and made our way to shore. The shortest route would have been straight across the bay to the tiny marina and wooden docks, but it was now low tide and a great sandbar lay bare, creating a sand island that virtually cut the harbour in half. We would have to skirt the rocks all the way around the bay to navigate around the bar. The sun now had chased the morning clouds away, and it was hot. Janet sat across from me in the back of the dinghy, huddled under her umbrella, which protected her from the direct heat. As we motored along, I cut close to the penguin colony as they perched atop of the rocks. Many of the birds stood with their stubby wings outstretched to help warm them from a morning of fishing in the cold waters offshore.

"Look, there are penguins in the water," Teri shouted while pointing off the bow. It was wonderful to see a flock of these graceful swimmers swim and, porpoise-like, break the surface as they were in hot pursuit of a tiny school of fish. On the eastern end of the bay, we passed through a fleet of rough-looking fishing boats moored to buoys. Huge sea lions occupied many of the boats; the beasts were sunning themselves on deck or on a boat's swim grids. The animals paid us no mind as we came close to snap some photographs. We skirted the edge of the sandbar, and once clear, we altered course for the docks. As we did, a pair of spotted eagle rays passed directly under the boat. Quickly, I turned us around to follow the rays into the shallows.

It took longer to get to shore than anticipated, what with slowing down to count and photograph all the creatures we had spotted, but it was enjoyable. However, our meandering course to the docks had not gone unnoticed.

Some of the small fishing boats and water taxis were moored along several long wooden docks. One particular dock had a roof that covered a pair of bench seats—this was the visitor's dock the Port Captain instructed us to use. It was here we could leave our dinghy whenever we went to town. As we approached the guest dock, a man, in the uniform of a park guide, was standing on the end of one of the other docks frantically waving at us. I was not sure what he wanted to talk to us about, but I would soon find out. I changed course to head over to see what he wanted. As we approached, he began to not shout but loudly speak to us, and from the tone of his voice, he was upset about something. I brought the dinghy to a stop, killing the engine so that I could clearly hear what the man was saying. He had much to say.

At first, even with the engine off, I had trouble comprehending what he was saying. He spoke too fast for my ear, yet slowly I pieced it together. Apparently, by slowing down to look at the wildlife, we had broken some of the Galápagos Park rules. The guide informed me I was to take the most direct route from our boat to the dock, and I was not permitted to stop to take pictures or look at the animals I may encounter along the way.

"No hay gira ilegal!" ("No illegal touring!") he said. Considering what he had said, I had no choice but to apologize and to promise never to do it again. I had heard stories of these guides complaining to the Port Captain that a cruiser was not following the rules, and the Port Captain would immediately evict the cruiser from the Galápagos, with no appeals permitted.

"Andy, why would they care if we looked at the animals on the way in? We have seen the tour boats right in there amongst the animals. What does it matter?" Janet asked after I had explained what I got out of the conversation with the park guide.

"Hun, they want us to either hire a guide to go with us or to pay a tour boat to take us out on the bay to see the animals. It's all about money," I said.

"But that's stupid. We paid to be here too!' Janet shot back.

"Yes, I know, hun, but they don't want cruisers here. They want people to visit the islands by flying in, staying at hotels or on charter boats. Aside from the park fees, these guides make nothing on us, and I don't think they like that much."

Maiatla was anchored within metres of perhaps one off the greatest snorkelling spots in the world, the Las Tintoreras, and it was off limits to us. If we wanted to snorkel there, we would have to go ashore and hire a local to bring us back out. Then, and only then, could we swim there. This did not make logical sense, unless you considered the dollars and cents they demanded from us for the privilege. Our encounter with the strict park guide left me feeling a bit frustrated and, in some ways, cheated.

Settling on a spot on the guest docks, next to a couple of decrepit skiffs, we made our landing. The water was low, so the motor had to be lifted out of it to get close enough to the dock. Tied alongside, I removed the engine's fuel line, placing it in my daypack. We had been told outboard fuel lines are a hot commodity in the Galápagos, particularly on Isabela, and would likely be stolen if left in the boat. Losing the fuel line would render the dinghy engine utterly useless and, for us, near impossible to replace while here.

I brought our daypack with Janet's tablet and bottled water, along with a spare sun umbrella. As we have learned since arriving in the tropics, you can never have enough shade. I had hoped to find an internet café from which I could send a message to family and friends and update our blog. Mark lead the way up the ramp, carrying a bag of garbage in one hand and a plastic sack of recyclable cans and bottles in the other. At the top of the ramp, several dozing sea lions, some with young pups, greeted us. The animals grunted and snorted at us, but refused to move out of our way. Fearing he may be bitten, Mark held the bag of cans and bottles out in front of him and gave it a shake, rattling the cans and creating enough noise to induce the animals to move to one side, clearing a nice path for the rest of us. Mark's action seemed reasonable, or we thought so anyway, but we were about to learn otherwise. No sooner had we stepped past the sea lions than a different park guide emerged out of the mangrove trees to chastise Mark for disturbing the animals with his bag-waving ploy. We had only been off the boat half an hour, and we were already getting a second reprimanding—this time for wildlife harassment.

Again, we had to agree not to molest the animals. Satisfied he had done his job to protect the wildlife, the guide pointed to the path and a barrel where he said we could leave our bottles and trash. I glanced at the trail he was pointing, and it was obvious just getting to the trash barrel without inviting the wrath of this or another park guide was going to be difficult.

Along the serpentine path, constructed of red cobble brick, perhaps every two steps or so, sat a giant, metre-long marine iguana having a snooze. The iguanas had recently returned from their morning foraging swim on the reefs and were now warming themselves on the hot bricks. It was interesting to see that some of the iguanas would raise their heads, then sneeze—an action performed as a means of expelling the excess salt they had ingested while feeding. The sneeze or snort created a wet salty patch in front of them. It was hard enough to step around the lounging lizards, but dammed near impossible not to step into puddles of fresh iguana snot.

"At this rate, I think we will be lucky not to get kicked off the island by the end of the day!" I said to Janet as we deftly tiptoed around the dozing lizards.

Despite all the obstacles to getting safely ashore, we were happy to reach the beach parking lot where a vendor was selling coconut drinks from a small stall. When a drink was ordered, the vendor would choose a green nut from a wheelbarrow. Then, with the big nut in one hand and a great machete in the other, he would nimbly chop a neat little hole into the nut, large enough to insert a drinking straw. If I were to attempt such a feat, I'm sure it would end with a finger or two left twitching on the ground. Neither Janet nor I are fond of the sticky liquid, but it does quench one's thirst.

A few days later, while sampling a coconut, Teri had an opportunity to get to know a little about Jamel, the nut salesmen, who looked a little like the Jamaican Rastafarianism and reggae musician, Bob Marley. In a hushed tone, in broken English, Jamal told Teri if we needed fuel for the boat, he could arrange it for a "good price, but don't tell anyone!"

Teri had inadvertently stumbled onto the island's blackmarketeer, dealing in diesel fuel and, as I would later learn, whatever else you wanted, legal or not. Whether it be something to smoke, snort or cuddle against, Jamal was your man. This industrious island entrepreneur would greet us eagerly with a big smile each time we came ashore, offering his services. I would come to wonder if the coconut-selling business was profitable for Jamal or was it a legitimate front for other illicit activities?

Taking advantage of Teri's island connection, I used the services of this "nut salesman" to acquire fuel. Ultimately, it was not any cheaper than if I purchased fuel through my agent, but it was less of a hassle, as there was no paperwork involved and I did not have to wait a week to get it. Whenever we went to town, I brought a couple of empty Jerry jugs ashore and left them with Jamal, next to his wheelbarrow full of nuts, and when we returned a few hours later, the cans were full. Easy! That is, if we weren't caught.

It was obvious, with how busy the docks and beach were while we were there, that this is an important centre for the town of Puerto Villamil. Across the road from the iguana-ridden trail stands a wooden building, which houses what looked to us like the Park's Ranger Station, complete with radios and official-looking vehicles parked about. A drop gate in front of the guides' shack controls the road leading to town. I was not sure if the gate was to control the people and vehicles going into town or to control access to the beach and the big concrete pier. The sand beach was marvellous. To one side, under a tall stand of coconut palm trees, we spotted a thatched roof beach bar with wooden stools. We soon discovered the shack served cold beer and delicious real fruit ice cream.

Aside from a few tourists lounging or swimming, the beach was mostly quiet. It was fun to see that among the sun worshipers stretched out on beach towels, dozens of sea lion lay alongside, as if mingling with the humans was the most natural thing in the world. The handful of park-like benches scattered about had all been claimed by lethargic sea lions, as everywhere else.

Near the beach, there is a concrete pier, which is used to load and unload supplies for the island, and as we would later see, this is a major production and source of entertainment for the islanders and tourists alike. Approximately every two weeks the supply ship, *Fusion,* from the mainland port of Guayaquil, would arrive and anchor well out in deep water. Then, using a small tug boat and flat bottom barges, shipping containers, one at a time, would be loaded onto the barge and pushed through the lagoon to the concrete pier for unloading. As we already knew, the lagoon is shallow, with numerous sand bars, so this operation could only be carried out during a high tide. Twice while anchored here, we would watch with great amusement the near frantic process of re-provisioning the island.

A common practice would be for the ship to arrive and load the first barge. Then as the tide changed and flooded in, the tug would charge for the dock until it ran hard aground. It would wait a few minutes for the water to rise, freeing the barge, and then at full throttle, it would charge forward again only to strike bottom closer to shore and come to a grinding halt. They would repeat this process until they were finally able to reach the loading dock. The tide only permitted a couple of hours to get as many containers ashore before the water became too shallow for moving the barges. This process would continue on each rising tide until all the ship's cargo had been unloaded.

We made our way past the park gate and down a dusty road. After half a kilometre or so, we reached a great concrete archway with a sign above welcoming all to the islands. The archway is the beginning of a new cobble brick roadway lined with palm trees and flower beds planted in the centre divider. Solar-powered street lamps illuminate the roadway at night. There are no buildings on either side of the road, just some dilapidated shacks further inland. As what often happens in third world countries, the roadway, an island beautification project, could have been planned out better. One of the first things I noticed was the new archway had been constructed too low. The low arch prevents most of the island's tour buses and cargo trucks from using the new roadway, forcing these vehicles to take a rough dirt track that bypasses this part of town.

Figure 47. The "welcome" arch at Puerto Villamil that was constructed too low for trucks or buses to pass.

Also on the ocean side of the thoroughfare, we saw building lots subdivided and for sale. At the time, the lots consisted of nothing more than black lava flows, crisscrossed with magma tunnels, and countless sinkholes, most of which were full of scummy rainwater. Several of the holes must have been connected to the sea, as they were full of young mullets swimming in tight circles around the bowl-like pits. Even if you were to backfill and level the land, it would be near impossible to tell if you built your new home right atop of an ancient magma dome that could collapse with the next earthquake or a passing truck.

Another kilometre down the roadway, a second archway marks the end of the paved road and the return to sandy dirt. It was here we started to see one-and two-story concrete buildings, some stores selling basic canned foods and household goods, happy young children playing in the streets, and packs of friendly but timid dogs sniffing around.

There are a couple of rustic hotels in this area, and every second shop or building is either advertising guided tours around the island or a restaurant or cafe. Most of the structures are masonry plastered in stucco and painted white, yellow, orange or blue, with either an equally colourful tin roof or red clay interlocking tiles. At the centre of the town stands a modern, white stucco church with a towering crucifix visible from most anywhere within miles. Next to the church is the town square and courtyard, which has meandering paths and decorative concrete pillars and arches. In the centre sits the typical town gazebo for music or stage performances.

We walked past the police and ambulance station. Mark, being a paramedic took particular interest in the old ambulance that appeared more like a hearse and   was perhaps a few weeks shy of achieving antique status.

Unlike the other big towns in the Galápagos, we found the atmosphere of this community pleasing and friendly, lacking the tourist harassment to buy something, anything, as we had found elsewhere. (The park guides notwithstanding.) With the dirt streets, it reminded me of pictures and movies I had seen of 19th-century California during the era of Mexican rule. The fictional, foil-wielding character Zorro would look right at home in the streets of Puerto Villamil—aside from the telephone poles, "free internet inside" signs and Toyota pickup trucks dusting by.

"I think I'm going to like it here," I said to Janet as we passed some local kids playing soccer in the street.

Walking until almost the last building on the dirt *malecón*, we found Jim's place. The Booby Trap is a two-story concrete restaurant separated from the roadway by a low brick, undulating wall. The place has an elevated and covered outdoor seating and a rooftop patio. At the time we were there, the building was still under construction; nevertheless, it was open for business and it was here I first met our cruising agent, Jim Hinkle.

Jim is well into his sixties and an American expat, who came to Ecuador in the late 1970s and stayed. He married an Ecuadorian woman by the name of Marlene, who was now scurrying about the restaurant's kitchen, making a meal for a pair of English-speaking women sitting at a corner table.

It was wonderful to be able to speak English again with someone fluent. Jim and Marlene proved to be pleasant and extremely helpful, and after he took all my paperwork, and my $15 check-in fee, he gave us information about the island, which left us all wound up wanting to get on with the exploring. Jim also provided Wi-Fi, which was a bit slow but adequate for our needs.

Figure 48. Marine iguanas lounging about the beaches and streets of Isla Isabela.

After having a lunch of American-style hamburgers and sending a flurry of emails at the Booby Trap, we decided to take a stroll about town to get the lay of the land. We needed to find a laundromat, a place to purchase groceries and, more importantly, since it was so hot out, beer.

We thanked Jim, but before we left, I told him of our run-in with the park guide who had warned us about illegal touring down at the beach. Apparently, Jim himself was not only a licensed guide, he was one of the first certified to run tours in the park when the park was first formed. Therefore, I was eager to hear his take on the matter.

After careful consideration and looking a bit perplexed, Jim said, "That seems a bit extreme to me, not being able to look at the animals as you pass by." He paused again for a moment before adding a warning. "Be careful!" he said, with all seriousness. "These people are protective of their livelihood. If he or anyone else reports you to the Captain, you may be ordered to leave—like right now—and there is nothing I or Bolívar could do to help you!"

While sounding apologetic, he concluded with, "I think you are safe to swim off your boat, but don't go too far away. Stay right next to it!"

Chapter 19

Horses up Sierra Negra and "The Wall of Tears"

"If you live a life of make-believe, your life isn't worth anything until you do something that does challenge your reality. And to me, sailing the open ocean is a real challenge, because it's life or death."
—Morgan Freeman

There is always something to do aboard a boat while at anchor, and often, just like at home, when you are busy and up to your ass in honey-do house chores, a friend will come by to distract you. Here on Isabela, it was not much different. Not long after we first arrived, I was on deck, lowering the dink in the water, when I heard a snort and splash next to the boat. Looking over the side, I came face to face with a young sea lion that was reaching out of the water in an apparent attempt to get a better look at me.

Quickly I tied off the dink, grabbed my snorkelling gear and made the leap from the boarding ladder. The splash roused Mark and Teri, who were relaxing in the cockpit reading. Both were curious as to what compelled me to rush by and jump ship. After clearing my mask of water, I searched under the boat, and there, with huge black eyes intently watching me, was the sea lion. I spent the following hour diving and chasing the sea lion around and under the boat, out and around the mooring buoy and back again.

It didn't take Mark long to decide to get into the game and make the leap. However, despite Mark and I teaming up in an effort to catch the sea lion in our aquatic game of tag, we never did. Sea lions are swift and graceful creatures, making our swimming efforts appear clumsy at best.

The sea lion came around most days to continue the game, and if I was not on deck, the sea lion would dive under the boat and blow bubbles, which were plainly heard inside. The bubbles were his way of announcing that it was time for me to come out and play—a call which I was happy to answer.

Janet and I would come to love this anchorage. It was calm, isolated with only a couple of other cruisers that came and quickly went. All of the other cruisers we met, seen here or on the other islands, were on the fast track to the Marquesas Islands, located in French Polynesian. After a quick trip ashore and a tour or two, they headed off back to sea. Most of them we would never meet, as they were too intent on rushing through paradise and getting on with it—a common trait that often infects the more recent netherworld escapees.

When you look at a map of the Galápagos Islands, or more specifically the ocean surrounding round it, you cannot help but notice how isolated they truly are from the rest of the world. To paraphrase Charles Darwin, he said that these islands were at the ends of the earth and as far removed from the rest of the known world as one could possibly be, in both distance and geological time. In many ways, he was correct. Accepting this, it is little wonder the creatures here, left unmolested and unadulterated by traditional species migration, have developed unique characteristics all of their own.

The maps or nautical charts show that the nearest significant landmass to the Galápagos is mainland Ecuador, in South America, which bears 1222 kilometres (660 nautical miles) to the east. It is another 1609 kilometres (1000 miles) north to México and the North American continent, our route of choice, and still over 7408 kilometres (4000 nautical miles) to the south and the sub-continent of Antarctica.

The nearest land mass to the west is the tiny island group of the Marquesas, which is a solid 5556 kilometres (3000 nautical miles) away over open ocean with nowhere to stop. The next nearest continent to the west of the Galápagos is Australia, and even on the most direct route, it was still almost 12,964 kilometres (7000 nautical miles) in distance. The average cruising boat that dares to venture between the Galápagos and Marquesas will be constantly at sea for three to five weeks, during which time they will likely experience every weather pattern and condition imaginable—everything from dead calms to full-blown tropical gales, augmented by a blistering sun or punctuated by spiraling waterspouts. Few people fully appreciate the vastness of the Pacific Ocean, or what it takes to challenge the largest ocean on the planet in a small vessel.

At its widest point, from Ecuador to Asia, the Pacific Ocean is over 16,093 kilometres (10,000 miles) wide, and over 12,874 kilometres (8,000 miles) long from the Bering Sea to the Antarctic Continent. Any voyage across this great trackless expanse is an aquatic marathon that will most assuredly test the mettle of both vessel and crew before the voyage is completed.

A few years earlier, I had made a voyage of 28 days from the Marquesas Islands to Cabo San Lucas, México, with my friends Mike and Kelly on a yacht delivery. Therefore, I was well aware what lay ahead for our Nordic friends, Pieter and crew, who were now perhaps a week into this epic passage, on their way to the Marquesas Islands, then onto Australia. In many ways, I wish I could have turned *Maiatla* westward and sailed along with them.

Mark and Teri only had 10 days remaining with us before returning home, so we made every effort to do as much as we could in their time remaining. Yet despite being in holiday mode, the everyday boat chores and maintenance were still our major focus.

Each day found us ashore shopping for fresh food items, such as lettuce, tomatoes, bread and, our ship's staple, beer, which would become ever scarcer until the next supply ship's arrival in a week's time. There are two larger grocery stores, as well as a public fruit, veggie and fish market near the centre of town. If the market or the big stores did not have what we required, it usually meant spending a great deal of time visiting the abundance of tiny stores. The price for goods varied greatly from store to store, and for us "gringos," it was usually several times higher than what the locals paid. The amount was often calculated at the time our purchase, factoring in the apparent scarcity of the item at the time.

Figure 49. Janet, Teri and Mark wandering the deserted dirt streets of Puerto Villamil, Isla Isabela, at high noon.

There are so many things to see and do on Isabela. Four major visitor sites are easily accessible from Puerto Villamil and all are free to visit, no guides required. The beaches and lagoons near Villamil were said to be the best sites in the entire archipelago to view migratory birds. Black-necked stilts and flamingos are two of the most common resident species.

The Villamil Lagoon, which was near our dinghy dock, is accessible down a short boardwalk that leads through the mangroves to a small floating swim platform.

Whenever we went, the boardwalk was usually awash with sleeping iguanas requiring of us to step with nimble feet as the lizards often refuse to move. Here in the lagoon you can swim with wild sea turtles, small reef sharks, juvenile sting and spotted rays. Janet and I would often swim here, but we were rarely alone as the lagoon is a favourite swimming hole of the local children, as well as tourists.

Fortunately, most of the swimmers were leery of venturing too far from the dock and the shallows. By heading further offshore where few ventured, Janet and I discovered undamaged coral reefs, larger rays and sharks. We also located a sandy patch where we encountered numerous sea turtles that appeared to be sleeping on the bottom. However, when we dived down to investigate, we discovered that it was not a sub-aquatic slumber party, but a turtle detailing centre.

Figure 50. Andrew with a GoPro, trying to get into position for a picture of a sea turtle at Villamil Lagoon, Isla Isabela.

The turtles came here to have their shells cleaned of parasites by a legion of tiny rasps. These fish that would scourer the turtle's shell, pulling and eating the sea lice and pests that cling to the shells and the turtle's leathery skin. The tiny fish were thorough as they nosed into every nook and cranny and even entered the turtles open mouth to remove parasites from the throat and nostrils. A symbiotic relationship that benefited both creatures, it was fun to watch as the turtles raised themselves off the bottom by standing on the tips of their fins, permitting the fish to scourer their bellies and under the base of their tails. As on San Cristóbal and Santa Cruz, there is a tortoise breeding centre. The Tortoise Centre of Isabela was completed in 1994 and houses tortoises from the populations of southern Isabela, many of which have experienced relatively high levels of poaching within the last 10 to 20 years at the hands of local fisherman. Here visitors can see both hatchlings tortoises and the older breeding animals.

Isabela Island is also home to a most remarkable landmark that, when viewed, will leave you numb with disbelief. El Muro de las Lágrimas—the Wall of Tears—is a thought-provoking historical site, usually visited by tourists staying in Villamil for a few days, as it is not easy to access. The wall is a 6-kilometre (3.8-mile) walk from town. It is possible to get a ride half way by using a taxi, but many rent bicycles. The sandy trail follows the beach to pass, shortly after town, the Villamil cemetery, which holds tombs of the first settlers, many of whom are intern in above ground mausoleums. Approximately half way to the wall, the trail passes another white sand beach, surrounded by lagoons where all four species of mangrove trees existing in the Galápagos flourish. The shorelines and swamps are lined with red, black, white and buttonwood mangrove trees.

The trail continues through a locked gate, then a dry zone until it reaches the wall further inland. The massive stonewall was erected on an abandoned U.S. Army radar site, constructed during World War II. In 1944, Ecuador took over the infrastructure left by the U.S. military, transforming it into a penal colony and transferring prisoners from the mainland to the Galápagos to complete their sentences. The conditions the prisoners were subjected too were brutal and extreme, ensuring many would never return to the mainland. To keep the prisoners busy and to punish them by hard labour, under the direction and watchful eyes of guards, the convicts were forced to quarry, cut and dress lava stones. The heavy blocks were carried for kilometres to construct the wall.

It was a gruelling existence made all the worse by the lack of proper food, clean water and shade from the hot tropical sun. At the onset of construction, the intent was to construct the prison walls; however, the sheer isolation of the island proved more than enough to contain the prisoners, who quickly learned escaping from the island was nearly impossible. Moreover, for convicts who were mostly from the mainland's big cities and lacking wilderness survival skills, fleeing into the highlands often resulted in death.

The suffering of the prisoners on Isabela under the equatorial sun carried on until 1959, and just as other notorious island prisons around the world, such as Devil's Island in French Guiana and United States' own Alcatraz Island, Ecuador's Galápagos' penal experiment was finally closed after 15 brutal years, spurred on by financial, rather than humanitarian reasons.

What remains today is a black stonewall that is approximately 20 metres (65 feet) tall, 300 metres (984 feet) long and over 10 metres (32.8 feet) thick at its base. The locals claim the wall emanates eerie cries and has a "heavy" energy surrounding it. Thousands died while labouring here, and a sun burnt sign at the entrance to the site bears a sobering quote: "Here the strong cry and the weak die." The sign is a mute testament to a period of human cruelty and torture—the dark history of a group of islands best known for the proliferation of life.

Mark and Teri rented bicycles to ride out to view this wall of shame. I would remain aboard *Maiatla* this day, but I would also visit the wall by bicycle after our friends had departed for home.

Figure 51. Mark and Teri at the Wall of Tears, Isla Isabela.

Figure 52. Top view of the Wall of Tears.

We were all pleased these sites were free to visit and did not require the services of a guide, but if we wanted to venture beyond the town or into the jungle, we were forced to become part of a tour group. Thankfully, the costs for most of the tours are reasonable. Janet has always been fond of horseback riding, so she was quick to agree to a trail ride through the jungle and ascending the mountain. Sierra Negra, which requires a 45-minute drive from Villamil, followed by several hours of horseback riding up the mountain, is a spectacular sight.

Also, nearby and located on the northeast corner of Sierra Negra is the Volcán Chico, which is a fissure of a parasitic cone that last erupted in November 1979, leaving fresh scars upon the land.

Here visitors can walk on relatively recent lava flows that crunch beneath your feet. The lookouts at the summit provide incredible vistas of the volcanoes of Isabela, as well as the nearby island of Fernandina. At the opposite end of the caldera, visitors who want to make a longer trek can view a system of fumaroles, known as the Sulfur Mine. Sulfur in the form of crystals has been deposited on the fumaroles for thousands of years. The land here smells of brimstone, eliciting visions of the islands when they first exploded into existence.

Mark and Teri decided a trip up the volcano was in order and joined Janet and I as we left the boat, early one morning, to meet the bus at the guides' shack near the dinghy dock. Our "bus" turned out to be a large truck that had open sides with bench seats in the back and a tin roof over head. We hadn't planned on a tour around town, but ended up shooting along dusty backstreets while making brief stops at various tiny hotels, some of which were located in the poorest of neighbourhoods. By the time our running around was complete, we had seen parts of the community that most tourist never see.

The perimeter of Puerto Villamil is Ecuador's version of row housing—interconnected single-or two-story concrete block, windowless homes occupied by the poorest folks of the island. Many of the people were elderly, who stopped sweeping their porches or looked up from chairs perched in the doorways and, with stone faces, watched us dust our way by.

After loading the last of our fellow riders, a young Japanese couple, we shot off, bouncing our way down rutted roads out of town, towards the green hills and jungle beckoning in the distance. For several miles around the town, the area reminded me of the floor of a scorched rock quarry, as countless burnt-looking and jagged boulders were strewn about.

Scraggly-looking vegetation with tenuous footholds sprouted from small depressions that have, over the past decades, accumulated enough dirt to support plant life. There were heaping black mounds reminiscent of the slag heaps and tailing piles often seen at abandoned iron or copper mines. From a human standpoint, the area inland of town, for many miles, was a virtual wasteland, having no redeeming value, and would remain so for countless millennium.

We quickly left the flat lands behind, climbing a winding road into the forest that skirts the base of the volcano. After almost an hour, we broke into a clearing and drove through a cattle guard and wooden gate onto what looked to be a cattle ranch. It was on this ranch we were met by our park guide and some mangy-looking animals.

Our horses were of short stature and came with obstinate attitudes, not to mention ass-eating saddles, and our trail guide did not appear any more hospitable than the horses. Well perhaps "guide" is not the best word to use. He, astride his own horse, was more of a herder than a guide. As what happens to most trail horses, they knew the way, both up and down the mountain, and all the stops in between. The animals would require little (if any) direction from us on our journey and rarely followed direction from us even when we tried.

Figure 53. Teri and Janet along with our guide prepare to ride up the volcano.

We would share this adventure with six other horseback riders, as well as some 10 others who decided that riding a horse was the lazy way to see the volcano. These crazy people assaulted the mountain on foot in a heat that could wither rocks, and several of them, mostly Asian, decided they were not going to be beat to the top of the mountain by gringos on horseback. From the moment we departed the corral, the race was on. Even on horseback at a steady walk, it was difficult to see anything as the scenery passed quickly by, leaving us barley enough time to take a photograph. As for the hikers, I'm sure they saw even less, as most who kept up with the horses had their heads down, huffing and puffing up the steep hill at almost a run. It made little sense to me why someone would pay so much money to run up a mountain chasing a horse. What they were attempting to prove escaped me, but it was obvious that sightseeing or communing with nature was not the objective.

One Japanese fellow, who at the start left his wife behind in the first few hundred metres, kept up his feverish pace the entire trip. Surprisingly, by the end of the day, he only missed beating the horses back to the ranch by a few minutes.

Our trail guide stayed close behind us, clicking his tongue and snapping his rope, which was his way of directing our horses to run or to walk, depending on the terrain or his mood. Flopping about in the worn saddles, we were not riding the horses so much as going along for the ride, like cargo.

Nevertheless, it was a great experience, and when we finally broached the top and dismounted the animals, it was breathtaking to witness the immensity of the volcanic caldera. A thick mist floated across the peaks, partially obscuring the view, giving the vista a surreal and primordial appearance. Mark and Teri carried on with the rest of our group on foot down into the adjacent valley onto a recent lava flow. Janet was not up to such a strenuous hike in the heat, so we opted to stay with the horses for the hour or so while the others were gone.

On the rim of Sierra Negra, Janet and I ate our packed lunch while lying on a grassy slope. Just a handful of metres beyond our outstretched feet was a vertical drop-off into the caldera. The cloudy air and a slight cooling breeze diminished the intensity of the sun, making for a pleasant picnic. From our lofty vantage point, we watched hawks sore below on the thermals. We ate while flanked by blossoming hillsides, fields thick and lush with green brush, dripping in dew and abuzz with yellow bees, black beetles and yellow and blue butterflies. Glistening in the pale sunlight and strung between stands of brush were countless silky spider webs adorned with dew pearls.

Endemic to the Galápagos, the queen butterfly is bright orange in colour, with black lines on its wings, appearing remarkably like the monarch butterfly of North America. Queen butterflies are seen mainly on the island of Isabela, and here on the mountain top swarmed a great congregation of the flighty insect. Not to be out done by its orange cousin, the Galápagos blue butterfly is found throughout all the islands, and this tiny, erratic creature appeared to be the nervous sort as it darted from flower to flower.

The rim was alive with critters, and we had it all to ourselves, or at least for the moment. It was an incredible day on the volcano, but the notion that this mountain is still volcanically active and could awaken at any time was never far from my mind—a thought I did not share with Janet until we were safely back aboard *Maiatla*.

Chapter 20

Guns Were Drawn and the House Sitter Challenge

"To move, to breathe, to fly, to float; to gain all while you give;
to roam the roads of lands remote; to travel is to live."
—Hans Christian Andersen

Travelling away from your home for extended periods of time often presents a conundrum as to what to do with your house—that is, if you have kept it despite becoming a cruiser. In our case, for the past three seasons, Janet and I have left our home unattended, with only our good neighbours, on either side, collecting our mail while keeping an eye on the place. Our daughter, Melissa, who lives an hour away, would also drop by the house every couple of weeks to sort through our mail, forwarding to us anything she may deem important. It was simple and worked, but that is not what we had done for this season, and we would come to regret it.

When underway from México to the Galápagos Islands, Janet sent me an email suggesting that her friend, who was going through some tough times, could house sit for us while we were gone. It made sense, and I agreed. The day after Janet boarded her flight to the Ecuador, Brent moved in and made himself at home. For the next five weeks, all went well, leaving us with no worries about our home. Going well that is until one day, while at the Booby Trap having beers and sending emails, Janet instant-messaged Melissa. At first their conversation was mother–daughter small talk, and then it came out.

I was busy emailing my brother, Steven, when Janet passed me her tablet and told me to read the messages from Melissa.

"Mom, I think there is something going on at the house with Brent," she said.

"What do you mean? Why? What is he doing?" Janet replied.

"Not sure, Mom, but the last time I was there, he didn't want me to go into the house. He said that I was invading his privacy and didn't want me in. I think he may be smoking pot inside, and he's got aluminum foil covering some of the windows."

"That's crap," I snapped. "He better not be smoking anything in our house, especially pot! Ask Melissa when she is planning on going down to the house next," I instructed as I handed the tablet back across the table.

A few minutes later, Janet had her answer. "Melissa says she and Morgan were going down later today."

I was a bit annoyed by the attitude of our house sitter. Here we were, having a great time in paradise, and this guy was causing us trouble back home. We gave him explicit instructions, and he knew smoking inside the house was expressly forbidden. I have never smoked anything, and coming back to a smoke-filled house was unacceptable. I didn't need this, not now.

"Great," I said. "Tell her that when she gets there and she finds that he has been smoking in the house, she's got to tell him to get his ass out!"

"Wait a minute, Andy. Don't get so excited. We don't know if anything is even wrong yet. Let me get in touch with Brent and see what's going on, okay?"

Janet wanted to handle this, so I decided to let her; after all, it was her friend.

"Andy, I see that Brent is online now. I will try to talk to him." Janet went silent as she typed. Instantly, Brent responded.

"Okay, got him," Janet said as she typed away.

I went back to my email. Several minutes passed as Janet and Brent exchanged messages. All was fine until I heard Janet curse before handing me her tablet to read the messages.

I read, and the more I read the madder I became. When Janet asked if he had indeed refused to permit Melissa into the house, this guy responded by saying that Melissa was harassing him by coming around the house, asking him questions and calling him. He went on to say that he did not want her to come around anymore to spy on him. The tone of his messages was aggressive. Although the atmosphere in the Booby Trap was already hot, it quickly grew 10 degrees hotter as I flushed with anger. I passed Janet's tablet back to her.

"What an asshole," I said. "Janet, you tell him that Melissa and her boyfriend will be at the house later this afternoon. Tell him that Melissa is in charge and what she says goes! If he gives her a hard time or refuses to let her into the house, she will tell him to get out and now!"

Janet was a bit reluctant at first, but I was insistent. She sent the message, and if I had any hope this silly episode was over, I was perhaps crazier than our house sitter. Brent's reply was instant and direct.

"No! I will not have her invading my privacy, and you tell her not to come!"

When I read this, I was livid. I took the tablet from Janet to type a message of my own.

"Brent, this is Andrew. I want you out of my house before Melissa arrives, and if you are still there when she does, I will have her call the police and have you dragged out of there. Do you understand me?"

Aside from typing in all capital letters, it is hard to sound angry or truly threatening through instant messaging. Still, I believe I had successfully conveyed my sentiment. I wanted him gone!

Again, Brent's response was instant. "Are you threatening me? I'll have my lawyer on you and charged, and the police won't do anything if you do call them anyway. I have rights, so I think you better speak to the Residential Tenancy Branch and a lawyer before you talk to me again."

At this point, I was ready to lose it.

"Let's get this straight," I typed. "You are not a tenant, you do not pay rent and you have NO rights in our house, so get the hell out and now!"

Brent responded by saying, "You people are weird! I'm not going to talk to you anymore." From then on he was unresponsive.

If I was hot before, I now feared I might have a brain aneurysm over this. I cursed aloud, startling Mark and Teri, who were at the end of the table from us Skyping with Teri's adult kids.

"If that asshole makes me get on a plane and he is still there, I'm going to take a bat to him and drag him out of the house myself!" I said as I swore again.

"Take it easy," Janet suggested. "Let Melissa and Morgan handle it, okay?"

I ordered another cooling round while Janet relayed to Melissa what had transpired. Using Mark's Skype account, I then made a voice call to Melissa, who was now already on her way to the house to confront Brent. I told her not to fool around with Brent; if he is still there, call the cops!

"Okay, Dad, but I think he will just leave. Morgan can make him," she insisted. Melissa's boyfriend of seven years is a towering muscular fella, who can look intimidating, and I have no doubt he can handle himself in a fray. Still, I didn't want either our daughter or Morgan in the middle of this. "I will call you when we get there, okay, Dad?"

Neither Janet nor I could believe what was happening and the stance Janet's friend of many years had taken. After I had killed another couple Pilsners, I placed another call—this time to the Nanaimo RCMP, our local detachment of the Royal Canadian Mounted Police.

As I explained who and where I was, and what was going on, the woman on the other end of the line stopped me to ask, "Is your daughter Melissa Gunson?"

At first I was a bit taken aback as to how she would know that, but as soon as I confirmed she was, the dispatcher instantly made it clear.

"I have your daughter on the other line, and we have already dispatched a patrol car to your home."

I thanked the woman and hung up. I tried to call Melissa, but had no luck. Her line was busy. Fifteen minutes passed before Melissa called me.

"Hi, Dad, the cops are here and trying to talk to Brent, but he is refusing to open the door or answer the phone, and I can't let them in because I think he changed all the locks on the house," Melissa said in half disbelief.

Apparently, not only had all the locks been changed, but all the windows were blacked out so the police could not even look inside. After trying all the doors and windows, an unlocked window leading into the living room was located, and expecting the worst with guns drawn, the police carefully crawled through the open window.

The police officers later told Melissa that they found Brent in my office with the door closed. He was Skyping to a friend and claimed that he did not hear Melissa or the police knocking. He also claimed to not have heard his cell phone or my office phone ringing.

Fortunately, the situation was diffused, and without further incident, an indignant and still defiant-looking Brent was given 10 minutes to collect all his belongings. As Brent was packing, the officer noticed a 45-kilogram (100-pound) bag of dog food in the middle of the kitchen floor, right next to the mattress on the floor where he had been apparently sleeping.

"Is that your dog food?" the officer asked.

Brent took a longing look at the bag before replying, "Yes, I was going to get a dog!"

Believing he was the victim here, Brent attempted to plead his case to the police officers, but they would have none of it. The police wasted no time in ushering Brent to his truck and ordered him off the property. As Brent pulled away, he shot dagger-filled stares at Melissa.

Aside from the place being a bit messy (he left the dog food), having the faint aroma of marijuana and having all our door locks changed, including the one to my office, most everything was in order. Apparently, my suspicions that he had turned our home into a drug lab proved unfounded. Perhaps the aluminum foil on all the windows was designed to keep the voices out of the house and from entering his head. Both Janet and I were shocked over how someone could take advantage of our good nature, especially as we were doing him a huge favour by letting his stay rent-free in his time of need.

Aside from the obvious frustrations, we were not too worse for the wear, but things could have played out much differently. Worst case would have been the meth lab scenario. However, nearly as dire would have been if I had accepted any monies in exchange for him staying in our home. He could have claimed to be a tenant, and it would have taken months to legally get him out. However, I'm not sure it would have gotten that far, as I would have reverted to my baseball bat solution long before then. We were thankful to have escaped a potentially ugly situation.

Unfortunately, our encounters with this nut job were not over yet. After an 11-month absence, Brent reappeared, and once again, he was physically ushered off of our property after we caught him sneaking around the house one evening. He had parked his truck down the street, in an obvious effort to hide from us. What he was doing there or what he had planned, we would never know, but there was little doubt he was up to no good. I later suspected he may have believed we had gone away for the winter as usual, and if we had, perhaps he would have decided to try and reclaim the house.

So ended our experiment in altruism and the use of house sitters. From now on, the house will remain empty when we sail—fewer headaches that way.

Chapter 21

Down into the Bowels of the Earth and Always Dip Your Banana Stalks in the Ocean

"The three great elemental sounds in nature are the sound of rain, the sound of wind in a primeval wood, and the sound of outer ocean on a beach."
—Henry Beston

After a trek ashore, we usually found ourselves at Jim's place, the Booby Trap. If not for a bite to eat, for at least a beer and some internet time. Jim was always pleasant to talk to and had been immensely helpful with not only information and stories about the islands, but also to find a mechanic to repair the faulty alternator on *Maiatla* at a reasonable cost.

One afternoon while at Jim's, I asked if there was anything else he could suggest we do while we were here. We had already hit most of the island's highlights and were looking for another exciting adventure.

Jim thought for a moment before saying, "Well, if you like climbing, I think I have a suggestion. My neighbour owns a ranch up in the jungle, and he has the only vertical magma tunnel in all the Galápagos Islands. He sometimes takes people out there and lets them repel down into the tunnel . . . I think it's something like 600 feet deep." He was struggling to remember the details.

Mark and I looked at each other for a moment, and I could tell by the way Mark was smiling he was in. "What do you think, hun? Wanna climb down into a volcano?" I asked Janet as she was eating one of Marlene's freshly baked brownies.

"No! But I wouldn't mind going just to see it with you if it isn't too hard to get too," Janet said, with some obvious reservations. This magma tube was not in any of the island's tour books and was not located on parklands, so this would be a unique thing to do and, as we later discovered, dangerous as hell. Still, it sounded like fun, well sort of.

Jim contacted his neighbour and arrangements were made for the four of us to meet him at the dock in two days. He would take us into the hills to his family's mountaintop ranch for a bit of spelunking, Galápagos style.

The morning of our trip, we awoke to find a strong wind blowing in from the south, causing *Maiatla* to pull hard on her bow anchor and the mooring buoy off the stern. Days before, I had let out more chain on the bow, permitting us to drift backwards until our stern was a dozen metres from a large, yellow mooring can, to which I tied the stern. I had concern because we had erected three large tarpaulins for sunshades, and when the boat sat broadside to the wind, the tarps acted like giant sails wanting to drive the boat sideways. The strain this put on the ground tackles was immense, as evidenced by the anchor chain, which was stretched out and rigid as a steel bar.

Still, pulled tight between the anchor and the buoy, *Maiatla* was rock solid, which proved to be helpful when the wind whipped in from the south, slamming us on the beam as it was doing this morning. I had every confidence that our big and heavy CQR anchor and chain on the bow would hold us in place. However the lighter stern anchor, with partial rope rode, which we normally use, has dragged in the past under these conditions. If our stern dragged here, we would swing dangerously close to a rocky reef, and if that were to happen while we were all ashore, the consequences could be disastrous.

I had seen a large charter vessel tied to the mooring buoy, so I was confident it would hold *Maiatla* in the worst of conditions, even with all the sun awnings in place. This morning in the gusty winds, I made the usual rounds, checking the snubber line on the bow and for chafing on the twin lines I used to secure the stern to the buoy. With all the tarps tightly secured, I felt confident in leaving the boat for the day.

The sky was heavily overcast with scattered rain showers. In the strong wind, the lagoon developed small whitecaps that were racing across its surface, making for a bumpy and wet ride around the harbour to the dinghy dock.

Despite the guide's warnings about "illegal touring," we stopped to drift for a few minutes to watch a pair of spotted rays circle around and stopped a second time to snap pictures of the penguins as they stood shoulder to shoulder along the rocky shore, their backs turned to the wind.

"If someone sees us, we are going to get into trouble again," Janet said, with some concern.

"If we get caught, I will just say our engine died and I had trouble restarting it," I replied.

Since the first day, when we had the run-in with the park guides, no one had said anything to us despite my testing the limits by swimming and snorkelling off the boat and discreetly touring around the bay in the dinghy. Late in the afternoon, after all the day tours had returned to the docks, I even made a stealthy motor up into the Las Tintoreras to look for turtles and sharks. If anyone had seen me, no one complained. After being there for over a week, I suspected the locals were either getting use to us or the Neo-Nazi guides had moved elsewhere.

We were met onshore by Ulisis, the ranch owner, who quickly ushered us into a pickup truck taxi, the back full of ropes and repelling harnesses. Ulisis had also arranged for us to have lunch at a restaurant at a jungle resort. Later, he asked if we would like to visit a farm where we could purchase some fresh fruits and vegetables. We all eagerly agreed.

With only one main road across Isabela, we found ourselves on the same road we had taken to get to Sierra Negra when we went horseback riding a few days earlier. Instead of driving all the way to the top of the mountain, the taxi made a sharp left turn into the dense jungle. The small truck bounced down the rut-filled muddy road. After half a kilometre or so, the trees thinned, revealing a couple of cow pastures. We came to a halt in a tiny clearing, just big enough for the truck to turn around before coming to a stop.

Ulisis helped Janet and Teri out of the back seat, then he unloaded the repelling gear out of the box. As soon as this was accomplished, the taxi pickup retreated down the road to be quickly swallowed by the jungle. With the noise of the truck gone, the sounds of the wild greeted our ears. Birds chirped or warbled while the bush rustled, as if countless insects and tiny creatures were on the move. The air, thick with humidity and laden with a light mist floating through the underbrush, smelled of damp earth and rotting vegetation. The pungent decay left a tart taste upon our lips. However, high at the treetop level, the upper branches swayed with the same stiff wind that had the harbour dancing.

In Spanish, Ulisis gave instructions in how to don the equipment, and as soon as everyone was geared up and wearing Styrofoam helmets, Ulisis led the way down a muddy trail that meandered towards a nearby hill. After crossing several murky rivulets that bisected the path, our guide stopped to show us a clump of ferns that, Ulisis said, represented the four endemic genera of ferns found nowhere else on Earth. He held out the leaves of each plant for the women to examine, cradling the plant as delicately, and with as much reverence, as one would a fragile and ancient treasure.

Yep, looked like a fern to me, and I can only assume pulling out a machete and hacking your way through the jungle, like you were in an old Tarzan movie, would be frowned upon.

With the heat, we were all sweating profusely, and by the time we climbed the steep hill and crested the top, my underwear was soaked, salted and royally chaffing. We had only ascended 50 metres (164 feet) or so, but from the ridge top, scarcely a few metres wide, we were treated to a mountaintop panoramic view of the south side of Isabela and its neighbouring islands.

Before us lay what looked to be unbroken jungle. Some 12 kilometres (8 miles) in the distance and far below, we could see Puerto Villamil, its streets and the harbour. We now felt the full force of the wind, which was cool and refreshing on our dripping faces. It was a miraculous sight, so we spent several minutes taking stills and video of the vista, as well as each other. When done, Ulisis instructed us to turn around while pointing to the small valley and three depressions in the jungle.

Figure 54. The crew is ready to repel down into the only vertical magma tube in the Galápagos Islands.

Ulisis went on to explain that down there were the openings of three magma tunnels, or shafts, each 20 or 30 metres (65.6 to 98.4 feet) across. He said his family had owned this land for many years and ran cattle here. Amazingly, they did not find the shafts until recently when mysteriously one of their cows went missing. The cow literally dropped off the face of the earth. During the subsequent search for the beast, they found the vertical shafts. The cow, the true discoverer of the only vertical magma tube in the Galápagos Islands, was eventually located on a ledge deep down in the main shaft.

As we visually searched the jungle below from the ridge top, the deep holes were invisible. Our guide moved us along to the far end of a knife-edge ridge where a metre or two (3.2 to 6.4 feet) on either side was a shear drop-off. Carefully moving along the ridge top for approximately another 100 metres (328 feet), we followed the trail leading steeply downward back into the jungle.

All of us were thankful Ulisis had constructed a handrail out of old rope to cling too as the slope was slick with mud. With some trepidation, we followed our guide down into the valley and up to the opposite side of the ridge. From this vantage point, we could now see a break in the tress below where Ulisis said the first of the shafts was located. He led us around the lip of the hole until we came to a rocky outcropping, and at its base was a small hole of 2 metres (6.4 feet) tall and about half as narrow. Again a rope handrail marked the path that we were to take. Ulisis disappeared inside; the rest of us paused for a moment to get our bearings, catch our breaths and take a drink from our water bottles. As I passed the bottle to Janet, I could see she was suffering from the heat and strain of the mountain hike. The trail ahead led nearly vertically downward, and I was fearful of her falling or not being able to get back if she were to descend much further.

It felt like it was miles back to the clearing where we were to meet the truck, and there were many hills to challenge us further.

"Hun, how you doing?" I asked as she took a long draw from the water bottle. "You know, if you have had enough we can wait here for the others to come back," I offered.

I wanted to carry on, but if Janet had reached her limit, we would stay. I knew the hard part was just beginning, and perhaps this would prove too much for her. Janet wiped the sweat from her brow and passed the bottle back to me, which I returned to my backpack.

"No, I'm okay. If we take it slow, I'll be fine. I've come this far," she said.

One by one, we dropped into the hole. The tunnel covered maybe 5 metres (16.4 feet) before the ceiling vanished. Inside, on a small ledge barely big enough for the four of us to stand side by side, we all gazed in wonderment at what lay before us.

It was a great cavern of perhaps 50 metres (164 feet) in diameter, with a dome ceiling high above where the apex or crown had once collapsed, permitting an intense beam of sunlight to pierce the earth. Great vines, as thick as a man's arm, firmly rooted in the jungle above, draped downward until they reached the sloping sidewalls of the cavern where they again took root. In an effort to reconnect with the jungle above, new shoots, thick with emerald leaves, climbed the fractured walls in a bid to regain the sunlight.

As if raining, large water droplets wept from the porous stone above, causing the dome and side walls to glisten and shimmer as if gilded in liquid silver. The air was earthy, damp and dense, making it more laboursome to breathe than the open air above. The rush of flowing and dripping water hauntingly echoed through the chasm, adding auditory stimuli that chilled the spine while completing the image one would expect when venturing into the bowels of the earth.

The cavern was a sight that could have inspired Jules Vern to pen *Journey to the Centre of the Earth* or serve for the opening scene of an Indiana Jones movie. All we needed to complete the adventure was to be pursued by a villainous doctor and poison dart-spewing Amazonians.

Ulisis called to us from somewhere below, breaking the entrancing spell and calm of the muted moment.

Figure 55. The hidden entrance to the vertical magma tunnel. Mark is preparing to follow **Ulisis** into the bowels of the earth.

"*Ven aquí abajo.*" ("Come down here.") His demand echoed from the walls.

Apparently, we were so enthralled with what was above we had not taken much notice of what lay below. The muddy trail we were on sloped steeply down for perhaps 30 or 40 metres (98.4 or 131 feet) where it abruptly ended at a ledge where Ulisis stood. From there, the trail became even steeper, and instead of a footpath, the trail was now a makeshift rope ladder, with wooden rungs that appeared to end at another drop off. It was here at the last drop off where the walls of the cavern narrowed even further, becoming vertical. The magma tube formed a perfectly round shaft that plummeted off into utter darkness.

Reluctantly, Mark and Teri took hold of the dirt-caked rope and did as our guide asked. I waited for our friends to get ahead some distance before turning to Janet to say, "So, babe, what ya think?"

I was surprised when she replied, "You first, but give me your hand."

It only took a few minutes to descend to the ledge where Ulisis was busy securing a pair of lanyards to a repelling rope, which lay atop the crudely constructed rope ladder. From there the trail sloped downwards, only to drop out of sight into a hole I suspected had no bottom.

Ulisis tested his pair of lanyards by leaning back with his full weight. Satisfied the knots would hold, he looked at us all and queried, "*¿Quién es el primero?*" ("Who is first?")

I looked at Janet, who quickly said, "This is it. This is as far as I go. I will wait for you here." She gave a nervous grin.

Figure 56. Janet on her secure perch where she remained while the rest ventured deeper into the mountain.

I agreed to go first, but only after I helped Janet find a comfortable place to sit—well, as comfortable as one can be on a narrow ledge just a slip away from oblivion. I took Janet's lanyards and made sure she was securely tied to the repelling base line in case she slipped, fainted or if there was an earthquake. It was at this time I remembered we were deep inside a part of a volcanic chain that was still classified as active. The last eruption of nearby Mount Wolf was a mere 33 years ago, mere seconds ago in geological terms!

Tensely, I took a good look overhead where I spied a surprisingly large number of boulders in the walls and dome that looked suspiciously loose. The scree or rubble slope we had descended likewise contained precariously perched rocks ranging from fist size to that of small cars, all appearing poised to tumble at the slightest provocation. An old high school geology lesson suddenly flashed back as I suddenly remembered the term "scree" comes from the Old Norse word for landslide. Perhaps this was not such a good idea after all.

With Janet safe for now, I joined Ulisis on the precipice where I secured my pair of lanyards, which were an arm's length to the base line, with cinch knots one atop of the other. The idea is to climb down until the lanyards become taught, then slide the knots down the base line to waist level, and then climb down some more. The theory is if you were to slip and fall, the cinch knots would tighten under your weight on the base line and arrest your fall. It was comforting to know how in theory it worked, yet in practice, with wet, dirty and worn lines, to me the probability of a failure looked good. Perhaps I should have enquired of Ulisis how he intended to rescue someone dangling from a single rope while suspended hundreds of metres in the air. However, with the language barrier, I deferred asking.

I copied Ulisis's example and tested my knots by applying weight to them, and as I did, Ulisis gave me one last set of instructions. He told me when I get to the bottom, I should not move around as there is another hole that drops straight down hundreds of metres. I was to carefully move to one side of the ladder and wait for him.

To make sure I understood, he walked his two fingers across his flattened palm, then with a fading scream, he simulated a man falling off a cliff. Fucking great, I thought.

Tied off, I began to make my way down the slope, kicking loose small stones and dirt, creating tiny avalanches as I went. After 30 metres (98.4 feet) or so, I found my ass hanging in midair over a blackness that appeared to have a substance or density to it. I searched for the next rung on the weather-eaten rope ladder and tested the wood slat carefully until I was confident it could hold my entire weight. I now understood why Ulisis was happy to have the biggest guy go first—I was the ladder's stress test. Step by step, over the rim I went to be swallowed by the complete darkness. I was thankful I had brought a headlamp and not accepted the handheld flashlight our guide was ready to provide, but the headlamp was only useful to see the next rung. I also brought gloves, the textured palms helpful in clinging to the slime-covered rope and ladder. After 20 metres (65.6 feet) or so, I paused to have a look around, but all four sidewalls were too far away to be illuminated by my headlamp and any hope of seeing the bottom at this point was obviously fruitless. I was suspended on a rope ladder, encased in utter darkness, depriving many of my senses. It reminded me of the night-time dives I had made while working on the oil rigs, descending to work on the well's blow out preventer located on the sea floor.

Figure 57. Andrew ready to hook on and continue his decent into the magma tube. (Janet took this photo from where she sat on her perch.)

Water was still streaming down, forming tiny waterfalls around the rim above. I was now more soaked than before, if that was possible, and not surprisingly, despite sweating profusely, I was now cold, as the temperature had dropped rapidly. The ladder shook from the weight and struggling of the others above as they too made their decent. As I looked upward to where I had come, illuminated by the faint daylight above, I saw silhouettes of cascading rocks and dirt as they broached the rim to plummet towards me. Fortunately, the rocks' momentum launched them far enough out to miss me as they passed by, just barely. I would not need the helmet in this instance; still I was thankful for having it, nonetheless.

Teri's foot appeared over the rim, sticking out, hesitantly searching for her next rung. I could not dawdle any longer, so I carried on down until a ledge covered in broken rock became visible. Back on relatively solid ground, I untied myself and carefully moved a few metres away from the ladder in the direction Ulisis had instructed, away from the now steady stream of falling debris. Nervously, I waited for the others to land.

Ulisis was the last to descend the ladder and join the three of us standing tensely in the dark. My friends likewise brought headlamps, but it was obvious they would be insufficient in exploring the cave. Fortunately, Ulisis brought the powerhouse. Ulisis unslung a potent flashlight from his shoulder and aimed it overhead to illuminate the sidewalls and a dome almost as large as the first one where we had left Janet.

Figure 58. Looking upward from the mid-point on the ladder. Teri can be seen approaching the next rim where the tube plummets straight down for another 30 metres (98 feet).

Ulisis went on to explain that we were standing in a massive magma chamber, with what looked like a single tiny opening in the ceiling high above, our point of entry and regrettably our only point of egress. Again from my high school geology lessons, molten rock underground is called magma, but when it reaches the surface it becomes lava. The rock walls here were smooth, as if having been plastered or polished, but instead of being solid black like the solidified lava flows above, the rocks were splashed with colours ranging from blood red to almost pink, as if stained by the very fires of hell, which by all accounts, it was. Embedded in the surface were billion of gold specks that danced when you passed your light overtop of them.

Ulisis called this room "the discotheque." At first, I was puzzled by his comment and thought perhaps I misunderstood him, but it suddenly became clear when he started to shuffle his feet and mouth a disco beat while flashing his light on the ceiling.

The dancing light brought to life the myriad of colours while the gold specks remarkably resembled a nightclub's mirror ball. We all laughed.

With the room better lit by all of our lights, it became evident we were standing atop a rubble pile, remnants of the partially collapsed ceiling. The thought of earth tremors giving us a shake kept crossing my mind.

"So how deep do you think we are, Andy?" Mark asked as he stared back up the long rope ladder and the distant prick of light, representing the surface. "Two hundred feet?" he guessed.

I was the first down, so I had some time to count the rungs of the ladder. It was easy to calculate how far it was back to the last landing, which was approximately halfway back to the surface.

"I'd guess an easy 250 feet, straight down, maybe a bit more," I offered.

Mark hadn't taken his eyes off the light above. "That's a long climb back up, and I wouldn't want to have to do it in a hurry or try and get a body out of here," Mark concluded, with a nervous chuckle. Being an advanced life support paramedic and trained in the art of rescuing people, I was not surprised he would contemplate such a thing, but I was a little concerned he choose to use the word "body," as in dead, instead of "patient," as in still alive! As we were the only four down here, I couldn't help wonder whose body he might be referring too? Being the largest, I would most assuredly give him the most trouble if it came to that.

"Yes, I know what you mean," I agreed, then added half-jokingly, "You know, I don't think you could get a tour like this back in Canada or the States. The liability insurance would be a killer."

Carefully, Ulisis led us down the rubble slope for a few metres before coming to a stop. He shone his light straight down into another shaft that was almost perfectly round and perhaps 15 metres (49.2 feet) in diameter. Ulisis told us that after they found this place, he had led a scientific *National Geographic* team down to this point. They repelled straight down another 200 metres (656 feet) to the bottom where they found the remains of several species of birds and reptiles, some of which are now extinct.

"Did you go all the way to the bottom?" I asked Ulisis.

Ulisis laughed, "*No! Muy asustado.*" ("No! Very afraid.")

As we moved back up the slope, we came across a large pile of heavy bones. I pointed them out to Ulisis, which brought a smile to his face. Ulisis raised his hands to his temple and spread his fingers to form horns and said, "*Mi vaca.*" ("My cow.")

Ah, so here were the remains of the discoverer of this magnificent magma tube.

I said to Mark and Teri, "I don't imagine there was much more than hamburger left by the time the cow got all the way down here, eh?"

We explored on, discovering three more large tunnels that penetrated the dome above. These horizontal tunnels were reported to extend for kilometres underground, leading further up the mountain. We were told by Ulisis that most of tunnels and shafts were still unexplored or mapped and he had no plans to explore further. Apparently the park's board has been putting pressure on Ulisis and his family to sell them the property so that they could explore further and open it up to thousands of paying tourists. Ulisis was adamant he would not sell; he wanted to leave the land to his children.

Figure 59. At 76 metres (250 feet) from the surface, Andrew holds one of the bones of Ulisis's lost cow. This photo was taken by Teri. And just 10 metres (33 feet) behind her was the next drop off, which went straight down another 200 metres (656 feet).

At the top of the rubble pile, Ulisis had us climb a low rock face, and at the top, hidden from view, was another small tunnel with a low ceiling, requiring us to hunch over to enter. Like most of the tunnels we had already seen, the floor was covered in broken remnants of what was once the ceiling. The collapse most likely occurred after the magma had drained away and the tunnels cooled and contracted.

At times, wading through puddles of water, we penetrated deep into the mountain. The tunnel grew smaller the further along we went until we were only able to proceed on our hands and knees. I was not sure how long it had been since we left Janet on the ledge above, but I was thinking we should start back. When I informed Ulisis so, he said he had one more thing to show us and it was right ahead.

We all crawled over one more boulder and under a rock bridge to find ourselves in a slightly larger room, but not large enough to stand. Here was Ulisis's pride and joy. On the tunnel walls and floor was some magnificent quartz crystal deposits. How these delicate crystals had formed here and did not get destroyed by the molten magma of subsequent eruptions, I could hardly guess. I found the formations fascinating, but I had my mind on returning to Janet's side, so after taking a few quick pictures, I lead the way back to the base of the rope ladder and began my ascent.

The long climb back out of the pit wasn't as bad as I had imagined, and I was happy to find a still content Janet perched on her ledge as I had left her. With everyone safely back on the surface, we hiked to a nearby ridge top to take one last look and to allow the hot wind to course over our muddy and weary bodies. Our guide led us back along the trail we had come until we reach a small hill, and atop of the knoll was a cabin.

Figure 60. Teri emerges from the bowels of the volcano.

The tiny one room shack only possessed two walls on the side that would normally face the prevailing winds—much cooler in the living room when you only have two walls instead of our customary four. Inside the cabin sat a table and chairs, with beds all made and ready. This was where Ulisis or one of his cowboys slept while tending cattle. Interestingly, some 20 metres (65.6 feet) away was a concrete block, duel outhouse with running water. It was there we washed off much of the mud that had accumulated on us. The twin stalls had doors, but no hinges. I had to lift one of the heavy wooden doors into place so that the ladies could use the facilities.

"Just knock when you are done," I said to Janet as the door slammed shut.

From the outhouse, it was a surprising short downhill walk (thank God) back to the clearing where the taxi was waiting for us.

Despite all of us being exhausted, our day was not done. Back on the paved road, we headed towards town. We only covered a kilometre or two before we hung a right turn, slipping back into the cooler jungle. Somewhere back in here was supposed to be a restaurant, and judging from the surroundings, I suspected it would be a rustic affair, but I would be pleasantly surprised. A kilometre further in the bush, we came across a neatly cropped grass field used as a parking lot. There were several coconut palms lining a gravel garden path, which led to, then through, a stone archway. Curiously, we all followed Ulisis under the arch and subsequent tunnel. Inside we found ourselves standing under a great thatched roof supported by a massive tree. Around the base of the tree were tables and stools set out in concentric circles, with seating for perhaps one hundred or more. A pair of young waitresses dressed neatly in white shirts and black slacks were making ready a table, apparently in preparation for our arrival. A similarly dressed fellow emerged from out of an adjacent stone archway to greet Ulisis with a handshake and a knowing smile. Ulisis then introduced us all to the manager.

"Your lunch will be ready shortly, but you have a choice of beef, chicken or fish," Ulisis said while the manager waited dutifully at his elbow. After we all placed our orders, we were told we would have time to explore the grounds before we ate. We wandered about discovering meandering trails through towering bamboo and banana groves, with the branches full of a variety of finches. We were delighted to spy, most everywhere, free-roaming tortoises. Most of the lumbering beasts congregated around man-made watering holes, which were strategically placed alongside the many foot paths.

The estate was well manicured, neat and tidy and large, as it covered many acres. In our wanderings, off in the back, we located what appeared to be little block bungalows, assumingly for rent, and we even came across a green, trimmed field, which had signage designating it as the tenting site, complete with picnic tables and taps with running water. I was also surprised to note we were the only ones there, aside from the few staff members who had greeted us upon our arrival. We suspected this was a newly constructed guest ranch, and we were perhaps some of its first visitors.

We had a pleasant meal, accompanied by endless jugs of ice-cold lemonade, which we all hit hard. The meal came with a reasonable price, and as was the custom here, our taxi driver ate with us, his meal placed upon my tab. I didn't mind, but this would surely impact his tip at the end of the day. It was now getting late in the afternoon, so Ulisis asked if we still wanted to visit a local farm for some produce shopping. Tired and now fed, I would have been content to head back to the boat for a nap. With Janet's heart set on getting some fresh fruit, we loaded back into the taxi and headed down the road.

We came to a stop at a locked gate, and on the opposite side was a man wielding a massive machete, chopping back bush alongside what I assumed was his driveway. Ulisis jumped out of the taxi, and after a friendly but animated conversation, the man unlocked the gate and waved us in. Inside the gate and around a bend, we came to a stop next to three elevated, tin-roof buildings that had rail-less front porches surrounded by tall shade trees. The ground surrounding the buildings was carpeted in a green grass cropped short by the dozens of chickens pecking and scratching.

Countless tree roots broke the surface most everywhere, creating tripping hazards if you didn't watch your step. The man with the machete followed us in, and with a smile and a handshake; he took us on a tour of his farm.

Figure 61. Janet posing in front of the farmer's home up in the mountains above Puerto Villamil.

Aside from the usual vegetable garden, the farm sported a field of perhaps an acre. The ground was thick with pineapples, all growing neatly in a row. Looking back to the truck, I noticed that, as far as I could see, the surrounding trees were heavily laden with fruit. I suddenly realized the farmhouse where this family lived was right dab in the centre of papaya and banana orchards. Despite the "third world" appearances of the homes (shacks) and the store that double as a barn, it must have been a pleasant place to live and raise children, and these people did appear to be content.

The girls placed an order for some pineapples and bananas, and with a quick chop and a slice with the great knife, the farmer made the harvest. I was stunned to see the farmer cut down a whole tree to reach the stalks of banana that were hanging some 3 metres (9.84 feet) above our heads. We eventually met the whole family, and by the time we departed, we had a couple of paper bags of papaya, pineapples and a stalk of bananas the size of a portly man's torso. The farmer wrapped the stalk in several layers of banana leaves and tied the bundle with a string. I like bananas, but this was too much, as it took both Ulisis and I to lift the heavy bundle into the back of the truck. The price we paid was no cheaper than what we would have paid in town, but it was fresher produce and a much more pleasant shopping experience. We had a peek into the rural lives of these marvelous people.

Figure 62. The farmer's "store."

We had the taxi drop all off at the Booby Trap for a cool beer, and it was here we thanked Ulisis for an incredible day and said our goodbyes. As I downed a cold pilsner beer, Jim spotted the banana bundle I had left at his front gate.

"I see you made it to the farm," Jim said, with some amusement. "Yep, do you want some bananas, Jim? We couldn't possible eat that many before they go bad?"

After seeing the farmer fall a tree for us, I felt obliged to take the whole bundle. Besides they were cheap by our standards, just pennies to the kilogram. After a second beer, Jim helped me split the stalk in half.

"There ya go, Jim. This should keep the Booby Trap in banana daiquiris for a year," I joked.

As I rewrapped the remaining bananas in the leaves, Jim said, "You better dump those leaves and wash the stalk in sea water before you get back to the boat. Probably some bugs in there you don't want aboard."

He gave a sound piece of advice—one we were aware of, as we always made it a habit of discarding unwanted paper products and wrappings to not transport bugs aboard. Washing of fruit in a bleach solution was also a habit and advisable.

I was tired. It was time to go, but Mark and Teri decided to stay behind for another beer and to try and Skype with their family back home. Janet and I called a cab and headed back to the harbour.

Back at the dinghy dock, after dislodging a sleeping sea lion pup from our dinghy, we loaded our gear. As I lugged the now much lighter half stalk of bananas down the ramp and stepping around the parents of the previously ejected pup, Janet reminded me be to dip the bananas in the ocean. Kneeling at the edge of the floating dock, I striped away all the protective banana leaves. Once bare, I carefully lowered the stalk into the clear water while giving it a hardy push to submerge the bananas. The reaction was immediate and explosive as dozens of panic-stricken, finger-sized cockroaches and chicken egg-size spiders sprung forth to commence flailing atop the water. There were so many bugs I was forced to let go of the stalk as many of the refugees were attempting to clamber up my arm to safety. I cursed as I ran my other hand down my right arm in an effort to dislodge three giant cockroaches that had already made it as far as the elbow.

"Holly shit! Janet you see that?" I said.

It took repeated dunkings to satisfy us that all the bugs either had drowned or had abandoned ship. It was startling to see the amount and the variety of insects and creepy crawlers that had made their home in the stalk. Dunking of the stalk provided a windfall for many of the tiny fish that lived beneath the dock. They were suddenly treated to a free lunch as only the quickest of spiders and cockroaches managed to evade the fishes feeding frenzy.

Back aboard *Maiatla,* the banana stalk found a home swinging from the main boom, adjacent to the mast where they were permitted to ripen.

Figure 63. Janet with her bananas hanging from the mast.

Chapter 22

The Night of the Iguanas

"Don't know who named them swells. There's nothing swell about them.
They should have named them awfuls."
—Hugo Vihlen

Jan and I, after shopping and a trip to the local laundromat, made the mistake one night of staying too long ashore. Mark and Teri opted to stay aboard the boat that afternoon for some alone time, which was hard to come by, even on a boat of *Maiatla's* size. It was nice to see the sunset from the beach. However, the drama of getting back out to *Maiatla* afterwards was not something we wanted to experience any more often than necessary. We usually carried a pair of headlamps in our daypack, so fortunately we were prepared for nightfall.

The town centre was alight and music blared from the many open-aired restaurants where most of the island's land-based tourists dined once the heat of the day started to wane. At the junction of Antonio Gil and Las Fragates streets stood Cesar's Restaurant. It was here we received a knowing wave from a waiter that served us lunch the day before. Mateo, a tall, young and extremely flamboyant Latino, with a single dazzling earring, spoke fair English, with a slight lisp punctuating his thick accent. No exaggeration here. While we dined and with more animation than usually customary, Mateo took great delight in bringing us up-to-date on his favourite American television show, *The Real Housewives of Beverley Hills*. The food was not great, but he was entertaining, and to top it off, they had respectable Wi-Fi for checking emails from home.

While heavily weighed down by two bundles of clean laundry and several bags of groceries, I attempted to hail a cab, but they passed right on by us. As usual they were either full to capacity or empty and had other places to be, prompting us to start walking the twisted mile back to the harbour. Unlike the busy downtown core, here on the outskirts, the streets were mostly deserted. As we made our way out of town, the dirt road grew darker as the less prosperous suburbs lacked street lighting, the only illumination spilling out from the barred windows of the little homes on either side.

Interestingly, here on Isabela, as is the case on almost all South Pacific islands, all of the electrical power is produced by a large diesel generator. Puerto Villamil's generator, which is the size of a diesel locomotive, is located inland on the outskirts of town in a block building, with two open sides. The roar of the engine can be heard from blocks away. The town of Villamil is only one missed shipment of fuel from reverting to candles or whale oil lamps—and not to mention horses for transportation. The Galápagos have a precarious grip on the 21st century, a hold that is dependent on shipments from the mainland.

We said good evening to a few pedestrians, young couples mostly and some preteens playing with soccer balls in the otherwise vacant streets. Somewhere along the line, we attracted a few scruffy, yet harmless, looking dogs that perhaps knew our bags contained food and a handout may be in the offing if they sniffed at our heals often enough.

"Don't worry, hun. One of the drivers will come back and pick us up after he drops off his passengers," I said while trying to sound optimistic, a hard thing to do when sweat is trickling down cracks and chafing.

In truth, I was not at all optimistic. In our short time on this island, I was surprised by the number of times an empty taxi cab sped right by regardless of how much arm waving I did. I could only assume that these drivers were not that hungry for paying fares or were late for a quickie with a lover, or perhaps they received some kind of perverted pleasure in seeing the gringos struggle down the road with great loads of laundry. Even when Jim, from the Booby Trap, called a cab for us to head home after a meal, they were often a no-show, forcing us to walk until we accidentally ran upon a cab parked alongside the road. The usual fare of $1 per person was probably not much of an incentive—especially when the Ecuadorian government subsidizes the taxis.

Isabela was unlike the other islands that we had already visited where many of the locals not only accepted the tourist occupation, but embraced it. Here on Isabela, I sensed many resented the intrusion. People resisted the changes brought on by the invading hordes from foreign lands, as they are force-fed an unpalatable diet of noise, bustle, bureaucracy, commercialism and pageantry. Often tourists are impatient and an ignorant mass that complain loudly when the expectant Disneyland- or Marineland-type atmosphere failed to materialize on cue. Isabela is the most recent major Galápagos Island to have surrendered its hinterlands to the netherworld, who demanded access to its wild and unspoiled lands, its essence, its heart and soul.

As we approached the parking lot of the harbour, I used the handheld VHF radio to inform Mark we could not find a taxi and were running late, but should be back soon.

"Okay, Andy. I've got dinner started and it should be ready by the time you guys get back to the boat," Mark said.

It was nice to know we wouldn't have to cook something when we got home. Teri and Mark took it upon themselves to perform many of the galley chores, something which both Janet and I were grateful. Our friends prepared some surprisingly good meals.

The public harbour and docks of Puerto Villamil are poorly lit and few people have any reason to loiter after dark. Even the normally ubiquitous sea lions that are everywhere during the day were gone. Aside from a few young pups I spotted hiding among the roots of some mangrove trees, the rest were all out to sea feeding for the night. Still we were not alone. Reptilian eyes were everywhere, and we were surrounded. There were legions of the iguanas, hundreds, if not thousands, of the creatures, lying on any surface that was still radiating the heat of the day.

On a stone curb, under a handrail lining the boardwalk, the youngest of the iguana clan congregated. Scores of tiny, finger-length lizards huddled together for warmth and protection from aerial assault. The young lacked the body girth of their parents, and when they sat with their legs pulled tight into their bodies in an effort to conserve heat, they resembled snakes more than lizards.

The cobblestone sidewalk leading us through the mangroves back to the dinghy dock was covered in the dozing lizards and all defiant, refusing to spend any effort or energy to move out of our way. Like lifeless gargoyles, with snotty spew marking their territory, they remained frozen and paid us no mind, lest we gave them a prod with our toes. And even then, they would only scud away as short a distance as possible. Ever so carefully, Janet and I took great steps around or over top of the lounging reptiles, as not to tread upon them.

It was now cloudy, making for an uncomfortably dark night, and from the dinghy dock, off in the distance, I could see *Maiatla's* masthead light shining bright, as if a distant star on the horizon. Mark remembered to turn on our beacon at sunset. A good thing—without it, finding the boat in the dark would be almost impossible.

There had been a couple of tour boats moored out near us, but they had retrieved their shore-side guests by sunset (smart move), pulled anchored and were well on their way to their next island. Past the open mouth of the harbour, we could still see one set of retreating lights as a tour boat was about to round the most southern tip of Isabela, headed for the wild West Coast.

We had the bay to ourselves once again. But, in the pre-dawn, a group of new boats will arrive to take their place.

Our boat was only a quarter mile away, as the booby flies or the iguana swims, but the tide was out, so I knew we had to take the long way home, skirting the perimeter of the bay to get around the sand bars, which would more than double the distance.

Eeriness took over the night, and only the sounds of buzzing insects swarming a nearby street lamp and the hissing of the distant surf as it broke upon the Tintoreras could be heard. After bailing out the water that had accumulated in the bottom of the dinghy from an earlier rain shower, I carefully placed our groceries and clean laundry in the bow, then dug out the fuel line from my daypack and connected the fuel tank to the engine. The tide was well out, so there was hardly enough water to float the now laden dink. Janet took her customary seat on the starboard side next to the engine. I took off my sandals, untied the dinghy and waded out past a row of grounded pangas until the water was deep enough to lower the engine leg. A few sharp pulls of the cord started the little engine, and after Janet warned me of a submerged rock dead ahead, we quickly headed out, past the last finger, to be embraced by the cloak of the night.

"Janet, can you shine the light off to the right a bit? I can hear some waves nearby."

Sure enough, as Janet did as I instructed, a line of white water revealed itself a few dinghy lengths to our right, the waves breaking atop of an exposed sand bank. I was driving strictly by feel, guided by the depth of the water and the shape of the harbour, which I had memorized from the chart. I'm not entirely sure if it was my mental image of the chart that was faulty or if it was the chart itself that let us down, but we had scarcely covered 100 metres (328 feet) before we ran solidly aground for the first time.

With Janet shinning the light around in a futile effort to find some sort of landmark as a guide, I stepped out of the dink into ankle deep water and commenced to perform the time and anchorage tested "Baja shuffle." While trying hard not to herniate myself as I hauled the heavy dinghy along, I shuffled my feet through the sand, dragging our overloaded boat over the first of many sand bars in search of water deep enough to refloat the dink and my concerned and vocal admiral.

"I'm never doing this again. From now on, we get back to the boat before dark, Andy!" Janet said, with all assertiveness. Under our present circumstances, a sound pledge and one Janet would strictly adhere too in the future. However, for me, tonight's lesson would soon be a faded memory, dooming me to repeat this night's folly two more times, or was it three? Not sure, as my "cruisetimers" may be kicking in again.

For those who are not familiar with the term "Baja shuffle," it's a dance we learned many years ago while cruising the Sea of Cortez and exploring México's Baja Peninsula. The many shallow bays of the Baja are the hunting and breeding grounds for skates and stingrays, and as Crocodile Hunter Steve Erwin found out the hard way, stingrays frown upon being messed with. Rays have poisonous barbs mounted on the ends of powerful tails that can drive a finger-length spike deep into your flesh. In Steve Erwin's case, the barb reached his heart killing him almost instantly.

Rays that come as large as a half sheet of plywood like to bury themselves in the sand to hide as well as hunt, making them hard to see even in daylight, never mind at night with your wife shining a beam of intense light into your eyes. Even more poisonous are stonefish, which also use similar tactics as their distant cousins the ray. To step upon a ray, skate or stonefish in the shallow water will most certainly ruin your day.

The local Baja fishermen taught us to shuffle our feet through the sand instead of taking a step. The shuffling action sends out a vibration and will usually frighten these critters away before you can even get close enough to tread on one. I have contacted several rays with the tips of my toes over the years, and fortunately, I have yet to receive a swipe of an angry tail or puncture from a venomous barb. Typically when a wader makes toe contact with a ray, he or she instinctively leaps high into the air while emitting either an ungodly scream, yelp or blasphemous utterance. Or at times, all three followed by a hasty retreat in the direction that you came from.

Figure 64. A string ray laying upon the bottom. Photograph taken at Gordon Rock, Santa Cruz Island.

After half an hour or more of a combination of pulling the dinghy and motoring, we finally made it to the halfway mark, which put us in the basin where some of the larger pangas and water taxis moored. But, with the deeper water, a new hazard materialized in the form of coral heads, dotting the anchorage. The locals know where all of these jagged submerged peaks are; we, on the other hand, had to rely on shinning the light into the water ahead of us. Janet would call out when she spotted one, of which there were many, in our path.

Aside from tearing a hole in the pontoons of the dinghy, striking the solid coral with the engine leg could damage the propeller or shear the pin that attaches the propeller to the drive shaft. A sheared pin would mean a long row back to *Maiatla*. A torn pontoon would have us swimming with the penguins. Luckily, the crystal-clear water provided a good view of dangerous coral head and an opportunity to spot several giant eagle rays flying in formation over the bottom a metre (3.28 feet) or so below the dinghy. After surprising some sleeping penguins and then burning their retinas with our bright lights, we made it back to *Maiatla* without further incidents.

Securely tied alongside, Janet scurried up the boarding while making the utterance: "Nope, not doing that again. If you want to be ashore after dark, you can do it without me!"

As we entered the cockpit, Mark's head poked out of the companion hatch and a delicious aroma filled our nostrils.

"You guys are back just in time. Dinner is ready, and we made spaghetti with a special sauce," Mark said, with much cheer.

"Yes, it smells great, and I'm starved," Janet stated as we dropped down into salon.

I poured myself a glass of red wine, and as I did so, I watched Teri busily stirring a steaming pot on the galley stove. Sitting at the table I noticed Teri had a sweaty, dishevelled appearance, not surprising in itself, as it was pushing 30 degrees Celsius (86 degrees Fahrenheit) in the cabin even before she started cooking. Still, I suspected her flustered and flushed appearance might have been the result of some other recent carnal activity.

"So, what did you guys get up to this afternoon?" I said while fishing for a clue to confirm my suspicion.

Mark replied as he helped Teri dump the water out of the spaghetti pot. "Well, we relaxed on deck for a while and read. Later, we cleaned our area of the boat and remade the beds with clean linen."

"Must have been nice having the boat to yourself for a change," I said as I took a sip of wine. "Glad you got some boat chores done, but I would have thought you'd have taken the opportunity to have a tumble in the sack." I grinned over top of my wine glass. My comment stopped both of our friends dead in their tracks. Mark and Teri locked eyes, then broke out into great smiles.

"We were planning to," Mark said, with a great grin, "but we got so busy. Then we thought that you would be back sooner, and we needed to get dinner started, so we didn't get to it."

Teri made the call and said, "Dinner is ready, but you need to serve yourself." She brushed a limp lock of hair off her face. From Teri's darting eyes and now ridged posture, I suspected Mark was lying to me. I wasn't surprised; I suspected that he would have told a different story if Teri and Janet hadn't been in the room.

"Nice to see you put my dinner ahead of your sex life, but I would suggest you plan your day out better next time," I counselled.

It was a great meal followed by more wine in the cockpit. To complete the day, Janet and I went for a skinny dip off the boat, then a cool shower before bedtime.

Chapter 23

A Farewell to Friends and a Maiatla *Crew Change*

"It is not that life ashore is distasteful to me. But life at sea is better."
—Sir Francis Drake

Our time with Mark and Teri was grand, but they were running out of time. Their netherworld jobs and families were beckoning. Despite their great reluctance, they were compelled to answer the call. Our last few days together while anchored at Puerto Villamil flew by as they attempted to see and do as much as possible before leaving. Janet and I on the other hand were mostly tuckered out, and we still had not decided how long we would stay there. This was our third island on our three-island permit, and so we believed that the next time we got underway, it would be when we departed for Panamá. Although Isabela was a magnificent island, it was not the best place to re-provision a vessel for what could be a 10-day ocean voyage. But due to our permit restrictions, we had no choice in the matter.

Since we still had another six weeks on our permit, we were not compelled to rush or to do anything other than relax and recuperate from all the trekking we had been doing. Living abroad in relatively cramp quarters, as found on most cruising vessels, can be a challenge—especially while in a harbour or at anchor.

Someone nautical once declared, "Harbours rot ships and rot the men in them." There is often more chaffing between shipmates while in port than at sea. When at sea, the crew has their schedules and duties; I'm on watch when they are sleeping. Seldom is everyone at the same place at the same time with nothing to do while underway. Someone is always on duty, in charge—the boat demands it. The boat demands stoic order regardless of any natural tempest at hand. Foul weather and adverse conditions can bring the crew closer together as they unite to fight a common enemy. The crew sweats and toils together for the common good.

However, when a ship is idle, swinging on the hook in a placid lagoon or backwater, the dynamics between the crew and the boat often change. The once working ship is now transformed into mere lodging as the crew stands at ease and relaxation becomes the principal focus.

Calms like harbours can encourage indolence that can eat away at a crew's cohesiveness. Fortunately, there was no such chafing between the four of us, and a sense of harmony had descended upon *Maiatla* in this magical place. Although we would greatly miss our friends, we were still looking forward to the day when we had our home once again all to ourselves and the freedom to scratch any intimate itch without regard to who may be peeling potatoes at the galley sink.

Mark had reluctantly booked passage on one of the high-speed, bone-jarring cattle boats laughingly called the "inter-island ferry." You too, for a measly $35 a head, can experience a mode of transportation that should come with a complimentary chiropractic adjustment at the end of the journey. We checked into flights from one island to the next, but it was cost prohibitive, and from the look of the tiny, well-worn planes, the ferry may well prove to be a safer bet.

Two days before Mark and Teri's 6 a.m. ferry, the weather had turned ugly. The skies were thick with guncotton clouds, grey masses that regularly sprung leaks to form a deluge and pounded the sea like machine gun fire. And if that weren't enough, the wind had increased from the south with solid authority, packing gusts in the 20 to 30 knot range. This was predicted to last for the next few days.

Our friends possessed a lot of baggage, and it occurred to us that getting them and their bags to the beach without getting soaked was not likely, so Mark opted to book a hotel room ashore for the night before departing. In the morning, they would take a taxi (if they could find one) to the dock for the ferry's crack-of-dawn departure—a prudent decision for sure under the damp and blustery circumstances.

We had plans for all to go ashore and have dinner together for one last time, but after seeing the dinghy sinking waves of the bay, Janet thought getting soaked before dining was not all that appealing. Besides, Janet was determined never to be caught ashore after dark, the vow she made the week before still ringing in her head. Therefore, with much reluctance, Janet stayed aboard where she said her teary goodbyes to our friends.

Clad in rain gear and baggage swaddled in garbage bags, I took our friends ashore for the last time. Reluctantly, between rain bursts and while trying to keep from getting swamped by the waves, we cast off from *Maiatla* and hoped for the best. It took twice as long to get to shore as normal, and we only had to bail out the water just a little. Secured to the dinghy dock, I helped carry their baggage (couldn't find a cab) towards the centre of town to find Mark's inexpensive hotel that he had booked online.

The Hospedaje Cerro Azul is a two-story white stucco building with blue trim, which I thought looked to have been recently repainted—a fact surely lost to the skateboard-sized iguana eyeing us from atop of the brick wall surrounding the courtyard. The desk clerk was pleasant, and he assured me he would have a taxi there in the morning for my friends.

The hostel is nothing fancy, but it is clean and cheap, at $45 a night, including a continental breakfast. The rooms are typically sparse, with minimal furnishing, but the building boasted a rooftop patio that commanded a lovely view of the town.

Down below is a common open-aired lounge, with a television and internet where guests could sit on a plush sofa or swing in a mesh hammock. The clerk led us up the stairs to the room, giving us a guided tour that was mostly wasted on us because he spoke Spanish far too fast for us to follow. The hostel did not look busy. The only other guest we saw was a young Ecuadorian man, dressed in jeans, a long sleeve, white shirt and open toe sandals. He was sprawled in a hammock; one leg draped over the side that lazily kept him swinging as he thumbed his iPhone. I asked the clerk if there were many other guests and excitedly, he said, "Yes, but they were all still out on tours and would be returning soon." As it turned out, the Hostel Azul was nearly full to capacity.

In the morning, Mark and Teri would catch the ferry, spend one more night in a hotel on Santa Cruz, then fly to Quito, Ecuador. They would have one night there, then a direct flight to Houston and on home to Vancouver—a milk run for sure and still the only way to get to or from this part of the world.

The following few days were strange, what with being on the boat all alone, but in a good way. It was like taking off a body cast and finally getting to stretch a sore muscle or scratch an itch that for weeks had irritated you because you could not reach it. It was sleeping in late, eating only when we were hungry, swimming off the boat and losing our clothing more than usual. Fortunately, the weather improved the day after the crew's departure, so we basked on deck and ate ripening bananas from the stalk that swung from the rigging.

It was glorious to do nothing for a while and to just be, read, write, or watch, from the cockpit, the incredible nature surrounding us in this magnificent place. We even reverted to taking turns reading to one another in bed. Life afloat was grand, but our solitude wasn't going to last long, a little over a week in fact, as the next wave of crew was about to fly south and join *Maiatla*.

Long before we departed México, Janet and I had decided we would love to have our two adult children join us for the trip through the Panamá Canal. As an added bonus, our oldest grandchild, who was eight years old, would accompany his father. So, our son, Thomas, his son, Damien, and our daughter, Melissa, planned to meet the boat on the Pacific coast of Panamá and make the crossing from the Pacific Ocean to the Caribbean Sea with us.

One leisurely evening, a month previous, while sitting in the cockpit back on San Cristóbal Island, Janet said, "Andy, wouldn't it be nice to have the kids here? Damien would just love all the animals, don't you think?"

I was not surprised by her question if that is what it truly was. I had been considering the same thing for some time now.

"Wouldn't it be amazing to get Damien to swim with the turtles and sea lions? You can teach him how to snorkel!" Janet said, with great enthusiasm. She concluded by adding, "Who knows if we will ever get back here again?"

Janet was right. The next day, I emailed the kids and asked them. Two weeks in Panamá or the Galápagos? The kids' reply was quick and decisive, so my next email was to our travel agent, my niece, Samantha. I gave her instruction to book three tickets to the Galápagos Islands as soon as possible and to get me a great deal.

During our week of solitude, Janet and I only went ashore twice, for shopping and to meet with our coconut/diesel fuel black-market distributor. We were also on a quest for fresh vegetables, beer and rum. It had been some time since the last supply ship, so most of the stores were running low on staples, forcing us to explore further afield for supplies. We left no back alley un-trod. In this town, you never knew where a store might be lurking. Eventually, we located a small hardware store where I hoped to purchase some stainless-steel bolts. The building was dark and airless, as the community generator was not running, so neither was the air conditioner. We had heard the fuel for the town's generator was running low and there would be rolling outages throughout the day until the next supply ship arrived. When that would be was anybody's guess.

The store's stock of nuts and bolts was meagre, and any hope of finding marine grade stainless was futile. It was too hot to stay indoors for long, but as we were ready to leave, Janet noticed a few food items for sale in the corner, so she stopped to check it out. There on the shelf were several jars of what looked like peanut butter, but the jars were not labelled. Janet took a jar to show me.

"Andy, do you think this is peanut butter? Kind of looks like it," she said as she tried to smell the contents through the closed lid.

"Don't know, babe, but I will ask." I took the jar and approached the counter where a middle-aged couple conversed in Spanish while keeping one eye turned our way. My question in English only managed to produce a confused look from the pair. I took out my smart phone and accessed my Google translation app to look up the correct words. Most times, I attempted to speak Spanish, but other times, it was easier to type in the question and let them read the translation. However, today I gave it a go and asked "*¿Es esta mantequilla de cacahuete?*" ("Is this peanut butter?")

The people broke out into great smiles and said, "*Sí, hecho aquí.*" ("Yes, and it's made here.")

Well, we found homemade peanut butter, and it was surprisingly cheap. Later we discovered, it was delicious on the fresh bread from the local bakery. Both the peanut butter and bread, I suspected, were organic.

Janet and I hit the Booby Trap later in the day to fill Jim in on our plans, letting him know our children would be arriving in a few days.

"You know, Jim, it would be nice if we could sail our boat over to Santa Cruz to pick up our kids instead of taking the ferry both ways," I said as Jim brought us another round of beer and a hot brownie. Marlene had been baking again.

"Can you ask Bolívar if it might be possible?"

Jim gave it a thought and said, "I don't know if it's possible, but yes, I will call him."

When we checked into the country, Bolívar was clear that our permit was for three islands only and no back tracking. I wasn't hopeful, but we had nothing to lose by asking. To our surprise, the following day, Jim called me on the radio with the good news.

"I talked to Bolívar. He said you can go and get your kids and bring them back here, okay?"

"That's great, Jim, but will I have to send them back to Santa Cruz on the ferry? Or can I take them back again?" I asked hopefully.

"No problem. Bolívar said you can come and go back to Santa Cruz as many times as you like, just as long as you check in with the Port Captain and our agents each time."

Well, it was unbelievable. Not only could we fetch and return our kids to Santa Cruz, we could also sail back to San Cristóbal to re-provision the boat before departing for Panamá next month. I'm not sure what had changed. Perhaps Bolívar trusted us to follow the rules and decided to loosen the mooring lines a bit. Or perhaps he liked how much money we were spending, what with getting our boat fixed and all the tours we were taking. Whatever the reason for the change, we did not care. It gave us a new sense of freedom—a freedom we were going to take full advantage.

This would have been good to know before Mark and Teri had to take the ferry, but we were happy, nonetheless. Two days before the kids were due to arrive, I dropped the tarps, pulled the main anchor, so we were riding on the mooring buoy only, and made ready for heading back to sea in the morning.

Chapter 24

Inter-Island Transit and a Winged Assault

"The position and extent of any shoal or danger discovered, especially of one upon which a vessel has struck or grounded, should be determined, if practicable, by five horizontal sextant angles between well selected objects."
—Admiralty Manual of Navigation

We received our paperwork from Jim at the Booby Trap late on a Thursday afternoon, with an intended departure time for dawn Friday. After issuing the permit, I was required to return to the vessel and depart within 24 hours, which is what we did. Not sure why we were told not to loiter on shore, we were just departing for a neighbouring island, not another country.

As dawn broke, we dropped the mooring lines and headed west through the anchorage bound for the open sea. During the night, the supply ship, *Fusion,* had arrived and it had taken up its station, anchored outside the harbour within a boat length of the channel marker. The crane had already started to unload containers onto the barge in preparation for shuttling them ashore, which would happen in about an hour when the tide commenced its flood. The harbour pier was already awash with car and truck headlights beaming in anticipation. The island's dwindling stock of tourist trinkets from the mainland, beer and diesel was about to get a boost, creating a festive-like atmosphere ashore, and I was sorry we were going to miss it.

Our departure was infinitely easier than our arrival in Puerto Villamil, as we now knew the way past the reefs and sand banks. Janet had no difficulty in piloting us out past the supply vessel to open water while I cleared away the lines and made ready to hoist sail. Despite the cloud overcast and early hour, the temperature felt hot and humid. What little effort I made on deck was all it took to get my shirt to cling to my body with perspiration. As *Maiatla* cleared the harbour, a cooling, light breeze filled in from the south.

Bracing my back against the mainmast and like a cormorant perched on a rock with outstretched wings drying in the sun, I lifted my chin and splayed my arms. The wind felt good, sending an involuntary shiver through my body.

The direction of the wind looked good once we motored past the outer islands of the Tintoreras. It would put us on a starboard tack and beam reach, *Maiatla's* fastest point of sail.

As we cleared the last of the offshore reefs and Janet altered course to the east, I optimistically hoisted the main and mizzen sails, but the anemic wind proved to be too feeble and would help us little. Reluctantly, we kept the engine running, as we had a deadline—we needed to be moored at Academy Bay on Santa Cruz before dark. We could not sail, so out went the fishing rods in an attempt to catch dinner.

I plotted the shortest route through the islands, which would take us between the mainland of Isabela and the offshore island, Isla Tortugas, the sickle-shaped volcanic crater. It was a deep-water passage, 6.5 kilometres (3.5 nautical miles) wide, and it was principally clear of any hazards—clear, if you do not include the half a dozen high-speed ferries making the twice daily trip and a rock the size of a pair of school buses poking out of the sea mid channel.

Roca Burra is an ancient volcanic plug that rises above the sea some 10 metres (32.8 feet) or so, with its roots planted 100 metres (328 feet) in the bottom. On the radar, the rock appeared like a small boat, but after I realized this boat was not moving and compared it to the chart, I recognized it for what it was. At half a mile distance and 20 degrees to starboard, the rock became visible to the naked eye. I altered course to head straight for the rock.

"What are you doing, Andy?" Janet was below making tea when she noticed the abrupt course change.

"Hun, I spotted what I thought was a boat on radar, but it's that big rock out here we saw when we first arrived. I thought I would use it to help finish aligning the radar," I said.

Janet stuck her head up out of the hatch, just far enough to have a look. After spying the rock, she said, "Don't get too close to it. You never know what may be around it, just under the surface." After that, the admiral dropped back below to get my breakfast started.

Janet was concerned and rightly so. Although the chart showed deep water right up to the rock, you can never be sure of what the cartographer who mapped this rock missed or left out. The first person to map this area was a 17th-century English Buccaneer by the name of William Ambrosia Cowley, who surveyed the Galápagos Islands during his circumnavigation of the world and published the first chart of the islands in 1684. Navigational charts are periodically updated and new rocks are added, often named after the ships that found them the hard way.

My chart showed it had been produced back in 1950, with some minor updates added over the years since. Any changes principally focused around the harbours or the most common shipping routes. Needless to say, a grain of salt, or perhaps a handful taken would be prudent.

Modern GPS (satellite Global Positioning System) has made modern charting more accurate, but laying the new accuracy over top of old charts can be a recipe for disaster, as the old and new technology often disagree. Over the years, I have seen islands marked on the chart up to 3.2 kilometres (2 miles) out of their actual position. I have been anchored in the middle of a bay only to have the GPS chart plotter tell me I was anchored 3.2 kilometres (2 miles) inland on a mountain top, and once, it told me that I was sailing along the centreline of main street as I entered the harbour, which was the case in Ensenada, México, a few years back. Janet's warnings did not fall on deaf ears, so I would have to make sure to slow right down and watch the sounder closely as I crept in for a good look.

While lying about on Isabela, I reread the instruction manual for the new radar with the intent of correcting the 15-degree misalignment. After figuring it out, all I needed was a fixed object directly ahead. This rock would work fine. After several minutes of pushing buttons, the rock dead ahead and our course line were now perfectly aligned on the radar. I gave a yep of success when it all finally worked. Almost two months after installing the new radar unit, I finally had it working correctly and could truly trust it when required.

With the radar now doing as it was supposed to, all of *Maiatla's* systems were once again operational, and I, as well as she, was happy.

"Well, I fixed it, babe. We got a working radar again. Screw the cup of tea. I think that calls for a celebration beer!" I said while perhaps sounding all too pleased with myself.

Janet again stuck her head out of the companionway.

"It's not even 10 o'clock yet and you want a beer?" Janet questioned.

"Ya, sure. Why not? It's hot out and as Jimmy Buffett says it's 5 o'clock somewhere. Hey, babe?" I received a blank stare for a few seconds before Janet relented. Reluctantly, she brought me a cold can nestled in a blue *"Mystery Tramp"* koozie and settled in the cockpit with me to watch the swell surge around Roca Burra.

The peak of the rock hosted a few black and white Nazca boobies, and on the rock's vertical faces, in the sun shadow, hundreds of tiny crabs scurried about. The blue and orange spider-like crabs were frightened into action by us motoring by, a few boat lengths away.

I snapped a dozen pictures, then said with some excitement, "Wouldn't that be a great place to snorkel. Bet there are some big hammerheads circling it."

In the channel between Isabela and Santa Cruz, the wind increased slightly due to the funneling effect, so I unfurled the headsail and trimmed for a broad reach. The high cloud cover burned off, producing a pleasant day for a sail as we bounced between 3 and 5 knots of speed. However, regrettably at our present speed, we would not make it to anchor before dark. After a couple of hours, I was forced to furl the headsail and fire the engine back up.

By 3 p.m., I started to lower and furl the main and mizzen sails in preparation of entering Puerto Ayora at La Bahía de la Academia on Santa Cruz. Sadly, fishing proved futile; the fish were not biting. The only thing our normally killer army truck-coloured hoochies attracted as they skipped along the surface was a pair of hungry Nazca boobies, which made a couple of expectant dives upon our lures. Usually, if I notice in time, I'd grab the line and jerk the lure away just as the bird was about to make its grab. If there were no fish to catch, this bird teasing could be great sport, as the birds would try again and again until they'd tire of the game. I have hooked a few birds over the years and had to reel them in. Often when hooked, the birds go stiff-legged, and with webbed feet, they ended up waterskiing behind the boat in a comical fashion.

I recall once, while crossing from the Nuku Hiva in the Marquesas Islands in the South Pacific, on my way to México, I caught a massive winged Frigate bird. The huge bird boasted a wingspan of over 2 metres (6.5 feet). It swooped down to scoop up my squid. To make its escape, the thief attempted to rise to a great height. The line, singing as it went, spooled off the fishing rod, as if I hooked a massive tuna. With the upwards pull of the line, the rod jumped out of the rod holder, and after tossing my nearly full beer can to the deck, it was only with great luck I managed to latch onto the butt of the rod before it sailed off into the blue yonder. As if battling a fish of epic proportions, I set the drag on the rod, leaned back against the cabin top and started to play my catch.

It must have looked like I was flying a kite, but this kite was seemingly furious at being on the end of the string. For several minutes, I struggled to reel in my prize, using my best technique as the bird frantically swopped from side to side, diving this way and that, in an effort to throw me. With no small effort, I managed to get the bird within a few metres of the boat, but the closer the bird came, the more frantic it had become.

What I was going to do with it when I had it in an arm's length, I was not sure. I had not thought things through that far as of yet, but now with its capture imminent, it suddenly occurred to me if the thrashing wings didn't beat the crap out of me, that sharp beak was most assuredly going to peck the eyes right out of my skull. I could cut the line and let him fly off, but leaving the hook to protrude from its beak may interfere with its ability to feed, which could cause the magnificent bird to starve to death. I have also seen sea birds trailing 10 or 20 metres (32.8 to 65.6 feet) of fishing line, which can be foul in trees or on dock piles, effectively condemning the poor creature to a death of slow starvation. No, I had to get the hook out of my bird!

Aside from the bird perhaps losing a few feathers and squawking with a permanent lisp due to the scar the hook would leave, I was determined to let my Frigate bird fly away unharmed. However, I was not so sure I would escape unscathed, and in fact, I was sure I wouldn't. As I continued to reel the last few metres of line in, the bird and I were given a reprieve as if by divine intervention, or perhaps the bird grew tired of the game of tug-o-war, because the Frigate spit out the hook. Without so much as a glance back at me, it soared off over the horizon. Afterwards, I had to wonder if the bird was truly caught on the hook or if it had a firm bite on the lure, refusing to release the line until confronted by an ugly beast that wanted the squid more than he.

Fishing in the Galápagos was frustrating, and what I found even more annoying this day was having to pull the fishing rods in every time a ferry or fishing panga passed close by, which happened every half hour or so. I didn't want to be caught illegally fishing.

Webster's dictionary defines fishing as "the sport or business of catching fish." Since we were never able to hook any of these Galápagos fish, I believe I could reasonably argue we weren't "fishing," but simply washing our rubber squids by dragging them behind the boat.

After rounding the last point of land, Punta Estrada, Academy Bay came into view, and I wasn't surprised to see it was busy as ever. I left the cockpit to have a clear look to see if I could pick our way through the anchored flotillas and find a mooring buoy or place to anchor. The big sailing vessel, *Lady Anne,* was gone and so was the National Geographic cruise ship, but there were plenty of other charter vessels I did not recognize filling the voids.

We toured the basin, trying to find a spot to anchor out of the swell that followed us in, but it was tight everywhere. I finally decided on the only spot available, which was right next to the mooring buoy we had moored to the last time we were here. Sadly, our buoy was taken by a rundown charter boat, and sad-looking it was, with its chipped dark blue paint. It had laundry drying in the breeze, strung on lines that spanned the aft deck, a sign the crew lived permanently aboard. Spiteful, they were too because no matter how many turns around him we did, or how intent my stares, the boat refused to give up the mooring. I received a cautious or perhaps indifferent wave from one of the shirtless crew members, who apparently had come on deck to greet the new neighbours while having a pee over the side.

I dropped the hook, then gave Janet the okay to back the boat down to bite the anchor in. All was good, so I quickly grabbed my paperwork, hailed a water taxi and made the trip ashore to meet our agent. Nothing had changed since our last visit, including the throwing of insults and finger gestures as my taxi narrowly avoided a collision with another boat as we approached the dock.

On the busy *malecón*, I found Loretta on the same bench she was sitting on the first time we had met, a couple of weeks earlier. Loretta appeared to be genuinely happy to see me, and she gave my hand an eager shake. Clearing *Maiatla* back into Puerto Ayora went smoothly. There was only an exchange of paperwork, my clearance from Jim and the handing over the fee. Mercifully, another inspection by the Port Captain would not be needed.

Loretta would handle everything. I explained my reason for returning and informing her we would only be staying five days, then sailing back to Isabela. All was in order, so I made a run across the street to the internet café to send the kids a quick message confirming our safe arrival on Santa Cruz and that we were waiting. I hailed a taxi to ask if I could book him for a tour of the turtle ranch and tunnels for the day after tomorrow. Terms and a meeting place were agreed upon, then I hastily returned to the boat.

First chore was to drop a stern anchor to keep the boat pointing in the right direction, and then I stripped off for a swim and to check the set of the two sets of ground tackle. Up went the shade tarps, and we finally were settled by sunset. It was a quick dinner, shower, and then bed. Only once during the night did I have to get up to close the hatches due to a sudden rain shower.

We would have one full day to ourselves before the kids arrived, but we could ill afford to lie around for the day, as we had to provision the boat before the crew's arrival. We didn't want to waste a minute of time shopping once the kids had arrived. The kids would be on the same milk run coming here from Canada as Mark and Teri had taken home, including the overnighter in Quito on mainland Ecuador. This would be my eight-year-old grandson's first flight on any aircraft, as well as his first venture out of Canada, so I know it was going to be an exciting adventure for him. Both Janet and I wished we could have shared that experience with him, but there would be plenty of adventures to share once they all arrived. We were going to make memories to last us all a lifetime.

Chapter 25

The Kids Arrive and It's Time to Wear a Tortoise Shell

"The waves broke and spread their waters swiftly over the shore. One after another they massed themselves and fell; the spray tossed itself back with the energy of their fall. The waves were steeped deep-blue save for a pattern of diamond-pointed light on their backs which rippled as the backs of great horses ripple with muscles as they move. The waves fell; withdrew and fell again, like the thud of a great beast stamping."
—Virginia Woolf, *The Waves*

It was late in the morning when Janet and I excitedly went ashore and hailed a taxi for the long, 45-minute ride to the far side of Isla Santa Cruz. The south side of the island is all lush and green with jungle that surrounds the handful of villages lining the Santa Cruz highway. Near the top of the mountain, the road passes over a natural causeway, perhaps three times wider than the paved roadway. The twin lane roadbed separates a pair of massive sinkholes called Los Gemelos (The Twins). Through a gap in the towering *Scalesia* trees, I was able to snatch a glimpse of one of the cavernous depressions as we sped by.

"Janet, we've got to bring the kids back here later in the week," I said as I strained to get a better look out the window before the vitas disappeared.

As we broached the saddle of Cerro Crocker, the landscape, over a kilometre or two, changed to one of red-brown earth, boulders and scrub brush, leaving behind the lush of the jungle. Once in the northern wind shadow of the mountain, it was noticeably hotter and dryer. Far too hot for most people from northern climates. The road ended at the pier where, a few weeks earlier, I had been picked up to take my Gordon Rocks diving excursion. Instead of jumping in a zodiac and ferried out to a boat, Janet and I would have to wait. With time to kill, we made ourselves comfortable in the shade of a tiny palapa serving cold drinks and food at the dock's edge. A Palapa is a traditional Mexican open-sided shelter roofed with palm leafs or branches, quite suited for the hot climates, not to mention cheap to construct as all one needs is a supply of palm trees. However, this palapa came with a modern tin roof.

The dock was as far as we were permitted to go. The airport lay across the Itabaca Channel on the tiny Baltra Island, and unless we had a ticket to fly, we were forbidden to cross. We would have to be content to wait here and greet each ferry as they landed to unload passengers. At the dock, there was a constant flow of baggage-wheeling people, boarding and disembarking the walk-on passenger ferries connecting the airport to Santa Cruz. Each ferry, or barges, would hold roughly 40 passengers under a roof that served as a luggage rack. Baggage was piled high atop the barge, in a way one would assume it would be possible for some to tumble into the sea if the channel turned rough.

At the time our children's flight arrived and had gone by at least an hour or so, I was starting to get worried. With no Wi-Fi service at the dock, I could not check for messages. The last one I had received from the kids, which said they were getting ready to board, was sent from the airport in Quito. I started to consider what I would do if the kids were a no-show, but before the thought process was completed, I spotted a ferry rounding the corner. There in the window, I recognized the smiling face of our beautiful 24-year-old daughter, Melissa. It was a glorious family reunion, as it had been months since we last saw any of the children. I received the biggest hug from my grandson, Damien. As typically happens when we needed one, there wasn't a cabbie in sight. I asked the family to wait in the shade of the palapa as I went in search of a ride, which I found in the form of a local bus. The small bus held 20 passengers, and after some difficulty interrogating the driver, I learned that for $3 a head, we could have a ride to Puerto Ayora. However, there would be many stops along the way. Always up for an adventure, I grabbed the kids, and we blended in with the working class people of the islands. There was plenty of seating which was fortunate, because here in the Galápagos Islands, no one is permitted to ride on the outside of the bus or in the rooftop luggage rack, unlike in Guatemala. We were happy for the ride, and to our relief, the bus was air-conditioned and everyone smelled as if they had remembered their deodorant that morning—a bonus! Again memories of public transportation in Guatemala flashed through my mind.

The ride back to our side of the island was pleasant, as it entailed a tour of some of the back streets of the tiny villages along the way, giving us an intimate look at the Galápagos version of rural life. Mostly, we saw dusty back streets, surprisingly clean, unpainted concrete block houses and happy street kids playing with sticks, soccer balls or dogs and stray chickens. Our children were tired as expected, but also excited. Young Damien hardly took a breath while regaling Granny and Granddad with details of his long flight.

It was late afternoon when the bus dropped us on the *malecón* of Puerto Ayora. We were all getting hungry, so a late lunch was in order, but first, I took all the kid's bags and loaded them onto a water taxi. Alone, I ran them out to the boat. I instructed the driver to come along side, just close enough to toss the bags onto the floor of the cockpit, and then return me to shore.

While I was playing porter, Janet took the kids across the street for a $5 lunch at our favourite "cheap" restaurant. For $30 including tip, we had a great meal.

After eating, we made our way to the taxi dock where Damien stopped to get his first close look at a brown pelican, which was roosting on the dock's handrail. Encouraged by us to get closer so that we could get a picture, he nervously sidestepped his way in until he was nearly rubbing shoulders with the indifferent bird. Further along the pier, Damien spotted a sea lion laying on a bench, then a small white tip shark swimming under the floating dock. He followed the shark until he spied a clutch of black marine iguanas sitting on the nearby rocks, sunning themselves. Our grandson was beside himself with excitement. His reaction validated our hopes that this trip would be a thrilling and memorable trip for not only Damien, but also Thomas and Melissa.

Figure 65. Damien first encounter with the friendly wild life at Academy Bay.

For Thomas and Melissa, who had spent most of their formative years growing up while living and travelling aboard *Maiatla*, it was a homecoming. For eight-year-old Damien, who was last aboard *Maiatla* when he was five years old, it would be a grand new adventure, and he was extremely pleased we had given him his dad's old cabin on the port side. Melissa wasted no time in claiming her old room in the V-berth, which left Thomas to bed down amidships, in the lower salon on the pull out couch. This was fine with him, as next to our Queen-sized in the master cabin, it was the biggest bed on board. We had a full boat once again; nevertheless, Janet and I were ecstatic.

By the time everyone settled, it was growing dark. The breeze that had been keeping the cockpit under the tarp cool was now waning with the sun. It suddenly grew warmer, so I suggested we all have a swim off the boat. I went in first, and although initially a little nervous, Damien took the leap, followed by his dad. Janet and Melissa decided not to swim, but to sit back and watch the fun. After an hour of swimming circles around the boat and checking out the fish that had already taken up residence in *Maiatla*'s shadow, Thomas finally had to order his son out of the water and to head below for a shower in preparation for going to bed. I would be the last in line for a shower, so I stayed in the water, floating about until the sky was filled with sparkles set atop black velvet. I was so full and happy at that moment, what with having the kids back aboard and in such a magnificent place, that it was hard restraining myself and keeping from busting with joy. Janet and I had them for the next two weeks, and I was determined to make the most of every moment.

We were all up early the following morning. As I made a breakfast of French toast and bacon, the kids sat in the cockpit, taking in the sights. They were particularly thrilled to see several marine iguanas swim past the boat, headed for the open sea, to feed upon the alga-covered rocks of the reef.

I had booked a taxi this morning to take us all on a tour of the tortoise ranch and magma tunnels, the same place where we had gone with Mark and Teri a few short weeks ago. After breakfast, I used the radio to call a water taxi, and in a few short minutes, they were alongside, ready to load. The harbour was busy this morning as new arrivals from the airport were quickly loaded into big zodiacs and ferried out to one of the many waiting charter boats.

On our way in, I noticed we had a new sailboat, a new cruiser, which had arrived either late last night or early this morning. I was pleased to see she flew the Canadian maple leaf off the stern. As we passed, there was a young couple, perhaps in their early 40s, tidying up the deck.

"Hey, babe, look. More Canucks," I said while pointing. "I will go over to meet them later; see where they are from."

Ashore, I was greeted by a wave from our driver, who I had arranged the tour with two days previous. I was a little surprised that the taxi waited for us, considering the problems we had on Isabela with cabbies. When the five of us, plus the driver, whose name was Rafael, were all crammed into the tiny pickup truck, we sped through town and headed for the hinterlands of Isla Santa Cruz.

Our first stop was Los Gemelos—The Twins—the massive craters we had seen on our way to the airport. Los Gemelos are located in the highlands of Santa Cruz Island, and despite looking like massive meteor impact craters, they are in fact sink holes.

The circular, 30-metre (98.4-feet) deep holes were created when the volcanic roof of empty magma chambers collapsed from tectonic shifts and erosion over eons of time. The craters are located 25 metres (82 feet) and 125 metres (410 feet), one on either side of the road. We parked on the west side where Rafael instructed us to get out of the truck and follow the trail that goes into the jungle. He would wait for us down the road, at the parking lot. After a short walk, the first of the great holes appeared in front of us. Surprisingly, there are few guard rails to keep people back, so it was easy for us to walk right to the edge to take some dramatic pictures. I kept a tight grip on Damien's hand as he cautiously leaned over the edge for a better look.

These geologic structures were impressive to see. The lush green of the surrounding forest, cascading over the rim of the crater, is in stark contrast with the immense grey and black volcanic rock walls. Los Gemelos is one of the many places on the Galápagos Islands where you slide into a different world or time. This area has a different climate from other parts of the island, and the biodiverse forest is comprised mainly of a species of tree unique to the Galápagos—the strange looking *Scalesia pedunculata,* which gives the impression that one is in a different epoch or, perhaps even, planet. Our guide, Rafael, called it the "broccoli tree" because the branches and leaves appear as huge stalks of broccoli. This area is also prime habitat for bromeliads, orchids, mosses, lichens and many of the endemic birds.

Figure 66. The whole crew at the "Twins," Los Gemelos: Melissa, Andrew, Thomas, Janet and young Damien.

Our short visit was rich with bird sightings, smells and sounds, especially the soft twittering of finches. After looking at the pictures mounted on the information boards, I may have seen a vermilion flycatcher, a small bird of some notoriety, one many "birders" would consider a prize sighting. We also were treated to several varieties of flowering plants close to the trail, something that was of particular interest to Janet and Melissa. Me? Not so much.

The place is decidedly worth the visit of a couple of hours for those who truly want to explore. We settled on only doing the short walk to the first viewing point of each crater, but you can do the full trail around the perimeter of both holes in one and a half hours. For someone who is a biologist, a naturalist or a birdwatcher, it is a great place to spend the day, but when you are eight years old, 30 minutes is long enough. After piling back into the truck, we moved on to the tortoise ranch.

Rancho Primicias is a different ranch than the one we had visited with Mark and Teri some weeks before; nevertheless, we found it just as impressive. The grasslands and scrub brush was awash in great tortoises either grazing or wallowing in mud puddles to escape the heat of the noonday sun. We walked the trails taking pictures and video of Damien approaching close to the beasts. Acting as a guide and interpreter, Rafael enthusiastically led us around. He was obviously proud of his island and the animal life, and he made sure that we didn't miss a thing. Apparently some of the other cabbies were not as engaging as Rafael. After letting out their passengers at the reception area of the ranch, most cabbies either stayed in their trucks or were sitting on the tailgates fingering their phone screens, flipping through messages or the like, while their travellers wonder on their own.

In some thick bush by a bend in the trail, Rafael stopped dead in his tracks while placing cupped hands around his ears. He listened intently for a few seconds before breaking out in a great smile and pointing off into the bush, gesturing that we should listen. At first, I heard nothing, but after a few moments, a faint, deep throated grunt or a moan floated amongst the trees. Rafael motioned we should follow him as he parted the bush and headed in the direction of the moaning. Doing as instructed, we left the trail. Perhaps a dozen metres into the thicket, we came across a muddy wallow and at the centre were a pair of mating tortoises. The large male was almost a third larger than his mate, and he was struggling to stay on top as his lover was slick with mud.

For Galápagos tortoises, mating can occur at any time of the year, with seasonal peaks between February and June in the humid uplands, during the rainy season. When mature males meet in the mating season, they face each other in a ritualized dominance display, rising on their legs and stretching their necks with their mouths gaped open. Occasionally, head-biting occurs, but usually the shorter tortoise backs off, conceding mating rights to the victor.

The preamble to mating is typically aggressive, as the male forcefully rams the female's shell with his own while often biting her legs. Mounting is often an awkward process and takes great care and effort. However, when successful, the male is helped to stay atop by the concave underside of his shell. As we were now hearing, during mating, the male vocalizes with hoarse bellows and grunts, often described as "rhythmic groans" (not unlike humans, eh?), one of the few vocalizations the tortoise makes. Other noises are made during aggressive encounters or when struggling to right themselves. Still, I wasn't sure if the grunting was his mating call or just the sound the old guy made while attempting to get his great bulk atop of the female.

From personal experience, the latter may be closer to the truth. Damien had also learned if he got too close to a tortoise, the animal would hiss at him while withdrawing into their shells.

Figure 67. Damien, his dad, Thomas, and Janet admire a Santa Cruz tortoise at Rancho Primicias.

After breeding, the females can journey for several kilometres to reach nesting areas in dry, sandy terrain. Nest digging can take the female several hours a day and over many days to complete. Often nest sites are abandoned before they are completed because she has decided the spot is no longer suitable. The Galápagos tortoises typically breed three or four times a year, laying up to 16 spherical, hard-shelled eggs the size of a billiard ball. The female covers the nest with a muddy plug comprised of soil mixed with urine. She leaves the eggs to be incubated by the tropical sun. Temperature plays a huge role in the sex of the hatchlings, with lower-temperature nests producing more males and higher-temperature nests producing more females. Because of this, Galápagos scientists are now concerned with what the long-term effect global warming may have on future tortoise populations.

The hatchlings emerge from the nest after four to eight months and measure 6 centimetres (2.4 inches). The Galápagos hawk was formerly the sole native predator of the tortoise hatchlings. Darwin wrote: *"The young tortoises, as soon as they are hatched, fall prey in great numbers to the buzzard."* With the hawk fewer in numbers today, feral pigs, dogs, cats and black rats now pose the greatest threat to the young tortoises. As an adult, the tortoises have no natural predators, apart from humans. Darwin also noted: *"The old ones seem generally to die from accidents, as from falling down precipices. At least several of the inhabitants told me, they had never found one dead without some such apparent cause."*

The Galápagos Island tortoises reach sexual maturity between 20 and 40 years of age. Depending on the environment, life expectancy in the wild is believed to be over 100 years and up to 180 in captivity, making it one of the longest-lived species in the animal kingdom.

Back on the trail, Rafael led us down a path that ended abruptly at a wooden staircase. The rickety steps led into a great hole in the earth—the mouth of our first magma tunnel. We spent the better part of an hour underground exploring several tubes, some only perhaps 30 or 40 metres (98.4 to 131 feet) long, but a couple were in the 1-kilometre range. By late afternoon, we were getting weary of exploring, so we headed to the concession stand for a cold drink. As we sipped bottled water in the shade, Rafael excitedly led Damien to the far side of the concession building where there were two large tortoise shells sitting on the ground. The original owners had long since abandoned the premises.

After a bit of coaxing, Rafael helped Damien to crawl into one of the shells to try it on for size and to see what the world would look like from the perspective of a tortoise. With his head and hands poking out one end and his feet sticking out the other, Damien struggled to lift the great shell off of the ground, but with a helping hand, he was able to do so.

"Come on, Granddad. You get in the other one!" Damien demanded as he attempted to waddle like a tortoise.

"Yeah, go ahead, Andy. Try it on. I wanna get some pictures," Janet said as she brought out the camera. Well, it didn't take much prodding for me to want to try, but I'm not a svelte young boy anymore, and it took some doing to wriggle my butt into the other unoccupied tortoise shell. It was great fun, and we all had a good laugh at my expense, but how often do you get to try on an authentic turtle girdle?

Once Damien and I shed our shells, we headed back to the truck and hit the road for home. On the way, we passed a sign indicating the road to Playa El Garrapatero. We had visited Playa El Garrapatero with Mark and Teri. I loved the beach, and I was sure the kids would also. It didn't take much convincing for everyone to agree to make one more stop.

Rafael dropped us off in the tarmac parking lot at the head of a trail. I asked Rafael if he wanted to come with us to the beach, but he declined stating, *"No, demasiado lejos para mi."* ("No, too far for me.")

Rafael's declaration should have been a reminder to me of our last visit, but for whatever reason, I ignored it. It is a beautiful trail, constructed of tan brick pavers meandering through some pretty impressive-looking terrain and vegetation. Huge prickly pear cactus, their trunks looking more like trees than any cactus I have ever seen, dominate the landscape.

Not to be out done, the reaching *Scalesia pedunculata*, the broccoli tree, compete with the cacti for supremacy.

Figure 68. Damien tries wearing his home on his back.

At the feet of the cacti and trees, thorny bushes provide a shelter for a variety of finches flitting in and out of the underbrush. As we made our way down the path, fluttering butterflies displaying vivid blues and yellows tempted us to wander off the path, but the needle-sharp thorns made it clear that any attempt to leave the trail would be at one's own peril.

In keeping with the less than hospitable-looking topography, at nearly every bend in the trail was a manchineel tree, the *manzanilla de la muerte*, "little apple of death."

"Oh, look, Granny, apples," Damien said while pointing to a bunch that were sitting along the side of the trail. Apparently, he had forgotten our earlier warning regarding the fruit and reached to pick up one of the tiny apples for a better look.

"Don't touch that, Damien. It's poisonous," Janet and Thomas excitedly exclaimed at the same time. Too late, Damien had picked up one before the warning had rung in his ears, but the instant he had heard it, he tossed the apple to one side, then wiped his fingers on his shorts. We immediately took a water bottle, rinsed his fingers and examined them. Fortunately, he did not appear to be any worse off for the encounter, aside from perhaps a few stressed nerves from everyone screaming at him. Disaster avoided and soon forgotten, Damien went back to chasing tiny lava lizards that were trying to sun themselves along the path.

We had not ventured very far when we started to see the wasps that we had encountered on our first visit with Mark and Teri, some weeks before. Thomas had been stung by wasps as a child, so to say he wasn't impressed by these buzzing hypodermic needles would have been a gross understatement, an aversion shared by us all. Whenever wasps were encountered, we used the umbrellas as shields while twirling backpacks and increasing the walking pace (running with fits of screaming mostly).

The heat and stinging reception aside, it was a beautiful walk to the beach, all 3 kilometres (1.8 miles) of it, and I was starting to appreciate Rafael's reasoning for declining to join us. When we finally broke out of the bush, we were amazed what lay before us—a pristine sand beach arching around a tropical bay full of azure water. Thankfully, a cooling breeze had engulfed us.

Inland of the beach are beautiful mangrove trees where ducks and pink flamingos leisurely trolled. We would soon see that the protected bay is home to an incredible array of birds, most notably, pelicans, mockingbirds, herons, grebes, penguins, oystercatchers and patillos. Black marine iguanas basked on the rocks or swam in the surf. Perhaps the most incredible part of this experience was that only perhaps half a dozen other people were in sight, most of whom were hundreds of metres away down the beach that stretched for perhaps 2 kilometres.

We made our way along the beach to set up our beach towels under the shade of some trees we made sure weren't sporting apples of death. Damien and I took to the water for a refreshing swim. Beyond the small breaking surf, we encountered cruising iguanas and darting penguins, so we spent an enjoyable hour following them about. Later on the beach, we ate a snack, and I pulled the top off a couple of beers while Janet, Melissa and Damien fed bread crumbs to fearless finches that ate right out of the palms of their hands.

"Right there, Janet. Do you see that little bay on the other side, next to the rocky point?" I asked while pointing.

"Yes, I see it. What about it?" Janet responded, with some indifference, as if humouring me.

"That is where I would anchor *Maiatla* if we were permitted to come here," I said, with all eagerness. "Can you imagine being here? I could see us hanging here on the hook for a couple of months, just swimming and relaxing. Can you imagine?"

Janet took a long pondering moment before responding. "Yeah, that would be nice, and it's too bad we can't."

For now, I would have to be satisfied with sharing Puerto Ayora along with all the others.

An incredible end to an incredible day, it was time to go and we all hated to leave, not just because it was the type of beach paradise most people dream of, but because we hated leaving when it meant having to face the heat and onslaught of wasps that would come with the trek back to the taxi.

We made it back to the *malecón* of Puerto Ayora without incident or having to use an EpiPen to counteract an allergic reaction to wasp stings. While waiting for a water taxi to take us back out to *Maiatla*, we saw a small dinghy coming ashore and it looked like it held the crew of the new Canadian yacht I had seen earlier. I went over to introduce myself and to hopefully get acquainted. John and Susan and their two children, 18-year-old Carl and eight–year-old Ellie, owned the yacht *Tigress* and were from Toronto, Canada. As I would later learn, John and Susan owned a kid's summer camp in back woods of Ontario, but they were taking their winters off to sail the world with their children. After transiting the Intracoastal Waterway of the American Eastern Seaboard, *Tigress* and her crew crossed the Caribbean to Panamá, then onto the Galápagos Islands, with plans to leave the boat in Fiji for the summer and return home to work.

Over the following week, we would get to know these people better, and in particular, Damien and little Ellie would become fast friends, hanging out and swimming together whenever possible. We made plans to visit the Grotto in the morning for a swim, so I extended an invitation for them join us, which they readily accepted.

We finally made it back to *Maiatla* as darkness fell, and we were all exhausted. After a quick dinner and a swim off the boat, it was shower and bed time. Tomorrow would prove to be another busy day.

Chapter 26

Of Mullet and Parrotfish, It's Off to the Grotto We Go

"One ship is much like another, and the sea is always the same. In the immutability of their surroundings, the foreign shores, the foreign faces, the changing immensity of life, glide past, veiled not by a sense of mystery but by a slightly disdainful ignorance, for there is nothing mysterious to a seaman unless it be the sea itself, which is the mistress of his existence and as inscrutable as Destiny."
—Joseph Conrad

We rose early the following day and got on the move, a tactic employed in an effort to avoid trudging around in the worst of the daytime heat. After breakfast, we all loaded our snorkelling gear into our backpacks. I hailed a water taxi and told the driver we wanted to go to a nearby point.

Not more than a couple hundred metres from *Maiatla* lay Punta Angermeyer, the southernmost tip of the harbour. The point is isolated from the rest of the town, as there are no roads; it is only accessible by the harbour water taxis. On the point, a cluster of red pantile-roofed buildings house a small and exclusive hotel and restaurant. Next to the taxi dock, constructed out of black lava rock, stands a circular room that is the kitchen of another exclusive hotel. The hotel boasts of an outdoor patio, cactus gardens enclosed by lava rock walls of over 2 metres (6.5 feet) in height. To keep out undesirables, the thick stonewall is capped with jagged rocks, in lieu of barbed wire or, as is typical in most third world countries, broken pop bottles or shattered glass. The bloodletting wall tops are a deterrent for anyone contemplating broaching the parapets to be sure, but the glass spikes are of no consequence to the tough-skinned iguanas that used the wall as a tanning bed and transportation avenue. I couldn't help wondering if the hide of a marine iguana would make for a durable cowboy boot.

The single-story, low-profile stone hotel appeared to have insufficient headroom for most guests, but perhaps this was an illusion. Still, with its round windows constructed of stone and mortar, arched gateways and thatched roof shading the entrance, the hotel could have come from some distant Hobbit Village.

The wide walkway leads inland between a series of Bed and Breakfast hotels, one of which is a white stucco, three-story hotel called the Blue Heron Villa. The complex is small, perhaps containing rooms for a couple of dozen guests, and for just $600 USD a night, you too can gaze at the distant sea from your own private balcony, constructed in the middle of a mangrove swamp.

We took a trail that meanders for half a kilometre before dumping onto a sand beach and connecting with an elevated wooden boardwalk, constructed to keep people from disturbing an iguana nesting area below. We stopped for a few moments to see a couple of iguanas scratching around, but if they were into egg laying, the effort looked half-hearted.

Figure 69. Janet on the trail to the Grotto, surrounded by towering cacti.

The walkway extends past a beautiful crescent-shaped beach that is popular with not only the hotel guests, but the locals as well. Despite still being early in the day, a couple of dozen sun bathers and snorkelers already had staked claim to the best sandy spots in the shade of some canting mangrove trees at the high tide mark. It appeared like a great snorkelling spot, but we would have to come back here another time if we wanted to explore. We were on a mission with a destination already in mind and that was the Grotto—the deep slash in the earth, which still lay some distance off hidden in the jungle.

Damien, in particular, was eager to reach the Grotto because we made arrangements to meet the crew of the *Tigress* for a swim and his new friend, Ellie, would be there. Leaving the beach, I promised the kids we would return another day for a snorkel, when I wasn't sure, as our time on this island was running short. We continued on the trail as it turned from sand to hard packed, red earth and wound its way through the underbrush past tall prickly cacti trees until we reached a small inland lagoon teeming with foreshore birds. Egrets and oystercatchers prodded about, and on the far side of the lagoon, a flock of white-cheeked pintail duck skirted the edge of the mangrove forest.

The trail cut between the water's edge and another massive stone wall and a building sporting several large round windows. The panes of the windows were constructed of old soda bottles laid in mortar so that only the bottom of the bottle could be seen from the outside. The combination of green and clear glass bottles serve as a sort of light prism to channel sunlight into the building, creating a "stained glass window" effect inside.

A crudely made sign at a large archway and heavy gate identifies the structure as a museum of some sort. The gate resembles one belonging on a medieval castle fortress, with massive wrought-iron hinges, and was secured by a heavy chain and keyed lock. For us, this meant any exhibits or treasures housed inside would remain a mystery. The trail continues over a wooden footbridge, which passes over a stream with muddy banks. On our adventure, the tide was out, exposing much of the soft mud bottom. We stopped on the bridge to have a better look. This first thing to catch our attention was not what we saw, but what we heard—a mysterious clicking and popping sound emanating out of the mud. While searching for the source of the sound, we noticed the mud contained thousands of tiny holes, and when we stood quiet and still, the occupants of the holes—the creators of the sounds—cautiously emerged.

"Look, Damien, fiddler crabs!" Janet said while pointing to the shy creatures, which either took flight or dived back into the hole each time anyone of us made a move or quick gesture. We spent several minutes watching the crabs forage through the mud with their tiny claws, looking for edibles while waving the other massive claw in the air to warn other crabs to keep clear. We weren't the only ones to have an interest in the crabs—a few metres away, standing stork stiff, was a pair of blue herons. The regal looking birds were steadily waiting to strike at any crab foolish enough to pop its head out or wander within striking range.

The Galápagos fiddler crab is like some strange cartoon character with its battleship grey body and bright orange right claw that appears like Popeye's arm, way out of proportion to its body. The intimidating-looking pincer is so large you would imagine they would topple over to one side from the sheer weight of it.

After a couple of more kilometres, we left the lowlands of the mangrove swamps behind to start climbing a steep slope. At the top of the slope, we came to a guardrail that stopped people from walking into a great crack in the earth. The Grotto, now our favourite swimming hole lay before us.

When we looked back in the direction that we had come, we were treated to a spectacular, panoramic view of Puerto Ayora and the adjacent bays. Beyond the town in the distances, the cloud-capped volcanic mountain, Cerro Crocker, lorded over the landscape it had created eons ago. To seaward, the nearby island of Coamaño, with its booby colonies, stood stark, and still further off, the distant Santa Fe Island appeared as a shimmering apparition through the tropical haze. Blowing from the south, a stiff wind simultaneously churned the ocean, creating whitecaps. A stiff breeze reached the hilltop where we stood.

We followed the trail to the wooden staircase, signed in with the park ranger while turning down his offer to rent us some snorkeling gear, then down to the water's edge we went. Care would have to be taken not to let Damien or anyone else swim or snorkel into one of the underwater tunnels, of which there were many (especially when the tide was ebbing), least one wanted to be carried out to sea. Considering the open ocean was a good kilometre away, I doubted anyone sucked underground would be able to hold their breath long enough to see open water again, assuming they didn't get caught up somewhere inside.

There was not much room on the tiny wooden dock, as several local kids, scrambling around in a playful manner, engaged in a pushing and shoving match to see who was going to go in first. We managed to find some room for our gear on the rocks off to one side, so Thomas, Damien, Janet and I, along with Melissa, suited up and made the leap from a rocky ledge into the first pool. The water was surprisingly cold, or maybe it felt that way because we were all overheated from the long hike and climb. The visibility underwater was incredibly clear. The canyon walls drop vertically into the water, then again plummet uninterrupted to the bottom.

Figure 70. Thomas and Damien swimming in the Grotto.

The first pool is approximately 50 metres (164 feet) long, with only one place to rest, a partially submerged ledge half way down the length of the Grotto. On our visit, the ledge held several local teens, boys and girls who were laughing while splashing one another. At the far end of the pool, on top of a rubble pile ready to challenge the second pool, sat the crew of the *Tigress,* who had arrived some time before us.

"Dad, I see Ellie," Damien excitedly called above the water to Thomas. "Come on, Dad, let's catch up to them." With Damien taking the lead, we all made our way down the length of the pool.

Despite being attached to the sea, the Grotto is principally filled with fresh water as it is fed by underground springs originating in the highlands, but there are layers of salt water. It was here, in the brine level, we found schools of large mullet and great parrotfish, grazing upon algae that clung to the rocks.

With Melissa close behind, I dived deep, passing through a pair of thermoclines, identified by the abrupt drop in water temperature that sent an involuntary shiver through me. I also noticed a shimmering line formed at the interface of the fresh and saltier ocean water. With some effort, I managed to reach the bottom and snatch up a handful of muddy sand to take back to the surface to show Damien.

Along the canyon walls, we peered under rock ledges where we found several tunnels leading off into the mountain. When I poked my head into one of the tunnels, I felt the slight but unmistakable pull of tidal flow, so I instinctively braced my arms across the narrow opening to prevent being drawn in any further. As the tunnel was over 8 metres (26.2 feet) below the surface, it did not present any danger for anyone swimming on the surface, and I doubted any of the young kids could get this deep. Still, I could well imagine that during an extreme tide in conjunction with a heavy rain inland, this tunnel could develop suction and, like a toilet bowl, flush an unwary swimmer out to sea. Melissa and I had great fun chasing schools of mullets and parrotfish. I wished I had brought a spear gun, but I knew the park guide wouldn't have taken too kindly to it.

Figure 71. Melissa diving deep into the clear waters of the Grotto.

Barbeque parrotfish is fine, and although the flesh of the mullet is reported to be a delicacy, I could never get past the stink of the skin to even attempt to fillet the fish. Unless you use gloves, the stench, despite repeated hand washings, will stay with you for days. As I've learned, the smell will wake you up from a dead sleep if your hand even gets remotely close to your nose.

By the time we finally arrived at the end of the first pool, we were all in need of some sun. Despite the heat and exertion of swimming, the cold water had us all chilled and we all needed a rest and warmth. This gave Damien and Ellie an opportunity to get reacquainted and play atop the rubble pile before we all made our way into the narrower second pool. It was a grand but exhausting day at the Grotto, and we were sorry it was getting late and nearly time to go. After making our way back to the wooden dock, I helped Janet climb the cliff to get out of the water. We found a place to sit and rest. While the kids continued splashing about, I pulled a pair of beers out of my backpack, popped the caps off of the cold bottles and took a drink.

Surprisingly, I had barely taken a couple of mouthfuls of beer before someone tapped me on my shoulder. Turning around, I came eye to eye with a park ranger, the same fellow who wanted to rent me a mask and snorkel. He told me in Spanish I could not drink the beer here. He instructed me to pour the beer out or leave. Reluctantly, I did as instructed, dumping the still cold brew between a gap in the rocks. I was a bit confused as to the reason. I can only assume they either did not allow glass bottles in the Grotto or didn't permit the consumption of alcohol in public places. Or perhaps he simply resented me for bringing my own snorkelling gear and sidestepping his obviously lucrative side business. Irrespective of the teetotalling environment of the Grotto (mainly no beer allowed), it was a grand day.

We were back at the boat for dinner. Then it was a quick trip ashore for a little night-time sightseeing and a shop for provisions. We planned on departing Puerto Ayora the day after next, so we needed to top up on some staples. On the *malecón*, we took a few minutes to watch the antics of the locals and scrutinized the trinkets spread out on blankets on the cobble bricks. The kids were now on a serious souvenir hunt, nothing shiny was given a miss, but we needed to make a quick cab ride up town to the fruit and veggie markets.

Being a typical kid, Damien became a little restless watching Granny and Granddad shop for fruit, so he and Thomas decided to wait outside of the store, as it was cooler outdoors. In the street, people wandered about on their business while competing with car traffic that moved a snail's pace. Equally bored with the whole shopping experience, I had left Janet and Melissa to sort through a table of veggies while I took up a station in the doorway next to my son. In the parking lot adjacent to the store selling eggs, there were three kids of around Damien's age kicking a soccer ball about. After several minutes of play, the local kids noticed Damien, who had wandered over to watch them. It was then the oldest of the three boys snatched up the soccer ball and approached Damien. At first I was a little concerned, but I needn't have been. Damien and the boy exchanged words. What was said, I could only guess, as I was out of earshot and doubted the young Ecuadorian boy spoke any English. I knew aside from saying "*hola*," Damien didn't speak any Spanish either, but whatever the language barrier, it was overcome. The kids invited Damien to play soccer with them.

Quickly they chose sides, forming two teams of two, and started to play. While watching the kids, I noticed the game had drawn the attention of what I assumed to be the father of one of the kids. He took it upon himself to position a pair of old wooden vegetable boxes to act as goal posts. It was enjoyable to see kids from different sides of the world play and get along. I know it's an old cliché, but adults could learn a great deal about getting along if they were to emulate their children. Thomas and I kept an eye on the raucous game while the women continued to shop. Eventually, the game came to an end when a parent called the boys to head home. The boys thanked Damien for playing with them and patted him on the back before running off.

With groceries in hand, we wandered around the corner to the open-air market where we snacked on chicken empanadas pulled from great boiling vats of honey-coloured oil. Finally, by 10 p.m., we made our way back to the waterfront to make one last stop for ice-cream at a supermarket. The treat was made from real fruit—blackberries and strawberries—and cream. It became a favourite of ours all the while on the Galápagos.

Back aboard *Maiatla*, Thomas and Damien led the charge for showers while Janet and Melissa put away the groceries. To keep clear of all the commotion below, I went topside. It was a clear night with nearly a full moon, its milky light illuminating the harbour waters. After watching a giant manta ray, clipping the boarding ladder with a wing tip as he swam by, I stripped off and dived in for a swim.

Chapter 27

Mad Dogs and Englishmen—a Pilgrimage to the Darwin Research Centre

"A man who is not afraid of the sea will soon drown, for he'll be going out on a day when he shouldn't. But we do be afraid of the sea, and we do only be drowned no and again."
—From *The Aran Islands* by J.M. Synge

Our last day in Puerto Ayora was spent making the trek from along the waterfront to the Darwin Research Centre, located at the far end of town. We had risen late, as the day at the Grotto ate any and all of our physical reserves, and for me in particular, simply getting out of bed took more effort than I thought I could muster. Nevertheless, I was determined to make sure the kids had every opportunity to see all the sights, so after making a bunch of "old man noises" while hauling my ass out of bed, I prepared breakfast for all. Damien, Thomas and Melissa sat in the cockpit switching between reading and watching a myriad of sea creatures swim, skull, flutter or float by the boat.

As I flipped the French toast in the pan, I called to Janet who was still on our bed in the aft cabin. "Hey, babe, you sure you don't want to come with us to the Darwin Centre to see some more tortoises?" Janet was sitting in bed, reading under the open hatch. It was already hot in the cabin and the lack of breeze outside and heat from the cooking didn't help.

"No, I think I'm all tortoised out. You go with the kids, but you do know that you will be doing it during the hottest part of the day, don't you?"

"Yes, I know, but the wind should fill in soon, and the centre is right next to the water, so it shouldn't be that bad," I replied.

I didn't believe it, but I had to offer a reasonable excuse for attempting something so stupid, and in truth, I was glad Janet had declined to come with us as she suffered from the heat most of all.

"I'll take my Tilley hat. I'll be fine," I said, as if all I needed was a big floppy hat for protection as I parted the gates of hell.

True to the admiral's prediction, we hit the pavement slightly after noon and there wasn't a cloud in the blue sky, nor a whisper of a breeze to dry the perspiration from our brows. The streets were mostly deserted, as the locals were all either hiding inside air-conditioned shops or had closed shop and were waiting out the heat, sitting at home or having a siesta.

Rudyard Kipling was a 19th-century journalist, novelist and the author of *The Jungle Book*. Kipling also wrote extensively on the subject of British Imperialism in India. And it was Kipling who first recognized a unique English trait. This "trait" or peculiarity was later redefined and set into song by the 20th-century English playwright and composer Noel Coward. This character trait, or perhaps it should be called a flaw, was well-known to me as I had apparently inherited it from my father.

Kipling and Coward, gentlemen and scholars of some notoriety, had recognized the unwillingness of English people to adopt the custom of taking a siesta during the heat of the day while in tropical climates. This observation eventually became entrenched in popular culture and literature by way of Noel Coward's song, "*Mad Dogs and Englishmen,*" which states, "*Mad dogs and Englishmen go out in the midday sun.*"

The song became popular in the 1930s and is an appropriate truism I cannot dispute, considering my own proclivity for engaging in epic foot marches when the sun has reached its blistering zenith.

I confess that both of my parents were from Lincolnshire, England, and my Anglo-Saxon roots reach back to the 5th century, so it all makes perfect sense. On solid ground, I can argue that venturing out into the tropical sun is in my blood, and because of my genetic predisposition, any suggestions from the admiral not to do so are all for nothing. Being of Anglo-Saxon ancestry, I am only doing what comes naturally—like going naked at the drop of a Tilley hat, for instance!

Thomas, Damien, Melissa and I, whenever possible, stuck to the shady side of the street. I had refused a taxi ride for two reasons. One was that Charles Darwin drive was a one-way street, and of course, we wanted to go the wrong way. To hail a cabbie would mean having to ride up the main street and circle much of the town to get back to where we wanted to go, which was a short walk down the road, according to my map.

"Honestly, Melissa, it would take longer to drive there than it would to just walk!" was the reply to my daughter's question. Melissa was already falling behind while looking like she was going to melt. Nevertheless, I knew it was Thomas who was suffering the most. Even as a kid, in the dead of a Canadian winter, he would sleep in his room with the window partially open. He never liked the heat, so Ecuador was a challenge for him.

Reason number two was that a taxi ride would cost $4, and I was well beyond thinking this country had already sucked enough money out of me. Besides, it wasn't far and there would be shade at the centre with cold drinks. Right? If I had an inkling of what was coming, I would have paid for the taxi and done so gladly. Or smarter yet, returned to *Maiatla*.

Well the "10–minute" walk to the gates of the Darwin Research Centre took us a blistering 30 minutes. However, we had made it. The arched gates with the embossed sign heralded our arrival, or so we thought. From the entrance, all I could see was a brick road disappearing into a field of thick scrub brush, with not a building in sight.

I asked the guard on the gate how far it was to the exhibits in the park, and when he stopped to consider my question and a faraway-glazed look flooded his eyes, I should have known to turn around and head home. Nevertheless, this was for the kids, so I forged on.

While we all stood in the shade of the wall catching our breath, a taxi pulled up and unloaded several passengers. I thought, "Oh, yes, we will get a cab now." While waving at the taxi driver, I excitedly asked the guard if we could drive in. Apparently, this fellow was still considering my first question, which he seemed determined to answer first.

As it turns out, no cars are permitted inside the gate; if you wanted in, you walked. Everyone walked from here and what the guidebook failed to mention was that the gate is only the start of a long driveway. In actual fact, it was as far to the exhibit centre as we had already come through town. Still, there were a surprisingly large number of people entering the gate, so we could only assume that it would be well worth the visit. With some reluctance, I waved the cabbie off, and we entered the gate. On the upside, the centre is free to visit.

The road is paved, and as we walked along, the dark brick did a fabulous job of absorbing the sun, radiating the heat and causing the air to shimmer with dancing mirages. The fluid images appearing like tiny lakes on the roadway were so convincing that I first thought perhaps the road was wet with puddles from garden sprinklers. Nonetheless, it is a pretty road and well thought out. Shade trees were strategically planted, staggering from one side of the road to the other, as if street lamps, with a similar spacing. If you wanted to run from tree to tree, you would have to repeatedly cross the road, not a dangerous action since no cars use it anyway. In our desperation for relief from the sun, we even knowingly took shade under the little "apple of death" tree, which grew to overshadow the sidewalk in one location. As we stood fanning ourselves, I called to Damien, "Don't touch the tree, bud, or look up. You might get sap in your eyes."

Apparently, in this country, even trees sweat, which could be seen in the form of sap oozing from the crotch of a tree's limbs—not unlike me. I was already soaked to the skin and commencing to chafe in intimate places as a steady stream of perspiration trickled into cracks and crevices, of which there are more appearing as I grow older. I had mistakenly wore Keagan sandals, which were normally fine for walking, but they left my flesh exposed, and now the tops of my feet were getting sunburnt, creating a hash tag pattern. Who remembers to put suntan lotion on their feet? At the halfway mark along the seemingly never-ending roadway, it curves to the right, and now visible through the thick bush is the water. We followed several people down a short trail until we broke out onto a beautiful little beach with a spectacular view of the harbour. There were kids playing in the breaking waves while others sat in the sand under colourful umbrellas. Despite being initially pleased at what we had found, my gut twisted as I realized nearly everyone we had seen on the roadway coming in, was going to the beach, not the Darwin Centre as I had assumed.

"So what do you think, guys? Wanna go for a swim?" I asked hopefully.

I was all for stripping off as far as we dared and jumping in. There was even a slight breeze, which we felt upon our faces that would have been cooling if we were not facing directly into the sun. From the beach, I could see *Maiatla,* secure on her moorings. She was close enough to swim too, and there was every possibility I might do just that. *Maiatla's* deck was hard to see under all the sun awnings she was flying at the moment, but I could well imagine Janet as she sat quietly in the shade of the cockpit, reading with a cold drink at hand, or napping as anybody with a modicum of common sense should be doing at this time of the day. Napping or swimming— neither of which we were doing.

"No, Dad, I don't want to be walking around the centre in wet, salty cloths," Melissa said. "Let's just keep going, okay?"

Well, that settled that. Now, with sand chafing under the straps of my Keagan's, it was back to the blistering road.

We finally reached the first of the exhibit buildings, which was locked tight with a big sign out front saying it was closed for renovations. Likewise, the nearby concession stand was also closed. There were still a surprising number of people walking about and not only dumb *turistas,* but also some locals and workers wearing tan-coloured uniforms. I stopped a fellow emptying a trash can. He told me the tortoise breeding centre was also closed, but a short walk from here were pens where we could see examples of tortoises from all the islands. And there, we would also find a refreshment stand. Great, another "short walk."

"Okay, kids, it's not far now, just down that trail. So, how are you holding up? Anyone want to go back?" I asked while secretly hoping they had had enough and it was time to turn around.

Damien spoke first, "Yeah, I'm okay. Can we go and see the tortoises, Granddad?"

At this point, the paved road gives way to a dirt trail, which thankfully led us to the concession stand first. After cold bottles of water and two helpings of ice cream and an appropriate amount of time to recuperate, we took a tour of three separate pens, which house a variety of tortoise species. There is even a pen containing a collection of land iguanas that looked striking different than their water savvy cousins, the marine iguanas. Apparently, there is lots to see at the centre, but during our time there, unfortunately, most of the exhibits were closed. In less than half an hour, we had seen all that there was to see, so it was back to the concession stand for another drink and ice-cream. Then, with much trepidation, we commenced the long trek home. Once outside the gate, I looked for a taxi, but as usual, when needed, there wasn't one to be had.

We retraced our steps back through town, shade-hopping while checking each store along the way for our favourite ice cream. We arrived back on the malecón in time to meet up with Loretta, who had our departure papers all ready to go. I informed Loretta there was a wind warning for the morning, and if it was blowing stink, I may delay our departure for a day or two. She said it wouldn't be a problem, but to let her know if we stay.

"So how was your day?" Janet asked as we all clambered back aboard *Maiatla*, sunburnt, chaffed and exhausted. My soul was as blistered as my feet.

"Fine, babe. How was yours?" was my reply as I headed below for a beer.

Chapter 28

A Return to Isabela's Penguins and Our Friend the Sea Lion

"Wherever we want to go, we go. That's what a ship is, you know. It's not just a keel and an hull and a deck and sails; that's what a ship needs. But what a ship is . . . what the Black Pearl is . . . is freedom."
—Captain Jack Sparrow

We departed Puerto Ayora as planned, leaving the crew of the *Tigress* to follow in a couple of days. The wind warning for the early morning had not yet materialized, so with a cautious eye searching the clouds for any sign of the pending gale, we cast off and got underway without a hitch—this time without having to dive and retrieve any ground tackle. I was still a bit concerned the gale that was predicted was stalking us and, like a predator, was waiting to pounce once we rounded the far point.

I wasn't concerned for *Maiatla*, 35 knots of wind on the right quarter is just a good day of sailing for us, but my grandson, Damien, had never seen foul weather before. A southerly blow funnelling between Santa Cruz and Isabela could build some ugly seas, making for a rough passage. I did not want to frighten him on his first real ocean passage. As for Thomas and Melissa, by the time they were both into their teens, they had countless gales and one hurricane under their belts, so I wasn't worried about them. Knowing Melissa, who took after her dad's own heart, she probably would have welcomed a bit of a blow.

If it blew, we would have to make a wide swing around the hidden reefs of the Las Tintoreras before altering course to head into the bay at Puerto Villamil and the anchorage at Isabela. Janet and I were now familiar with entering and leaving Isabela's tight anchorage, but driving directly for shore with a gale on your tail can be a dangerous business. If the roller furling jams or the engine dies at the wrong moment, you can find yourself on the rocks or beach before you may have time to react. Far too many boats and lives have been lost in such a way. All these thoughts crossed my mind long before we raised the hook to depart.

Fortunately, the stiff winds did not materialize right away, and we had a pleasant sail on a tight port tack reach. I brought out the fishing rods and showed Damien how to set the gear, and he would later experience the joy of reeling in his first tuna, a small skipjack that we released.

When Thomas and Melissa were young and voyaging the coast of México, they devised a unique pastime to amuse themselves. The kids would make tiny surfboards out of cardboard and wrap them in electrical tape to make them waterproof. Then, taking pipe cleaners, twist ties or other such things, fashion a man, a stick figure, to mount upon the surfboards. The kids attached fishing line to their surfers and dropped them over the side of the boat. It was great fun as the surfer dude skipped along the wave tops created by *Maiatla*'s wake. The children even learned to perform tricks with their surfers. A sharp jerk of the line as the surfer was on the backside of a wave would causes the surfer to shoot up the wave and do a complete flip in the air before landing right side up and carrying on. The kids and I spent countless hours designing and building tiny surfer dudes and playing with them alongside. In truth, I had almost forgotten this game we used to play to amuses ourselves on long passages, but Thomas had not.

Figure 72. Thomas and Melissa on the passage from Santa Cruz to Isabela.

Once underway and all was quiet, Thomas disappeared below to return a short time later with all the materials required to build a new surfboard and rider.

"Damien, I'm going to show you how to build a surfer dude," Thomas said as he set all the components on the cockpit seat in preparation for assembly.

With great care, my son taught his son how to build and launch a miniature surfboard and rider. It was heartwarming to see my son and grandson playing as Thomas and his sister had done so long ago. For Janet and I, a lifetime had seemed to have passed, well a generation's worth at least.

On our second date after meeting in 1982, I took Janet sailing in English Bay in Vancouver, as was customary for me at the time. It was a cold but sunny January morning after New Year's when we sailed from the inner harbour out into English Bay in the company of dozens of other hardcore, winter sailors. It was a beautiful day, but not much wind. The surrounding mountains were covered in a fresh dumping of snow, and while we drifted along, we could see, from high above, the Grouse Mountain ski hill was as busy as ever. My buddy and girl-hunting sidekick at the time, Campbell Gilbert, came along as crew. Cam was my wingman the night Janet and I had met, so I thought it would make Janet more comfortable having him along to chaperone. However, only a little.

Figure 73. Damien playing with the "surfer dude" that his dad had made him as we approach Isla Tortuga, at the southern end of Isabela.

I possessed dreams of voyaging around the world, so if I liked a girl well enough to ask her on a second date, it was usually to my boat for a day of sailing. My reasoning at the time was if they didn't like boats, succumbed to sea sickness while strolling along the dock or did not believe sailing around the world was the grandest idea ever, our second date would be our last.

At the time, I was a professional diver working on the oil rigs in the high Canadian Arctic, living on the drill ship *Explorer 4*. On my days off, my parents and I would take off on our 1969 Columbia 36 to explore the wild British Columbia coast, fishing and scuba diving as we went.

I was 22 years old and my whole life revolved around the sea. I knew what I wanted out of life and saw little logic in getting involved with a woman, any women, who dreamt of horse ranches and not sea horses. So needless to say, a sweet wind blew into my life that day, and on our second date, Janet stole my heart. Although she wasn't initially on board for a world cruise, she did decide I was workable.

So here Janet and I are, some 33 years later, in the Galápagos Islands with our two adult children and our eldest grandchild. Who would have thought after all these years and divergent trails, paths and courses we have taken, willingly or not, they would have led us to this magnificent place in time? Three generations of Gunsons were on a voyage of a lifetime, sharing the sail between Santa Cruz and Isabela Islands.

The forecasted gale never did appear, so we had a pleasant and uneventful sail to arrive at Isabela long before dark. Once settled in, I made a quick radio call to the harbour master and to Jim, our agent, letting them know we had arrived safely. Thankfully, we were already known to all, which meant a visit and inspection was not necessary.

Coming back to Isabela was a bit like coming home, and it was pleasant to be back in a quiet anchorage devoid of the constant flood and ebb of noisy tourists. We had anchored right in our old spot, with our stern tied again to the yellow mooring buoy. Using the excuse of needing to check the anchors' set, I jumped in for a swim, not that I needed a reason to make the leap and neither did the kids.

One of the first things I eagerly wanted to do on Isabela was to introduce the kids, and in particular Damien, to our favourite sea lion. That is if our playful friend with flippers remembered to come by and make a house call. After all, we had been gone for over a week and perhaps he had forgotten our game. I needn't have worried because on the morning of our first day back, he came for a visit and knocked.

I was standing at the galley sink clearing away the breakfast dishes when I heard the unmistakable telltale "knock" of the bubbles he would blow while under the hull of *Maiatla*. I ran on deck to peer over the side, and there he was staring back at me with those big puppy dog eyes.

"Damien, grab your mask and snorkel. We are going to go swimming with our friend the sea lion."

We wasted no time in leaping overboard. At first, Damien was a little leery of being in the water with a creature as big as he was, so he stayed close to his dad. However, after watching his granddad chase the sea lion as fast as he could, never able to catch him, Damien became more at ease and was soon joining in by pursuing the friendly sea lion around and under the boat. The two, who were kids of a different species, came nose to nose a couple of times as the sea lion went around one side of the keel while Damien ducked around the other. It was hilarious to watch, as both would realize a head-on collision was imminent. Bubbles, arms and fins flew as they frantically put all engines in reverse.

The sea lion came around most every day, and on some days, he brought a friend. It was twice as much fun to see Damien chasing one sea lion while the other followed behind, close enough to get kicked in the face once in a while. Our stern mooring buoy was also a source of amusement. The sea lions would swim tight circles around the buoy while we chased them. Between our games, they would often sleep or sun themselves on the buoy, waiting for us to come back into the water.

The stern mooring line became a favourite hangout for Damien, as well as for the rest of the crew. The line had some slack in it, so when you sat on it, you would be almost neck deep in the water. But when a swell passed by and the boat surged forward, the line would be drawn tight. While fighting to keep your balance, the line would lift us clear out of the water. It was kind of a vertical swing powered by the ocean swells, great fun for all, and particularly a favourite game of Damien's.

Figure 74. Damien playing with our sea lion friend that came daily to play.

Having a sea lion visit the boat regularly was not an uncommon event for the crew of the *Maiatla,* as it has happened before. Some seven years previous, while cruising the Hawaiian archipelago, Janet and I spent a blissful week anchored behind the reef on the tiny island of Ni'ihau. The isolated island is called the forbidden island because you require written permission to visit, permission we did not have. I have always been a big believer that "it's better to plead ignorance and ask for forgiveness later than to ask for permission first." A tactic that doesn't work so well in some third world countries, which I learned on our voyage to Costa Rica. Apparently, my lack of judgment resulted in our making an illegal landing and being caught naked on a beach and held at gunpoint by Nicaraguan Marines. I blame Captain Morgan for that dilemma.

Janet and I had a marvelous week anchored out on Ni'ihau, swimming daily on a magnificent coral reef. During our time at the island, we had received only three visitors. The first was a pair of men with rifles, hunting wild boar in the sand dunes near the boat. They gave a wave and moved on. The second visitor was a lone dark-skinned man on horseback, who had a casting net to fish along shore. He too paid us no mind.

Our third visitor was from a friendly monk seal that followed us in when we first arrive. Once anchored, I dived in to see if I could approach him. Before I knew it, I was chasing the monk around the boat while never getting any closer than an arm's length of him. Our monk seal returned around 9 a.m. each day to continue the play. Janet and I would don our masks and snorkels and attempt to play tag with him, but no matter how hard we swam, we were always it!

Figure 75. One of the two playful friends who loved being chased around the boat.

Back on Isabela, the sea lions were not the only creatures that came around for a regular visit. As often as not, the little penguins came chasing the schools of tiny fish that had taken residence under *Maiatla*. One afternoon while Damien and I were in the water with a sea lion, a single penguin shot by apparently on his way to our buoy, so we followed. Around the buoy's thick anchor cable, schools of tiny silver and yellow fish had congregated, and they were what attracted the little penguin. We watched as the penguin commenced to chase the fish around and around the buoy. It was funny to watch as the penguin never seemed to get close enough to eat any of the fish, but he stayed in hot pursuit while making dozens of dizzying, high-speed turns around the buoy. I wasn't sure if the little penguin was inept at hunting, or if he was just playing or tormenting the tiny school of fish. I had the GoPro camera in the water and was able to get some fantastic footage of the penguin powered merry-go-round.

Even underwater, I could hear Damien laughing almost uncontrollably as he watched the penguin's antics, and when I resurfaced, I noticed that we too were being watched. I called to Damien who was floating on the surface directly in front of me. He was head down, with his face in the water intent on watching the penguin going round and round.

"Hey, Damien, look up!" I called. My grandson first spun around to look at me. Then he flipped back around to see what I was pointing at, and when he did, he came nose to nose with our sea lion, who had been sitting on top of the buoy resting. The sea lion was fascinated with our antics.

Playing with the sea lions became a routine, as either a first thing in the morning or late in the afternoon swim with our friends. Or if they were a no-show, we would swim along the side of the boat, hang off the anchor chain or stern line and wait to see what else came along. Usually, we did not have to wait long.

Chapter 29

Concha de Perla—a Jewel of a Lagoon

"The Sea is the last free place on Earth."
—Ernest Hemingway

Despite swimming and snorkelling off of the boat each day, we still weren't permitted to venture into the nearby Tintoreras islets, which were so tantalizingly close. Unless we paid for a tour, we would not be able to see their wonders. However, nearby, I knew of a place I suspected could be almost as good, and we would be free to visit on our own.

A short walk from the dinghy dock at Puerto Villamil, at the parking lot where our coconut blackmarketeer has his stand, there is a large sign which marks a hidden trail. The winding trail leads through the mangrove swamps until it spills out onto a peaceful saltwater lagoon. Although the bay is unnamed on the chart, the sign reads "Concha de Perla," which translates to "Pearl Shell"—a fitting name for a lagoon that only could be describe as a jewel. The sign displays pictures of prominent wildlife a visitor might expect to see at the lagoon while stating that "Concha de Perla" is surrounded by dense red and black mangroves trees and the shallow waters provide refuge for resting and feeding sea turtles. The sign also states visitors will see rays, flightless cormorants, penguins, pelicans, lava herons and other species. After reading this, we naturally had to check it out.

I had hoped the *Tigress* and her crew, or in particular Damien's friend, Ellie, would be here by now. They planned on spending one more day in Santa Cruz before sailing to Isabela, but there was no sign of them yet. We had been expecting them before dusk the previous day. I tried to contact them on the radio, but no joy on that account. I was starting to consider they might have passed this island by. We would have to wait and see.

We arrived early in the afternoon at Concha de Perla while carting our snorkelling gear, which included wetsuits and dive weights to help us get deep if desired. Damien led the charge into the mangroves where the dirt trail quickly changes into an elevated sidewalk, constructed of weatherworn planks and posts. Here, the knurled and twisted mangrove trees have no respect for the pathway as thick branches challenge the guardrails while forming a dense canopy overhead. At several locations along the trail, we were forced to duck as to not bash our heads on low-hanging limbs that often provided a roost for herons and red-throated frigate birds.

Frigate birds are graceful flyers as they possess long slender wings, not unlike a glider plane. In flight, they are easy to identify by their forked tails, hooked beak and overall sleek appearance. During nesting season, the males are often seen with their throats puffed out like a bright red balloon, a means to attract a mate. Frigates are also notorious pirates of the skies, as they are lazy and prefer to steal another bird's catch rather than hunt for themselves. You will often see gangs of frigates harassing a gull, albatross or booby, snatching a meal from its grip or forcing the tormented to drop its catch, the frigate catching the meal long before it strikes the water. Even worse, these shameless buccaneers will often torment another bird to a point where their victim will regurgitate its last meal, throwing it up just to escape its pursuers.

As you get closer to the lagoon, the roots of the mangrove trees emerge from a salt-white sand and are bathed in clear seawater—a scene similar to our time in Costa Rica. However, the difference here is, instead of having crocodiles resting atop the thick mangrove roots, cute sea lion pups hide among the twisted shoots, waiting for their mothers to return from the open sea. Even though there are no crocs, there are still plenty of reptiles all underfoot. On our walk, we found most of the sidewalk was thick in lethargic iguanas, which, true to their nature, were defiant and refused to move. After taking a moment to look to see if any park guides were about, using the toe of my shoe, I attempted to nudge a large beast out of the way, but he would have none of it. The iguana snapped his head to one side while shooting me a steely glare.

"Andy, it looks like it's going to bite you. You better leave it alone," Janet said as she remained behind, using me a shield in case the lizard made a lunge for my jugular. It was a momentary standoff, but after perhaps sensing my determination and fearing a swift boot, the black devil decided to slowly move off into the water to disappear under the boardwalk. With the largest obstacle now out of the way, Damien moved on, but he was extra careful not to approach too close or to step upon the remaining normally docile creatures.

After 100 metres or so, the sidewalk abruptly ends at a ladder that descends a few rungs to a small floating dock. The view from the dock is spectacular as the lagoon is perhaps 100 metres (328 feet) wide by 1000 metres (3280.4 feet) long and filled with the most beautiful translucent aquamarine water. The outer limits of the lagoon are marked by a barrier of rocks, a rubble reef appearing as if intentionally set like a breakwater to create a pond or boat anchorage. We had seen similar structures in the Hawaiian Islands, but there, the open-sea ponds are artificially enclosed by rock walls (*kuapu*) and controlled by sluice gates (*makaha*) that connect the pond to the sea. The pond's fish stocks and water are replenished by the cycles of the tides.

The Hawaiian ponds are elaborate fish traps created by great feats of engineering while employing massive amounts of labour, performed and maintained over generations. Moli'i Fishpond is one of the largest fishponds in all of Hawaii, encompassing 125 acres and ranging in depth from 1 to 9 metres (4 to 30 feet).

Located on Oahu's windward (east) coast, the fishpond is estimated to be between 600 to 960 years old. Concha de Perla is a fine example of a Hawaiian fish trap, except this trap is in the Galápagos Islands and was wholly constructed by Mother Nature.

The waters in the lagoon looked clear and, in most places, only a couple of metres deep—a fantastic place to snorkel. It would have been all the better if we had the place to ourselves, but unfortunately, that was not the case. The end of the boardwalk, dock and floating dock were covered with local people, men, women and children, all looking to escape the heat of the afternoon by taking a swim. Undeterred, we all changed into our snorkelling gear, and when a gap appeared between a knot of playful teens, we jumped in and quickly made our way out into deep water, away from most of the other swimmers and snorkelers.

For island people, who I suspect grew up with the sea at their doorsteps, I was surprised how many of them didn't appear to be all that skilled at swimming or snorkelling. Many played and thrashed about like dogs that had been tossed in for the first time. Because of obvious insecurities, many of the locals stayed close to the floating dock, not venturing too far away or into the deep water of the outer lagoon. The locals' lack of confidence in the water proved fortuitous for us because on the far side of the lagoon where the waves broke violently upon the reef, there was no one. Once our kids had cleared their masks and adjusted their gear, I lead the way to the far side where I hoped to find some rays and perhaps some sharks to show Damien.

A few metres from the dock, the bottom changes from rocks covered in coral to flat sand that quickly drops off to 3 or 4 metres (9.8 to 13.1 feet) deep. Much of the coral close to shore is dead, as it had been walked upon countless times or picked over by careless or ignorant individuals. Walking on coral kills it.

The sand felt coarse and there wasn't much to see, so we continued on and headed outward towards the reef, which I hoped was in better condition. At the halfway mark, the water shoaled as a rock ledge appeared. As we swam over the rocks, the rush of the incoming tide accelerated in the shallows. At first, I grabbed Damien and Janet's hands and attempted to help them power swim into the current in an effort to get beyond the shallows. From the rock ledge, I could see the bottom sloping downward, getting deeper, so I knew that the current would be weaker there. However, it was no use; the current was too strong. Looking about, I decided on another course.

"Janet! Kids, go to the left and follow this rock ledge towards the shore. Looks like the current won't be as strong there," I said.

My assumption was correct, and the closer to the shore we swam, the weaker the current became, and apparently, I wasn't the only one to have made this discovery. The rock ledge split in two forming a trench 2 metres (6.5 feet) wide and perhaps a metre (3.2 feet) deep or 3 metres (9.8 feet) from the surface. In the still waters of the trench, resting on the bottom was a grey stingray, partially obscured by sand. Coming to a stop, I pointed out the ray to Damien and Janet. Once they had a good look at the creature, I dived down and, ever so carefully, touched it with a gloved hand.

Disturbed but not startled, the ray gave a leisurely flip of its barbed tail and, with sand cascading from its back, slowly swam away.

We continued to swim, finding more trenches filled with an incredible variety of marine life, including healthy patches of hard and soft corals. Apparently, either not many ventured out this far or the people who had were perhaps more appreciative of the reef and took greater care to not damage it.

Gold and silver-striped wrasse, blue neons and bright yellow guineafowl pufferfish peered at us with tiny black eyes from holes in the rocks. Likewise, watching us as we cruised by their lairs where juvenile moray eels, brown and green, red dragons and banded eels, all with jaws agape, tracked our every movement. Moray eels are mouth breathers, so they always appear menacing, constantly opening and closing their mouths, showing rows of razor-sharp teeth as they breathe. To me, they always looked like they are out of breath or panting like a heat-stressed dog.

Back home on the West Coast of Canada, we have an ugly cousin of the moray that possesses the body of an eel, with the jaws and head of pit bull. Wolf eels can grow to be over 2.2 metres (7.2 feet) long and be as thick as a fat man's thigh. Despite their fearsome appearance, wolf eels and moray eels are usually timid and not normally dangerous to swimmers. I have fed crushed sea urchin by hand to giant wolf eels and stroked under their chins, as you would scratch a kitten. In reality, morays and wolf eels are intelligent and inquisitive, with a playful nature.

Still, as a precaution, I reminded everyone not to stick their hands into any hole without looking into it first, lest you want to lose a finger or two. Why would you stick your hand into a hole, you may ask? Well, moray eels and pufferfish are not the only ones that like to hide, spiny lobsters like to also, and this clawless cousin of the Atlantic lobster is almost as tasty.

Schools of yellow and black surgeonfish ignored us as they grazed upon the algae-covered rocks while, in stark contrast, agitated black damselfish, with ivory-coloured lips, charged and bit us if we came too close to their nests. The toothless bite is more annoying than painful, unless of course they score a direct hit upon your unprotected inner thigh.

In the shallows along the shore, we discovered schools of tiny fish of all shapes and colours, surging between boulders and rock crevices or attempting to hide among stands of soft corals. The delicate, fernlike corals appeared as if drawn in pastels of every imaginable colour.

Unlike the hard corals most people are familiar with, which are made of calcium carbonate, creating the hard and often sharp exterior, and have a creature living within, soft corals are different. Octocoral, commonly known as soft corals, have a flexible skeleton made of a protein called gorgonin. Their skeleton also contains calcium carbonate, but only in small clumps called spicules. The polyps of soft corals have eight tentacles, hence the name octocoral, "octo" meaning eight. We had to be careful not to brush against the delicate plant-like corals, as not to damage them. However, these living organisms are not without some defences. Some are armed with thousands of stinging tentacles, not usually dangerous to swimmers, but carelessly brushing against them can result in a nasty rash. Not to mention, they often transfer parasites to unprotected skin, which can also irritate the hell out of you in more ways than one.

After leaving the ocean, it is always recommended to have a complete shower as soon as possible. The reason is the ocean is the primordial soup, the genesis of all life on Earth, and after you take a leisurely swim in the ocean, you will emerge cloaked from head to toe in hundreds, if not thousands, of every tiny pint-sized thing that slimes, slithers, oozes and bores in the ocean. You are now their new host. Welcome aboard! Under high magnification, the likes of these creatures that now call you home, resemble everything imaginable, from every space alien movie that you have ever witnessed. I believe that if we truly took note with what collects upon our skins while in the ocean, we would never dare to don a bathing suit ever again. Swimming naked is worse!

I remember an incident that occurred some years back while snorkelling off an island of Nuku Hiva in the South Pacific. Mike Keller, Kelly Keller and I had been preparing a yacht for sea that we were hired to return to San Diego. We had all been working hard, so we decided to take a break and go for a snorkel out at the point. Kelly declined to go, but Mike, my friend, and the other Mike, the boat's owner, thought it was a good idea, and off we went. We found the perfect place to snorkel on a reef below a great rock wall, which protected us from the surf surging by. As we were dressing in, it dawned on me that I neglected to bring a weight belt. Without the belt, it would be difficult for me to dive deep and stay down. Apparently, my large lung capacity (30 per cent greater than average) and some buoyant belly fat (what percentage above average I dare not guess) would make it difficult to keep my butt on the bottom.

To combat the buoyancy problem, I dived down and chose a pretty pink and red rock, the size of a large lettuce and shoved it inside of by baggy shorts. Aside from looking like I was an advertisement for some wildly successful male enhancement drug, the problem was solved.

We had a fine swim. Sometime later, back in the dinghy on the long ride back to the boat, I started to notice my groin was on fire. Not a jock itch or athletes foot kind of fire, but a "holy crap I've got lit briquettes in my pants, and there is a major bush fire underway!" kind of fire.

I yelled to Mike to stop the dinghy. As soon as I could, I leapt to my feet and ripped my shorts off and began frantically checking out the goods for damage. Well, it was instantly recognizable that I had a major bug infestation as we could all see the little beasts, with their antenna and claws, scurrying for cover as I attempted to brush them off of me.

To make matters worse, the nice soft pink and red coral that covered the rock and took the roughness out of its sharp edges had oozed some sort of poisonous mucus, which I was now doing a magnificent job of smearing into every nook, cranny and scrotum crease in my effort to evict the unwanted colony of bugs.

To add insult to injury was the laughter coming from my friends while I was undergoing a natural napalming of my genitalia. It took a couple of dips in the ocean and a hot soapy shower back on the boat to delouse myself. It itched for a solid week. Okay it may not have been my finest hour, but I learned a valuable lesson that day.

Figure 76. The penguins were cute and paid us no mind, as we were able to swim right up to them.

I followed Damien, who dived after fish as we made our way to the rocks of the eastern shore of the lagoon. While checking out a hole to look for lobster, I heard Damien squeal in excitement. When I looked, a black and white little penguin first circled him and then Melissa before taking off in a hurry, heading for the mangrove trees nearby. Melissa and Thomas took turns finding things to show Damien, seashells, sand dollars and the like. We were all having a grand time.

We all moved inshore as far as we could without leaving the water. At the edge of the lagoon, the black lava rocks rose out of the water, and there, sunning themselves, were hundreds of marine iguanas. If we were careful, we could swim right up to them, close enough to touch them if we dared. The iguanas perhaps assumed we were simply some type of cycloptic sea lions, so they decided to pay us no mind.

Standing in among the loafing lizards were flightless cormorants airing their stubby wings, the birds appearing as if they were some sort of security attachment guarding the iguana colony. Also in the mix were a few Nazca boobies with their green feet.

The surprisingly antisocial birds were pecking and squawking at their iguana neighbours as they demanded more room to preen. It was as if the Nazcas were human children in the back seat of a car, screaming at a sibling not to touch them, even if they weren't.

We spent some time in the shallows with the swimming iguanas. Then, when I noticed the current had slackened, I suggested we head further out into the lagoon to see what else we could find. Led by an excited Damien, we crossed the rock ridge, and there was our first sea turtle. It sat on the bottom, grazing on some weeds. Grabbing my grandson's hand, we dived down, and Damien ever so carefully reached out to touch the shell of the hawksbill turtle. The animal was almost as big as he was and didn't appear to mind being touched.

In the deep water, beyond the ledge, we encountered several more sea turtles, some swimming, others resting or feeding on the bottom. One particularly large turtle was getting a thorough cleaning. The animal was on the bottom, but had extended its fins to lift itself clear of the sand, permitting tiny fish, wrasses, to swim under its belly and pick off its parasites.

We encountered spotted eagle rays and stingrays, and it was here Damien had his first encounter with a live shark. I had already talked with Damien about what to do if we saw a shark, so he was prepared, but obviously a little nervous when the metre long grey reef shark swam in to check us out. We stayed still while maintaining eye contact. The shark encounter would be one of a few that day and each was exciting. We had all spent the better part of 3 hours in the water, and some of us were getting tired and a bit cold despite wearing wetsuits. I suggested we start to head back to the beach, but first, I wanted to make a little side trip.

This was not my first dive in the lagoon, as Mark and I had explored Concha de Perla a couple of times when we had first come to Isabela. On the west side of the lagoon is a cluster of thick mangrove trees growing atop of many small islands or rocks clumped close to together. The trees of each island have grown together, creating a thick nearly impenetrable canopy. However, underneath at the root level, there are channels and tunnels we could swim through while penetrating deep into the mangroves. We discovered a watery labyrinth hidden under the mangroves. When we dived in the clear water, we could clearly see the maze of channels and archways comprising this island chain, but these channels were not visible from the surface, as the drooping branches touched and penetrated the water's surface.

I took Damien's hand and told him to stay close to me. After taking deep breaths, we dived and headed for a gap in the rocks and where the surface was a tangle of tree branches and roots, creating a tunnel. At the entrance, I gave a hard push, shoving Damien down and under the branches while propelling him through the split in the rocks.

After a couple of metres or so, we resurfaced in a small patch of open water inside the mangroves canopy. Janet, Melissa and Thomas soon followed. It was incredible swimming through the mangroves this way. We followed the channel for a short way, exploring, and often, we were forced to dive under tree limbs and branches to carry on. In some parts, where the channel narrowed to a point, we could touch both sides with our arms outstretched.

Figure 77. While exploring the reef, we disturbed a stingray that took flight to find less crowded waters.

I don't recall who asked, but someone made an enquiry about snakes. A reasonable question considering that we were swimming through a South American jungle. Nevertheless, these islands only have three species of land snakes, one being the Galápagos racer, which is a constrictor and hunts fish. The racer is said to be only mildly venomous and is considered non-aggressive and harmless to humans.

As in most of the world's tropical seas, here in the Galápagos, there is a sea snake that is notoriously venomous and can grow up to 80 centimetres (31.5 inches) long. The yellow-bellied sea snake is an aquatic snake, living its entire life cycle at sea, feeding on surface dwelling fish and eels. This sea snake is an ambush predator, with its young born at sea or in mangroves or tidal lagoons. Normally shy, they present little danger to humans, as they are not aggressive and possess tiny mouths that make it difficult to bite something as large as a person. Still, I suppose you could have one clamp upon your lower lip or earlobe. With those facts out in the open, everyone was more or less back at ease, but I did find myself looking up into the branches and around the tree roots a little more carefully.

We never did bump into any sea snakes, but Nick and Marina had the good fortune to encounter one while swimming at nearby Tortuga Bay. Nick and Marina were snorkelling, admiring a school of translucent needle fish, when Marina spotted something on the bottom that looked like a piece of rope—except it moved! Her survival instincts kicked in, and by the time she realized that it was a yellow-bellied sea snake, she was already half way to the beach, leaving a sizable wake. Safe in the shallows, Marina took a moment to search for Nick, who had been just seconds ago by her side. There treading water some 30 metres (98 feet) away was Nick, but he was nowhere near where she had seen the snake.

"Did you see the snake?" she called out to him.

"Why do you think I'm way over here?" he answered.

Marina just gave me a blank look when I asked, "Did you get any pictures?"

There were thousands of juvenile fish darting between the densely-packed mangrove roots, which was not surprising as many species of fish use the mangroves as a nursery, affording protection to their young from large predators. However, not all the fish we encountered were tiny. As we explored the deep channels, we came across several giant blue-chin parrotfish and a massive box pufferfish that was as large as a medium-size dog. The pufferfish possess tiny pectoral fins that appear to be woefully inadequate for propulsion and a leathery skin spotted with sharp spines, which it could erect by puffing up if agitated. This fish bore huge black eyes the size of silver dollars and clearly wasn't impressed we were following him through his maze.

We had not gone far when the ebbing tide began to tug upon me. Fearing it would increase in strength and suck us deeper into the mangroves, and perhaps into places that we didn't want to go, I decided it was time to leave, so we searched for a tunnel that would lead us back to the lagoon. By the time we made it back to the floating dock, we were all exhausted, and as we found out later, someone with a thinning hair line had sunburnt the top of his head. We stopped at the beach concession stand by the coconut salesman and had an ice cream, and for me, a beer to wash it down. So far the lagoon had been a real highlight for the kids, and Damien couldn't stop talking about swimming with the turtles and saying, "Dad, did you see me touch that turtle? Did ya? Did you, Granny?"

We would have a serene night on the boat. A lovely breeze had taken hold, and the air was cool after the sun disappeared. Thankfully, no rain fell this night, so we were able to leave all the hatches open and windsocks in place. Being as exhausted as we all were, we all slept like the dead.

Chapter 30

Breeding Tortoises, Flamingos and Our Wayward Taxi Driver

"A sailor is an artist whose medium is the wind. Live passionately, even if it kills you, because something is going to kill you anyway."

—*Webb Chiles, sailor*

The day after our Concha de Perla Laguna diving expedition, we awoke early as the plan was to head to town to visit the tortoise breeding centre before the heat of the day set in. I also needed to talk to Jim about arranging a couple of other tours. The kid's time with us was so limited, and with the likelihood of all of us being here again slim to none, we needed to make the most of it. Therefore, with that in mind and against my frugal, cruising principles, I decided to loosen the purse strings a little and splurge for a special excursion. We had heard so many good things about Los Tuneles from others on shore that we decided it was a must do for the kids, and I would need Jim to recommend a tour group.

I was the first up that morning, so after making a cup of tea for Janet, I stumbled topside to greet the new day here in paradise while rolling up the cockpit windows, which we normally dropped during the night to keep the seats dry if it were to rain. There was no sign of rain, but the decks glistened with heavy dew, which felt cold on my bare feet. After checking to make sure the anchor snubber line was not chaffing, I looked aft and noticed something was wrong with my makeshift flopper stoppers. The heavy line that suspends the two canvass buckets and lead weights was missing.

Apparently, I had become complacent about checking for wear and the line chafed through, right at the end of the pole where the line passes through the block. It wasn't the first time it had done this, and I dare say it won't be the last. The swells that had been wrapping around the point had subsided, so it was not a problem at the moment. However, I decided that I'd better make a dive to retrieve the gear before the swells pick up and the boat begins to roll, which usually happens in the middle of the night. If that were to happen, Janet would demand that I do something—and now! I made a mental note to get the lost gear after we returned from town and have the flopper stopper back in place before nightfall.

It was shaping into a decent-looking day. To the south, the tumbling clouds were breaking up, creating hollow shadows that shifted as if fleeing the early morning sun.

The great volcano Sierra Negra was hidden this morning in what appeared to be grey floss, all fluffy and flowing, with slanting sun rays catching ethereal wisps of clouds. Hidden under the dense cloud cover, it occurred to me that that mountain, under its concealing cloak, could have vanished and travelled anywhere it wanted and I would have been none the wiser. I have seen a whole island at sea vanish behind a squall's dense mass. I wondered now, had we not sailed on, would we have seen the island return from its travels once the squall quieted? Odd thoughts this morning for sure, and I obviously needed to pay more attention, looking for both chafing and wayward landmasses.

I had hoped to find *Tigress* anchored right next to us, but no such luck. A glance to seaward in search of a sail was similarly fruitless. Disappointed as I was, I didn't expect to see them, as they would not have dared to enter at night if they could at all help it, and to see them arrive this morning would have entailed them hauling anchor before midnight last night at Santa Cruz. No, they would not have done that either. While still scanning the seas, I heard a voice call to me from the cockpit. It was Damien, and he had his head stuck out the front window.

"Hey, Granddad! What ya doing?"

"Morning, buddy. Come up here, and I will show you," I said.

Damien had taken to boat life well, which I had no doubt he would, considering his lineage. He enjoyed sleeping in his dad's old cabin, and I made sure he learned as much about being a cruiser as I could. I had him help me check the engine oil before start up, and he lent a helping hand as I checked the alternator belts for tension. Like most kids his age, he drank it all in.

"I came up here to look to see if this line here was getting worn from being pulled on all the time," I explained. Damien knelt to take a serious look at the line I had indicated.

"But why have you tied the rope to the chain, Granddad? Isn't the chain stronger than the rope?"

"Yes, buddy, the chain is stronger, but the line has a special purpose. It's like this: See how the anchor chain is pulled real tight? Well, the chain is made of steel and it does not stretch, and when the boat is pushed by a swell, it jerks hard on the chain which can damage the anchor windless—this machine here that pulls the chain back in to pick up the anchor. The 3 metres (9.8 feet) of line, we put on stretches a lot, and it acts like a shock absorber so that the boat doesn't jerk so hard. By tying the line around the cleat here, the stress is taken off of the anchor windless and transfers the strain to a strong part of the boat. You understand, bud?"

After a closer inspection of the windless and twin snubbers, Damien agreed it was a good idea.

"Another thing, bud, on a sailboat, we don't call them ropes, we call them lines, sheets, guys or halyards. Every line on a boat has a proper name, just like your proper name is Damien. Get it?"

I could see the wheels churning in his head before he asked, "So we have no rope here then, right, Granddad?"

"No, not exactly, bud. We have one rope and it's sewn into the luff of the mainsail, and even it has its own name. It's called the 'boltrope' and that is the only 'rope' on *Maiatla*. Cool, eh?"

I pulled back the mainsail cover on the boom next to the mast to show Damien the boltrope. My eight-year-old grandson seemed to comprehend, but to test my assertion that everything had a name, Damien, in a playful manner, pointed to various lines and asked what their names were. After several minutes of playing this "name game," he was duly impressed. Our game was interrupted by another call.

"Dad, mum wants to know if you're going to cook pancakes and bacon this morning?" It was Thomas's turn to stick his head out the window and call to us on the foredeck.

"Yeah, bud, we will be right there," I said. "I was just teaching Damien the ropes."

I'm not sure if Damien truly understood the joke, but he laughed as if he had.

"And oh, yes, mum also says the shower sump isn't working again," Thomas added before disappearing back below.

As our lives are on shore, there are certain routines and chores that cannot be avoided, and meals, dishes and home maintenance are always a constant.

After breakfast, it was a quick trip ashore, and as if by some miracle, we caught a taxi in the parking lot. We decided to take advantage of our good fortune. I instructed the driver to take us straight to the *Tortoise Breeding y Centro de Visitantes,* the Tortoise Breeding and Visitors Centre. The visitor centre was located on the far west end of town, a little over a kilometre past the Booby Trap. The cabbie dropped us off in a nearly deserted parking lot, next to a circular sign that read *"Centro de Visitantes"* and depicted a pair of giant tortoises in the midst of humping their brains out.

"I think this is it," I said to everyone.

The lot contained only two other trucks and one tour bus. Not a bumper crowd; the place was obviously not busy. But that's the way we like it. For some strange reason, I was reminded of what my father said when our family visited Disneyland in Florida, where the parking lots span several acres and were normally full to capacity. So, at the breeding centre, after we all piled out of the truck in the deserted parking lot, I jokingly said, "Remember where we parked kids!"

Aside from generating some confused looks, my humour failed to get the intended response. Okay, it failed miserably.

"Andy, we are a long way from town. How are we going to get back?" Janet asked, sounding a bit concerned.

"I'll take care of it," I said.

I leaned into the still open door of the taxi and asked the driver if he could come back in two hours to pick us up? He readily agreed, or I reasoned so, as he did not speak any English. To ensure his eager participation, I paid him double our agreed upon fare and shook his hand. Off he went, with a smile.

To our delight, and contrary to the Galápagos policy of sucking every last dollar from each and every tourist, the centre is free to visit. The breeding centre is modern, with a gift shop and small air-conditioned interpretation centre. The displays depict the life cycles of all the island's tortoises and the modern hazards that they now face. Man and all his trappings, in the form of domestic livestock, cattle, dogs, cats, pigs and the imported rats, presented the worst threats to the tortoises survival out in the wild. We walked around several open top pens containing tortoises, with each successive pen holding animals of increasing ages and size. The tortoises ranged from a year old to the eldest that we were over 70.

Aside from the lady in the gift shop, there was hardly anyone around, just a handful of Ecuadorians taking pictures of the reptiles and a pair of young women in their 20s raking tortoise poop in one of the pens. Tortoise poop was everywhere! Where the people were from the bus, I could only guess. I approached the two women and asked them in Spanish how old the largest tortoise was. The massive brute stood nearby, eating leaves and grunting at a young male, warning him to stay away from his breakfast. I was surprised to get my reply in English. The ladies were from Minnesota and were here on a working holiday as volunteers at the breeding centre.

Each of them were here for a month. They roomed with local families and worked at the centre four or five hours each day with weekends off. The girls informed me they had to pay for their own flights, but room and board were provided. Noble no doubt, but when they were told they would be working directly with the tortoises at the breeding centre, they were not informed that 90 per cent of their time would be taken up by collecting poop and hauling leaves to feed the animals.

Near the end of our tour, we came across several elevated pens capped with a fine steel mesh and inside were the youngest tortoises of the centre, ranging from a few days to a year old. Each of the tiny tortoises had a white number written on its back for identification. Thomas lifted Damien so that he could see properly into the cages.

It was fast approaching 10 a.m., and despite the thick leafy canopy overhead, the heat was building. We were relieved to find the entrance leading to the cool air of the interpretation centre. Inside the small building, no bigger than a double car garage, we found the bus tour people. Sitting on the floor were two dozen children of perhaps 10 to 12 years of age, and all were intently listening to a lady describing each exhibit. The children were on a field trip from the local school, and they were here to learn how to protect their greatest resource, the tortoises.

I'm sure we would have all found the lesson informative, but since it was conducted in Spanish, most was lost to our ears. An hour after our arrival, we had seen all we could see, so we decided to wander further up the road to where Jim said we could find a little lagoon where pink flamingos feed. The road was hot and dusty, but while the pond was worth the visit to see the birds, there was little wind and the clouds had burned off. With the sun scorching, we made a hasty retreat to the parking lot to wait for the taxi to return.

We made ourselves comfortable on a wooden bench carved out of a single log, while taking a hit from my water bottle, I mistakenly placed my Tilley hat upon the ground, but only for a few minutes. When I went to return the hat to my head, I looked inside. There, scurrying around the hat, were hundreds of tiny ants.

If my faith in Isabela's taxi drivers had been shaken before, it was surely crushed this day. We waited an hour past the agreed upon time, and our driver was a no-show. To make matters worse, once the school bus had departed, no one else arrived by taxi, bus or foot. My map of the island showed a wilderness trail that cut through the jungle, past a mangrove swamp and ending at the beach near the Booby Trap. It would be the shortest route back, and I believed it would be much cooler than trudging down the open road, so off we went into the jungle. As expected, the tree cover protected us from the direct sun for part of the kilometre-long trek, but at the midway point, the trees thinned and then vanished altogether, leaving a red gravel path surrounded by midnight black volcanic rock of which, as if just vomited forth from the volcano, expelled a nauseating amount of heat. I cursed the taxi driver and all his confederates who provided me an excellent opportunity to test the limits of my patience and creative range of my profanity. I just had to make sure I was out of ear shot of Damien.

On the upside, the walk through the mangrove swamp and past the lagoon proved interesting as it was wick with waterfowl, more flamingos, and marine iguanas everywhere. At the edge of the lagoon the path transformed into an elevated boardwalk, which cut across the shallow waters, connecting several small islets near the middle. It was a pleasant walk, but as we had often witnessed in the Galápagos when we were there, the maintenance of the boardwalk was lacking. Nevertheless, apparently someone had come along and tried to rectify this problem by removing any planks that were suspect. We had to watch our step, as every few metres or so, one or more rotten planks had been removed, leaving a gaping hole that could swallow a person whole. It wasn't until reaching the end did we hear the sound of a generator and that of an electric skill saw cutting wood. I was pleased to see one man busy replacing the missing planks, but I had to wonder how long ago they had removed the boards before getting to this stage of repair.

The boardwalk finally spilled out onto the sandy beach road 100 metres (328 feet) from the Booby Trap, and Jim's cooler full of frosty Pilsners and freezer stuffed with ice-cream. Back on the beach road, the onshore breeze helped to evaporate the perspiration from our bodies, so we took a moment to let the wind revive us.

"Look, Granddad, more iguanas," Damien excitedly called out as he pointed to one side of the trail next to the road. We all watched as several large iguanas emerged from the dense brush to cross the road and head for the nearby ocean. As we crossed the road to follow, I noticed a street sign on the corner announcing that this particular junction of the road is known as "Iguana Crossing," apparently aptly named. The white sand beach here stretches for a couple of kilometres in either direction. There is a large outcropping of black rock, jutting out of the sand and into the sea. This was where the migrating iguanas we had seen crossing the road were headed. Upon the rocks were hundreds of iguanas ranging from a few inches long to the titans of the beach, large enough for a child to ride, if he dared.

Well, okay, maybe not that big, but the big ones were too large for *Maiatla's* barbeque. I had attempted to take some pictures, but as I was looking through the viewfinder of my waterproof Canon camera, I noticed the image appeared hazy. For the second time this morning, I cursed this reoccurring problem. I first noticed this issue shortly after arriving on San Cristóbal Island, a couple of months previous. The air here is so humid that if you leave your camera exposed to direct sunlight, even for a few minutes, the inside of the lens hazes up, making subsequent photos appear as if taken from the inside of a steam room. The only way to correct the problem is to either leave the camera for 20 minutes inside a pocket or to dip it into the sea to cool it. I was frustrated, as here was a great opportunity to get some impressive shots of these monsters, posturing for each other, and the camera was useless. I had learned to open the camera each night and place it into a Ziploc bag of dry rice to absorb the moisture. A tactic I had forgotten to do of late, and I was paying for it now.

Safely at Jim's tables, I ordered a round of cold waters for all, me included, but I also ordered a cold beer. While enjoying the respite, Janet heard me, in a hushed tone, curse once again. She gave me a questioning look, then asked, "What's the matter now?"

I pointed out into the street, and there coming down the road was our wayward taxi driver. Using a single digit, I gave him a not so friendly wave as he shot by. Some weeks later, Janet and I met a journalist from mainland Ecuador. The pretty young lady asked in excellent English how we were enjoying our visit to the islands. "We love it here," both Janet and I said. "The people have been great, but it's expensive," I added, but I'm sure the journalist already knew that. I did not tell her about the Nazi-like park guides we had met, but I did have a few words regarding the taxi drivers on Isabela and about a particular one that I had paid to return to pick us up at the tortoise centre.

After hearing my tale, she smiled before saying, "You should not have tipped him to come back as that is a sure way to make sure that he won't." She attempted to explain the Latino mindset behind her assertion, but she quickly lost me in their unique brand of logic. These people have a different way of looking at the world, one we from the netherworld of north often find hard to comprehend.

Jim gave me the name of a tour guide to book our tunnel adventure planned for later in the week. The tour office was on the way back to the dock, so we stopped in and made the arrangements. I also asked Jim to line up another excursion for Melissa and I to the vertical volcanic tunnel, again for later in the week. Janet was done with rock climbing, and it was far too dangerous for Damien, so Thomas decided that they too would stay back on the boat and hang out while Melissa and I went spelunking. With plans made we started our long walk back to the dinghy, and not surprisingly, we couldn't find a vacant taxi anywhere.

From the roadside, we spotted another sailboat enter the bay, circle around and drop anchor. To Damien's delight, it was *Tigress* and her crew.

Chapter 31

Los Tuneles, Isabela's Subsea Tunnels

"It isn't the oceans which cut us off from the world—it's the American way of looking at things."
—Henry Miller

Our kid's time with us was rapidly coming to an end. In a few days, we would have to drop the mooring, haul our anchor and head back to Santa Cruz. When we do, we would be departing Isabela for the last time, as we would not be returning, not anytime in the foreseeable future anyway. In Santa Cruz, we would, with great reluctance, put Thomas, Melissa and Damien on a plane bound for home; thus, ending their Galápagos adventure and once again, leaving Janet and I to our solitude.

However, for now, we finally had a chance to get together with the crew of the *Tigress*. Unfortunately, they didn't have plans to stay long on Isabela, only a couple of days in fact. *Tigress* was bound for the Marquesas Islands, and there was a nice weather window developing. The El Niño-inspired contrary southwest wind that had been plaguing the offshore waters of the Galápagos Islands was yielding to a stronger southeast wind, a perfect bearing to launch *Tigress* on its way. It was a window of opportunity of which John and Susan desperately needed to take advantage. Damien's reunion with his friend Ellie would be a short one.

Melissa and I invited the crew of the *Tigress*, Captain John and his son, Carl, Ellie's much older brother, to repel down the vertical magma tube with us. Susan volunteered to stay aboard *Tigress* with young Ellie, who promptly invited Damien over for a day of swimming off of *Tigress* and playing games down below, an agreeable arrangement for everyone.

Melissa and I were on shore early, with Carl and John, to meet our taxi to take us up to Ulisis's ranch. Ulisis was pleasantly surprised to see me again and to return with my daughter for his repelling adventure. After a brief instruction on how to use the gear, we headed back to the ridge top, then down into the volcanic magma tube. Ulisis had his spiel for his guests, and the adventure went on as it had with Janet, Mark and Teri, some three weeks previous. For me, it was just as thrilling the second time, and for Melissa, it was an adventure of a lifetime, as she had never done anything like this before.

It was a grand father–daughter day in the mountain, one I shall cherish for the rest of my life, and from the grin on her face once we resurfaced, I suspect Melissa will also. Back on *Tigress*, Damien and Ellie had an amusing day of swimming and play, and as I suspected, our sea lion friend came to visit and swim with the kids. Janet and Thomas took a day off to loaf about, reading, napping or pecking at some minor boat chores. Thomas was a bit uneasy having his young son off on someone else's boat for the day. After all, we had only known these people for a few days. "What if they sail away and take Damien?" Thomas asked me only half-joking.

I could well appreciate his concern as Kirstin, his wife and Damien's mother, left Damien in Thomas's charge. A continent away from his home in a foreign county, Thomas was especially protective of his young son.

I had to remind Thomas that cruisers were special people, and we were all family out here. I had every confidence in Susan and Ellie to take good care of my grandson. I reminded Thomas of all the times he went to friends' boats to play while we were sailing in México's Sea of Cortez and he was only 13 years old. Many of the older cruisers, who missed their own children or grandchildren, semi-adopted ours. It was not unusual to hear a knock on the hull and to see our neighbours alongside, who'd say, "We are going into town for ice cream. Do Thomas and Melissa want to come?" In San Diego, one Christmas, a similar knock on the hull came, with a request to take our kids to the zoo. Thomas may have been having a "teenage" moment, so he had declined, but nine-year-old Melissa gleefully went and had a magnificent day with Rob and Fiona from SV *Dazo*.

"Don't worry, Thomas," I said. "They are anchored right over there! They aren't going to shanghai Damien!"

The day went well for all, with the only negative note arising when Melissa neglected to put on enough sunscreen and had badly burnt her face while on the ridge top.

That evening as we finished dinner, I received a radio call from *Tigress*; they were pulling anchor and getting underway. We all went topside to wave goodbye and to wish them fair winds and a following sea. John and Carl were on deck, clearing away the ground tackle, but they stopped working only long enough to give us a wave. Susan was on the helm, but we could not see Ellie. Damien called over to ask where she was. Susan gave us a sad look while pointing down below, rubbed her eyes as if she were crying.

"Sorry, buddy," I said as I patted Damien on the back. "Looks like Ellie is too unhappy to come up and say goodbye. I think she is going to miss you."

"Yeah, it was fun playing with her," said Damien while looking and sounding a little hurt. However, as soon as *Tigress* had passed, he turned to me to ask, "Are you going to make French toast for breakfast tomorrow, Granddad?" It would appear sailor Damien had captured his first heart in a foreign port.

Everyone returned below deck to clear away the dishes. I asked Melissa to pour me a glass of wine. I set a cushion against the cabin top so that I could sit comfortably while facing aft. For the following hour, until the sun finally set, I watched *Tigress* clear the outer maker, then hoist all sail, bearing due west. They were departing with a 15-knot breeze on a beam reach. Perfect conditions to commence what will be a month-long sail to their next island, hidden somewhere over the horizon. I could still see the top of her mast as the last of the daylight failed. It has always been tough to say goodbye to cruising friends, even ones you'd just met. We had an early night, as in the morning, we were expecting the tour boat we had hired to come and take us all to go snorkelling at the Los Tuneles.

Despite being exhausted from the day of repelling into the volcano, I had trouble sleeping, and it did not help matters when three sets of rain squalls appeared during the night, forcing me to close all the hatches and ports, only to reopen them a half hour later when the squall passed. I lay awake for the longest time, listening to *Maiatla* and the sounds of the night: the creaking of the mainsheet as the boat gently rolled; the clicking sounds of krill feeding on the algae that grows on the hull; and the spouting and breathing of unseen sea lions as they passed the boat on their way in or out of the anchorage. Sea lions barked and boobies squawked—a protest in the night, perhaps addressed to an encroaching neighbour. Not unsettling noises in the least, but together they were a reminder of all the life surrounding us and where we stood in the world, a place that we were all happy to be, or at least for now.

I wasn't the only one having trouble sleeping. Melissa's sunburn turned out to be more severe than we first though. Janet lathered our daughter's face with a burn free ointment, so much so that Melissa's face resembled a glazed donut. Every year when Melissa joins us on the boat, despite being careful and constantly reminded by Janet and me, she always gets burned somehow and somewhere. She was getting close to the end of her trip, and we were hopeful this year she would be spared, but no such luck.

Damien received his wish, and it was bacon and French toast for breakfast. We had pulled our diving gear together the night before, so we were ready to go once our ride showed. Sadly, Melissa would have to forgo this trip, as we didn't want to risk her being in the sun, out on the water for a full day with the burn she already had. With a miserable look, she waved to us and said, "Have fun." We loaded onto the motor launch and raced out of the harbour.

We were not the only people headed out to Los Tuneles; we had to share our ride with a small group, eight others, mostly younger folks and a couple of children. As they spoke Spanish and little English, I assumed they were from the mainland here on holiday. They had loaded up on shore and, in a friendly manner, welcomed us when they took us off of *Maiatla*. A crewman offered us all a life jacket if we wanted one, but they were not mandatory. Thomas put one on Damien, but the rest of us declined.

The high-speed sports boat came with a two-man crew. A friendly dark-skinned deckhand named Juan and the boat's captain, who Juan introduced as John Travolta. It was shocking when the driver turned in his seat to great everyone; he truly was a spitting image of the famous actor. He too was friendly. I called him John, as his real name was too difficult for me to get my tongue around.

Juan spoke good English, and he made sure to translate everything for our benefit. Jim's recommendation was a good one.

The ride west along the coast was a fast and wet one. Janet and I took a seat in the stern of the boat in the corner where we learned waves and spray boarded whenever the boat rolled to starboard, but we did not mind, as the water was warm and the air already hot. We were bound for Cabo Rosa on a deserted and barren stretch of coast, which lay 24 kilometres (13 nautical miles) to the west of Puerto Villamil. John Travolta took great care to drive the boat up each swell to minimize the boat's pounding, an effort the inter-island ferry captains refused to do. After a half hour out, the boat slowed as we approached a pinnacle that stuck straight out of the sea. Roca Union lays some 2.4 kilometres (1.5 miles) offshore, and it is an impressive site. We watched the 3-metre (9.8-feet) swell running, pounding the seaward side of the rock with a relentless battering. Still the rock refused to submit and remained stoic and unmoving. White water surged and tumbled around the rock in a seething bubbling mass.

Juan informed us that this rock was a favourite fishing spot of the Nazca boobies, which fish closer to shore than blue-footed boobies, an adaptation that allowed the birds not to compete for the same food source. Juan went on to say that during El Niño, in years like this one, anchovies become scarce and the big fish have to look elsewhere for food, but that this rock causes an upwelling of the nutrient-rich Peru Current. Roca Union is a fish magnet, so life abounds here. I would have jumped in for a snorkel if Captain Travolta had permitted me. It would have been magnificent, I'm sure. The boat made a few circles around the rock before racing off, but this time we were headed back towards shore and our first snorkelling spot.

The shoreline here is low, less than a metre above high tide. The low-laying geography extends for many kilometres inshore. The land is comprised of black volcanic rock, broken and covered by a thick growth of mangrove trees. John Travolta ran the boat straight for the shore and rocks until we were almost aground, then he made a sharp turn around a barely submerged reef and slowed as we entered a tiny cove of a couple of hundred metres (328 feet) wide.

The cove is protected from the surf by a point that deflects the swell. I could see the sea bottom under the boat, but I was disappointed that the water clarity was not good; in fact, it was downright murky. I suspected the turbidity was caused by recent rain runoff. So far, I was not impressed, but I didn't want my disappointment to affect Damien's experience, so I remained upbeat about the snorkel. We suited up and hit the water, and with Juan as our in-water guide, we were off to explore. As we followed Juan towards the mangrove-encrusted shore, he stopped short and then swam in a tight circle. Juan had found one of the dozens of sea turtles we would encounter in the protected bay. For over an hour, we explored in the 2- to 3-metre (6.5- to 9.8-foot) deep water where we encountered not only turtles, but bat and stingrays, moray eels and countless other fish. Near the point, Juan led us to a submerged cave and instructed us to dive and have a look inside. When we did, we saw four large grey reef sharks resting on the bottom of the sandy tunnel. Off in the distance at the back of the cave, perhaps 10 metres (32.8 feet) away, the sunlight beamed in through a pair of openings, creating an ominous-looking shadow as a large shark was silhouetted against the intense aquamarine glow. The additional entrances permitted the current to flow through the tunnels, which is what made the spot so attractive for the sharks.

Some sharks must constantly swim to keep oxygen-rich water flowing over their gills, but others are able to pass water through their respiratory system by a pumping motion of their pharynx. Sitting on the bottom with their nose pointing into the current aids in this process, as it allows them to breathe with far less effort.

Back on the surface, I said, "Ah, Damien, you just got to see this. There are sharks in the cave. Do you want me to help you get down and have a look?"

Needless to say, he was in. I instructed Damien to take a deep breath, and then taking his hand, we dived in together. Once at the entrance of the cave, I pulled Damien into the hole, but only a little ways. I stopped and pointed to a 1-metre (3.2-feet) shark resting on the bottom, close enough for Damien to reach out and touch it if he wanted—not surprisingly, he didn't.

Thomas and I took turns helping Damien to dive to see the sharks. It was amusing seeing how excited he was by it all. Damien was positively giddy with joy. It made my heart smile. I heard a call from Juan; he wanted us to move on. Juan then led the others through a narrow split in the rocks that spilled out on the backside of a tiny island. Janet, Thomas and Damien followed, but I took a few minutes to make one last dive led by my video camera. Inside the cave, I manage to video a close-up shot of one of the sharks. I sank to the bottom and crept forward with my GoPro in hand. However, the shark decided I had gotten close enough. With a sharp flick of his tail and in a whirl of sand and sediment, he shot off and out one of the distant holes.

I was undeterred, as the other three sharks were still on the far side of the tunnel, so I went in hot pursuit, in an effort to record some more video. By the time I realized it, I was nearly out of breath and only midway through the tunnel. I decided it was easier to carry on than to turn around and head back. I hoped the holes on the far side were as big as they looked and I was able to get out that way. If not, I was sure I would be looking much like a member of the Blue Man Group by the time I back tracked and got out.

A good two minutes after I entered the submerged tunnel, the sharks exploded out of the far entrances with me hardly a tailfin behind. I believe I may have elbowed one of them out of the way in a near frantic bid to reach the surface. In my excitement to make some good video, I had pushed my breath-holding limits. On a good day, if I take it easy, I can push my time into the two-and-a-half-minute range, but barely—

still, decent for a guy who is a five-spot over 50 years old. In my heyday at 20 years old, and attending the College of Oceaneering in Wilmington, California, my commercial diving school, I held the class record for the longest breath hold. Timed by the instructor, performing a "dead man's float," with my face in the water, I held my breath for four minutes and 10 seconds. It's interesting to consider that they say you start to go brain dead after three minutes without oxygen. Guess that could explain a few of my own personal quirks. I believe I could have lasted a little longer, but as I lay there, face down in the water and butt in the air, I heard a classmate yell, "He's cheating! He's breathing through his asshole!"

Figure 78. A cave full of sharks.

I dammed near drowned as I started laughing while still underwater.

Back on the surface I could no longer see the group. The little islands I had just swum under were larger than I had first thought, so I decided that it would be quicker to take a couple of deep breaths and head back the way that I had come.

Back on the right side, I found the gap the group had swam through. The tide must have changed because I was given a push as the stiff current took hold of me. Swimming hard in an effort to catch up, I wasn't focusing on what was ahead or thinking of what may be coming my way. When I reached the narrowest part of the short passage, a torpedo-like object with black beady eyes was racing directly at me hell-bent for leather. If it weren't for the agility and a sudden dodge to the right at the last possible moment, the sea lion and I would have had a messy head on collision.

Don't know who looked more startled, but if he had crapped himself, at least he would not have done it inside his wetsuit.

Figure 79. A wild seahorse.

By the time I caught up to everyone, Juan had found something else of interest and something I had never seen in all my years of diving. Next to the massive root of a mangrove tree, with its tail wrapped around a root, was a live seahorse. It didn't look real, appearing more like a rubber bathtub toy. I suspected that it had been placed there for the tourist to view and to photograph, but when I moved in close, the incredible little creature moved. The seahorse, looking as though it were made of mahogany, was approximately 10 centimetres (4 inches) long and would fit in the palm of my hand.

We would encounter other seahorses on the way back to the boat, as well as egrets, flightless cormorants, blue-footed boobies and even penguins—lots and lots of penguins. The marine life here rivalled if not exceeded that of Concha de Perla. Unfortunately, the poor visibility made for some difficult picture taking. It was a great adventure, nonetheless, but once back aboard the boat, I learned we were not done, not by a long shot.

John Travolta fired up the boat, and we raced back offshore to round the point. On the far side, we paralleled the shore for a few hundred metres. Looking inland, I could see hundreds of tiny islands protruding barely above the surface, and it looked like a great place to snorkel, but the problem was the swell.

The 3-metres (9.8-feet) waves charged towards the shore until they hit the shallows where they grew to monstrous proportion before breaking in a roaring flurry of sea foam and spray. We were walled off from shore, or so I though. Our boat came to a complete stop and when I looked over at Juan and John Travolta, I recognized the look in their eyes as they stared over their shoulders at the incoming swells.

No, they can't be, I said to myself. They were timing the swells as I do when attempting a beach landing in our dinghy. No sooner had the realization crossed my mind that they were going to take a stab at running in than Juan yelled "Hold on everyone!" And with that, Captain Travolta thrust the twin throttles forward to the stops. Like a bat out of hell, we took off, racing directly towards the surf and rocks. They had obviously done this many times and knew exactly where the cut was in the reef. With ease, we hitched a ride on a big wave and surfed in, the white water and black rocks menacing us on either side, until we hit a patch of calm water on the inside. We had safely arrived at Los Tuneles, and the journey in alone was well worth $79 USD each for the trip.

Figure 80. Damien has a close encounter with a lazy sea lion at Los Tuneles.

Los Tuneles is an area consisting of hundreds of acres of tiny islets, many of which are joined together by natural stone archways and Venetian-like channels and moats, crisscrossing the landscape. Much of this incredible topography was formed when a series of old magma tubes near the surface collapsed, creating an intricate array of water-filled channels and bridges.

Ever so carefully, we navigated the placid waterways, not much wider than the beam of our boat, until we came to a natural dock or landing spot. Juan led the way ashore so that we could walk over stone bridges, studded with tall cacti. Unlike the turbid waters where we had just snorkeled, the water within these channels was crystal clear as if you were looking into a massive aquarium where parrot fish and hawksbill turtles leisurely swam. I asked Juan if we could snorkel in here. He said no, but we could further out. We ate the lunch provided, after which we loaded back into the boat and moved to our next snorkelling destination. We did not have to go far.

Still behind the protective reef and in the tranquil clear waters, Juan tied our boat to a mooring hook set in a tiny rock that rose out of the sea. The tiny pinnacle rose out of the water next to a small island infested with penguins. It was here we would spend another hour exploring. Back in the water, I was pleased to see that the submarine geography matched what we had seen above the water. What lay before us were countless tunnels, archways and a pearl white sand bottom that reflected the sun's piercing rays, creating a sparkling starburst that rippled with the wavelets. This time, Juan stayed aboard the boat and the group was free to swim and explore on their own. Janet, I and the kids had a great time, and when Juan finally called us all back to the boat, I had to force myself to leave. I could have spent days here. It was better than I had imagined.

Our departure from behind the reef and our bolt back to the open sea through the surf were no less exciting. We charged up massive waves that were threatening to break upon us. The trip back to the harbour was dull by comparison, but no one minded. We were all exhausted, and from the looks on everyone's faces, they were happy to be so.

Figure 81. Damien and Janet take a moment to rest and have a look at a few stray penguins. Directly below is one of the entrances to the shark cave.

After dinner aboard *Maiatla,* we reviewed the pictures we had taken, and it was almost as exciting to view them as it was to be there. I watched Melissa as she studied the pictures, and I could see she was heartbroken to have missed it all.

"How's the face, hun? Feeling any better?" I asked after shutting down the laptop and slideshow.

"Yes, Dad, that stuff mum put on is awesome. It doesn't hurt, and I don't think I'm even going to peel," She added hopefully.

"Well, hun, tell you what. If your burn is much better by tomorrow, how about just you and I go back out to the tunnels. What do you think?" I didn't need an answer I could see her reply in her blotchy-gooey face.

After a single day of rest, because I sorely needed it, Melissa and I hitched a ride with John Travolta for a visit out to the tunnels—and this time, the surf was much larger than the last. What a ride!

The second go at the tunnels was as grand as my first, and I enjoyed leading Melissa through underwater arches and long tunnels. We even managed to flush out a lobster, the first I had seen in the Galápagos, only if you don't count the ones we eyed at the fisherman's market.

Figure 82. Melissa and Andrew exploring ashore at the Los Tuneles—a great father–daughter day

The spiny lobster was perfectly barbeque sized, and I caught and releasing him twice, just to keep in practice, mind you. If the local guides got upset with us for "illegally" looking at a passing manta ray in the harbour, I could only imagine how incensed they would be if I started hauling live lobster aboard and dipping them in garlic butter.

Lathered in sunscreen, Melissa fared well, having no further complications with the sunburn, and it was another proud father and daughter adventure that will last us a lifetime.

Our time on Isabela came to an end with all the suddenness of a lighting strike. The morning after my last visit to the Los Tuneles, we said farewell to Jim and Marlene at the Booby Trap and thanked them for all their help and kindness.

We were all saddened with having to leave Isabela. However, we all knew this day would come. At first light we dropped *Maiatla's* stern mooring line, pulled anchor and headed back to Santa Cruz.

Chapter 32

The Countdown to Our Panamá Departure, the Preparations Begins

"The sea will grant each man new hope, and sleep will bring dreams of home."
—Christopher Columbus

With *Tigress's* southeast wind still blowing, *Maiatla,* with all her sails set, had an awesome tight reach back to Academy Bay on Santa Cruz. It was a fun last sail with Damien and the kids, but our fishing efforts continued to fail us. As I watched Isabela in *Maiatla's* streaming wake, I could not help wonder if or when we would be this way again. I also wondered where *Tigress* was and how they were progressing. It would be another 10 days before we departed the Galápagos for good, and I thought it funny that we would most likely be over 1852 kilometres (1000 nautical miles) away from here, in Panamá, a good week before Tigress would raise the first of the Marquesas Islands.

On our voyage from México to Vancouver back in 2002, via the old clipper route, we endured 34 continuous days at sea, 12 of which we were battered by the remnants of Hurricane Alma. At that time, it was just Janet and I, Mark, a 14-year-old Thomas and a 10-year-old Melissa to handle *Maiatla* on that voyage home. We knew all too well what the family aboard *Tigress* was facing now. Such is the vastness of the Pacific Ocean.

Our stop in Academy Bay would be one of indeterminate duration, as we had not made any decision as to what to do or where to go next once our loved ones had left us. On the kids' last night in town, we dined on the street after it was closed to traffic and walked the back alleyways late into the night, searching for the perfect souvenirs to take home. Damien found a small hand-carved iguana, and Melissa purchased a pair of Galápagos shot glasses for her collection. Thomas found an "I Love Boobies" t-shirt, which he purchased for his wife Kirstin, along with a sarong or pareo with an intricate tortoise and iguana pattern.

It nearly broke Janet's and my heart to put the kids back on the ferry bound for Baltra airport, but it was time for them to go home and Janet and I to get moving.

With the boat officially back to a crew of two, for a week and a half anyway, we had much to do. There was no time to mope over our family's departure. By the time Janet and I were back aboard *Maiatla*, the kids were already in the air.

The boat was ominously quiet and lonely, an experience reminiscent of the first time Janet and I found ourselves empty nesters after the last of our children moved out. Back then, Janet and I grappled with paradoxical feelings of great joy and profound relief all tightly wound in deep sadness and uncertainty. For me it would take many months for these feeling to pass, as for Janet, she hit the "Yay" stage long before I. Back on Santa Cruz, our first order of business was to decide where to do our major provisioning and where we were going to spend the next week. Janet and I ate dinner in the cockpit to take advantage of the evening breeze. It was time to discuss and agree upon a plan.

"When do the girls arrive?" Janet asked as we settled into the cockpit, with plates of spaghetti leftovers balanced on our knees.

"A week next Sunday. They fly into Baltra."

"So we have to stay here and wait for them?" she asked while sounding none too happy about the prospect. "Wish they could get here earlier so that we could just go to Panamá. It's too busy and noisy here," Janet added, looking around the bay at all the boats and anxious-looking people on the move.

"Yes, me too, babe. I want to get moving as well, but we can't ask them to fly all the way here and not spend at least a few days doing a bit of sightseeing. It wouldn't be fair," I said.

At the most, we could give them five days to see what they can after that we would have to sail. We had a preliminary date to transit the Panamá Canal and needed to get there as soon as possible, as we might have to wait up to a week before we were permitted to transit. Apparently, the big cargo and cruise ships take precedence over us. Go figure.

I shared Janet's gaze around the bay that appeared to be even more congested than the first two times we had visited. The novelty of Academy Bay was wearing off, and it was in stark contrast to the peaceful solitude of Isabela that we had just left behind.

"Wish we could go back to San Cristóbal. It's a better anchorage, and I liked the town there," Janet said as if she was just thinking aloud.

"Why don't we head back to San Cristóbal and wait there, babe? I can email the girls and tell them to take the ferry and meet us there? I'm sure they wouldn't mind spending a night on Santa Cruz before catching up to us on San Cristóbal," I offered.

After a bit more discussion, it was decided. We would do as much of the re-provisioning as we could here, of all the non-perishables, in quantities that would sustain us for at least another month. Many of the goods we required could be found here on Santa Cruz and at reasonable prices, cans of beer and bottles of rum especially. Well, cheap for the Galápagos—not so for everywhere else. Typically, we were finding the costs running often double if not triple of what they would be back in Canada. The $15 USD jars of small peanut butter we found on San Cristóbal were a bargain here at just $12. Beer and rum ran twice what I would normally pay.

However, we would wait for our next stop on San Cristóbal and then a day or two before heading to Panamá to take on perishable foods like eggs, fruits and vegetables, all locally grown so costing less than they would be back home. It was settled; we would go ashore in the morning and email the plans to the girls and our agent, Bolívar.

"You do remember that it rained a lot more on San Cristóbal. Don't you, babe?"

"I don't remember that," Janet said, searching her memory. "Well, it's now the dry season, so it shouldn't be that bad," she assured me.

I hoped Janet was correct because I did remember the once daily, and the four times at night, when it poured a rain of biblical proportions.

I guess Janet must have slept through that part of our stay on the island. Even with the threat of more rain, I too preferred to wait on San Cristóbal, as there was reported to be some fine snorkelling around the point in the harbour and I knew a local pirate who would take us out there.

Janet was still not back to her old self. She fatigued easily and struggled with constant back pain. We were both worried the long passage to Panamá would be too much for her. So much so, she gave serious consideration into flying home with the kids.

It was over 1852 kilometres (1000 nautical miles) to the Pearl Islands off Panamá, and with the El Niño winds, the normally broad reach was looking more like a marathon beat up wind the whole way. In 20 knot winds, the ride would be rough, with the boat hard on the wind. A week and a half with the boat on its ear is punishing, but I was hopeful the winds would behave themselves. Janet had also heard the heat in Panamá was even more gruelling than it was in the Galápagos, and she was dreading even hotter days. I loathed the idea sailing for Panamá without Janet, but if she was not up to it, I understood and would have to let her go home if that's what she needed. However, in the previous weeks, Janet seemed to be getting stronger and perhaps more tolerant of the oppressive climate, so with some serious reservations, for better or for worse, she opted to stay on the boat.

But the winds and heat would not be our only antagonists on the leg of our journey. The head currents we were expecting would play a pivotal role in the navigational puzzle as we made our way east, across and against no less than four major currents, each able to create swirling back eddies and vortices.

For more than a couple of weeks, I had been studying the charts, monitoring the winds and real-time currents, some of which reached speeds of 2.5 knots. This may not sound like a lot, but as a head current, if we average 6 knots, our real-time speed is only 3.5 knots. The difference is, instead of averaging 278 kilometres (150 nautical miles) per day towards our destination, we would only be averaging 135 kilometres (84 miles) a day, thus adding four full days to our journey. The best route to Panamá would change daily, as the winds and currents played their games while taunting and mocking us. I will have to be sharp on my navigation to accomplish the journey in the 10 days I allotted.

With or without Janet aboard, I decided some help on this open ocean passage would be handy, so when Mark and Teri decided to fly home from here, I contacted Kara, and she was eager to rejoin the crew. Kara was a veteran *Maiatlain,* who, at the tender age of 18, joined us for our 2007 cruise from Vancouver, BC, Canada, to the Hawaiian Islands and back again. That particular voyage is chronicled in my book, *The Tahiti Syndrome, Hawaiian Style.*

When searching for crew for the Panamá voyage, Kara was at the top of my list. She had already proven herself worthy on what was a long and difficult voyage. As a testament to the brutality of the return voyage from Hawaii that year, a fellow Canadian-cruising couple departed Hawaii four days behind us, also bound for Vancouver. Sadly, they would never make it home, as somewhere between Hawaii and Vancouver, the sea had claimed them.

Considering the potential conditions that now faced us, we may well need the kind of moxie that Kara would bring. That is if getting married, baring two children and adopting a "white-picket fence" life had not made her soft. I did not know when I invited her that Kara had recently separated from her husband of seven years, which would later present problems of their own.

After Kara had accepted the position, she told me she had a girlfriend who would "kill" to come along and her name was Ashley. I was leery at first, as it was risky taking on someone that I had never met, nor possessed any sailing experience whatsoever. We would have the girls for a whole month, and if Ashley proved to be a handful or decided that she hated offshore sailing, it could taint the experience for everyone. With Janet's delicate condition, I did not want to stress her any more than necessary. I would sail shorthanded before signing on someone who was miserable, uncooperative or, worse, a troublemaker.

I eventually relented to Kara's pleas and assertion that Ashley would be a suitable crewmate. I prayed she was right and the girls would behave themselves. Signing on a pair of, let us say, high-spirited 27-year-old girls as crew may be asking for trouble, especially in foreign ports. Ashley would prove herself the character and a source of much amusement and bewilderment. In the end, as it would turn out, the girls would prove to be a godsend.

With our sights set on getting back to San Cristóbal as quickly as possible, we completed our shopping and met with our agent, Loretta, who informed Bolívar we were on our way back.

At sunrise, three days after dropping the kids off, we dropped the mooring lines and headed east. I was hoping for a pleasant sail between the islands, but in the morning, the wind failed to materialize, leaving us to motor over a glass calm sea undulated by a long swell from the southeast.

The conditions were not entirely unexpected, as the weather report predicted less than 5 knots of wind between some of the islands. With a hope that the forecast was correct, I left our shade tarps up to protect us from the sun. If the reports were wrong and a freak gale was to materialize out of nowhere, I would have a frantic time getting the tarps down before they were damaged. As it turned out, no wind would visit us that day.

The sea conditions were pleasant enough if you did not mind the constant hum of the diesel engine. The sea rose and fell with a gentle ease, a condition often referred to as an oily swell, creating a comfortable motion that would be conducive to taking a nap.

The duality of the images the sea now displayed was astonishing. When gazed upon at just the right refractive angle, the sea's reflective image was that of the sun surrounded by spectral clouds, fleeting and translucent cotton pads scudding by. It was as if two sets of suns and clouds existed simultaneously—one set overhead and the other beneath our feet—giving the perception that the deck of *Maiatla* was merely a suspended platform floating freely in the stratosphere. Yet when switching your gaze upon the sea to that of a right angle, the mirrored universe of sun and clouds vanished and a new world of the blue abyss appeared as if gazing through a window.

The sea is blue and more so on days like this one. At the surface where the sun's rays first strike the water, you detect a pale tint of azure, a colour known as Alice blue. Gazing further, you see piercing streaks of golden light, penetrating the depth, and with each fathom counted off, the sea morphs through every possible shade of blue imaginable. The sunlight gifts us with cascading blue shades that touch the entire visible blue spectrum until plummeting into the depths of Oxford and midnight blue, just before attainment is achieved in the form of the black of the deep abyss.

"Andy, I see wings over there."

From the helm seat, I followed Janet's gaze and her pointing finger, which drew my attention to a disturbance in the water a handful of metres off to the starboard.

Not one, but two parallel large fins cut the surface, and from the course they were on, they would bisect our path if they, or we, did not alter in the next few seconds.

"Are they dolphins or sharks?" Janet asked as she leaned outside the shade of the cockpit in an effort to get a better look.

The fins rose and dived in unison not unlike a pair of swimming dolphins, but the distance between them never varied or fell out of sync as they swam along.

"I think it might be a manta ray, honey, and a big one at that," I finally said after having a good look myself.

We didn't have to wait long to see for sure because, moments later, our paths crossed, and aside from sinking only enough to clear our keel, the animal's course was unwavering. The giant manta ray, from wing tip to wing tip, was about as wide as *Maiatla*, a good 4.2 metres (14 feet). The water clarity was perfect, and we were able to see every detail of the white and black devil ray. I was even able to see a parasite with a long tail stuck to the ray's back. The sailing conditions may have been poor, but for wildlife viewing, they were perfect.

On the seven-hour voyage back to Puerto Baquerizo Moreno, on San Cristóbal Island, we spotted dozens of manta and stingrays, Galápagos dolphins and countless sea turtles of various species. A large whale shark, perhaps half the length of *Maiatla,* appeared. I quickly spun the boat around to have better look. However, the biggest fish in the sea would have none of it and quickly dived to a great depth to escape us.

It was all exciting, and I desperately wanted to grab my snorkelling gear and jump in to take some pictures, but it was not a smart idea on a couple of accounts. The first was that we needed to get into harbour before nightfall.

Although I now knew all the hazards around Puerto Baquerizo Moreno well, there was no point in tempting fate by making a night landing. We usually avoided these at all costs. The other reason was that it was only Janet and I aboard, and if I were to get into trouble in the water way out here or if Janet were to lose sight of me, that would not be good.

Although over the years I have made the leap when we were alone, we tried not to make a habit of it. If we had one other crew member on board, Janet would usually do all the driving while the crew member would keep a constant watch on me in the water. It is the safest thing to do, and since I did not want to find myself treading water while watching Janet sail away, searching for me in the wrong direction, I tried to limit my swims to only when we had a hand on board.

It killed me not to dive in this day, with so much wildlife about, but discretion prevented me from doing so. I would have to be content to take pictures from the deck while Janet drove and made sure I had a cold one in my koozie at all times. Such a good wife.

We found our old anchoring spot empty, along with the mooring buoy Eric had used when we had first arrived on San Cristóbal, some nine weeks earlier.

It was hard to believe we had been in the Galápagos for so long, and yet, in some ways, it still felt like we had just arrived. I secured a double line to the mooring ball. Then as I rechecked my knots, our old friend, Danny, and his taxi, *La Perla Negra*, pulled alongside.

"Hola *amigos,* welcome back. I wasn't expecting to see *Maiatla* again." Danny leaned over the rail to give me a welcoming fist pump, a big smile and wave to Janet. "Is there anything I can do you, *amigo*?"

"Yes, sure, bud. If you wait a minute, I'll give you the stern anchor, and if you can drive it out that way and drop it, that will save me launching the dinghy tonight."

After two attempts, we had the stern anchor set and the boat tensioned between the anchor and buoy. I slipped Danny $10 and tossed him a couple of bags of garbage before he raced off to answer the call of a crew looking for a ride ashore.

Well, we had safely arrived back at our starting point, and it was time to settle in. Janet went below to throw something together for dinner while I checked the tarps to make sure nothing had loosened up. That done, over went the boarding ladder and I dived in for a refreshing swim before dinner.

Chapter 33

The ARC Invasion Begins and Galápagos, Bulls or Tiger Sharks, Take Your Pick!

> *"The sea is no place for timid or arrogant men, nor fools!"*
> —Andrew W. Gunson, SV *Maiatla II*

We had a surprisingly peaceful night back in Puerto Baquerizo and not once did I have to get up to close the hatches due to rain, which I hoped affirmed Janet's assertion that San Cristóbal Island was now well into its dry season. I was still holding judgment on that at the moment. Despite the serene conditions, Janet insisted I put up the pole and flopper stopper—my first order of business. Then it was a call to Danny, who took us ashore to meet with Bolívar so that we could send emails to the kids and Kara to let them know we had made it safely to the anchorage. The town appeared much as we had left it over a month previous, but the anchorage was now busier than we had expected, not with charter boats but cruising sailboats. Finally, there were some like-minded sailors that we could exchange sailing stories. Fellow vagabonds, and from the number of U.S. flags flying, I suspected they spoke English, a bonus for sure. The cruisers were spread out all over the place. Some were even tucked in tight among the fishing fleets and even more anchored dangerously close to the reef and beaches.

My first guess was that there were at least 15 new cruisers anchored all about, and in hindsight, we were so fortunate to have found our buoy empty when we arrived. I noticed right off that many of the new boats displayed a characteristic that people new to cruising often display, which was odd since we were well out into the deep blue sea, the domain of experienced Bluewater sailors. Still this group displayed the typical misguided belief that it is safer to anchor as close to shore as possible for protection and that there is safety in numbers, meaning the closer you cuddle to your neighbour, the better.

It is a syndrome that I have seen countless times on our voyages, but rarely have I seen this complex shared by so many people in one place that were not part of a vacation charter/party fleet, out on a holiday cruise. I was confused; however, my befuddlement wouldn't last, as it would become clear when we went ashore.

I called Danny on VHF14, and he wasted no time in coming alongside to take us to town for our check in and walk around.

"That explains why all these boats are here now. Janet, look at the sign on the Hotel Miconia," I said while pointing.

There hanging from the upstairs balcony was a large banner that read: "ARC Around The World Rally." Once on the dock, Janet and I wasted no time in heading over to the hotel to find out what was going on. The normally tranquil waterfront hotel, where we had spent so many quiet evenings having ice cream and using the internet connection, was abuzz with people, English-speaking people in matching t-shirts sporting the ARC logo. Waiters were busy setting tables for what looked like a planned outdoor banquet and party. I spotted a lady wearing an ARC Rally Committee t-shirt and approached her. The woman was pleasant, but too busy for idle chatter when she discovered that this sailor was not part of their rally. However, what I did learn was interesting as well as disturbing.

The World ARC is an around the world race spanning 15 months, covering some 48,152 kilometres (26,000 nautical miles). They typically follow the downwind, trade wind routes from east to west while avoiding any areas fraught with political or economic strife—including the pirate infested waters of Somalia and the southern Red Sea. This group commenced their journey six weeks earlier on Saint Lucia in the Caribbean, so they were fresh at it. They call it a race, but it is more like a loose cruising club, boaters, mostly brand new to the cruising world, who sail together for mutual support and encouragement. They planned fixed stops of a specified duration; the Galápagos was their first offshore destination on what would still be a long voyage. Considering until recently, most around the world racers took up to nine months to circumnavigate the world, often without stopping anywhere. The ARC's planned 15-month itinerary would not be what I would call a leisurely cruise. The ARC fleet had scheduled spending only seven days in the Galápagos before following in *Tigress's* wake to the Marquesas Islands.

The rally woman informed me they had upwards of 40 vessels, most were U.S. registered, and they were still expecting another 17 to arrive here in the port in the next few days. Fortunately for us, some of the rally members were bypassing San Cristóbal Island altogether and were heading straight for Santa Cruz or Isabela. If all the traffic was not enough, we would soon realize that many of the boat crews lacked serious sailing, navigation and, more importantly in our bay, anchoring skills. This apparent lack of experience for some was probably the reason they joined such a rally in the first place. The sea is no place for timid or arrogant men, nor fools which this fleet had its share of—all of the aforementioned. The following week proved entertaining if nothing else.

During the ARC week, we witnessed not only multiple breaches of anchoring etiquette, but also several vessels dragging anchors, as well as plain ignorance to the use and purpose of clearly laid navigational buoys. "What is anchoring etiquette?"

you may ask. Well, there are some unwritten but hard and fast rules that every cruiser should make himself aware if of he or she wants to get along in any anchorage.

Like many things in life, common sense often dictates how one should or should not behave, but as often happens, common sense is not all that common. Combined with a strong sense of integrity, common sense also conveys a sense of what is right and wrong. Distinguishing between what is right from what is wrong allows us to make the next decision about what we should and should not do in relation or retaliation. When there is no written rule or law, common sense and etiquette will often dictate who is right if and when a dispute arises. And rest assured that it will arise in any crowded anchorage, as it did here in Puerto Baquerizo, and frequently.

The list of possible infractions is long, but high on the list are:

- Anchoring too close to another vessel that got there first.
- Anchoring with different configuration than other vessels in the anchorage (single anchor or double).
- Shouting above engine noise.
- Anchoring directly upwind of vessels and barbecuing odiferous meals on deck.
- Shining a spotlight directly at anchored vessels at night.
- Running a generator early in the morning or late into the night.
- Creating a wake in an anchorage that can spill another cruises drink.
- Allowing a dog to continue barking for prolonged periods.
- Playing loud music in proximity to others.
- Incessant cell phone ringing.
- And the worst infraction of all, hosting a party and not inviting your closest neighbours.

And, of course, there is the "That's the spot" effect!

"That's the spot" effect is a strange phenomenon that occurs the world over. Imagine sailing into a large beautiful bay that is deserted. You pick a perfect spot and drop the hook. You are all settled in and sitting topside, having a sundowner cocktail and admiring the view, when all of a sudden you see another sail round the point and enter your bay. All is good as there is plenty of room. However, instead of anchoring on the furthest side of the bay in an effort to obtain their own piece of solitude, the newcomer motors right over and anchors as close as humanly possible to you. So close that not only can you engage the couple in a quiet conversation, you know every time they activate the electric flush toilet.

It's as though the spot you are in is the only spot to be in and there is some primeval imperative to get as humanly possible to "That's the spot." Boats will gravitate together in this way, and whether it's simply human nature to want to be close together or ignorance in being able to choose a worthy spot of their own, I can only speculate. Aside from possibly irritating a neighbour, this kind of mindset can often be dangerous if, when hit by an unexpected gale in the middle of the night, a vessel directly up wind of you starts to drag, which has happened to us more than once. A tactic of mine whenever anyone appears to want to anchor too close or atop of my own anchor is to tell them that I'm not happy with them being there, and if that doesn't work, it's time to strip off, wander around the deck in the buff, with a beer in hand, while attempting to chat up the fellow's wife. Whenever I have had to resort to this tactic, the newcomer either hauled anchor and got the hell out of there or we just made some new friends.

Aside from getting snubbed by the ARC sailors, Janet and I had fun on our own, wandering along the beach in search of barbecued chicken and corn on a stick or swimming off of *Maiatla* and playing with the massive schools of fish under the boat. We even located a masseuse working out of one of the hotels, so I treated Janet to a couple of sessions over the week to help alleviate some of the back pain she had been experiencing. However, it was not all fun and games, as I had to make *Maiatla* ready for a long sea passage. We ran the watermaker to make sure that the tanks were topped up and that we had two fresh five-gallon water jugs on deck ready for an emergency. I ordered more fuel from Bolívar and just in case, Danny sold me two more 10-gallon jugs of fuel to strap on deck. If I needed to motor all the way to Panamá against a 3-knot head current, I wanted enough fuel on board.

Everything was coming together until the wind generator started making a funny grinding noise, as if a bearing was going. Not wanting to do any more damage than necessary, I flipped the switch to short the unit out, which should have stopped the blades from turning. However, the shutoff failed. When the wind blew, the generator would start, then suddenly slam the brakes on, causing the blades to come to a stop with a great bang. The violent braking sent a shudder down the mizzenmast into our aft cabin.

When windy, every 30 seconds or so, the generator would speed up, then bang! It was bad enough to listen to during the day, but at night, it made sleeping near impossible. In an effort to manually stop the blades from turning, I made a gizmo. I spread a wire coat hanger out to create a loop, which I duct taped to a broomstick. I then taped the broomstick to an unused staysail halyard on the mizzenmast and hoisted it up the mast. The loop captured one of the blades, preventing it from spinning, silencing the banging altogether. I would miss the power from the wind generator, but I could compensate for the lack of charging capacity by running the genset or the main engine when required. The wind generator would have to wait to get to Panamá before I attempted to make the repairs.

Janet and I made sure we had downtime each day to do something for ourselves or do nothing at all, if that's what we wanted. Late in the evening, we had reverted to reading to one another in bed or watching a show on the computer, movie and popcorn time in the cockpit. It was wonderful slipping back into our couple's routine aboard with no one else's needs to consider but our own.

I had wanted to hire Danny to take us around the point to where Darwin had first landed in his ship, the *Beagle,* so long ago. From shore, it appeared to be a fine snorkelling spot, and we were eager to check it out. Since the first day we arrived, some serious waves had been beating the reef off the north shore, so snorkelling there had not been possible. Then one day when I ventured topside, the surf was gone; this was our chance. Excitedly, I called below through the aft cabin hatch to Janet, who was still sitting in bed drinking her morning tea. I startled her when I stuck my head inside and said, "Hey, babe, surf is down. Wanna go for a snorkel on the point? I'll call Danny. What ya say?"

After some contemplation, Janet said, "I don't know, maybe."

"Ah, come on, hun. At least come for the boat ride if you don't wanna to go into the water," I pushed. Janet tried to look past my big head and out from under the deck tarp.

"Is it sunny or cloudy?" she asked.

I glanced to one side to check it out. "Mostly cloudy, babe, and it looks like they will be sticking around."

We had little rain since we first arrived; only a couple of light showers during the day, more evidence to prove Janet's assertion about the dry season was correct. A point I was now happy to concede. Still, the cloud cover here in the shadow of the volcano was nearly constant but not unappreciated, by us anyway.

"Okay, but if it's too rough or gets too hot, I wanna come back," Janet relented, none too enthused.

It only took a radio call to get the *La Perla Negra* alongside, and we were loading our snorkelling gear into the boat.

"Before I take you out to the point for snorkelling, I want to show you something," Danny said as we cast off and got underway. Instead of heading to the north side of the harbour, we charged at full throttle towards the large barrier reef that extends almost two thirds of the way across the harbour.

The reef prevents any boats with a draft of more than a metre from entering on that side at low tide. Arrecife Schiavoni (Schiavoni Reef) at low tide is not hard to see as the white-water breakers pounding the reef are unmistakable. At night, I enjoyed the roar of the distant surf, as constant here as any creature's heartbeat. To help keep vessels out of harm's way, there are a pair of lit, floating channel buoys, one at either end. There are only two entrances into the harbour: the one to the north, which is how we had arrived and exited; and a narrow passage between the southern point and the reef. The narrow cut in the reef is only usefully to small fishing boats and to people with local knowledge, as it is only a fraction of the size of the northern channel.

Looking over the side of *La Perla Negra*, the water shoaled as we approached the reef, and just when I was about to suggest to Danny that he may want to slow down, he came to a stop and killed the engine.

"Watch this," Danny said as he grabbed a small orange float, roughly the size of a basketball. The float had a short length of line attached to a supporting eye. Moving to the bow of the boat, Danny began to swing the float as if it were a medieval mace and commenced to vigorously attack the surface of the water with the float. Janet and I watched, a bit confused at first, but then it suddenly became evident what Danny was doing. He had only struck the water three or four times before we saw the first one come torpedoing in. It was shark and a big one that was 2 to 3 metres (6.5 to 9.8 feet) in length. After a few minutes of pounding, three or four more sharks of similar size joined in to circle our tiny boat. I could not help but look back over my shoulder at *Maiatla* as she was still surprisingly close. I suddenly remembered my nightly swims. The reality is that if the sharks were here, they were over there also. I have always known in all likelihood that sharks were nearby, but I was now wondering how many of these big boys had come in to sniff my toes while I was trailing in the current, dangling from a line while mindlessly gazing at the stars.

It was hard for me to tell what species of shark these were. They were too big to be grey reef sharks, and they definitely were not hammerheads. I concluded they were either Galápagos, bull or tiger sharks. The sharks circled the boat as if expecting a meal and most likely they were. The pounding of the buoy resembled the sounds created when fishermen discarded the carcasses of cleaned fish as they were tossed back into the sea. It was conditioning as exemplified by Pavlov's dog, like ringing a dinner bell on Walton's Mountain and John-boy and the family come a running.

In the Galápagos Islands, Galápagos sharks often gather in large groups and will usually be the most abundant species on a reef. With an average size of 3 metres (9.8 feet) and an aggressive attitude, they typically dominate over the other species of sharks found in the area. While only one fatal shark attack has ever been attributed to the Galápagos shark, it is considered highly aggressive and a hazard to divers.

The bull shark is commonly found worldwide in warm, shallow waters, along coasts and in rivers. The bull shark obtains a maximum size of 3.5 metres (11 feet), with a single record of a female specimen of exactly 4 metres (13 feet). These sharks are known for their aggressive nature and predilection for warm shallow water, particularly in brackish and freshwater systems, including estuaries and rivers. Recently, marine scientists have determined bull sharks are likely responsible for more attacks on humans than any other sharks, including the great white.

Lastly is the tiger shark, which is a relatively large macro predator, capable of attaining a length over 5 metres (16 feet). Tigers are found in many tropical and temperate waters, and they are especially common around central Pacific Islands, like the Galápagos. Its name is derived from the dark stripes along its body, resembling a tiger's pattern, which fade as the shark matures. The tiger sharks are solitary, mostly nocturnal hunters, and the most likely one to be checking me out on my midnight swims. A notable distinction of tiger sharks is they possess the widest food spectrum of all sharks, consuming a variety of prey ranging from crustaceans, fish, seals, birds, squid, turtles and sea snakes to dolphins and even other smaller sharks. The tiger shark has been known to eat inedible, man-made objects that linger in its stomach, giving it the reputation for being a "garbage eater." Again, these sharks can be aggressive and have been known to attack divers.

I hoped and suspected that these guys were Galápagos sharks for no other reason than they seemed to me, anyway, to be less of a man eater than my other choices.

"That is cool, Danny," I said. "Can you put the boarding ladder down so that I can go in and get some video?"

Danny gave me a strange look, knitting his brows in puzzlement. He was silent for a few moments before asking me to see if he had heard me correctly.

"Captain Andy, you want to go into the water with the sharks here?"

"Yes," I said. "I do."

Danny shot a sideways look at Janet, then muttered something unintelligible in Spanish while bringing his index finger to his temple and giving it a couple of twirls. I did not need a translator for what Danny was saying or thinking, but I was serious. I was about to push my point when Janet decided to speak her mind.

"Andy, if you want to swim with these sharks, you will need to do it when I'm not here." Janet was adamant. "If you want to take me back to the boat or come back out later, you can, but I don't want to be here."

Well, the admiral had spoken, and she was not supportive of my quest to swim with these big sharks.

In her defence, Janet had a bad experience some years back while we were spear fishing off Ni'ihau in Hawaii. Janet was at my side when a large and aggressive white tip shark came in to swipe the fish right off the end of my spear as I was placing my catch into a game bag. Janet fled back to the safety of the dinghy as I bolted after the shark, which stole my fish and now had my expensive spear gun in tow. Janet was so distraught over the incident she could not pull herself back into the boat. What made matters worse was that I was now nowhere in sight and *Maiatla* was anchored miles away, on an island out in the middle of nowhere. So naturally Janet's mind envisioned the worst. In the end, I retrieved my gun. The shark had jammed it in a crevice, ripping the gun out of the fish as it fled. I conceded the loss of the fish and was forced to make Janet a promise to never again bring my spear gun along on a snorkelling trip. The rule became, "If Janet was in the water, the gun was out." Janet didn't even like to have the spear gun in the dinghy when we went snorkelling, least I be tempted.

I would have to come back if I wanted to dive with Danny's sharks. With that, we were off to the nearby Lido point, located half a mile to the north, for some snorkelling. We passed the popular surfer's beach, Playa Carola. Here we would normally see big breaking waves, but this morning, the water appeared subdued. As we rounded the point and motored along the north shore, it was obvious the swell still bore some authority. The swell beat on the cliff side, rebounding back out to create a confused sea—not the best conditions for snorkelling because, as the water surged in and out, you ran the risk of being hurled upon the barnacle-encrusted rocks. We carried on for half a mile until we reach the protected waters of Darwin's little bay.

Janet and I wasted no time in suiting up and jumping in. With the waves churning up the beaches on the north shore, the water visibility wasn't great but descent. While holding hands, Janet and I explored the shallow waters of the bay where we found several sea turtles resting and feeding on the bottom. We assumed we had the bay all to ourselves, but to our delight, a pair of friendly sea lions decided they would escort us as we explored. It was a pleasurable morning, but after an hour or so, Janet became tired, so we waved at Danny who was drifting nearby, keeping an eye on us.

"Hey, hun, I'm going to stay in the water for a bit longer. I want to swim out of the bay and along the outer shore and see what's there, okay?"

"Okay, but be careful. It's pretty rough out there," Janet countered.

It didn't take me long to leave the flat waters of the bay behind and find myself in the washing machine that was the north shore. The 2-metre (6.5-feet) swells rolled in, first lifting me up, then quickly dropping me into a deep trough. The swells continued on until finally it pounded into the vertical face of the cliff, only to rebound out to assault me once again. The water was turbulent for sure, still the marine life, the schools of colourful fish were mind-blowing. Several times I found myself drawn in too close and was nearly tossed upon the boulders breaking the surface as each wave came and went. It was exciting snorkelling, but also extremely tiring. I swam perhaps a quarter mile along this shore before becoming too fatigued to carry on. Reluctantly, I spun about to look for Danny and Janet in the boat. There they were a dozen metres away motoring along. I knew Danny could not bring the boat in close to shore to pick me up, as it was far too dangerous, so I swam out to meet them.

Danny was quick to get the boarding ladder in the water and help me back into the boat.

"So how was it? Any fish?" Janet asked while handing me a towel to dry my face.

"Yeah, it was pretty nice, lots of fish, and I stuck my head in a few holes, but couldn't find any lobster," I said. "A bit rough, though. I got some nice barnacle cuts from scraping against the rocks." I rolled to one side to show Janet the cuts on my left leg, which now was smeared with running blood.

I wore gloves to protect my hands and a "shorty" wetsuit protected my arms, torso and upper thighs, but my calves were exposed and vulnerable, and I have countless scars to prove it.

"So, how was your little cruise, see anything?" I asked as I dropped my weight belt to the floor and peeled off the gloves.

"Oh, yes," Janet said, with excitement. "Lots of boobies along the shore and others diving in the water, but did you see the sharks?" Janet queried.

I paused for a moment to take a drink from our bottled water before asking. "What sharks?" now I was curious.

"When you were swimming, Danny struck the water again and called in a couple of more sharks, like he did on the reef. We were close to you then, so I'm surprised that you didn't see them."

I took a moment to contemplate what Janet had said before replying. "No, hun, didn't see a one, but they probably saw me," I glanced at my still bleeding leg before adding, "or at least smelled me."

Three days later big swells returned, negating any future snorkeling trips to the north shore or out to the reef to swim with Danny's sharks.

By the end of the week, we had had our fill of the ARC people and were happy when the day finally arrived for some of them to move on. They started early, and I had turned the VHF radio to the channel they had appropriated. It was amusing to listen to the farewell calls and often heated chatter between boats that had fouled each other's anchors. Janet and I sat on deck, with our morning cup of tea, to watch the show. As the first boat headed for the harbour entrance, Janet noticed that his present course was going to take him dangerously close to the reef.

"Andy, it looks like he is going to pass on the wrong side of that channel marker. Do you think he knows where he is going?"

I looked to where Janet was fixated and saw a large boat motoring towards the reef and buoy. It was a long way off and hard to tell from that angle, but the boat did appear to be heading the wrong way.

"He does look a bit close to the reef, but he sailed into here through the right channel, so I would assume he knows how to get out," I said, with some reservations. No sooner had I said that than we watched the boat make an abrupt starboard turn and then spiral into a complete circle. I grabbed the binoculars for a better look.

"Hun, you were right, and it looks like they found the reef the hard way!"

Concerned, Janet asked, "Did they hit it?"

"I didn't hear a bang or see the mast shiver as it usually does when a boat like that hits a rock, but his depth sounder either went off or he looked over the side and shit himself when he could suddenly see the bottom."

For over 20 minutes, we watched as the boat, still on the wrong side of the channel marker, slowly pick a path over the shallow reef. Almost miraculously, they made it back into deep water and continued off towards the west. Just when we thought the show was over, the captain of the boat came booming over the radio with a warning for the rest of the fleet claiming the channel marker was not painted in the correct colours and that he had almost ran around because the Ecuadorians marked the channel wrong.

After cursing the Ecuadorian government for their careless mistake, the cruisers signed off. Throughout the day, we watched three more vessels choose the wrong side and narrowly escape grounding. I had taken a close look at this buoy when we had first arrived, and although the colours indicating which side a vessel must pass were faded, the shape of the cardinal buoy, which also indicated which side was the safe side, was unmistakable to me, at least. But to these would-be world cruisers who nearly lost their boats on the reef, it was apparently not so obvious.

"Hun, if they don't learn to read buoys better, I doubt they will make it all the way around the world and get back to the States," I said. I paused to watch another boat bounce over the reef. "Not with their boats anyway."

Despite being blown off by an ARC organizer earlier in the week, I still hoped to mingle with some of the other cruisers, but that too would prove fruitless, as what encounters we did have with them, proved to be short. As soon as the ARC members learned that *Maiatla* and her crew were not ARC affiliates, we were politely but instantly dismissed. This particular rally was cliquey, and its members saw no benefit in associating with the likes of *Maiatla* or her crew. The twisted netherworld ideals and conceptions proved to have been deeply entrenched in this lot. Still, these folks had just started, and they had a long way to go, so with some luck, they may be able to shake the grasp of the netherworld and free their souls, and hopefully acquire some seamanship skills and manners along the way.

With all the ARC cruisers in the bay, the place was crowded enough, and when I spotted another mast rounding the point, I was not thrilled, even less so when they closed in on *Maiatla* and prepared to anchor. Appearing to be of a 1930s vintage, the 14 metre (45.9 feet) long *Freyr* was wooden yawl, with tall rakish spars flying a Norwegian flag. She was a pretty boat, with sharp, fast-looking lines, and from the look of her well-varnished topsides, she was well cared for. Once I finished admiring the boat, I turned my attention to the crew of seven, who were skillfully furling sails and making ready the anchor for dropping. Aside from noticing the proficiency of the crew, I was also struck by their overtly fitness and tall stature, which was even apparent from my distant vantage point.

As the boat approached, I snatched up the binoculars to have a better look, and I was surprised at the sight. The crew was comprised of three men and four women, all in their late 20s or early 30s, all extremely tall and cut as if they spent a great deal of time in the gym. In keeping with the Nordic registry of the boat, they were all, men and women alike, richly blonde. I had to admit they were a fine-looking Viking crew.

The *Freyr,* with a Nordic princess on the helm who deftly brought the boat into the wind, gave the order to drop the anchor, then neatly backed down to set the hook. From the direction the boat had come, I could only assume that they had just completed the crossing from Panamá. It didn't take the crew long to complete tidying up the boat, and once that was accomplished, they commenced to tidy up themselves, which involved stripping off completely naked and organizing a washing party on the foredeck. Without any obvious signs of self-consciousness, the crew took turns bucketing water out of the sea and dumping it over one another while taking turns soaping up and rinsing.

The men, as usual, finished up first and retreated to the aft deck to dry off and change into clean clothes. The ladies took longer as their long hair demanded more attention. It was nice to have new neighbours.

Later at the internet café, I met the crew and their blond captain, who had a sing-song accent, melding Ws into Vs when she spoke. A tall handsome lady that I had to look up too in more ways than one. I do not recall her name, but she informed me that they had sailed from Norway some six months previous, with plans of circumnavigating the world, changing out crewmembers as they went. Apparently, the Yawl *Freyr* was a charter boat owned and operated by a sailing society in Norway whose mandate was to maintain the countries sailing heritage by taking youths on training voyages—a noble cause to be sure.

The captain also informed me, the *Freyr,* aside for short layup periods for refits, has been constantly sailing around the world with different crews since 1962. An impressive claim of which I had no reason to doubt. I would have no further contact with the crew of the *Freyr* during their short four-day stay on San Cristóbal Island, but I would see them every evening while having a sundowner in the cockpit, which coincidentally was the same time the crew liked to take to the foredeck for their daily evening bath.

It would be many months later while making notes that I discovered that the boat was named the *Freyr* after the Norse goddess of love and beauty, or fertility and success, depending on the source. Either way to me, the boat was appropriately named.

Chapter 34

The Panamá Crew Arrives

"The true peace of God begins at any point 1,000 miles from the nearest land."
—Joseph Conrad

On Saturday, February 27, the girls arrived on Santa Cruz Island safely and checked into a picturesque but inexpensive hotel near the *malecón*. They had an uneventful flight down from Canada, but they did make a new friend on the plane, Joshua, who was moving back to Panamá after living some years in the States. They all made plans to meet again once the girls had arrived in Panamá aboard *Maiatla*, in a month's time. Kara and Ashley spent the next couple of days touring the sites as we had done, with the tortoise ranch, Rancho Primicias, Tortugas beach and Los Gemelos (The Twins) being the highlights. In some ways, I wished we could have been there to greet them and show them around, but Janet and I suspected they would enjoy some time on their own while on this adventure. We would all be thrust together in comparatively tight quarters soon enough. We had the girls for the better part of a month, so we will have plenty of time for togetherness later.

We have known Kara since she was a teen, and thus, we harboured some protective, parental feelings for her, but we did not want to cramp their free spirits. Santa Cruz was safe enough, and as long as they exercised due care, they would be fine. Besides, what trouble could a pair of pretty and gregarious 27-year-old girls get into in the Galápagos Islands? Not much, we hoped. However, Panamá City would prove to be an entirely different matter where trouble would find them in a big way.

Kara and Ashley booked a ferry ride to bring them to San Cristóbal for Monday afternoon. The day before, I was up early in an effort to complete the preparations for their anticipated arrival. I still wanted to finish cleaning out the V-berth, which was where one of the girls would sleep, while the other would reside in the portside cabin, Damien's now vacant room. After clearing away the breakfast dishes, Janet and I retired to the cockpit to enjoying our morning tea while watching the town and harbour wake up. The sun had yet to breach the peak of the volcano. Instead, the mountain was backlit with a crown of mottled clouds and scattered rain at its peak. A stiff offshore wind filled in with the rising sun, creating a chop that spread across the water. The wind was warm, but not uncomfortably so. It was going to be a pleasant day.

"When are we actually going to leave, Andy? It's almost March, and we have flights booked out of Panamá at the end of the month. Don't we need to get going?"

Janet was as anxious as I was to get back to sea, but since Kara and Ashley had come a long way, it did not feel right to rush them off as soon as they arrived without giving them a chance to see some of these magnificent islands.

Figure 83. Kara and Ashley take a selfie upon arrival

"Not sure, hun, maybe in three or four days. I would like to get the girls to help with the final provisioning and maybe take a tour or two with them, like we did with Marina and Mark when we first arrived," I said.

"I don't want to go back out to Kicker Rock or anything, and with all these cruisers in town, most of the tours will be booked up anyway. Don't you think?" Janet was right in that respect. Ever since we arrived, the VHF radio had been alive with chatter from the ARC people, talking about what tours they were taking today and asking who could give them a ride to wherever. Over half the fleet had already departed, but there were still boatloads hanging about.

"I don't think the girls have the money to do a bunch of stuff, hun, but maybe we can call Bolívar and get his taxi buddy to take us around the island for a second time, now that you are feeling better and more acclimatized to the heat. We might enjoy it more and perhaps we can get to see that beach we missed, you remember? Puerto Chino," I suggested.

"Which beach was that?" Janet asked. "They all blend together after a while," she added.

"You remember, hun, when we took the taxi to the far said of the island when it was too hot and we left the others to walk to the beach. And we headed back to the restaurant and banana plantation to wait for them. Remember?"

"Oh, I don't know, maybe," Janet said while doing a mental search. "I'll see how I feel then," she said as she glanced past me to look at large ARC catamaran anchored nearby. She studied the 18-metre (59-feet) cat for a moment. "Wasn't that cat further in shore last night?"

When I had a look at the big catamaran, it was not in the position it had been the previous night. It was much closer, and when we watched carefully, it appeared to be coming even closer by the minute.

"Yep, I think your right, hun. Think she is dragging her anchor," I said as I leaned out the dodger to get a better look. We had watched the big cat come in two days earlier, choose a section of open water close into shore and prepare to anchor. When it became apparent where they intended to plant the hook, with cupped hands round my mouth, I called to them.

"Hey, skipper, there is a rock rubble pile right under you. If you anchor there, it will get fouled. You'll never get it back up."

The crew of the cat appeared to be a middle-aged couple and a pair of teen boys. The couple briefly talked among themselves, then gave me a friendly wave, powered up and moved to the far side of the bay, looking for a better spot to anchor. Believing it was all settled, I slipped below for a while, but when I returned, the cat was back and they had already anchored between a pair of their fellow ACR cruisers. I was surprised that his neighbours would have permitted him to anchor so close. If they had given it some thought, they would have realized that, considering the water there was 12 or 14 metres (39.3 to 45.9 feet) deep, there was no way the cat could have laid out enough anchor rode for a good set. As it was, they were less than two boat lengths away from the vessel in front of them and less than one boat length away from the one behind. Not a good position to be in, and I suspected that when the tide and wind shifted, they would be bumping into each other. However, that was not my worry. We were far enough away.

Well, I was wrong again, as this morning the wind was blowing perfectly, swinging all the other boats, so that when this cat commenced to drag, it was going to miss all the others and come straight down on us. Not fast mind you, but at the present rate of drift in this wind, I estimated that we had 20 minutes before it was upon us. Sort of a slow-motion collision. Nevertheless, with each vessel in the 20-ton displacement range, the possibility of some serious damage was likely.

"Is there anybody aboard, Andy? I don't see anyone. Maybe you should go over and check."

"Yes, maybe because I think I saw all the crew from those three boats leave with Danny this morning," I replied. "First, I'll get on the radio and tell the ARC organizers that one of their boats is dragging. Maybe the owners can be found on shore."

Jumping down the companion stairs to the radio, I snatched up the microphone. As I was making the call, Janet shouted to me, "Andy, there is someone aboard the cat!"

I left the radio and returned topside to see what was up. Fortunately, one of the teen boys had remained aboard, and he had noticed their vessel-dragging anchor. For the following hour, we listened to the teen call ashore, looking for his parents. Thankfully, the teen had the presence of mind to start the engine and motor the boat slowly forward to keep in position. Sometime later, his family returned. After making several more attempts to re-anchor unsuccessfully, to our relief, they finally conceded defeat and made their way back to the far side of the harbour. I was delighted they did not do this dragging business in the middle of the night. Not surprisingly, over the next few days, we witnessed three other boats drag, but fortunately, they were nowhere near us, so we only watched and listened to the excitement on the radio as each event played out.

With the morning excitement over, I had chores to do. One was to check the set of our stern anchor, the one Danny had placed for me when we arrived. At the time when we dropped it, I took the bitter end of the rode, wrapped it around a winch and gave the rode a hard pull. With the bow securely tied to the mooring buoy, I was able to give the anchor a good tug to make sure it was bought into the bottom properly. Normally when the anchor is dropped on a sandy bottom and pulled, you can feel the anchor slide across the sand for a few metres until the chain straightens out as the flukes dig in. However, this time there was no sliding, so I suspected the anchored had caught a rock, the same rock rubble pile that I had informed the cat about and that I had seen while snorkelling around the boat last time that we were here. I knew when Danny tossed the anchor, it would land uncomfortably close to the end of that rock pile. Now I was sure that my hook was fouled in it.

"I'm going to dive the stern hook and make sure that we can get it up when we want to leave," I said.

Janet was still watching the cat off in the distance, motoring in circles, trying to find enough space to anchor.

"Thought you were going to wash the girl's rooms and hang the bedding out to air?" Janet said, with some expectations.

"I will, hun, but I want to check the anchor first, and besides, it's time for my morning swim. You wanna come in with me?"

Janet declined the invitation.

Donning a mask and snorkel, I leapt over the side to swim to the stern of *Maiatla*. Grabbing the taut anchor rode, I took a deep breath and, hand over hand, pulled myself downward to the bottom. The stern anchor consisted of 30 metres (98.4 feet) of rope and 10 metres (32.8 feet) of chain. With the water so clear, I could easily see to the bottom and where the line switched to chain. Shooting downward, my ears popped with the increasing pressure. By the time I reached the chain, I was at my limit somewhere below 10 metres (32.8 feet). Still pulling myself along, I followed the chain until it disappeared under a large boulder located at the edge of the thick rock rubble pile.

Releasing the chain, I swam over the top of the boulder to find the Danforth anchor on the other side. I could see it was still attached to the chain as it emerged from underneath the great boulder. I was about out of breath, so wasting little time, I grabbed the chain and, placing both of my finned feet against the side of the rock, pulled. Despite all my effort, I could not clear the chain. Now frantic for air, I bolted for the surface, spiralling upward with my right arm stretched out above my head in case I came up under a boat or unsuspecting sea lion.

If anyone had been watching, they would have seen me explode from the water, with a full two thirds of my body shooting clear of the surface, while blowing and gasping for air as if I was a breaching whale.

After a brief rest and to watch a few zodiacs full of tourist shoot by, I made three more dives to the bottom in an attempt to dig the chain out from under the rock. However, with no luck and now exhausted, I returned to *Maiatla* to implement Plan B.

"So, you get the anchor clear?" Janet asked as I clamber back aboard.

"No, it's fouled. It looks like someone took a 2-ton rock and placed it directly atop of our chain, and it's pretty deep, so I don't have much time down there to dig it out," I said, perhaps sounding a little frustrated.

Janet had been tidying up below, but had returned to the cockpit for a break moments before.

"So what are you going to do then?" she asked as she handed me my saltwater towel, which was lying on the cabin top. I could save the rode and anchor by unshackling them and leaving the chain behind, but as far as I was concerned, leaving expensive galvanized chain on the bottom was not an option. I knew what I had to do. Janet handed me a bottle of cold water.

After downing a long draw, I said, "It looks like I'm going to have to drag the scuba tanks out of the bilge and make a dive."

Janet now looked concerned. "You haven't used the tanks in a couple of years. Would the air still be good?" Janet asked.

"If they were full, I wouldn't trust them anyway," I said, "but I'm pretty sure both tanks are empty, so I will have to get out the diving air compressor and fill them up." I handed Janet back the water bottle and climbed out of the cockpit to head to the stern lazarett where my compressor had been neatly stored some years ago. As I went, Janet called to me, "When was the last time you had the compressor running?"

"Oh, about two or three years ago," I said.

"Is it even going to start?"

"I guess I'm going to find that out!" I said, not sounding too hopeful.

Nothing ever comes easy on a boat. All I wanted to do was retrieve the stern anchor, which should have been relatively simple. However, this day, to accomplish that, I had to spend a few hours standing in the hot sun overhauling the fuel system of my Honda air compressor so that I could fill the air tanks to dive and dig the chain out from under a mountainous rock.

Back on the bottom, with an hour's supply of air strapped to my back and burrowing like a gopher with gloved hands, I was not amused. However, a barbeque-size hawk fish appeared fascinated by my efforts while he hovered over my left shoulder the whole time while periodically darting in to snap up some of the sea bugs I was digging up. I was surprised how long the project took, but after digging a hole big enough to crawl into, I gave the chain a few hard jerks to finally pop it free.

With air still to burn, I decided to explore the nearby reef to look for bugs. I hoped a park guide did not motor by to see bubbles on the surface and charge me with illegal diving in the harbour and unauthorized sightseeing. I guess I could always claim that I was recovering my anchor and that anytime a fish or ray passed by, I closed my eyes so as not to violate the parks sightseeing rules.

By the time I climbed back aboard, most of the day had gone, and I was beat and worse for not having found any dinner. Again, Janet greeted me with a drink, but this time it was a cold beer.

"So, it was harder than you thought it would be?"

"Yep, hun, she was sure stuck, and I'm glad I got the tanks out because I never would have gotten the chain out free diving from the surface. It was deeper than it looked," I said between guzzles of beer.

"How deep was it?" Janet asked

"The depth gauge said it was 39 feet at the bottom, which surprised me because I didn't think I could get down that far. I mean, I did it in diving school, but that was 40 years ago when I was a couple of pounds lighter," I said.

Janet smirked when she replied, "Only a couple of pounds?"

Since the day was already shot, I decided to let the girls clean their own rooms when they arrived.

The day of the girls' planned arrival on the boat, Janet and I took it easy. Going ashore alone, an hour before the ferry's arrival, I planned to wait at the hotel and kill time by sending emails and updating our blog for family and friends back home. Good internet proved to be an elusive animal in the Galápagos, so updates of our travels had been sparse. I also made contact with my Panamá Canal agent, Erick, who would arrange to have our boat inspected, measured and pay all our transit fees, as well as arrange for a pilot to guide us through the historic canal. I was to contact him again when we were close, and he would set the wheels in motion.

I was on the rooftop patio well into my second post on the blog, as well as my third beer, when a pretty woman, near my own age, approached and asked if she could plug her phone into my laptop to charge. Her name was Cathy and at her elbow was her husband, Terry. The couple took the table next to mine, at the railing overlooking the harbour, and introductions were made all around. Opportunities can presents itself in strange places and ways, and this opportunity came with a request for an electrical charge.

As I learned, Terry Shiels and his wife were from North Carolina. He was a videographer and a producer of travel documentaries for such markets as the Discovery Channel and public television stations. Terry was now retired, but he managed his own production company under the moniker *Shiels Production*. He was now in the Galápagos filming his latest documentary on the islands.

"My last documentary just got picked up by the travel network, as it was about motorcycling across Vietnam," Terry excitedly explained. Apparently, Terry was eagerly looking for retirement projects, and as it so happened, I had a pitch for him, one featuring two Nanaimo sailors rounding Cape Horn and visiting Antarctica. After some further discussion, he found my proposition interesting. We traded cards and agreed to get in touch to discuss the venture further, once we all returned to the netherworld.

I said goodbye to my newfound friends and, hopefully, my new video producer. Once I was again sitting alone, I suddenly realized I had forgotten about the girls, and when I looked to the ferry dock, it was obvious that the ferry had come and gone and, more importantly, Kara and Ashley were nowhere in sight.

"Shit," I said aloud, startling the young waiter behind me, who was clearing off Terry's now vacant table.

"*Gracias*," I said as I quickly tossed a few dollars on the table, shoved my laptop back into the bag and bolted down the stairs on a quest to locate my crew.

I searched the immediate area and stores along the *malecón*, and after coming up empty handed, I stopped by the pier's guardrail to scan the waterfront for a second time and consider what to do next. It was then I remembered I had brought the handheld radio, and if I had the forethought to have turned it on, I would have heard Janet calling me from *Maiatla*. The girls arrived safely on the boat almost half an hour earlier. Relieved all was well and that I would not have to call these girls' parents and tell them I had lost their daughters, I hailed a water taxi and headed back to the boat.

Once aboard, I received a great hug from Kara and was introduced to her beautiful friend, Ashley, who appeared nervous and perhaps just too bubbly, so much so I instantly began to fear she might be a bit overwhelming for me. Choosing crew for a long ocean passage is always a difficult one, as even the smallest personality quirks can be like fingernails on a chalkboard in a cramped vessel. Kara swore Ashley would be fine, and as it turned out, I need not have worried.

"Anyone want a drink?" I asked as I made my way below, leaving our new crew to continue telling Janet of their travels.

Figure 84. Ashley and Kara take their inaugural skinny dip.

"What you got?" Kara asked as she stuck her head through the open hatch.

"I've got cold water, coke, orange juice, beer, red wine and rum!" I said.

I heard the girls chuckle and say, almost in unison, "Rum and coke, please."

As I made the drinks, a loud splash boomed next to the boat. While I was playing bartender, the new arrivals decided to cool off by going for a swim.

"Hey, Janet, can you grab my camera and get a picture of us in the water?" I heard Kara say.

I returned topside with the drinks to find the clothes the girls had been wearing in a pile on the seat and Janet standing outside the cockpit snapping pictures of them as they splashed alongside.

When Kara saw me, she called out, "Andy, you will have to change the title of your next book from the *Naked Canadian* to the *Naked Canadians.*" While treading water, she laughed. If I had any previous reservation whether either Kara or Ashley would fit in as *Maiatla* crewmembers, at that moment they instantly evaporated.

Chapter 35

Farewell to the Galápagos Islands and Back on the High Seas

"I taste once again the greatest joy which small boat cruising can offer:
the satisfying contentment of an anxious passage successfully achieved. . . ."
—Eric Hiscock, Wandering Under Sail

We spent the balance of the week reconnecting with Kara and getting to know Ashley by going on a road trip up to Cerro Mundo, the volcano, and down to Puerto Chino. We also made an excursion to the south coast of San Cristóbal to an unnamed beach thick with black marine iguanas where we snorkelled with sea turtles.

Just as I had seen on Isabela with my grandson Damien, this bay was a marine cleaning station for turtles of all kinds. We saw one particularly large bruit, a green sea turtle with an old propeller scar across its back perched on the bottom. Like a car on a mechanic's hoist, the turtle extended its flippers and lifted its bulk clear of the bottom so that the tiny Bluestreak cleaner wrasse could swim underneath the turtle's belly to pick at what bugs were hiding there. Other turtles, most with white barnacles clinging to their shells, swam slowly in tight circles, permitting the quick and agile hordes of wrasse to dart in, nip a meal and retreat in a flash. Some of the turtles were all but obscured as hundreds of the tiny fish, engaged in a feeding frenzy, swarming about like one would imagine a pack of veracious piranhas attacking a bloody carcass.

It was amusing watching nature at work, but at times, it was more humorous watching the girls' reactions, especially Ashley, whose melodramatic personality was comical and, at times, puzzling. Ashley possesses a child-like naiveté that effervesces whenever she encounters something new or exciting, which here in the Galápagos Islands was most of the time. It must have been exhausting for her, as often Ashley seemed to be on the verge of an orgasmic-like spasm, losing bodily control. She would shake her arms and hands while vibrating with anticipation of an event as simple or as common as leaping from the boat into the sea or swimming with reams of tiny fishes.

A big hit with the ladies was the tree house where they were able to swing Jane-like from long ropes and slide down the 8-metre (26.2-feet) "fireman's pole," which was installed to presumably give the high-rise occupants a quick escape in case of bush fire, high winds or sudden mosquito attacks. After some coaxing from the girls, I decided to give the quick way down a try. It was a dizzying height, but never one to run from a challenge and with the girls egging me on, I grabbed the pole and started my slide.

I had barely cleared the deck when I realized I had made a grave error. I knew all too well, why firefighters wore long, thick pants and not swimming shorts when they slide down the pole. A fact that I had carelessly neglected at this time. The pole was slick with a coating of grey dust, but that did little to alleviate the friction as my leg hairs were first bound, then mercilessly ripped out at the roots, causing my eyes to weep, and to add insult to injury, the abrasion branded me by creating a scorching first-degree burn between my legs and knees. Kara and Ashley quickly followed me down the pole, but they were smarter than I as they were better attired.

In the basement of the tree house, some 3 metres (9.8 feet) underground, among the tree's great roots, hung a hammock next to a porcelain toilet bowl complete with a brush and a tiny fragile-looking table sporting a Spanish farmer's almanac. The room owned a *Silence of the Lambs* atmosphere, as it was painted sky-blue with alternate walls blood red and had deep gouges that appeared suspiciously like fingernail scratches. The remaining décor was reminiscent of some of the torture rooms created by a few of America's infamous mass murderers. Like the tree's own testicles, a pair of massive cork fishing floats encased in hemp netting hung from the ceiling next to an arched brick alcove with a recessed shelf. Alter-like, an old kerosene lamp was on display on the shelf, which also held coins of various countries, a form of tiding or donation, perhaps.

Figure 85. Kara starts her slide down the tree house's "fireman's pole."

The coins I thought were a placating tribute to the spirits of the tree to ensure the visitors deliverance from the pit.

To aid the visitor in their departure was a street sign that pointed to the only exit and read, "*UNA VIA*" ("ONE WAY"). The mood lighting was provided by several old, green wine bottles with dripping candles and a single 25-watt bulb dangling from the ceiling on a kinked electrical cord suitable for hanging yourself if your silver donation failed to secure your release.

With great effort, Ashley was determined to climb into the tiny, child-size hammock, which she only managed with Kara's help and only after they curbed their incessant laughing. It was obvious Kara and Ashley were the best of friends and intuitive to each other's often-illogical thoughts and sense of what they deemed funny.

Kara last sailed with us some nine years previous when she was a young but worldly 17-year-old on our voyage to and from Hawaii. I spent many a long but pleasant watches with her in *Maiatla's* cockpit, discussing her hopes and dreams for the future. Kara talked of purchasing her own boat and sailing the world. Whether the boat or a husband and kids would come first, she was not sure at the time. As for most of us netherworld captives, the course we chart for our lives often does not go to plan. Upon her return from her voyage to Hawaii, Kara reunited with a high school sweetheart and married. A career in federal corrections and a stint as a union rep followed, and somewhere in there, she managed the time to bear two beautiful boys. She never did buy that boat, and here, almost 10 years after our late-night talks of adventure, she was estranged from her husband and trying to decide if her marriage was worth saving. As I learned all so long ago, the deck of a small vessel is the perfect place for introspective thought and deep soul searching.

Kara's husband, Travis, was watching the kids while she took a break to help clear her head and perhaps find a way to stay, or not. I was hoping this voyage to Panamá would help give her some perspective, and for a little while, a chance to dream and play as if nothing else mattered. However, unfortunately, the fickle finger of fate was about to give Kara another deep poke in the ribs, as if to remind her that she was child of the netherworld and any escape from the fold, if at all achieved, is often fleeting.

Ashley was a project coordinator for a Vancouver architectural firm and had never been married. A free spirit in every sense of the word, she had done some travelling abroad, living in England and backpacking through much of Western Europe. She had travelled over vast areas of the United States, including Hawaii, and had even ventured to Jamaica and Cuba. Ashley obviously had contracted a similar affliction as my own, with the principal symptom, a case of fevered wanderlust. At the time of her invite to join *Maiatla*, Ashley was deciding if she wanted to travel on a work permit to New Zealand to see how the people down under lived. Now, here, Ashley was on *Maiatla* and what better place to make life-altering decisions than with your best friend on a yacht in the South Pacific?

This voyage would be a life-altering experience for both of them, and Janet and I were thankful we had them along, as their help and fun-loving spirits would be invaluable on a voyage that would prove an exciting, yet trying one.

On Friday, March 4, we departed Puerto Baquerizo, San Cristóbal Island, at the crack of dawn. The warm wind was light out of the east-southeast and right on the nose, of course. The pallid morning sky had some thin cloud cover that we would later be thankful for, as it tamed the wild heat that typically comes with being on the open water. I had no trouble getting the stern anchor back aboard, thanks mostly to my little diving adventure a few days before. Casting off the mooring ball was easy and, apparently, to the amusement of a pair of young black sea lions that chased the tails of the moorings as I pulled the lines in. The animals blew bubbles and snorted a farewell (or were they snorts of derision?). As we throttled up, Kara and I removed the mainsail cover as Ashley took the helm to drive us out of the harbour and pass without incident, the same cardinal buoy that gave the ARC cruises so much difficulty.

Once clear of the bay, I took over the helm as the girls attempted to hoist the mainsail right away. It had been some years since Kara had worked the deck; nevertheless, with some direction from me while sitting in the shade of the cockpit and with a little trial and error on the girls' part, the sail finally went up in jerks and grunts between fits of laughter. Although there was not enough wind to sail, the big main made for a decent sun awning in the early morning, throwing a long shadow that covered most of the portside of the boat.

I could not help but cast a long glance back over my shoulder. The Galápagos is a snorkeler's paradise and a magical place I fell in love with, especially with the abundant and friendly marine life. I had no idea if I would ever again sail in Darwin's shadow, which he had cast so long ago over these enchanted islands. I wondered if the ghost of Darwin and the *Beagle* still ply these islands, their waters, running before their winds. Charles Darwin left his indelible mark on these islands, just as these islands had imprinted their mark upon my soul. There was much that we had not done in the islands, but one in particular would leave me with a knot in the pit of my stomach, a void. I never did get to sample Guinea pig on a stick, which was a pity.

We motored eastward along the coast, staying close to shore to see some of the sites. As we slipped past Kicker Rock, three baby manta rays leapt clear out of the water, performing acrobatic somersaults before landing in a resounding splash that I was sure carried for a mile or two over the calm water.

On shore, inland of towering sea cliffs and rising out of the arid landscape, stood dozens of black volcanic cinder cones. The jet-black peaks stood in steep contrast to the sea cliffs plastered white with thick layers of booby and frigate guano.

Nature's whitewash is prized shit (literally) in many places of the world. The white streaks of guano are the accumulated excrement of seabirds, sea lions or cave-dwelling bats. As manure, guano is a highly effective fertilizer due to its exceptionally high content of nitrogen, phosphate and potassium—nutrients essential for plant growth. The 19th-century guano trade played a pivotal role in the development of modern intensive-farming practices and encouraged the formal human colonization of remote bird islands in many parts of the world. Guano had been harvested on the Galápagos Islands, but surprisingly, despite the massive bird colonies, deposits did not draw intense commercial development, as it had in other South American countries, like Chile.

We encountered a pair of dive charter boats and a larger sailboat, a charter I believe, that appeared to be heading to mainland Ecuador. Once clear of the harbour, we dropped the fishing hooks in the water, in hopes of catching dinner. I was no longer worried about being caught fishing illegally, as expulsion was the penalty; we had nothing to lose since we were leaving anyway.

The big swell we had been watching wrap around the point for the past week had vanished, leaving a pleasant and gentle sea. Agreeable conditions for our first day, and it gave the girls a chance to gain their sea legs, which I was sure they would need before this trip was over.

We motored for half the day until the wind filled in from the east, permitting us to sail hard on the wind under full sail. We were cleaving the water at a respectable 5 knots, but it was on a heading of 22 degrees magnetic, which was putting us too far north of our rumb line to Panamá. By late in the afternoon, we lost sight of land. When Ashley first realized the land was gone, I feared that she was going to have an anxiety fit. But after a halting pause to let the realization sink in, she was fine. Loosing site of land un-nerves some people, but for me, I find it comforting because, as the netherworld sinks below the horizon, all I now have to worry about is my *Maiatla* world and her people.

Everyone settled into their watches, and thankfully, the girls slid comfortably into their routine, which for now entailed napping in the shade and listening to the water rush by. We fished all day, but with no success. It would have to be fried chicken with our fresh salad. After dinner, we all gathered in the cockpit to watch the sunset and to hopefully catch a glimpse of the illusive green flash. It was a beautiful fiery sunset, but some last minute cloud materialized right along the horizon, foiling any chance of see the green flash.

We spent the night continuing to sail hard on the wind, a steady 10 knots out of the east-southeast, putting us on a starboard tack. Not long after sunset, the few clouds that spoiled the flash dispersed, leaving a perfectly clear sky sparkling with a brilliance of stars that can only be viewed in the great desolate places of the world. I have witnessed such sights before in the middle of the Qatar desert on the Persian Gulf, on the tundra north of the Arctic Circle and resting at the base of *Maiatla*'s mainmast, here on the great expanse of the ocean. With the boat sculpting a bioluminescent wake, we charged on into the night.

A 1-metre (3.2-feet) wave pattern, a short choppy sea, set in making for an uncomfortable night of sleeping. Janet was already suffering from the jerky nature that was hard on her back and she feared that making this crossing was a mistake. In conjunction with the disagreeable waves, we were also battling strong countercurrents, forcing me to alter course and dodge about to look for weak spots. I would soon figure out the weakest currents were located closer to the equator. I was trying to stay south of our rumb line, but this tactic would prove difficult to do, as we were getting set to the north at an alarming rate.

The girls were assigned the late-night watches, Kara from 12 a.m. to 4 a.m. and Ashley from 4 a.m. to 8 a.m. Both the girls did surprising well on their watches by keeping the boat moving in the right direction, and despite the choppy condition, neither succumbed to seasickness.

Figure 86. Ashley and Kara settling in for their first watch at sea.

Considering the survival of the boat and crew was in their hands, I was a bit surprised that, aside from an initial overlap, Kara and Ashley decided each would stand their watches alone. No ships were sited on our first night at sea, so I was not called on deck for collision avoidance. However, I did wake up when the boat slowed or when *Maiatla* called to me requiring a sail trim. The air was cold comparatively that night, so much so that we all had to wear a shawl or wrap ourselves in a blanket while in the cockpit. My watch was uneventful, but I did have a few boobies follow the boat and hunt by our boat's running lights. It was fun to watch as they hovered some metres above the deck and then, like dive bombers, launched themselves into steep dives whenever the boat spooked a fish. The fish positively glowed with bioluminescence as they attempted to bolt away, making for an easy target when sighted from above.

The dawn of Saturday, March 5, broke clear and bold, and we were treated to the sight of a pod of feeding dolphins cruising by, but they did not get too close or stay long, as they were too busy having breakfast. The sea and wind flattened out, so we reverted to motoring, which we would continue for the better part of the day.

"So guys, we are 160 miles from San Cristóbal Island now," I called up the companion steps to the ladies that were now all resting in the shade of the cockpit after breakfast. I was sitting at the galley table, looking at the charts and plotting our course of the previous 24 hours. Without fanfare, in fact, we never noticed that we had, sometime during the night, crossed from the South Pacific to the North Pacific. Our morning plot put us 3.2 kilometres (2 miles) north of the equator, running parallel to the waist-belt of the Earth that headed straight for a tourist beach in

Ecuador. A look at the course easily showed where we met a strong cross current or when we encountered a back eddy that helped to push us along.

With *Maiatla* motoring for the better part of the day, our second day at sea was a replay of the first until we encountered a pair of ships late in the day. With some excitement, Ashley spotted the first ship on her afternoon watch. I showed her how to track it on the radar as it passed within a couple of miles. On Kara's watch, we hooked our first tuna. Kara reeled it in, but it was too small, only a few pounds. We threw it back to be caught another day.

Figure 87. Ashley trimming the big headsail when the wind did finally fill in.

The sea settled out once again, making us all happy. The girls prepared a spaghetti dinner that we ate in the cockpit as the sun set. With 1287 kilometres (800 miles) still ahead of us, we primed ourselves for our second night at sea.

Chapter 36

A Burial at Sea

"Everything can be found at sea, according to the spirit quest."
—*Joseph Conrad*

On Sunday, March 6, our third night at sea, was mostly uneventful. The wind died early on, so we kept on motor sailing hard into the wind, with the headsail furled but leaving the main and mizzen up to help us along and to dampen the roll. Immediately after dinner, I attempted to get on the ham radio to send emails and receive a weather update; however, I was only partially successful. Mail and replies to my most recent post downloaded fine, but the weather never came in and I was unable to send a position update or our log of the previous day. I made a second attempt in the morning, only to have similar results. No joy! All I could do was hope the atmospherics would be more conducive to propagation in the late afternoon. For now, friends and family would have to imagine what we were up too and keep the faith.

My watch ran as usual from 8 p.m. to 12 midnight. After giving up at my frustrating attempts to communicate with the netherworld, I bounded topside to relieve Ashley from her uneventful evening watch, only to find Janet and Ashley laughing and talking. What about I wasn't sure, but their conversation was distracting enough for neither of them to notice one of nature's great wonders displayed just beyond their reach.

The sea appeared leaden, heavy with only a gentle groundswell rolling under the boat and under sail and Perkin's power, *Maiatla* was boldly pushing her nose through the waves without hesitation, and in doing so, she churned up a brilliantly intense, bioluminescence light show. Lunging over top of each swell, like a sprinter attacking hurtles, *Maiatla* shot water out to each side, water that exploded with light of such intensity it illuminated all the sails in rhythmic flashes.

After pointing out the lightshow, I took Ashley by the hand to the foredeck and into the bow pulpit, which overlooks the bowsprit and the racing water below. I never tire of seeing *Maiatla* nose her way into the waves, churning up the black sea, forcing it into life. The intensity of the sparkling blue-white light is always most brilliant in the leading edge of each bow wave, looking as if each wave, each ripple or crest, is electrically charged, injected and energized with neon.

For Ashley, this was her first time witnessing such a spectacle, and she was similarly awestruck with the scene. It was as if the sea was attempting to mimic the incredibly bright constellations high above. From aloft, it was easy to imagine the boat appearing as a Roman candle as it shoots across the tranquil black sea. After some time, Ashley and Janet went below to bed. Ashley would need to be up in a few hours for her 4 a.m. watch. I remained topside for my watch, but not before pouring myself a mug of wine to ward off the chill of the night. I don't normally drink while on watch, but for some reason the immensity of the moment demanded it.

I made myself comfortable in the lee of the cockpit. While I continued to watch the water, I became lost in contemplative thought and began to scroll through nearly forgotten childhood memories. It was after a second mug of wine when it suddenly struck me—I needed to complete a task that I started many years ago. My father had passed away three months short of the arrival of the 21st century, followed some 10 years later by my mother. I have been carrying both of my parents' ashes on board *Maiatla* all these years. Our two children, Thomas and Melissa, grew up on board knowing their grandparents were squirreled away on a shelf next to our cruising books and movie DVDs. Janet and I had made it a practice of sprinkling a few ashes of each of my parents on our sailing travels. Hawaii, México, Costa Rica and, of course, the coast of B.C. All have adopted some of the last earthly remains of Maurice and Marion Gunson. I had been saving the last few ounces of ashes for when we crossed the equator. Since my parents loved to travel as well, it occurred to me that leaving the last of their remains on the border between the North and South Seas and under this indescribably beautiful night sky not only seemed appropriate, but also I believed that this night commanded it. Perhaps my parents, looking at us from above, had decided it was time that I finally laid them to rest. Yes, this would be the night.

Down in the main salon, and behind the flat screen TV, stood the pale blue cardboard urn, my mum's urn, in which we had placed the last remains of my father. Mixing the two, I received some measure of comfort knowing they were nearby and together, their life's dust commingling in death. I retrieved the urn to return to the cockpit where I leaned over the cockpit coaming, and using a headlamp, I studied the container that had been bouncing around with us for oh so many years. It looked scarred from being hurled about and stained from the cold North's condensation and the humid South's mildew.

Holding the urn in outstretched arms, I reminisced for the longest time, streaming the thoughts we do when trying to conjure up images of long lost loved ones. I had been fortunate to have been at both of my parents sides when their time came. Lung cancer suddenly took our father in 1999. Dad passed peacefully as anyone could pray for with his family at his side; and Mother, in 2010, surrounded by her children and latest great grandchild, and with an empty chair set closest to the bed for our father.

Mum died in a drug-induced coma, saving her of the pain of the bone and breast cancer.

After her death, I was not as distraught as I thought I would have been. Partly due to the knowledge that her suffering was over, but also due to something I had witnessed at the time of her passing. Moments after Mother took her last breath, there was an intense flash of light that appeared to have originated within the room. Like a bolt of lightning, the light shot out through the open doorway into the hallway to finally vanish after passing through a ceiling light fixture. The spectral light caught all of our eyes as it fled. My brothers, Steven and Greg, and sister, Jackie, all believe we witnessed our mother's soul passing on.

With moist eyes, I turned my attention to the glowing waves, waiting for the right moment. When that would be, I did not know, but I was sure that when the time came, I would know it. I didn't have to wait long, because as if ordered, *Maiatla* suddenly slammed into an especially large wave, creating an explosion of blue-white light. Quickly, I wrenched the lid from the urn, and not unlike releasing a genie from a bottle, a cloud of fine dust burst forth to be quickly grabbed by the wind and disappear into the black of the night. As the water glowed below, I leaned outboard to pour the remaining ashes from the container. Once empty, I dropped the urn into the sea, which spun around twice before vanishing in *Maiatla's* wake.

The remainder of the watch was uneventful, but it was hard not to reminisce about my parents for the balance of the night. Janet later expressed her disappointment for having missed the solemn event. I apologized because, in retrospect, after joining the Gunson family some 30 years earlier, Janet loved them as I had and they were her parents as well.

I woke Kara at midnight, then went to bed to join Janet in the aft cabin, only to be nudged awake around 3 a.m.

Whispering as not to wake Janet, Kara said, "Andy, I think I see some lights."

It only took a few seconds for me to respond. I leaped out of bed, perhaps more out of reflex than by conscience action, and still half asleep, grabbed a robe to stumble after Kara. Up in the cockpit, we peered off in the direction Kara was now pointing.

"Andy, I saw a light off in the distance, way off, I think, but I can't find the boat on the radar," Kara said, with a level of frustration ringing in her voice.

I could not see any lights, so I turned my attention to the radar. Commencing on the 38-kilometres (24-mile) range, I tuned it in, but nothing showed on the screen; it was a clean and speck-less sea ahead. I switched the range downward while pausing at each to look for any sign of vessel, but nothing. By the time I hit the last range, I was beginning to consider Kara's lights were a distant star, a ship heading away from us or simply a phantom. As I pushed the buttons to fine tune the screen for the last time at the quarter-mile range, a tiny black dot materialized off in the direction of Kara's reported light. If I wasn't fully awake seconds ago, I most assuredly was now— the dot was only a few hundred feet way and closing fast. I snatched up the binoculars, which were resting on the cabin top, aimed and focused. What was not visible before was now in sharp focus. Through the binoculars, I recognized three weak but distinctly separate lights all in a vertical line, as if mounted on an unseen pole. Down here, this light combination usually indicated a fishing boat. Through the binoculars, I suddenly saw our phantom, which turned out to be an 8-metre (26.2-feet) fishing panga with a pair of Ecuadorian fisherman frantically waving at us. Illuminated by the tri-lights, I could see them trying to tell us they had a net in the water stretching across our path.

"Shit, Kara, throttle down and put the engine in neutral," I ordered in a bit of a panic. *Maiatla* slowed as I disengaged the autopilot and threw the helm over hard. No sooner had we made a 90 degree turn than I spotted, a few metres away, a line of white cork floats supporting the top of the long drift net. Now that I had a clear line of sight on the net, I throttled up.

"Kara, keep the lamp shinning on the floats until we get past them."

As instructed, Kara took a position to best see ahead and to shine the light, but when she did she noticed something.

"Andy, I think that boat is chasing us," she said as she peered aft.

When I looked over my shoulder, I could see the three white lights above a big white bow wave coming our way. Coming across people and boats in isolated locations on the high seas always puts you on your guard, and out here, 644 kilometres (400 miles) from the Ecuador and Columbia borders, was no exception. Seconds later, the fishermen were alongside wanting to talk. It was a hard to hear over the noise of their engine, but I was not about to slow *Maiatla* to have a pow-wow with these fellows in the dead of night. After some yelling and hand signals, it became clear all they wanted was some cigarettes. I asked them if everything else was okay and did they need any water, but they just smiled and waved us off. A benign encounter, but out here, you can never be sure.

I assumed these guys had not come all the way out here, hundreds of miles from land, in such a little boat. They must have a mother ship nearby, so we would have to be vigilant not to run down another fisherman who may be working with the lights off. The rest of Kara's and Ashley's watches passed without any more excitement, but the next day, when no one was watching, I secretly pulled out the 12-gauge shot gun and filled it with eight rounds of shells in preparation for closing in on the coast of Columbia and crossing the cocaine highway.

It was a stretch of the passage that worried me. In this part of the ocean, being so close to the coast of Columbia, we not only had to watch out for "go-fast" drug boats, but the much bigger and slow moving "Bigfoot" drug submarines. During the 1980s, go-fast boats became the drug-smuggling vessel of choice in many parts of the world, especially Columbia. These boats can be detected by radar, which was another reason we constantly ran the radar at night. However, in the 1990s, Columbian drug cartels started using semi-submersibles to smuggle drugs. These subs were slower but nearly undetectable by radar, as they ran with their decks totally awash. This was accomplished with a snorkel for air intake and engine exhaust.

Apparently, the first time the U.S. Coast Guard found one containing drugs, authorities dubbed it "Bigfoot" because they had only heard rumours that such things existed. None had been actually seen until in late 2006 when a "Bigfoot" was seized 145 kilometres (79 nautical miles) southwest of Costa Rica, carrying several metric tonnes of cocaine. In 2006, U.S. officials said they detected three. By 2008, they spotted an average of 10 per month, but it was suggested only one out of 10 was intercepted. By 2009, the U.S.A. detected as many as 60 narco submarines, which were estimated to be moving as much as 330 metric tonnes of cocaine per year. Costing up to two million dollars each to construct, these submarines can move enough cocaine in a single trip to generate more than 100 million USD in profit, making the submarine business a lucrative one. Thus the likelihood of *Maiatla* coming in close contact with a drug sub was good. However, we would most likely never know it, unless we were to ram one.

Our fourth day at sea, we spent motor sailing into 8 knots of wind and a bit of a choppy sea. The high cloud cover made for a pleasantly cool 29 degrees Celsius (85 degrees Fahrenheit) in the boat and cockpit. As there wasn't much to do while motoring, the crew lounged about between their watches, reading, listening to music or carefully sun tanning on the cabin top under the main boom. Fishing still remained a futile effort, so it was chicken and rice, with a green salad, for dinner. Since we had been running the engine a great deal, we ran the watermaker quite a bit so that everyone could have a daily shower or two, which helped to keep the boat smells to a minimum, as it had been particularly hot and sweaty. Despite all the mechanical difficulties, we were forced to deal with after arriving in the Galápagos, the boat and engine ran well and everyone was happy. Even Janet seemed to be doing better after the first couple of days of turbulent water, but that was about to change.

Still, life on board became a familiar routine. Below are two log excerpts I sent home to family and friends.

Log: Monday, March 7, 2016 Position: 03.43N 85.45W

0800 hours. Well, we had a rough night. Fifteen knots on the nose, with up to a 2.5 knot current also on the nose. Motor sailed all night. No ship sightings, but tracked a rain squall on the radar. It missed us. Also saw sheets of lightning off in the distance, which was surprising as we had clear skies above us.

The girls succumbed to a bit sea sickness last night. It was rough and hot above, especially below deck. Ashley moved to sleep in the main salon, as there is less motion there than up in her cabin in the V-berth. The seasickness meds were working today, and the girls were back to their old talkative selves. Despite the rolly conditions, I cooked French toast with bacon for the crew for breakfast. That's it for now, love to all.

Andy and the crew of the *Maiatla*.

Log: Monday, March 7, 2016. 2200 hours

At 0800 hours, on my watch, we killed the engine and hoisted some more sail. We have been sailing at 6 to 7 knot all day on a heading varying from 30 to 45 degrees magnetic, not the best heading for us, as Panamá is at 52 degrees magnetic from here, but it's the best we can do now.

I suspected the head current would decrease the further we sailed north, and it seems to be bearing out, as we only have approximately 1 knot of head current now.

Will have to tack back to the south later so that we can better lay Panamá when we get closer to the coast.

By 1500 hours today, we were still pounding hard into the waves on 32 degrees magnetic and the wind has increased to 20 knots gusting to 25. At this writing, we are exactly halfway from the Galápagos Islands, so we are about 722 kilometres (390 nautical miles) from the north coast of Panamá; the canal is another 277 (150) further. Looking forward to a rough but a good mileage night.

Take care, bye from the crew of the *Maiatla*

We had been spending most of the time sailing with our port rail in the water. All the bouncing from the waves had made for a rough ride, so much so that Janet was having a difficult time sleeping.

Our bed in the aft cabin is a queen and orientated so that we have to sleep crossways to the boat, which means when the boat heels hard on one tack or the other, we tend to either slide down to plant our feet on the footboard or bang our heads. Therefore, a common posture we take entails sleeping like a starfish, all spread out to prevent from rolling about. Normally in extreme heeling cases, to go to sleep, we would grab a couple of pillows and place them against the head- or footboard to lay on and curl up, or at least, I would. But for Janet, it's always more difficult. Her back pain often requires her to lay out straight, and this is difficult to do if we are forced to lie in line with the length of the boat while heeling, because the width of the bed is not sufficient for her to do so.

The voyage to Panamá had us on our ear most of the time, heeled on a starboard tack. Janet's difficulty sleeping led her to sleep deprivation, which played havoc with her moods and her ability to cope. When I found her in the aft cabin crying one afternoon, complaining she could not get comfortable enough to sleep, I knew I had to do something. After giving it some thought, I told Janet I would now make her a new bed.

"How are you going to do that?" she had asked between sobs. I still wasn't sure how, but I gave it a try. I scrounged around to see what I had to work with and quickly found the cushion back on the galley table was the perfect size to extend the width of our bed. However, I needed a plywood support, but short of cutting a cupboard door or floor hatch, I had no wood to work with. Peering into the V-berth, I spotted what I needed. Some years earlier when I had to replace the worn out bed lee cloths, designed to keep the crew from rolling out of bed, I found a readymade replacement at my local Canadian Tire store—vinyl net truck tailgates, both strong and the perfect size.

When Janet saw me return to the cabin with the tailgate net and an electric drill, she insisted what I was doing wasn't necessary, but I didn't listen. I was on a mission. I screwed some stainless-steel pad eyes into the side of the bed and into the opposite wall and door jamb. Then I tied and stretched the net out at the correct elevation to accept the galley table cushion, which now made the foot of our bed over 2 metres (6.5 feet) long. Perfect for Janet to stretch out and with the wall lined with pillows, it made for a pretty nifty bed. Now Janet could be more comfortable while trying to sleep in our heeling boat. Janet reluctantly tried my bed modification, which proved to be a great improvement, and I was pleased to see her sleeping better when it was rough.

Log: Tuesday, March 8, 2016 Position: 05.13N 84.13 W

Approximately 418 kilometres (260 miles) west of the northern Panamá coast. Over 644 kilometres (400 miles) to the canal still.

Well, we had just spent our fifth day at sea. Wind out of the ESE most of the night, so we sailed all night hard on the wind at 6 to 8 knots of speed. All watches were uneventful.

No ship sightings, but lots of lightning to the north. At 1600 hours, this afternoon, Kara spotted a freighter. The large freighter was headed NE, passed us 3.2 kilometres (2 miles) out. Later, to our starboard, we tracked a second ship we sighted just 9.6 kilometres (6 miles) out. The second vessel came within 6.4 kilometres (4 miles) and looked to be moving slow, but I couldn't tell what kind of ship it was. We altered course for a bit more sea room. I went below and told the girls to keep an eye on it

We work hard at collision avoidance, especially at night, and the closer we get to the Panamá Canal, the more ships we expect to encounter.

Once the ships were no longer a hazard, we went back to our original course, motor sailing into 10 knots of wind with 2-metre (6.5-feet) swells. It is a little rough with the wind chop, and the girls just took their sea sickness meds in preparation for tonight. The sun is near setting as I write my log and try to prepare dinner. Sausages and mashed potatoes and green salad.

I changed the engine oil filter last night and drained the water traps for the diesel. When completed, we ran the engine for a few minutes to make sure all was well. Well, it wasn't until I started the engine this afternoon. The engine ran for a few minutes, then died! Although, not likely, perhaps the fuel injector pump packed it in again, as it had while sailing to the Galápagos.

"Great," I had said under my breath. We may have been engine-less again until Panamá. However, as it turned out, I didn't bleed all the air out of the fuel lines when I cleaned the filters.

Engine has been running 2 hours now and no problems. The girls were sharing the watch this afternoon, and for something to do, they held what they called "a dance party." (As each girl listens to her own music through headphones, they wriggle and play air guitar or drums.) Looks funny to see them gyrating around to tunes only they can hear. I have surprised Kara a few times during the night when I came topside to check on things only to find her all alone, beating away at her imaginary drum set.

Been too rough for fishing, so we haven't done any for a few days. Last two days have been noticeably hotter, both day and night, which is not a surprise, as it's supposed to warm up as we close on Panamá. Not looking forward to more heat than what we are used to.

Figure 88. A selfie taken during a "dance party."

Weather GRIB claims calmer weather ahead, but the GRIB seems to lie a lot. Oh and Ashley was showing off her *Maiatla* "love bites" today. She has many dark bruises from being thrown into things as the boat rolls about. She needs to learn to hang on better.

The girls found an empty rum bottle on board (not sure where it came from), wrote a note and made big deal on video, casting it adrift. The girls are a source of constant amusement, even when seasick.

Anyway, all is well. Goodbye for now, Andy.

Chapter 37

Swimming Naked with Pilot Whales

"I strive to make a life for myself that I do not require a vacation to escape."
—Anonymous

Life at sea is often day after day of monotonous routine until one day it is not! During our six days at sea since departing the Galápagos Islands, we had a mixed bag of weather, ranging from flat calms to gusting 25-knot winds. Fortunately, aside from spotting a rain squall and lighting storm off in the distance, gales have been pleasantly absent. A blessing since whenever we did have wind, it was always on the nose. Two-hundred years of pilot chart observations indicated we should have, for this time of the year, a southerly wind putting us on a beam reach, a fast and comfortable point of sail. Not the east, nose-slapping winds that had plagued us, which were most likely the result of our strong El Niño year.

Figure 89. Janet and Ashley share a quiet moment on a calm sea.

Dawn found us motoring along on a flat calm sea, without a shading cloud in sight. We were blessed, or cursed, with an unbroken sky from horizon to horizon and only a single burning white orb to mar the monotonous blue heavens. By 10 a.m., the heat was already oppressive, so early on, the girls gave me a hand and we stretched a tarpaulin over the main boom to shade the amidships and cockpit. Janet was hiding out below in our cabin, trying to stay under the open hatch, which was funneling in some air as we motored along.

"Okay, babe," I said as I popped my head into aft cabin. "I've got the tarp up and wind socks in place, so you should notice a bit of a differences now."

"I feel a bit of a breeze, but it isn't much," Janet replied. "Damn, it's hot!" she added as she glanced upward to the open hatch to see if she could feel any air movement on her sweating brow.

"Hey, hun, later in the day, I will need to transfer fuel to the day tank and to do that I will have to stop the engine, so if there still isn't any wind, I thought we could all go for a swim. Maybe after lunch, what ya think?" I asked as I sat on the edge of the bed beside her.

Janet fanned her face with the book she was reading.

"Yes, a swim would be nice, but let's do it sooner as opposed to later."

I didn't need a lot of convincing. "Okay, how about now?" I said.

Leaving Janet on the bed, I bolted topside to where Ashley and Kara were sitting in the newfound shade of the cockpit. They were busy listening to music and gyrating to another one of their "dance parties."

It was technically Kara's watch, but during the daylight hours, we were informal and often shared the watch duties, easy to do if you were lounging topside anyway. I said nothing to the girls as I sat next to the helm and throttled down the engine. As the boat lost way, I put the old girl into reverse and revved her up. The propeller bit into the water, then began to cavitate, with the formation of air bubbles behind the propeller. The propeller shot the bubbles under the hull creating an upwelling of foaming water around the boat until we finally came to a complete stop.

"What's up, Andy?" Ashley asked, with some concern.

I just smiled and said, "It's time for a swim. You guys coming in?" I didn't wait for an answer. I left the cockpit to retrieve the boarding ladder and quickly hung it over the side. It was a marvellous day for a swim, but to make sure we weren't going to get left behind if a breeze were to blow up, I told Kara to put the helm hard a-starboard, and then tying one end of a long line to *Maiatla's* rail and the other end to *Maiatla's* life ring, I tossed it into the water. Running forward, I pulled a mask and snorkel out of the dive gear box on the foredeck, stripped off my shorts and t-shirt, climbed the rail and prepared to make the leap, but not before I had a good look over the side.

Over the years, I have seen things like big sharks and other lurking creatures following the boat or taking advantage of the shade the hull provided, so I found it prudent to have a look before jumping overboard while at sea. Nothing was seen from the deck, so I jumped. By all accounts, it was a spectacular day in the tropics;

the sea was as smooth as glass, with only a slight groundswell rolling under the boat to remind us we were—on the ocean and not a lake. Remarkably, the sea was as clear as a pool and the water temperature almost matched the air, which was in the low 30 degrees Celsius range. It felt more like a hot tub than the sea. After the bubbles had cleared, I donned my mask and had another look under the boat and below my feet for anything that could eat me, but I saw nothing. With the water perfectly clear, I could easily see down 100 metres (328 feet) or more. There wasn't a fish of any size in sight.

When I looked back towards *Maiatla*, the boat appeared as if it was floating in air. At that point, I noticed I had forgotten we had a fishing rod out and there, hanging perhaps 30 metres (98.4 feet) below was my green squid, dangling lifelessly on the line.

I swam back to the boat to grab a camera as I needed to get some pictures and video of this. Back at the boarding ladder, I climbed partway out and called Kara to grab the camera from the bookshelf below, which she did and handed it to me. I flopped back into the water and commenced to take video of the boat on the surface and the scene under water. I was preoccupied with getting some shots when I heard Kara call to me.

"Andy, can you get some video of us jumping off the boat?"

When I looked, I saw that both the girls had likewise stripped off and were ready for a mid ocean skinny-dip.

"Just a second, Kara. I'll back up a bit to get more of the boat in frame."

Kara had swum mid ocean once before on our voyage to Hawaii, so she did not hesitate. When I told her I was ready, she climbed over the life line, and holding her nose, she screamed and jumped. Ashley was quick at her attempt to follow, but hesitated once she reached the rail. As predictable as the geyser Old Faithful, Ashley's anxiety flared up as she started to vibrate while making a cooing noise. I knew then, this could take a while.

"Come on, Ashley, just jump. The water is warm," Kara called to her friend.

Ashley was bouncing where she stood, and I'm sure her arms would be going as well if she didn't have to hang on to the boat as it rolled from side to side on the swell.

"How deep is it here?" Ashley asked, with a nervous chuckle as she stared down into the water.

"Oh, about 2 miles deep," I said. "But don't let that worry you, as you can drown in only 6 inches of water."

"There isn't anything down there that could bite me is there?" she asked between more cooing, bouncing and nervous laughter.

"Nope, nothing you have to worry about anyway," I said. "Just jump."

Ashley was a little nervous, and I guess she had every reason to be. We were over 483 kilometres (300 miles) from the nearest land, and if we were to get separated from the boat, we would surely all perish, as it was unlikely another vessel would come this way anytime soon, never mind be able to spot a head-sized object in the water from a distance. Swimming out here is no small feat of courage to be sure.

Another 10 minutes or so passed while Ashley weighted out the pros and cons of jumping as opposed to climbing down the ladder and slipping into the water. I'm sure staying aboard was also crossing her mind. In the meantime, Janet appeared on deck in a two-piece bathing suit and leapt over the side.

"So, what's with the bathing suit, hun," I asked when Janet swam over to me.

"I saw you had the video camera going, and I though at least one of us should have some clothes on."

Figure 90. Kara, Janet and Ashley passing around the beer cans as they tread water 2 miles deep.

Perhaps encouraged by Janet's leap or simply shamed by the being the last one left aboard, Ashley finally demanded that I count down from three. When I did, she jumped while I video recorded her flight through the air and her plunging descent into the abyss. We all cheered in acknowledgement of her conquering a real fear.

It was leisurely fun to hang off the buoy, and it made it easy to pull ourselves back to the boat if it were to drift off too far. For the following hour we swam, dived from the boat and rested on the buoy, taking in the grandeur of the moment. I slipped back aboard for a few minutes to switch on the fuel pump for the transfer while we were swimming.

That done, it was time for a barley water. While hanging off the life ring, floating some 15 metres (49.2 feet) from the boat, like winos on a park bench, we talked and laughed as we took hits off the beer can that we kept passing around until it was empty.

Every time I went back aboard to check on the fuel level, I brought back another cold brew. Whenever a beer was finished, we filled the can full of water, and like a descending depth charge, we watched it for several minutes as it slowly sank out of sight. It was easy to see the can well beyond 30 metres (98 feet) before losing sight of it in the dazzling starbursts created by the rays of sun penetrating into the depth.

We had a grand time, but my last check of the fuel tank was indicating it was nearly full, so I informed everyone we would have to get moving soon. I tossed the girls another beer while taking a seat on the cabin top, just to have a look around, and it was fortunate that I had. Looking off into the distance, I first saw a great splash, then an arching fin cut through the water. Bracing myself against the roll while shielding my eyes from the sun, I stood to have a better look.

"What d'ya see, Andy?" Janet asked as she passed the beer on around the life ring.

"I saw a splash and a fin." And no-sooner had I said it there were more splashes and more fins. "Holy shit!" I said. "It's a pod of dolphins, looks like hundreds of them, and they are coming this way."

As animals approach, I heard both Kara and Ashley ask, "Do we need to get out?"

"No, you don't have to, but if you want to, go ahead or just stay close to the boat. I'm grabbing the video camera and coming back in," I said.

Despite looking a little anxious, everyone stayed in the water. After grabbing everyone's snorkelling gear, I passed the equipment down the ladder to Kara, who passed it all around. Donning my own mask and turning on the GoPro, I leapt back in the water. Despite the excellent visibility, there was not much to see at first, but after a few minutes, like homing torpedoes, the first of the dolphins shot past. Then moments later, we were surrounded. I feared that they

Figure 91. Bottlenose dolphins came close in to say "hi" and check out the crew of *Maiatla*.

would pass us by, but the animals appeared to be as fascinated with us as we were with them. For over an hour, we swam around the boat gawking at bottlenose dolphins swimming around gawking at us.

There were even several females with some inquisitive young ones. The babies, not much bigger than a football, were most likely getting an eyeful of their first humans.

It was an incredible interaction with these playful animals that at times were an arm's length away. The girls clung tight to the life ring, mesmerized by the show.

I attempted to chase the dolphins with the camera, at times travelling quite far away from the boat. I was tiring, so it was time to climb back aboard and get moving. As I swam back over to Janet and the girls and approached the boat, I noticed Janet waving frantically at me while pointing off into the distance. Looking to where Janet was pointing, I stiffened while staring in disbelief at a bizarre sight to be sure. A spike of adrenaline energized my body.

Off in the distant underwater haze, I could see a dozen or so black objects, perhaps three times the size of the dolphins. However, they were not swimming. The animals were floating vertically in the water column. Some of them were at the surface, yet others were 5 or so metres (16.4 feet) deep.

It's funny how your mind works. My first fleeting thought was the dolphins were standing on their tails to form a line of attack. However, they were too big to be dolphins. I floated on the surface with my face in the water as the black shadows grew closer, drifting on the unseen current. I heard a muffled call from Janet asking what they were, followed by the assertion that we should get out of the water. Still mesmerized, I watched until I finally realized what they were. And I was right, they were not dolphins at all, but a larger cousin of theirs.

Pulling my head clear of the water, I excitedly yelled at the girls, "It's a pod of sleeping pilot whales."

As the whales drifted even closer, their size became more apparent. These animals were between 3 and 5 metres (9.8 to 16.4 feet) in length, and the reason they appeared to be standing on their tails was because they were. When pilot whales sleep, they do so vertically, dozing while slowly bobbing to the surface every few minutes for a breath of air, then sinking back down to repeat the process.

The dolphins did not appear to mind sharing the sea with either us or the whales, and for almost another hour, over 50 pilot whales drifted by until I moved too close with the camera and woke a few of them. If they did not know we were there before, they did now. However, they did not appear to be alarmed. It was like they were waiting for everyone to wake up, and then ever so causally they swam away, but at a pace I could keep up with. So, without any hesitation, I followed.

It was extraordinary to be able to swim within an arm's length of these magnificent mammals. I could see every scar and skin blemish as I followed for as long as I dared—until the boat looked to be a long way off. Reluctantly, I was forced to give up the pod and make my way back to Janet and the boat. A wise decision considering we were still a few hundred miles from the nearest land and to miss the boat would not be good.

Figure 92. Pilot whales sleep vertically bobbing to the surface to breath

Figure 93. We were able to swim in amongst them at an arm's length without them becoming alarmed.

As I made my way back, I could hardly believe how lucky I was that Janet loved me because if she didn't, it wouldn't take much for her to jump back aboard and sail off, leaving me with my whale friends. Divorce, pirate style. Not exactly like walking the plank, but equally effective. Finally back at the boat, I could still see the whales off in the distance, but the dolphins had vanished. We all had one more swim around the boat before getting out, but when I passed the stern, I notice something that gave me reason to pause. The squid jig was gone.

The fishing line was still dangling, but no lure. When I first saw the dolphins, it occurred to me that I should reel in the hook, but I didn't believe it would be an issue with them. I have trolled through great schools of tuna and dolphins feeding on herring, and I have never hooked a dolphin, as they were always too smart to take the fake bait. The possibility of a young one swimming away with a hook stuck in its mouth made me feel ill. I hoped it wasn't so.

Figure 94. After waking them the pod slowly swam off.

Perhaps the line fouled with a drifting whale, and it simply snapped? Since there was nothing I could do about it now, I tried to put it out of my mind.

With all safely back on *Maiatla,* we got the boat back underway, all the while chattering of our once in a lifetime encounter. We had the video and sunburns to prove it.

I have had many such encounters in my lifetime, with giant manta rays, elephant seals, whale sharks and big hammerhead and tiger sharks, but this was perhaps the best ever.

Later, as everyone showered, I poured a glass of wine, then made spaghetti with meat sauce for dinner. Waiting for the pasta to come to a boil, I peered out the window above the stove to see if I could get one last glimpse of my whales, but it was for naught. While sipping on wine and stirring the sauce, I could not help believe that it could not possibly get any better out here than this.

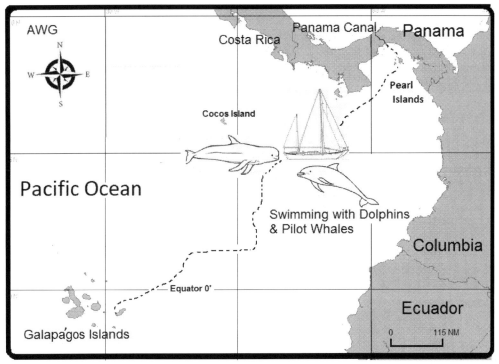

Figure 95. Map depicting the location of our encounter with the pod of dolphins and sleeping whales.

Chapter 38

Archipiélago de las Perlas—Archipelago of the Pearls

"Every minute, the future is becoming the past."
—Thor Heyerdahl

The following couple of days were mostly uneventful. On Thursday, March 10, during my watch, I started to see an ever-increasing number of flying fish take to the air, often frightened into flight by *Maiatla's* approach. I also saw sea turtles of greater numbers resting on the surface, often with cheeky seagulls perched upon their backs, mooching a free ride. The turtles and gulls indicated we were nearing land, and in fact, we were less than 322 kilometres (200 miles) from raising land, Punta Mala in Panamá. Then we had another 161 kilometres (100 miles) to the Pearl Islands, which would be the first opportunity for the crew to have a well-deserved rest.

Later, on Ashley's watch, she sighted a couple of fishing boats with drift nets out. They had two-man crews huddled under makeshift awnings made of multi-coloured blankets, which they wrapped themselves in at night. An hour later, she detected on the radar a large freighter about 22 kilometres (12 nautical miles) out. After tracking it for 10 minutes, I determined we were on a collision course. I called the ship on the radio using the standard high seas calling channels, but they failed, or they just refused, to respond. It was a massive ship with its bow stacked high with colourful containers. I was reasonably sure this island-size ship would not be able to see us once it came within a mile or so. When the ship closed the distance within 3.2 kilometres (2 miles), I altered course 90 degrees to starboard to get out of its way. Travelling at 20 knots, it passed to our port at less than three-quarters of a mile, and seeing how big it was, we would have been like a snail under a truck's wheels. The ship wouldn't have felt a thing and would've been fine; us on the other hand could not have been that hopeful. Best to give this brute a wide berth.

Later with Ashley still on watch, she had two fish strike the gear. The first hit on the starboard side and ran wild until it spit out the hook before we could get the rod out of the holder. Then 20 minutes later, a second fish hit on the port side. I heard the reel run out of line as I lay in my cabin. Running topside, I arrived in time to see Ashley reach for the rod, but she was too late. The fish stripped the remaining line from the reel, and when the line came to the end, the 100-pound test fishing line broke, startling Ashley with its firecracker-like snap. The rod whipped back, almost striking her in the face.

We never had a chance to see the fish, but whatever it was, it was big, VW bus big, and probably too large to bring aboard anyway, a tuna perhaps. Nevertheless, it would have been fun to play with or, at least, see. We might not have lost the fish if Ashley had remembered the first rule when a fish strikes, and that is to slow the boat down right away. I gave her a hard time about forgetting this. All in good fun, of course. No fresh fish for this dinner, so I cooked chicken and potatoes, with frozen mixed veggies. The crew dined in the cockpit, a common arrangement, as below decks was usually sweltering after the stove had been on.

In the evening, while attending to the ham net and sending our position report to be posted on the internet, I discovered an error I had been making for the past six days, since we crossed over to the north side of the equator. When I filled out the latitude part of my position, the coordinates were followed with an "N" or an "S," indicating whether we were north or south of the equator. Simple, but when we crossed back into the north, I neglected to change that one little letter. The result of this negligence was when our vessel's position was posted on the web at SHIPTRACK, the Google map placed us on a perfect course to land in two days on the north coast of Chile. Like Captain Ron from the movie of the same name, perhaps we should have "pulled in somewhere and asked for directions."

It was a quick fix, but it may have been baffling to anyone tracking our progress.

Somewhere before midnight while alone on watch, I made a cursory inspection walk around the deck, checking the rig tension and looking for sail and sheet chaffing, and for any flying fish that may have come aboard. With the foredeck in good order, I made my way to the stern where I noticed the dinghy was again getting soft. The starboard pontoon resembled a partially deflated balloon. Apparently, the patch I put on the dink back on Santa Cruz was leaking.

As a result of being partially deflated, the dink was now sagging in the davits, permitting it to sway from side to side in sympathy to the rolling of *Maiatla*. A closer look revealed a new rub mark on top of the inboard pontoon—a chafe spot that would quickly hole the dink if left to continue. I needed to run a pair of lines from the end of the davits, run them under the dink and draw them up tight, but that would entail precariously crawling out to the end of the davits, which would have me hanging my ass out over the water as *Maiatla* was steaming along at 6 knots.

To fall over this night would mean certain death. I could hear Janet inside my head giving me shit if I fell overboard because I was not wearing my harness and clipped on. Before securing the dinghy, I made my way back to the cockpit to get a harness and gear, no sense in pissing off the admiral by getting myself killed. All clipped on, I climb out over the rushing water.

The chore proved much more difficult than I had first anticipated, as the boat was lurching about and I needed both hands to run the lines around the dink and tie the requisite knots. Twice I was almost launched from the end of the davit as *Maiatla* slammed into a pair of particularly steep waves. I had wrapped my legs around a davit, locking my feet together, which was all that saved me. As I took a moment to watch the bioluminescent water race by, slightly over a metre (3.2 feet) below, it suddenly occurred to me that perhaps my harness lanyard may be a tad too long. If I were to fall, I would still be attached to the boat, but some 2 metres (6.5 feet) behind, dragged on the surface of the water until someone woke up to discover me missing.

Still better than getting left behind, but the thought of looking like trolling bait gave me an unsettled feeling. Once the dink was secured and with a new set of bruises between my legs, I returned to the cockpit for the balance of my watch, leaving my harness on while clipping the lanyard to the cockpit jack line, just in case.

Eight days after departing the Galápagos Islands, we were only 80 kilometres (50 miles) from Punta Mala Panamá and 267 kilometres (166 miles) from the Pearl Islands. The wind had finally shifted to the north, giving us a great sail on a port tack under full sail, ripping up the sea at 6.5 knots on a tight reach, and we were not alone. Right before sunset a massive pod of pantropical spotted dolphins passed by, some taking the time to ride *Maiatla's* bow wave.

The spotted dolphin is often mistaken for the more recognizable bottlenose dolphin. The spotted variety has a dark grey back and the adults are spotted. They are active and prone to making large, splashy leaps from the sea. It is a common "breacher" and will often clear the water by 2 metres (6.5 feet) or more, achieving some significant hang time in the air. The animals love bow-riding, and other types of play with boats is common. Unfortunately, the dolphins did not stay long with *Maiatla*.

Our other guests were not so welcoming. To the north and south of us, and as if we were driving up the median of a massive highway, there was a string of freighters inbound and outbound from the Panamá Canal—a never-ending parade of ships of all sizes, a genus of tankers, bulk carriers, containerships, cruise ships and the odd gun-toting naval vessel to round things off.

We had a tense afternoon dodging all the shipping. When night fell, it became even more intense as the wind and waves built up and all we could see of these giants were tiny running lights often obscured by rain, cloud or waves. It is on nights like these the radar earns its place on the boat, and it is priceless.

I sat my usual trick at the helm till midnight, but after being rousted from a warm bed several times before 2 a.m., I decided it would be easier to stay up and nap in the cockpit when the opportunity presented itself. I had a busy and restless night, first with Kara then Ashley, and not only tracking the shipping to keep from getting run over, but performing multiple sail changes as a series of mini gales, with wind lulls in between, hammered through. I was cold, rain-soaked and exhausted. I curled up on the lee side in a blanket, napping between sightings as one of the girls scanned the blackness, then turned her attention to the radar screen. I was relieved not only to witness the first streaks of the pending sunrise, but also to see, according to the chart, we were leaving the busy shipping lanes behind. The long line of ships making their turns either towards the canal or for the open Pacific and away from us.

Figure 96. Kara and Ashley looking for marine life as *Maiatla* motors along towards the Pearl Islands on a calm sea

I remained in the cockpit at the helm until well after daylight when Janet finally arose and brought me a hot cup of tea. The wind abated with the rise of the sun, and it was looking like the day would be humid and overcast. I hoped it would leave us enough wind to sail the rest of the way. However, time would prove we would not be that fortunate. This was the morning of our ninth day at sea, and if all went well, we would soon be anchoring in the lee of a nearly uninhabited tropical island, with our own private sand beach to play on.

The first of the Pearl Islands, as you approach from the southwest, is Isla San José. I chose this island as the one to receive our footprints for a day and provide the crew a quiet place to rest up from what had been a hard voyage. A long voyage such as this, in hindsight, often resembles one long day with a series of catnaps along the way. Every muscle in my body ached from fighting the near constant motion of the boat, and contrary to what I told Ashley and Kara, I had my own series of *Maiatla* "love bites" in the form of bruising, mainly on my legs and hips, as well as some serious butt chaffing from my ass sliding back and forth along the seat with each roll of the boat.

A prolonged voyage can leave holes in the butt cheeks of your shorts, that is, if you were wearing any. In truth, damp butt cheeks stick very nicely to polished wood cockpit seats, the suction limiting slippage, not unlike the knotty-non-skid cloths often placed upon galley tables or the sucker-tipped arrow striking a glass pane after being launched from a child's toy bow and arrow. However, since the boat rule that everyone had to use a "sweat towel" under naked flesh was strictly enforced, the butt suction technique was seldom employed. *Maiatla's* cockpit came with comfy seat cushions, but when it was particularly rolly, the cushions tended to slid off, dumping their occupant onto the cockpit floor—a heart stopping jolt if you happen to be napping at the time. Janet also suffered from the motion much more than the rest of us, still she managed not to show it most of the time.

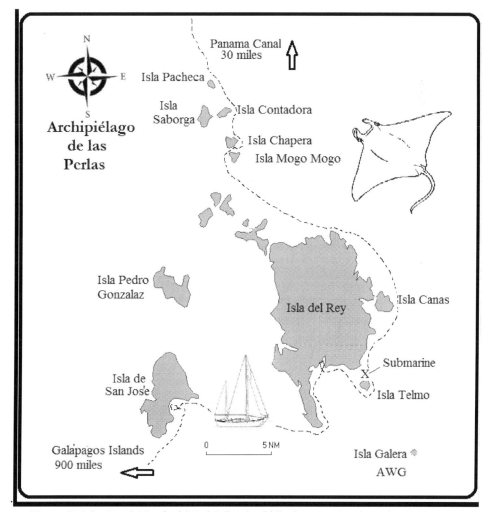

Figure 97. The Pearl Islands, *Maiatla's* first landfall after crossing from the Galápagos.

The Pearl Islands are a group of 200 islands and islets, principally uninhabited, lying some 56 kilometres (30 nautical miles) off the coast in the Gulf of Panamá on the Pacific side. The most notable island is Contadora Island, which in the 1970s and '80s was known for its resorts and many homes owned by wealthy Panaménians, who flew out from the nearby Panamá City. However, the islands have since fallen on hard economic times, and many of the hotels and homes have been abandoned.

Contadora's history stretches back to the 17th century when it was used by the Spanish conquistadors as a place to unload and take inventory of the booty they plundered from the Inca Empire before shipping it back to Spain. Hence, it was given the name "contador," meaning "counter" or "bookkeeper" in Spanish. Two years after the Spaniards arrival, all of the Native Indians on the Pearl Islands were either dead or enslaved.

The largest island, at 234 square kilometres (90 square miles), is Isla Del Rey ("Island of the King"). Isla Del Rey has several small towns, most notably San Miguel. It is easily larger than the other Pearl Islands combined and is the second largest island in all of Panamá, after Coiba, which lies on the Pacific north coast.

Privately owned, Isla San José, our first destination, is the second largest island in the Pearl Islands and has an area of 44 square kilometres (17 square miles). The 2000 census placed its resident population at 10, but this number has swelled, as a newly constructed hotel has flown in guests as well as staff. The cruising guide reports the island is also populated by thousands of wild pigs and deer, which can be seen scavenging on the island's some 50 sand beaches in the early morning hours or late in the day. Left unmolested and with my shotgun in hand, I'm sure I could find a volunteer for the B.B.Q. or Luau on the beach. I would have to see how "private" this island is. I also discovered a re-occurring theme involving the U.S. Military. Here in paradise, festered a netherworld malady.

From 1945 to 1947, a special unit of U.S. Army tested chemical weapons and arms on this, then deserted, island. When the military finally decided to vacate, they left behind some parting gifts in the form of at least eight unexploded 500-pound and 1,000-pound bombs. The U.S. Military admitted the larger bombs contain phosgene and cyanogen chloride, and the smaller ones contain mustard gas. Other reports claim that, aside from the particularly nasty chemical weapons, deadly Sarin and VX nerve gas were also extensively tested here. After WWII, conventional bombs, unexploded ordnance and thousands of insidious chemical mines were left lying around the islands. A clean up eventually ensued, which involved dumping an unknown but, reportedly, large amount of munitions into the sea surrounding the islands.

We were back to motoring; the wind died and the sea laid down, as if it too needed a rest. I finished my morning tea, then retreated to bed. Janet took the watch while I slept like the dead.

I awoke in the early afternoon, and on the distant horizon, our island rose out of the sea. It was a welcoming sight that signalled this part of the journey was coming to end. It was still overcast and hot, but the forward motion of the boat offered some relief in the form of apparent wind.

Everyone was sitting in the cockpit as I made my way topside. The crew appeared tired, yet happy (or was it a look of relief?). I believe the girls were as happy to see land as I. After giving Janet a kiss, I wandered forward to have a better look at our island, Ashley and Kara followed. No sooner had we reached the pulpit than I heard Ashley cry out, "Hey, there is a big fin over there. I'm going to get my camera."

When Kara and I looked to where Ashley had indicated, we could not see anything other than a great swirling ripple in the otherwise mirror-smooth water. We didn't have to wait long, though, because as soon as Ashley returned it resurfaced. There, a few boat lengths away, was a dorsal fin, an immense fin, protruding over a metre (3.2 feet) out of the water, and it was coming our way and fast. I assumed the creature wanted to have a look at us. It was a whale shark, bluish-grey, with dollar-size white spots, and of prehistoric proportions. Before I could say "holy crap," the shark, rivalling the size of *Maiatla,* sank to pass directly under the boat and carried on. I instructed Janet, who was on the helm at the time, to turn the boat around and give chase. However, it was no use, the whale shark dived out of sight, and that would be the last we would see of him. It was then I noticed how murky the water was.

The sea was a muddy-brown colour, as if a nearby river was dumping silt-laden rainwater. But it was not dirty—the brown colour was created by billions of plankton organisms, the whale shark's favourite food.

A filter feeder, the shark swims with its mouth agape swallowing whatever passes through its strainers. We made several circles hoping to spot the animal and maybe jump into the water for a free ride upon its back, as I had done on similar animals in the Sea of Cortez three years back. However, after 10 minutes of zigzagging, we went back to our original course although the girls and I stayed on deck in hopes of sighting other marine life. Not wanting to miss another opportunity, I retrieved a mask, fins and snorkel and had the GoPro video camera ready to go. I didn't have to wait long. Ashley, with her sharp young eyes, detected a pair of manta ray wingtips way off in the distance. Again Janet made chase, and when we had slipped in close enough, we saw a majestic-looking manta that must have been at least 3 metres (9.8 feet) across, swimming right at the surface.

"Janet, head over that way so that we can get in front of him. I'm going to jump in and see if I can get some video," I yelled as I pointed in the direction I wanted her to go. Minutes later, I made a leap, put my fins on and swam like a madman, heading off in search of the giant ray. The first metre of surface water was warm, but down a bit, the water turned downright cold, a big surprise. By the time I arrived to where the ray was, it had gone. I looked back towards the boat and, following Kara's and Ashley's directions, took up the chase, but due to the murky water, I couldn't see more than 2 metres (6.5 feet) ahead.

Peering across the surface, I spied the pair of fins a few metres away, so I resumed swimming as hard as I could, but I could not catch up. After 20 minutes or so, I learned I could "track" the ray by following the cold water trail it left in its wake, its great bulk drawing the cold water to the surface as it bat its massive wings. However, even though I could follow the critter, it just would not let me get close enough to see it. After swimming in great circles or backtracking, I developed the distinct feeling the manta ray was playing with me. I stopped to catch my breath when it suddenly occurred to me there could be other critters out here with big teeth, and I would hate to be mistaken for a lame seal in the murky water. A wave of uncertainty crept over me. On the surface, I spun around and there, off in the distance, way off, was *Maiatla* doing circles, with the girls still on the foredeck, trying to keep track of me while giving directions to Janet. After half an hour, I was exhausted from swimming flat out, so reluctantly, I decided to abort this hunt and to return to the boat. Once safely back aboard, we resumed our course.

An hour before dusk, I piloted *Maiatla* past a tall rock spire guarding the eastern approach to Ensenada Playa Grande and our bay on Isla San José. We dropped the hook in among several other sailing boats and a big sports fisherman. If all the company wasn't dishearten enough, the pair of Sea-Doos racing around, which belonged to the big hotel on the beach, were enough to spoil the remaining peace and privacy of our island. Still, it was a beautiful bay, with a crescent sand beach surrounded by a thick jungle, garnished with canting coconut palms. Despite the presence of the hotel, we could only see a handful of people on the beach. Thankfully, the hotel architects designed a "low key" structure, which blended kindly into the rocky cliffs of the point and the surrounding jungle.

Once the sea-bound dirt bikes headed home, the sound of the jungle birds drifted out to the boat. Not perfect, but the place will do, and the bonus was the unsecured internet from the hotel that we were able to log onto, as long as we were sitting in the cockpit.

Our first order of business was to swap the Ecuador courtesy flag for the Panamánian flag. Ashley and I went on the foredeck for an impromptu ceremony and flag raising. That done our next order of business was to take a swim, so I placed the boarding ladder over the side and jumped in. What a surprise was waiting for me. The water here, as it was when we chased the manta ray, was thick with brown plankton and cold, retracting testicles kind of cold. As I resurfaced from my leap, I noticed there was a strong current running past the boat, so I had to swim hard as to not get carried away.

"How's the water, Andy?" Kara asked as she and Ashley were about to come in.

I lied, "It's great and warm, but hang that jib sheet in the water so that we have something to hang onto, as there is a bit of current." I tried not to let my teeth chatter. I later concluded there was a nearby upwelling of deep cold water, created by the strong current that was colliding with the island.

Kara jumped and the screams and expression on her face gave it away. Kara was so shocked by the cold water she forgot to grab onto the line. I had to grab her to prevent her from being swept away. Seeing and hearing Kara scream was Ashley's motivation not to jump, but to her credit, after much theatrics, she did manage to climb down the ladder and, ever so carefully, slide into the water.

Janet and I made dinner while the girls logged onto the internet, and for the first time in almost 10 days, they were able to update their Facebook accounts. I also took advantage of the connection to send our Panamá agent a message informing him we had made the crossing safely and would be in Panamá on Sunday afternoon, five days from now.

Figure 98. Ashley drops the Ecuador courtesy flag and raises the Panamanian flag.

Kara was eagerly messaging her two young children to share some pictures so that they could see what their mother had been up to. For Kara, what started as an exciting chance to directly share her travels with her family and, more importantly, her two young boys turned into an evening of gut-wrenchingly guilty feelings and recrimination, as the netherworld brought Kara some devastating news.

"What's the matter, Kara?" Ashley asked as she was the first one to notice Kara sinking demeanor as she sat in the corner of the cockpit, thumbing through her cell phone.

The news was not good, Travis, Kara's estranged husband, who had been looking after their boys while she was off sailing the world, had been admitted into hospital, and the boys were now staying with Kara's mother. The diagnosis was stomach cancer, most likely brought on by alcohol abuse. Travis was a good father and provider for his boys, a hard-working pipeline welder who also liked to party hard, which can be the bane of remote camp life. The demon bottle was not satisfied with bringing a possible end to his marriage, it was now striving to terminate his life. The long-term prognosis was not good.

We had made good time in getting to the Pearl Islands, so much so we could spend four days here exploring and playing. However, after hearing of Travis aliment, I approached Kara when she was alone.

"Kara, we can head straight to Panamá, and you can get a flight home right away if you want," I said, seeing the anguish in her eyes.

Kara sank into a deep soul-searching silence while looking for answers as to what to do. Carefully, Kara regurgitated the thoughts she had racing through her mind ever since she received the news of Travis's illness. Now, she dared speaking of them to me.

"No, I don't think so. They boys are okay with my mum, and there is nothing I can do for Travis anyway. I still need time to think this through, and I don't want his cancer to be the reason that we get back together. It would be the wrong reason."

Kara obviously still possessed strong feeling for Travis; however, they were not the same ones she had when she first married him. Kara was torn, but I believed she may be right. She needed this time to prepare herself for when she had to go back home to face not only one personal crisis, but two.

I have always known that Kara was of strong character and possessed a wise old soul that she could draw upon in a time of crisis, and this was most assuredly one of those watershed-times.

We only spent part of the next day here, on Isla San José, exploring a few of the deserted beaches off our stern and tracking deer, pigs and iguana trails in the sand. It was nice, but the cold water and horde of people, combined with the news of Travis, all served to sully the mood of the boat and rightly so. Perhaps wrongly believing we could sail away and leave all the bad news and netherworld behind, we all agreed it was time to move on. Besides, I was sure there were better spots around the next headland. So, early in the afternoon, the day after our arrival, we pulled anchor and got back underway.

From our bay on Isla San José to its neighbouring island, Isla Del Rey, the distance was only 17.7 kilometres (11 miles), and according to our cruising guide, there was a nicely sheltered bay around the southernmost tip of the island where I planned to anchor. It was close by, so we thought we'd have no problem making it before dark. Once clear of Isla San José guarding spire, a stiff breeze filled in from the north, permitting the girls to unfurl the big headsail and sheet it home. It was a magnificent broad reach sail between islands. We passed several fishing pangas and a feeding pod of dolphins, and both human and fish paid us no mind as we raced by.

Our timing was perfect. As we rounded the wooded point, the water calmed, the wind died and an idyllic anchorage came into view moments before the sun sunk out of the sky. In went the headsail and I fired up the engine. I already had some chicken ready to barbeque after we finally get the hook down. However, as the 18th-century Scottish poet Robert Burns wrote, *"The best-laid plans of mice and men often go awry"*—a sentiment that applies to cruisers more often than not, and tonight, for the crew of *Maiatla*, there would be no exception.

The roar of huge engines carried for miles over the placid waters as a jet-black 15-metre (49.2 feet) long "cigarette" boat tore around the corner, racing at, what I would guess to be, over 40 knots, launching a 5-metre (16.4-feet) high roster tail of water in its wake. It was growing dark, and even though we lost sight of the speed boat in a hurry, we could hear it race up the coast, apparently on an urgent matter. We manoeuvred *Maiatla* close inshore where we spotted a sturdy-looking dock with navigation lights on the end.

"Looks like an official-looking dock there," I said to Janet, who was driving and following my directions as I searched for just the right spot to drop the hook.

"According to the guide book, there is a Panamanian Navy station just inland. It's probably theirs," Janet replied.

After making a few tight circles, I figured we found the "sweet spot"—it would offer the most protection from the wind and be out of the ocean swell that wrapped around the headland.

"Okay, looks good here, babe. Stop the boat, and I will drop the hook," I shouted over my shoulder as I ran to the foredeck. As an afterthought, I added, "Kara, can you hit the spreader lights so that I can see what I'm doing?" It was more of a command than a request.

As I cleared the ground tackle in preparation to drop, I became aware of the roar of the big speed boat, and it was getting louder quickly. Assuming the tourists were still racing around, I didn't give it any more thought, other than I hoped they'd quit it soon so that we could enjoy a peaceful night.

The anchor chain began to run free, and the hook had scarcely hit the bottom when the cigarette boat shot out of the black night. It slowed and, scarcely out of the range of my spreader lights, circled a mere few boat lengths away, mostly obscured by the edge of darkness.

A call in Spanish boomed out, but I did not understand what the voice was saying, partly because the background was filled with several other voices, all conversing in Spanish. I gazed towards the boat as it crept closer. When they finally entered my encompassing spreader lights, two men on the foredeck became visible. They were all dressed in deep blue or black, as if cat burglars, and they were cradling in their arms some pretty intimidating automatic weaponry.

My sphincter tightened and the air became heavy and hard to breath. My first thought was that these were drug smugglers or just plain old fashioned pirates here to plunder. The boat came to a stop a few metres away. Then a similarly dressed man, back in the cockpit of the boat, spoke in quick staccato bursts. He was obviously directing his sharp sounding questions at me.

My mind flashed to my own shot gun, which was safely, and most uselessly, sitting atop of my shelf in the aft cabin. I instantly dismissed running below to get it because, with five more men standing in the back of the boat holding their own collection of fully automatics rifles, quick draw holsters and side arms strapped to their thighs, I was seriously out gunned. The man called to me again, and he was obviously distressed I had not responded to him the first time.

In my research of these islands, I came across a recent warning posted on the Noonsite web page, which tracks pirate attacks around the world, including, and more of interest to us, the Pearl Islands. The report stated that two years previous, two sailing yachts at anchor were approached in the dead of night by fishing pangas. The yacht's crew were rousted out of bed at gunpoint by four men, then held as their boats were looted.

It was obvious these people that were now checking out *Maiatla* were more than just fishermen turned seaborne robbers. These guys were well funded and organized, so I was back to considering they may be drug smugglers, but if they were, what could they possibly want with us?

When I gave the man, who was doing all the talking, a good hard look, I noticed he had a pair of chevrons on a shoulder patch. That is when I finally breathed a sigh of relief.

It was a Panamánian Navy patrol boat, and once I managed to produce enough spit to speak and get my juvenile Spanish going, I finally understood. Apparently, we were now anchored in a restricted area, exclusive for the Navy, as they had a base ashore.

I explained that I believed we could anchor here and that we were tired after just arriving from the Galápagos—a bit of a lie. The commander of the boat asked who we had on board, and I explained it was myself and my family. The men all looked over at Janet, sitting on the helm, and Kara and Ashley, who were standing looking all demur next to the cockpit. The commander asked if there was anyone else inside.

I replied, "*No, señor, sólo nosotros. Mi esposa y mis hijas.*" ("No, sir just us. My wife and my daughters.") Again a bit of a lie, but I was banking on looking like a good family man and not a smuggler.

The sailors were talking among themselves, then I heard one of them mention "documents." Sensing that we were about to be boarded, I again felt a knot tightening in my bowels, as I wondered what would happen if they found the shot gun locked and loaded ready to repel boarders, which was laying in plain sight.

Thinking fast, I apologized for my ignorance and asked where I could anchor for the night. At the same time, I stomped on the switch for the anchor windless, starting the anchor back on its way up, in hopes of making a quick getaway. Again, there was some more talk on the navy boat. Then the commander finally told me to follow the coast a couple of kilometres and anchor off the town of La Esmeralda. The anchor clanked aboard, and with the girls giving the sailors a big smile and a wave, we said, "*Buenas noches.*" ("Good night.")

Then, with a big smile on my face and being careful not to move my lips, I told Janet to throttle up and "get us the hell out of here!" We raced off in the direction of town while the patrol boat shot off in the opposite direction.

It was after 9 p.m. in a rising wind and waves when we motored past the town of La Esmeralda, which did not have a harbour, just an open roadstead. We quickly decided in this wind, the town was far too exposed, so we carried on another of couple of miles. Using the radar, we made our way into the calm waters of Rio Cacique and the river's mouth. In 3 metres (9.8 feet) of water, we dropped the hook and settled in for the night.

It was a late dinner and almost midnight before we were all showered and ready for bed. I made one lap around the deck to check the snubber and anchor, then gazed at the first quarter moon-half moon as it peeked through the broken cloud cover.

The wind was warm and pleasantly so. I could see the masthead light of another sailboat anchored nearby, which I found encouraging. I was glad to see I wasn't the only one to believe the river would make a good anchorage, and if real pirates or drug smugglers were to make a raid in the middle of the night, at least there may be some help close at hand. Unless, they, just over there, were the pirates!

Chapter 39

Isla Telmo and the Ancient Submarine

"The sea hath no king but God alone."
—Dante Gabriel Rossetti

The morning daylight revealed our nearby anchored pirate threat for what it was—a big catamaran, with a U.S. flag fluttering off its stern. She had a white hull, with a blue stripe, and the boat looked vaguely familiar to me. The cat had anchored a great deal further up the river than we were. However, in the pitch of the previous night when we had arrived, I dared not attempt to travel too far in, as the river was shallow and I feared we'd ground on any shifting sand bars. It was barely past 6 a.m., and the big cat already showed signs they were preparing to get underway. I had hoped to have talked with them to see if they had any suggestions as to where the best anchorages were and if they knew of any trouble spots in the islands to avoid, but any hope of a parlay vanished when the chattering of their anchor chain resounded over the calm water.

It was looking like it was going to be a beautiful day, and I was eager to get underway, but the crew were all still in bed, and they would want to be fed first. As the cat got underway, I slipped below to get started on some French toast. Arriving at the galley stove, I noticed Kara and Ashley were now both awake and in the V-berth quietly talking. Ever since Kara had received the bad news concerning Travis, she and Ashley had been seriously talking. It was obvious Kara was torn as what to do, and both Janet and I felt for her, but there wasn't anything we could do, other than be there if she wanted to talk or put her ashore when she was ready.

I was whipping the eggs in the bowl when I heard a voice in English calling our name. I peered out the window above the stove to see the big cat motoring slowly past.

Leaving the eggs in the sink, I shot topside, and there on the foredeck of the cat was a middle-aged woman in a bikini, bronzed solid from having spent years in the sun. She was trying to get our attention. Seeing me, she cupped her hands and yelled, "Hi, *Maiatla,* we saw you last year in Huátulco. Remember us?"

Shielding my eyes against the sun, I searched my memory for a moment, then it clicked in. We had met these people while they were anchored in Bahia de San Agustin, México, and the reason I remembered them was they were anchored almost on top of one of the finest examples of a coral reef we had seen in all of the Pacific Coast of México. I waved as if they were dear old friends and then quickly asked where they were going to anchor next. The woman shouted a location I did not recognize, and before I could ask her to repeat it, they had moved too far away to converse. All I could do was wave a goodbye and hope we may be heading in the same direction.

Looking back towards shore, I could see the Rio Cacique, which was now flowing heavily with muddy water. Presumably the swollen river was the result of the rain squall passing over us in the early hours of the morning. The Rio Cacique is one of half a dozen rivers on Isla Del Rey that is navigable in a small boat like our dinghy. It would have been fun to have taken the time to explore inland, motoring the winding river, penetrating deep into the jungle. However, we didn't have the luxury of time, as I had another destination in mind.

It was after 10 a.m. by the time we had the hook back aboard and worked our way down stream. When I was sure we were clear of a nearby reef, we altered our course to the east. A light offshore breeze filled in, so the girls unfurled the head sail and sheeted it home. The big sail gave the engine a little boost. A couple a miles ahead of us proudly stood a small island, half a mile from shore. The gap between Isla Del Rey and Isla San Telmo is shallow and, according to the charts, littered with boulders and a reef, measuring some 2.3 kilometres (1.25 nautical miles) long. I studied the chart, then the gap through the binoculars, and what I saw there I didn't like. The tops of black rocks speckled the surface, leaving no obvious path or channel through the reef, and to add to the level of difficultly, from a navigation standpoint, the ebbing tide was churning white along the shorelines and overtop of the submerged rocks.

Isla San Telmo is a small island measuring 1.73 square kilometres (0.67 square miles)) in area. It is the smallest of the many volcanic islands in Las Perlas and lies in the southeast corner of the Archipelago. The bay formed between the pair of islands is reported to be full of marine fauna, including mollusks and fish, and I assumed it would be perfect for spear fishing. However, if I wanted to hunt, it would have to be on a subsequent visit. Still, the prospect of diving here was only part of the draw of the region. Some years earlier I had seen a TV documentary detailing the adventures of a Canadian research team who came here to explore the remains of a mysterious submarine that was reported to rest on the beach of the island that now lay before us. Being so close, I had to have a look.

The wreck of the submarine has been known to local fishermen for as long as they can remember. A German dive team located the wreck, which is exposed at low tide, and concluded it belonged to the Japanese. They theorised that it had wrecked here when the Japanese intended to destroy the strategically important Panamá Canal in 1942, during World War II. It was conjectured the attack on the canal was aborted after the submarine developed mechanical problems and was subsequently abandoned by its crew after running it aground. The Japanese, who later examined the vessel, adamantly denied the sub was theirs, deepening the mystery.

In the late 1990s when Jim Delgado, the curator of the Vancouver Maritime Museum, was in Panamá, a local fisherman took him to the rusted and weed covered metal body that was only visible at low tide. Jim Delgado did not believe the fisherman's assertion the wreck was a Japanese submarine of World War II vintage. He explored the wreck and recorded its dimensions, but could not link it to any known vessels, as it resembled more of a vessel of science than a war machine.

After five years research, it was finally identified as the "*Sub Marine Explorer*," one of the world's first submarines, an underwater craft designed by Julius H. Kroehl, a German engineer who reportedly died from the bends while operating this craft. Established as a pioneering vessel, the submarine performed underwater explorations during the 19th-century. Richard Wills, an American Civil War submarine specialist, confirmed the details regarding the *Sub Marine Explorer* that were published in a scientific article in 1902.

Investigations revealed there were several technical problems in the vessel, which had resulted in numerous tragedies, and the submarine became known as the "iron coffin." As the story of the submarine was widely circulated, Delgado set out to explore the submarine further, and in 2002 and 2004, he produced the documentary I had seen. I knew Jim Delgado from the Vancouver Maritime Museum in connection with my work with the Underwater Archaeological Society of British Columbia. Back in the early 1980s when I wasn't working as a diver on the oil rigs in the Arctic, I volunteered to perform survey and search and recovery work for the society on many of the thousands of shipwrecks along my home coast of British Columbia, so I felt a natural connection to this Panamá wreck.

The *Sub Marine Explorer* was a submersible built between 1863 and 1866 by Kroehl and Ariel Patterson in Brooklyn, New York, for the Pacific Pearl Company. The craft was hand powered and had an interconnected system of high-pressure air chambers or compartments, a pressurized working chamber for the crew and water ballast tanks. The submarine was brought to the Pearl Islands to harvest oysters and the pearls they contained, but the deep water caused problems with decompression sickness, an ailment not yet known to the divers at the time. It was commonly called the "bends" due to the contorted bodies of its victims; the sickness usually left the crew with aches and pains, then paralyzed or dead. At the time, the illness was often referred to as the "fever" and created a problem for the company. The lack of enthusiastic crew, combined with the overfishing of the pearl beds, led to the abandonment of *Sub Marine Explorer* in Panamá in 1869. Further plans were made to take the sub to México to work the pearl beds of the Baja, but nothing came of them. How the *Sub Marine Explorer* found its way back to Isla San Telmo is still not known, but here it was to explore, if we could find her.

The sight of the reef was impressive, but one we would have to avoid. Janet altered course so that we could round the southern end of the island in an effort to find the beach containing the rusting hulk that was the *Sub Marine Explorer*. Keeping an eye on the depth sounder and swirling currents, we carefully hugged the shore of the tiny island of Isla San Telmo. Steep cliffs made landing on most of the island all but impossible. The shore was a fortress of black basalt rocks, streaked white with bird droppings and tattered-looking nests from the last breeding season. Inland, the dense jungle, bristling with twisted vegetation and mat of tree roots, appeared lush, green and decidedly impenetrable and a place where herons and brown pelicans roosted. It would be a great area to explore, and we would give it a try once we found our wreck beach, but I was going to be disappointed.

As we approached the top of the island, along the reef side, a crescent-shaped white sand beach materialized—the *Sub Marine Explorer's* beach. But, instead of being elated, my heart sank. Despite the ebbing tide, the water was still high, covering much of the beach, and to make matters worse, the island divided the rapidly flowing tide, creating a cataract of swirling white water, making anchoring here virtually impossible. I scanned the beach and offshore water for any sign of our submarine, but there was nothing to indicate it was ever here.

Perhaps low tide may still reveal her, but since we could not just circle around and wait six hours, the search for the sub would have to wait for another day. With much regret, I instructed Janet to power up and keep going.

We spent the rest of the day motoring and hugging the shore of the massive Isla Del Rey. The wind deserted us, so I decided to put up all the tarps for shade in preparation for our next anchorage. Our next destination was located in a chain of low sand and coral islands at the northern tip of Isla Del Rey, the location of several reality TV episodes of *Survivor*. The deserted Isla Mogo Mogo lay 42 kilometres (26 miles) away, and I was eager to snorkel its reputed pristine reefs and tread upon its fine as flour sand beaches.

Chapter 40

"That's the Spot" and the Ghosts of Tourists Past

*"Cruising can best be described as the art of sailing to nowhere in particular, at a pace
that's hardly discernible and living as locals, not simply travellers passing by."*
—Andrew W. Gunson, SV *Maiatla II*

We had a pleasant day motoring northward along the coast of Isla Del Rey. The water shone like diamond under the tropical sun and under a sky that refused to be marred by any cloud. We fished all of the way, but with all the luck of previous attempts. We even tucked in behind a tiny island to drift while jigging for bottom fish; still, it would be chicken for dinner. It was hot and out came the spray water bottles to mist our faces, and as usually happens, a water fight ensued, but briefly because even this playful activity seemed to be too much exertion in the heat and required another run to the cold beer chest.

Once clear of the big island, an archipelago of tiny islets and sand beaches appeared, through which we had to carefully navigate until reaching the narrow gap between Isla Chapera and its equally enchanting Isla Mogo Mogo. From the deck of *Maiatla,* on the north side of the pass on Isla Chapera, we could see, separated by fingers of jungle, no less than five tiny coves boasting five tiny beaches, any of which we could claim for our own. On the south side of the pass lay Mogo Mogo, with its own sets of beaches, and a reef spanning the entire length of the pass—a coral reef perfect for snorkelling. Flanked by a pair of mesmeric islands, it beckoned us to explore.

Unfortunately, we were not alone. Anchored partway between the islands, swinging on its hook, was a large catamaran. At first I hoped it may be our friends from the Rio Cacique, but it was not. Still, whoever it was didn't matter, as there was plenty of paradise for the both of us. Not wanting to encroach on our new neighbours, I decided to anchor at the far end of the channel, on a sand shallow some 100 metres (328 feet) or so beyond the cat. I gave a friendly wave to a middle-aged couple, who sat in the cockpit sipping sundowners. A weak and grimacing expression one would give a sausage-fingered doctor moments before a rectal exam was their less than an enthusiastic response to our arrival.

We made a couple of tight circles to check out the bottom before setting the hook.

"What do you think?" I asked everyone after shutting down the engine, allowing the wilderness sounds to envelope us.

"Wow, this is beautiful, Andy," Kara said as she and Ashley stood on the foredeck taking pictures.

"When can we go ashore?" Ashley asked between picture snaps.

"It's getting late, and I've got to pump the dink up and get the outboard on and running, so I will say tomorrow."

It was breathtaking for sure, a picture usually reserved for a calendar's mid-winter months, an image designed to torture snowbound northerners.

"That's the spot!" I said to myself. Our own piece of paradise. I wasted no time in dropping the boarding ladder, and to our great pleasure, the water was warm; however, the ebbing tide through the pass was brisk and could sweep us away if we permitted it. After a quick swim, we were out and it was a time for a celebratory drink. We had rums all around as the sun set behind the island. I was bringing the boarding ladder up for the night when I noticed our neighbours in the cat were getting underway. I was curious as to where they would be going at this time of the day, but I wouldn't have long to guess. Once the hook was up they motored over towards Mogo Mogo and re-anchored on the east shore, a good mile away from us. I can only presume that even at over 100 metres (328 feet) away from them, we had encroached on their "That's the spot."

It was a beautiful evening full of stars and a big Panamá moon. A light northerly breeze, heavy with the heady funk of raw earth and exotic plants, carried with it the chirps, buzzes and rustles of the night-time jungle. The wind socks funnelled the freshening night air into *Maiatla*, cooling her innards and making for a reasonable comfortable night below decks. It was as peaceful an anchorage as we could have hoped for, and as I made my rounds to check the ground tackle before bed, I sat for a moment in the pulpit to watch a school of tiny fish on the surface. The minnow-size fish were attempting to hide in the boat's shadow, cast in the bright moon light.

I was impressed with these islands, which truly lived up to their gem of a name. I could easily spend a whole season here exploring, diving, snorkelling and just playing Robinson Crusoe on our choice of isles. Running and swimming naked as the world's first humans, content to be here with my own Eve in paradise. This is the place I could bag and barbeque a wild pig or two between bouts of lobster-hunting on the reef, a cold Pilsner in a koozie at hand.

Both Janet and I were looking forward to spending some time on our own, hanging out and being one with each other, having no real place to go or be. This was the part of our cruising life I believe Janet had missed the most over the past four years, as we were always on the move. We had been voyaging through Central America, not cruising. Cruising can best be described as the art of sailing to nowhere in particular, at a pace that's hardly discernible, and living as locals, not simply travellers passing by. One boater once confessed to me that she knew she had finally become a cruiser when she realized she didn't know what day of the week it was. My reply was, "I think you've finally made it as a cruiser when not only do you have to ask what month it is, but don't because you don't care anyway!"

Unfortunately, this idyllic dream life would have to wait a little longer. The netherworld was calling. We had flights booked for home at the end of the month, a little over two weeks away, and we still had to book our passage through the Panamá Canal, which, according to my agent, could take up to a week after our arrival. We could only afford a couple or more days here, and even that may be cutting it close. Any serious exploring, adventuring, cavorting or cruising in the Pearl Islands would have to wait until next season.

Later, as I lay sleeping in my cabin, I was awoken by the rumble of an engine and chatter of an anchor chain, the sounds resonating through our hull, invading my dreams. The unmistakable sounds of a new arrival filled our cabin, and the boat sounded close. Being careful not to wake Janet, I slid out of bed to peek out a port hole and saw a set of running lights close by, but not too close. Illuminated by intense moonlight, with Mogo Mogo as a back drop, was a ketch of perhaps the 13-metre (45 feet) range. Framed by *Maiatla's* rectangular porthole, the boat appeared surreal. Had it not been betrayed by the subtle and graceful movements of the ship and swaying palms, the ghost ketch would have looked as if were painted upon a velvet canvas. The crew seemed to know what they were doing and considerate, as they all spoke in hushed tones, whispering as if fearing to disturb the serenity of the place and our sleep. In the morning, I would be pleasantly surprised to see the new arrival was a Canadian boat with the odd name of *Blowing Bubbles,* from Ontario.

Once they killed their engine, I slid back into bed. I lay for some time staring out of the deck hatch above, past the rustling wind sock, to gaze upon the few stars that were visible in the bright moonlight. Above were the unmistakable three blue-white stars of Orion's Belt, shimmering as if to demand notice. For centuries sailors have used Orion's Belt to locate Sirius in the constellation Canis Major, the Greater Dog. Out of the approximately 6,000 stars visible to the naked eye on a dark night, Sirius is the brightest star in the night-time sky and one of the 58 most commonly used stars for celestial navigation. Sirius was hidden to me now, as the mizzen mast blocked my view.

Janet never stirred from her corner of the bed where she lay under a single bed sheet, oblivious to all, as she had taken some pain killers and sleeping pills before bed. The voyage from the Galápagos was hard on her, so she was thankful for the calm, motionless anchorage to sleep and recuperate.

At the time, the full impact of the voyage on her was not truly evident to me until it was driven home that night when we had slipped into bed. As we lay beneath a single cotton sheet, I had suggested to Janet the trip was not that bad and being able to swim with the pilot whales and dolphins was well worth any discomfort. Janet's response was immediate and emphatic. "No, it wasn't!" she declared, with all seriousness.

My heart sank to hear this. Knowing how excited she was and how much she enjoyed the dolphin experience, her statement spoke volumes to me. This was the first time that I truly came to grips with the possibility that Janet had just made her last ocean passage on *Maiatla*. As I lay alongside her in our great aft cabin, I could not help but fear that perhaps I also had made my last offshore voyage. I could not imagine I could continue on sailing without her. Only time will tell.

In the morning, we found ourselves in the company of two other vessels. The Canadian ketch of the night before, *Blowing Bubbles*, and an equally odd name for a boat, *Zoonie*—a sleek sloop, an Oyster 406, with a British Ensign fly limp off its taffrail. The Brits arrived at daybreak, and they too anchored as if they wanted to cuddle. I guess everyone knew "That's the spot!" Both yachts were far enough away, as long as the weather did not pipe up, so I wasn't concerned.

After breakfast, I launched the dink and headed to shore. Isla Chapera isn't entirely deserted. There is a manned weather station located on the point. The big beach on the far side of the islands is a favourite spot for hotel guests from the nearby island of Contadora. They could hire a local fisherman or a water taxi to take them out to one of the "uninhabited" islands to be marooned for the day with a picnic basket, on their own private beach, or semi-private anyway. The girls and I walked the trails connecting each tiny enclave, circumnavigating the island until we located a pair of swings hanging from the limb of a great tree. One swing had been constructed of old rope, presumably lost by some fisherman at sea, the rope now tied to a smooth driftwood log to form a seat. The second swing was a worn tire, dangling waist high from a branch on a similar old rope—a gift left by people unknown, perhaps by other cruisers or a fisherman who needed to amuse his children while the nets he set offshore were doing their thing.

Ashley and Kara took great delight in taking turns pushing each other on the swings all the while laughing like giddy school children. While the girls played, I wandered further down the beach, through the bush, until breaking out onto another tiny beach where I found a couple, a Caucasian women and a black American, sprawled out on a blanket in the shade of a coconut palm. The frisky couple were enjoying each other, as well as the view of the shallow azure waters and a sail boat anchored off in the distance. Startling the couple as I scrambled out of the bush, I apologized for the intrusion while informing them I was just passing through.

Instead of being upset at having their solitude shattered, they were pleasant and quickly struck up a conversation by first asking, "Where the hell did you come from? Our boatman said this island was deserted!" The woman said this while still looking surprised.

I pointed out to *Maiatla* and over the following half hour I explained of our latest adventure and how we came to be here. Claudette and Ernest, from North Carolina, were on their honeymoon and seemed genuinely interested and more than impressed by our tale. They still had more questions, but I felt the need to leave them to their solitude. As I was ready to excuse myself, an idea struck.

"Hey, guys, when your boat comes back to get you, can you ask the driver if he would be willing to come back tomorrow to pick us up off of my boat and take us shopping on Contadora?"

Figure 99. Our graceful beach landing on Isla Chapera.

They promised to ask, then I carried on back to look for the girls. As promised, just before sunset a panga came alongside, and Claudette and Ernest introduced me to the driver, Jesus. Just an observation, but every fifth person in Central America was either named after Christ or one of the Saints or Apostles. After quick negotiations, we were set; Jesus would be back at 9 a.m. tomorrow to take us about 5 kilometres (3 miles) to town. After waving goodbye to the newlyweds, it was time for a swim, dinner and a family update email via the ham net.

True to his word, Jesus arrived on time, and we were quickly loaded aboard and on our way. Janet, this morning, was feeling ill, so she decided to stay behind to watch the boat. A great act of courage on her part considering what happened the last time I left her aboard all alone while I ventured ashore to play. The Costa Rica Papagayo incident (freak gale force winds) at Cabo Blanco was still fresh in my mind, and as if the vivid memory of the terrified sound of Janet's voice on the radio wasn't enough, my right elbow was still giving me pains when extending it a certain way. I hoped Janet's volunteering to stay aboard alone was a signal that her memory of the horrendous incident was fading. This area of Panamá was known for its mostly benign weather, so the likelihood of a sudden gale slamming through was almost nonexistent. Still, I worried.

The high-speed panga made short work of the ride over to the former, exclusive resort island of Isla Contadora. As we approached the tall wooded islands from the south, we could see several sail boats anchored in the lee of the long island. All were flying foreign flags from other oceans, so they most likely had just transited the canal and were on their way to the South Pacific. *Maiatla's* eastward journey was an exception.

We passed along the eastern shore where a great bay opened up. Its protected waters revealed a sickle-shaped beach ringed with towering coconut palm trees—a perfect place for a holiday retreat. Hotel Contadora Resort was constructed in 1976, with 250 luxury rooms, two kidney-shaped pools with swim up bars, four restaurants and a separate ballroom for special events, which sat high upon the southern point, surrounded by jungle flora and fauna. Behind the lobby was a hanging garden and tropical rainforest, with pools where birds and colourful parrots came to bathe. The whole complex is surrounded by 25 acres of tropical gardens and walking trails, and on the north side of the beach were several Spanish luxury villas for wealthier guests.

The complex was truly elegant and a place of play for the affluent Panamánians and other international jetsetters, who could land their private planes at the airport within walking distance of the hotel. However, I would hazard a guess and say few walked, and instead were chauffeured to their rooms in golf carts. Today, from the panga offshore, it was easy to imaging the opulence of the place. To see the once magnificent hotel in its present condition was, to say the least, sad. The hotel closed its doors some 10 years previous and was abandoned. The ravages of weather, time and vandals had taken its toll. The red pantile-roofed, three-story building was a shell of its former self. Its only occupants were of the rodent, lizard and winged variety, including bats of which Panamá has seemingly an unlimited variety.

As if to advertise the finality of the hotel, south of the main lobby, with its tail still in the water, was the *La Perla 7*, the water ferry that formerly ferried guests out to the island from the mainland. The 25-metre (82-feet) high-speed craft was holed below the waterline, stripped of all things useful and decorated in colourful Spanish graffiti, no doubt thanks to the island's bored youth and budding artists looking for a canvas. Once we landed on shore, I hoped to have an opportunity to visit the defunct hotel.

Jesus motored us around to the north side of the island to land us on the beach, Playa Galeon, in front of a set of dilapidated waterfront restaurants and bars, most with sprawling waterfront patios. A majority of the beachfront businesses were closed, permanently from the neglected look of some of them. Others were open, but the staff, sporting white shirts and aprons, outnumbered the customers. We unloaded our shopping bags, along with a pair of empty fuel cans. Reluctantly I paid our driver $30 for the trip here while arranging for a pickup time. I was worried we would have a repeat of the disappearing taxi driver we had experienced in the Galápagos. However, I sensed Jesus was hungry, and he would most likely be waiting right where we had left him.

We wandered up a path past a dry waterfall and pool; the colourful mosaic tile basin full of dead palm leaves looked like the only time it had seen water in recent years was during the summer rain showers.

Figure 100. The gutted structure of the once five-star resort, Hotel Contadora.

We followed the trail as it wound its way up the hill to the end of the main street, which would take us to the centre of the town and the island life encompassing the community grocery store. This trail met the end of the road at a turnabout.

On the left side of Contadora's Main Street is a tall fence separating the street and its pedestrians from landing aircraft at the island's airport, and on the other side is an endless row of tourist shops, restaurants, guided tour booths, with hawkers all offering the "best deals" to anyone they did not recognize. The latest census put the town's permanent population at a meagre 250 souls. Again we noticed the number of shop keepers outnumbered the wandering tourists, so to say we stuck out, making us an easy mark, would be accurate. The waterfront gave me the impression of an aged street-walker with fading makeup, stinking of desperation while burdened with the sobering knowledge her best days were far behind her. Time for a discount?

"This should be fun," I said to Kara and Ashley, who were two steps behind me, checking their phones to see if they could connect with free Wi-Fi, without success. Although the tourist centre of the island appeared in financial shambles, the Hotel Punta Galeon, constructed on the rocky point overlooking the bay, was the exception, as its grounds were neat and tidy and had a restaurant busy with its guests.

After haggling a little at a t-shirt shop, for $80 we had wheels for the day in the form of a four-seat golf cart. I drove with the jerry cans next to me. The girls were perched on the rear seat, which faced backwards so that they would have an unobstructed view of where we had just been.

We needed to find a place to shop for fresh vegetables, steaks and, more importantly, beer and rum, as the boat was running low of such things. We would have normally stocked up our liquor supply at our last port of call, in preparation for a long voyage, but since the cost of alcohol in the Galápagos was atrocious, we sailed with the bare minimum. Like our rum, our diesel fuel was also running low, so we brought with us a pair of 5-gallon jerry cans to fill, in case we needed them to get to Panamá.

After asking for directions, we found the grocery store and loaded up on fresh supplies. I took great delight in choosing some fresh steaks for a later barbeque. I also found fuel, and with the jerry cans full of diesel, we carried on with our exploration. Our road trip around the island of Contadora showed us a world of contradiction and stark contrast. Elegant homes with neatly trimmed hedges and shimmering swimming pools stood next to the crumbling ruins of once equally stately neighbours, now rapidly consumed by the advancing jungle.

The island boasted several beautiful beaches and parks open to the public, and we visited each in turn. On the north coast was the tiny, member's only marina and yacht club, with its manicured lawns and tiny club house. The road in and out of the club was steep, so after doing a drive through, I was forced to take a couple of runs at the hill to get our gutless gas-powered cart back up the driveway. Surprisingly, I had not had to kick the girls off and have them walk or even push the cart up.

We encounter few people or vehicles as we scooted about, but when we did run into someone (figuratively), we stopped to ask for direction or to just say hello. Although the island is small enough to walk to most anywhere, we quickly learned few, if any, of the locals or long-term tourists walked, as the heat was oppressive. New arrivals walked for about a week, and then they relented and rented wheels to get around. I learned long ago to look to the natives to see how best to survive and scavenge from the inhospitable lands, and here, in the jungles of Panamá, a sturdy gas-powered golf cart is as essential to a cruiser as a spear and an ostrich-egg water canteen is to the Bushmen of the Kalahari Desert.

We traversed the island from the far north, then down to the south where we knew the abandoned hotel was located. I was surprised at how narrow the island is, which became apparent when we were forced to navigate along a narrow dirt road, flanked by the end of the airport runway on one side and a steep drop off into the sea on the other. The asphalt landing strip nearly bisects the island, with the terminus of each end stopping short of the beach on the north side and a cliff on the south.

On the south side of the airport, we found a rugged dirt trail leading into the bush. Stopping the cart at the cliff side, we took the opportunity to take some photographs of the several yachts anchored close to shore. There was a nice breeze blowing and a thick cloud cover had moved in, taming some of the heat. Protruding from the shore below us was a partially collapsed steel and concrete jetty around which the sea surged through its crumbling pylons. The pier was, in its time, substantial with little expense spared in its making, but like most of the island's infrastructure, it too had fallen into a state of disrepair. Now the massive structure is all but useless, for the human inhabitants of the island anyway. For the bird population, it is another matter, as it makes for a perfect nesting place and perch for a variety of sea birds and lizards. The paint that once protected the steel from the harsh elements has now been replaced by streaks of white guano and fist-sized flakes of rust. Against my better judgment, I took a chance and climbed out onto the deck of the pier, sending scores of roosting birds noisily into flight. While stepping carefully and under my meagre weight (okay, maybe not so meagre!), the structure let out as a warning, an ominous creak and groan while swaying.

"Andy, the dock is moving. It don't look safe," Ashley called to me from the safety of the shore. Kara was busy next to her taking pictures, perhaps believing if her captain went down with the dock at least she could get some YouTube video out of it.

Not wanting to push my luck, I snapped some photos, then beat a not-so-hasty retreat to the safety of the shore.

"I would hazard a guess and say that dock will not survive another good storm!" I said as soon as I was back standing on solid ground. After considering the condition of the pier further, I was indeed fortunate it had not collapsed under me. Then I said, "How about a beer!"

The reply from Kara and Ashley was as I suspected, so we wasted no time in breaking into the cold case and popping some tops. The road carried on from there, continuing to deteriorate as it developed deep ruts with sandy patches, indicating that we were getting close to another beach. At first I feared I may get the cart stuck in the sandy loam, and then I remembered I had two sturdy girls in back to push us out of any such difficulty. We continued on the road, which turned inland into thicker bush until it suddenly thinned out to reveal the shattered remnants of what we would later assume to be the staff housing for the hotel. The roofs for most of the buildings had collapsed, with access to the doors blocked by thick tangles of jungle vines and needle-bearing bushes resembling barbed wire. A twist in the road brought us out onto the beautiful beach where I parked the cart at a point I was sure I would get stuck if we ventured further.

The beach was Playa Larga, and it was as we had seen from Jesus's boat when we had arrived. The graffiti-covered ferry sat beached and battered and far beyond salvaging, and the once neatly groomed beach was covered in dead palm leaves and broken coconuts, mixed with an odd assortments of manmade flotsam and jetsam. It was shocking to see how many discarded 1-litre water bottles had found their way here. After climbing through the ferry's innards, we loaded back into the cart to further explore the remainder of the hotel.

Leaving the road behind, I drove onto the brick cobble pathway, once the exclusive domain of the hotel guests. We scooted past a three-story stack of rooms, all with missing windows. In this setting, it felt as though the building was watching us drive by, but it couldn't have, as all its eyes had been gouged out. We shot past an abandoned volleyball court towards the hotel lobby where a large gaping hole beckoned us to come inside. Without hesitating, I drove though the archway onto the tile mosaic floor to finally stop in the centre of the massive lobby, not far from the check-in desks. I couldn't go any farther, as the floor was covered in broken tile, glass and remnants of ceiling beams and light fixtures. Above us, electrical wiring dangled like jungle vines along the walls.

Figure 101. With the pools now filled with dirt, the once opulent hotel is in shambles.

The roof of the lobby had remained a tall peak, which created an echo whenever we spoke or the cart crushed the debris under its balloon-like wheels. Next to the registration desks sat a shallow pool, a basin for the water that once cascaded down an artificial stone embankment.

The overhead beams, ornately carved in some kind of Incas hieroglyphics, were still beautiful works of art, and we were surprised they too had not been looted. Perhaps the only thing saving them was that someone would need a crane to remove them, causing the complete collapsing of the massive roof structure. Stomping my foot on the accelerator, I took the girls on a guided tour of the lounge area and then the kitchen, out past the pools, swim-up bars and back inside to tour the dining room and gift shops.

As we sped past the hotel desk for a second time, in an effeminate voice, thick with lisps, I called out to an imaginary desk clerk.

Figure 102. The former hotel ferry is beached in front of the hotel and is slowly being claimed by the elements.

"Phillipe, I have here two hot Canadian chicks fresh from the sea and eager to abuse some margaritas while salsa dancing with our beefcake cabana boys. Isn't that right ladies?" I said, with all seriousness as I glanced over my shoulder. Behind me Kara and Ashley both laughed, desperately trying to keep from falling out of the cart as I launched the cart into series of burning donuts in the centre of the lobby. As the tires squealed in protest from the sharp turns, I continued with my monologue.

"Oh, wait, I may have that wrong! Maybe it was to abuse the cabana beefcakes and have salsa with the margaritas?"

I kept up the persona and running commentary as we continued to speed through the hotel's buildings and grounds. It was an enjoyable time, but after an hour or so of poking about, it was time to go, especially if we wanted to make a couple of more stops. Back on a dirt trail, we made our way out to the extreme south point where the grand ballroom once stood. I parked outside the concrete structure next to an arched doorway.

When we wandered inside, the grandeur of the place became evident. The floor remained tiled in a checker-board pattern, and across it, appearing as pawns on a chessboard of godly proportions, stood metre-thick (3.2–feet) columns that had once supported the roof structure, but now only reach into the sky. The roof was all but gone; it had been either salvaged for local use or perhaps burned away—the latter more likely, as the floor was littered with sections of burnt timbers and broken pantile.

The dirt trail continued, and so we followed it until reaching a point that if we ventured any further, would most assuredly get us stuck. Moments before turning around, a beach broke into view. We parked our cart next to a massive old tree, and there, we saw, nailed a metre above the ground, a sign in Spanish and English:

Figure 103. The main lobby of the once grand hotel.

"Las Suecas,
Stop!
Nudist Only, Nudista
No watchers/voyeurs"

We had found Las Suecas, or as it translates, "The Swedish," and the only official nude beach in all of Panamá. As expected, the beach was deserted, so we didn't feel self-conscious when we started to strip off, not that we would have been self-conscious anyway. I had quickly lost my shirt and shorts and headed for the water and made the plunge.

The water felt cool and refreshing and there was a small rock island just off shore that looked like a good place to swim to and sit upon. I was going to suggest to the girls we head out that way but when I turned back towards the beach, I saw a strange sight as Kara and Ashley appeared to be engaged in some sort of game of tug-o-war.

Kara was bracing herself as Ashley had a firm grip on Kara's shorts at the left hip and was forcefully pulling at Kara. Curious, I returned to the beach to see what was going on. As I approached the pair, Kara called out to me, "Hey, Andy, my zipper is stuck and I can't get it to undo!"

Ashley gave another hard jerk nearly pulling Kara off of her feet. I took a moment to examine the zipper upon Kara's hip, then as instructed, gave it a try. Whether due to sand or salt in the zipper or just a simple wardrobe malfunction, the zipper of Kara's skin-tight, hip-hugging shorts refused to budge. After several more minutes of tugging, Kara final said, "Just rip it! Break the zipper, Andy!"

At first I was a bit reluctant, but when she began to tug at the zipper to part the teeth, I lent my hands to the job.

We spent the following hour taking dips, drinking beer and exploring tide pools. We thought it was a nice beach and a pleasant day, and with the cloud cover still hanging around, we didn't worry about getting too much sun. We had just decided to dry off and head back to town when, on the far end of the beach, where we had parked our cart, another golf cart rolled to a stop. At first, the couple in their late fifties didn't appear to see us, but when they did, they suddenly made a beeline back to their cart.

At first, I assumed the sight of a couple of naked bodies had sent them into a tizzy, but apparently it had not. Back at their cart, they dug out a blanket and towels, headed to the shade of a palm, spread their blanket and stripped.

On our way back to our cart, we all exchanged greeting and pleasantries.

Darrel and Cathleen were from Minnesota, and to my delight, after hearing our story of our travels, Cathleen said to me "You should write a book," followed by, "I'm a book editor and publisher."

I was thrilled with this chance encounter. As we talked, a second couple discovered our hidden beach. The pair of fellows broke out onto the beach some distance away. The first young man, who was perhaps in his late twenties, immediately dropped all his clothing and dived into the water. The second fellow, who was around the same age, hesitated, but after some coxing from his friend in the surf, he pulled off his clothes and trotted towards the water.

Kara was standing by the water's edge, and Ashley was sitting in the sand facing me. From her position, Ashley had not seen the pair of fellows, so I called to her to tell her to turn around. When she did, she saw the second man making for the water while trying, not to successfully, to hide an erection. I laughed while asking Ashley what she thought. After taking a second hard look, she turned back to me and said, "The length is impressive, but it lacks the girth."

I talked a few minutes more to Darrel and Cathleen, then she handed me her business card. I thanked her and said we needed to be getting on our way. Back in town, we found a rustic-looking restaurant for dinner. There, we accessed the internet to update blogs and Facebook. Kara received an update on her husband, Travis. He was still in the hospital and undergoing chemo, but the prognosis was looking favourable—a turn in which, I'm sure, Kara found a measure of comfort. Despite his illness, Kara had confided in me she did not want to get back together with him, which, on some level, came with guilty feelings. This time aboard *Maiatla* gave her an opportunity to solidify her thoughts to possibly help her chart out her new life as a single mom of two.

After a nice meal, we made our way back to the waterfront in hopes of finding our water taxi. Thankfully, Jesus was waiting for us. We shared our day's adventures, along with a couple of beer, with Jesus, and we were back at *Maiatla* before dark. Janet also had a relaxing pleasant day, but she was happy to see us pulling alongside.

I barbequed the steaks while the girls told Janet of some of the haunting images that abound on Isla Contadora.

Chapter 41

A Typical Beach Day and Kara's Gut-busting Maiatla *"Love Bite"*

*"Every man's life ends the same way. It is only the details of how
he lived and how he died that distinguish one man from another."*
—Ernest Hemingway

It was a Wednesday morning, not that it would normally mean much to us, but I had decided we needed to be in Panamá on Friday morning to meet with our canal agent and get ourselves in the lineup to transit the canal. This would be our last full day on Isla Chapera and the Pearl Islands for now. With one more full day to explore, I organized a snorkelling excursion around the south side of the island in the morning, then over to Mogo Mogo's passage reef for the afternoon. Isla Chapera's reefs would prove to be interesting, but displayed the usual damage caused by too many tourists walking on or picking at the coral heads while collecting sea shells to take home. I suspected the hotel guests that are frequently ferried out here were mostly to blame.

Generally, I have found long-term cruisers show more respect and have learned how to view the reefs while causing minimal damage. Many I know will refuse to apply sunscreen, at their own peril, in order not to introduce toxic chemicals into the delicate environment. A recent study, February 2016, published in the journal *Archives of Environmental Contamination and Toxicology*, found the chemical oxybenzone has toxic effects on young coral, causing DNA damage and death of coral, among other problems. Oxybenzone also exacerbates coral bleaching, a process by which coral reject symbiotic organisms and lose their colour. Bleaching has been particularly prevalent in recent years due to rising sea temperatures.

Currently, somewhere between 4,000 and 6,000 tons of sunscreen enters coral reef areas around the world each year, according to the U.S. National Park Service. A massive amount of sunscreen considering how little it takes to have a toxic effect upon the reef. According to the new research, toxicity to fish and coral occurs at a concentration of 62 parts per trillion, the equivalent of a drop of lotion in an Olympic-size swimming pool.

I recall swimming at the Grotto in the Galápagos and seeing a thick sheen of oil floating atop of the water left by tourists swimming before us, disgusting to consider the slick was well above the 62 parts per trillion to commence killing the coral. Still, there is hope, as sunscreens with titanium oxide or zinc oxide do not seem to affect the reef in a negative way. Alternatively, if not wearing a wetsuit, one can wear a UV protective, long-sleeve shirt with a hood for snorkelling, which also protects from abrasions caused by accidentally brushing against the rocks or coral. Any colour other than grey or black will do as it does not bode well to look too much like a seal floundering about. Nature has no end of predators, villains of the deep, that love to cull the sick and infirmed from the schools of fish.

Despite the ravages of tourism, snorkelling on the reefs of Chapera was fun, as we saw some colourful fish. We also spotted several sea turtles lounging on the bottom and were fortunate to witness a congregation of several large groups of eagle and spotted eagle rays performing flybys for our amusement. The girls gave chase, but they soon realized any attempt at pursuit was futile as well as exhausting.

The east side of Chapera's proved to be a bit more difficult to snorkel due to the strong current whipping around the headlands. Despite the change in the tide's direction, switching from flood to ebb, the water always appeared to be flowing into the pass although at varying strengths, as governed by the magnitude of the tides—a condition, I suspect, which had to do with a strong westerly flowing surface current.

The girls soon fatigued, so it was back to the boat in time for lunch. After a short siesta, Janet and I took the dink for some alone time to snorkel on the back side of Mogo Mogo's passage reef. Kara and Ashley protested at being left behind, but Janet and I wanted some one on one time without having to keep an eye on inexperienced stragglers. Reluctantly, the girls dropped their petitions to come along and settled for rum drinks, sunbathing on deck and writing in their journals.

Mogo Mogo's passage reef is much shallower than on the Chapera's side of the pass, less than a metre (3.2 feet) at times; however, the coral is thick and healthy and harbours great schools of tiny colourful fish and invertebrates. For the most part, we thought, this reef, vibrant in pastel colours, appeared to have been unmolested by humans. The strong currents that tested our resolve on the opposite side of the pass were pleasantly absent here, making for an enjoyable swim in calm clear waters. We had a great time holding hands and slowly swimming along, with our faces in the warm water while taking in all the marvels of the bio-diverse and healthy reef system.

Often the most colourful or the strangest-looking creatures are among the smallest, so not only is a keen eye required to spot all the pretty fish and crustaceans, but also necessary to avoid getting stung or bit. We may treat the ocean and its reefs like a playground, but the marine environment can be both hostile and deadly to humans. Sharks, thanks to movies like *Jaws*, have instilled a healthy fear and a respect for sharks of any variety, but they are not the only sea critters humans need to be wary.

A prerequisite for anyone diving within the ocean is to know what sea critters are harmless and what may cause excruciating pain and then kill you long before you have even had a chance to get out of the water to seek medical attention. Being on an uninhabited island out in the middle of nowhere, where proper medical attention may be days if not weeks away, adds to the imperative of knowing what you can and cannot touch. On our little excursion off of Mogo Mogo, we encountered both stonefish and scorpionfish. Masters of camouflage and "ambush" predators, hiding motionless on the bottom, this pair of poisonous fish come armed with needle sharp spines that can inject you with toxic venom strong enough to kill an adult human.

Along with the deadly venom in their spines, which can cause excruciating pain or death, or both, scorpionfish and lionfish take a different approach to their stony-looking cousins, as they are festooned with sweeping fins decorated with floral-like colours. As pretty and docile-looking as they are, scorpionfish and lionfish are not to be messed with. Nonetheless, with a good "shake 'n' bake" recipe, they make a fine main course.

Not surprisingly, it's not only the finned multiplicity of sea critters that swimmers need be wary of, as even the innocuous-looking plants and corals can pack a wallop. Fire corals have a bright yellow-green and brown skeletal covering that possesses bare tentacle-like stingers able to inflict a nasty "burn" upon naked flesh. Even a pretty little sea shell may be hiding a poisonous dagger ready to harpoon anyone foolish enough to pick it up. The marine cone snail has one of the most powerful poisons in nature and is prevalent in most all tropical waters. As there are over 500 varieties of cone snails, most of which are harmless, it can be a crap shoot if you were to commence stuffing cone shells in into your short's pocket or tuck that pretty little shell between your bikini top and boob for safe keeping.

It was a great afternoon of snorkelling, with the only disparaging note occurring when Janet noticed the anchored dinghy moving further away. When I looked, the dink was sailing off towards the pass, propelled by the stiff breeze. Quickly I swam after it, only catching the dink when it had reached mid channel where the current was the strongest. I clambered back into the dink and collapsed into the bottom while panting breathlessly. I had just swum a distance of at least an Olympic size pool at a sprint, and my lungs and legs both ached from the exertion. I was also parched and now regretting not leaving a couple of cold beer in the boat, or at least a water bottle I needed to rest, but that would have to wait. For every second I sat there, the current drew me deeper into the pass, which, in a matter of minutes, would spit me out the far side of the island. Going on an unintended cruise was not an issue or concern, but leaving Janet to tread water, wondering if and when I would come back to get her, was.

When I pulled up the anchor line, I cursed to see my anchor was gone. The shackle I had used to secure it to the line must have either broken or somehow released itself. I thought, *Okay, this would not be a problem.* Because I had a good idea where we had anchored, I didn't think that finding the lost anchor would be too much of a chore. All I needed to do was start the engine and motor back, but that would prove more difficult than first thought. No matter how many times I pulled on the cord, the little 3.3 Mercury refused to start. Not having the luxury of time to strip the engine down to troubleshoot the problem, I set the oars and started rowing hard against the current. A full 20 minutes after chasing the dink, I finally spotted Janet treading water right where I had left her. Undeterred at seeing me swim off in hot pursuit of the dink, Janet kept poking around the reef, chasing blue neons while waiting for my return. Eventfully, we found the anchor, and after cleaning the fuel filter, the engine started, but it now sputtered like a chain smoker with only one lung. The motor stayed running long enough to motor the half mile or so back to *Maiatla*—a good thing, as I was done rowing for the day. Mogo Mogo is a great place to snorkel, and it would have been a leisurely day if not for our fleeing dinghy.

Back aboard *Maiatla* as I lay in the cockpit with a water bottle, I was aware of the pains in my legs from my hard and frantic swim, not to mention my burning biceps from the hard row back to Janet. I hurt, so I decided to take it easy for the rest of the day. I lay down in the shade while ensuring I had a steady supply of *cerveza fría* (cold beer), which was easy, as all I would have to do was call below to one of the girls and suddenly another cold brew would appear nestled in a "*Mystery Tramp*" koozie.

Earlier in the morning, before we departed on our snorkelling trip, I went for a short walk on the beach, and it was there I met the couple from the British yacht anchored nearby. Rob and Barbara, aboard *Zoonie,* they were three years into their circumnavigation of the world. The retired couple had spent the last two seasons sailing the Caribbean and were now on their way to the South Seas, and they, like us, had decided to do a bit of exploring on the Pearl Islands. After a quick exchange of itineraries, Rob said he had met the crews of the other boat in the bay and had suggested a beach trash-burning fire and potluck for that evening. "Just snacks and whiskey, nothing fancy," he insisted.

In many places, for cruisers, proper trash disposal can be difficult, if not downright impossible. And if you don't want to set it adrift or toss it into a ditch alongside the road, what often happens is you take it ashore, dig a hole, burn, then bury it. This custom can also be used as a rallying call and a great excuse for sundowners on the beach with other cruisers. By the time the sun was setting, from the three boats anchored nearby, we had made a cordial group, sitting around a campfire, sharing cheeses, crackers and an assortment of meat sausages.

The other Canadians were from Hamilton, Ontario, and, like the Brits, had spent the last two seasons island hopping in the Spanish Main. After only having met that day, they were already making plans to sail in company across the great expanse of the Pacific. As I listened to them all excitedly talk about their intended South Seas destinations, I could not help but feel a bit left out, as *Maiatla* was headed the other way.

It was a great evening of comradeship and salty storytelling. I believe Kara and Ashley received some measure of inspiration from these adventurous people. It was a chance meeting of travellers that perhaps would inspire Kara and Ashley to view their own young lives from a different perspective, a view not so harshly tainted by netherworld demands and expectations.

When Barb and Rob of *Zoonie* left the Pearl Islands, they sailed on to Bahía de Caráquez, Ecuador, where they set off on a land tour that took them on a hike through the Amazon and up to visit the ancient Inca ruins of Machu Picchu. Then they crossed the South Pacific and encountered a typhoon, which had nearly sunk *Zoonie*, requiring a refit of the boat in New Zealand. Despite their initial intentions, Kyle and Shelley of *Blowing Bubbles* parted company with *Zoonie*, crossed the great expanse of the South Pacific to New Zealand, then northward to the Marshall Islands where they spent Christmas of 2017. The last I heard from them, they were making plans to sail north further still to, of all places, Japan.

The morning's first light found us pulling anchor and moving off. We exchanged waves and departure wishes to our new found acquaintances, who, in all likelihood, we would never meet again. I set *Maiatla* on a course, taking us passed Contadora and its ghost hotel, then by Isla Pacheca and its tiny sister island, Isla Pachequilla, the northernmost uninhabited islands of the archipelago. Even though the wind was nonexistent and the weather reports were not promising wind anytime soon, I was hopeful, so I ordered the girls to remove the sun tarps and set the mainsail. We may not be able to sail, but at least we could look like we were trying. It kept the girls busy, and under normal circumstances, it would have been a good decision. However, as it turned out, it would have been best if Kara and Ashley stayed put in the cockpit.

After folding the tarps and as the girls fired back and forth a giddy banter, Kara commenced to remove the mainsail cover. When she needed to reach up the mast to grasp the zipper, she stepped onto a mast step to help her reach. However, when she put her full weight upon the step, the screws pulled free of the wooden mast, causing Kara to fall against the main halyard winch which protruded from the mast. From the cockpit, I heard the blow and the wind getting knocked out of Kara as she fell hard. Fortunately, Ashley was able to catch Kara and stop her from falling overboard.

I rushed from the cockpit to help. Hearing all the commotion topside, Janet stuck her head out of the companionway to see what was going on. Upon reaching Kara's side, it was obvious that she was still having trouble catching her breath while winching in pain. All Ashley and I could do was support her until she composed herself to a point where she could help us walk her back to the cockpit. After placing Kara on the bench seat and having her lay down, I had a good look at her abdomen, and I wasn't happy with what I saw. The winch caught her in the midline between her navel and her upper pubis area, and it was already turning black with deep bruising. I left Ashley to comfort Kara and went below to fetch some ice packs, Janet followed.

"Is she alright?" Janet asked, deeply concerned.

"Not sure, hun. Looks like she took a hard hit, and I'm a bit worried that she may have done some serious internal damage. Wouldn't be good if she had ruptured her spleen or has caused some serious internal hemorrhaging. She could be bleeding out, and we may not know it until it is too late."

I pulled two ices packs out of the freezer and asked Janet to grab a pair of tea towels from the galley drawer to wrap around the ice.

"We will have to keep a close eye on her for now and maybe get her to the hospital in Panamá as soon as we land," I said.

I was seriously afraid for Kara, as she had sustained a hard blow. In all the years of sailing, this was only the second serious injury inflected on a *Maiatla* crew member. Three years previous, Al, aka Raúl, caught the boom in his head, splitting his skull open. The blow nearly knocked him unconscious while spewing blood over the deck. Raúl's bloodletting had happened back in the California's Channel Islands and required my shaving Raúl's head and steri-stripping the wound. Aside from some minor additional brain damage, Raúl would be fine, or, at least, no worse off. However, I sensed Kara's injuries could be much worse. Panamá City was still at best six hours away, but we had little choice in the matter. We could possibly turn around and go back to Contadora where there was a clinic and, if the need be, a flight to the mainland for better medical care. I decided to see how she did over the next half hour, and if she showed any signs she was worsening, I would turn around and radio Contadora to get a water taxi to come out and ferry her to the island's clinic.

Back in the cockpit, I gave Ashley the icepacks to apply to Kara, as well as some Tylenol for the pain, but first I had another good look at Kara's belly. The bruising was deep blue and black, but it seemed to have stopped spreading. She said the area felt painful when I probed with some rigidity, but after a bit more prodding, I began to suspect her injuries were nothing more than a world-class bruise. I hoped so, anyway. We would hold our course for now while keeping a close eye on her.

When Janet and I started cruising on the high seas and exploring the deep wilds of foreign countries with the children many years ago, we were very concerned for their welfare. We needed to be as medically self-sufficient as possible. To that end, we both took first aid and CPR courses, and with the help of our cruising family doctor, we put together a medical kit that was about as complete as we could possibly make it. Our medical kit includes the latest antibiotics, pain killers and even morphine. If the need arose, we were prepared to suture wounds, set bones or perform an emergency appendectomy—with the help of a doctor on the other end of the ham radio, of course. I was sure missing having Mark, *Maiatla's* resident paramedic, aboard.

With Kara settled with water, pain killers and ice, I now had time to have a look at the mast step to see what went wrong. The step had been torn off the mast, but it quickly became evident that it was hardly Kara's fault. The three 1-inch screws securing the step to the mast had pulled out, and now upon examining the threads, I could see the pulped wood still clinging to the screws threads. Years of being in the tropics were to blame, as water had seeped into the threads and the heat and humidity had created dry rot, weakening the fasteners hold. It was only a matter of time before the step let loose, and unfortunately, it had been on Kara's watch.

The rest of our journey to Panamá was, thankfully, uneventful. The wind remained allusive, along with the marine life. We should have been positively giddy with anticipation at being so close to our destination; a new country and adventure awaited us just over the horizon. However, Kara's accident set a somber mood for the crew, filling us all with a new anxiety. For now, all we wanted to do was get to the dock in case we needed the hospital. It would be a tense few hours before our voyage would be over. Kara was now resting comfortably on the bench seat next to me, but the contorted lines in her face told the story. Behind the helm, I leaned on the throttle to eke out a few more revolutions of the propeller, in hopes of getting to Panamá perhaps a little sooner.

Chapter 42

Panamá City and Back to the Netherworld

*"Panamá is a strange destination. Part of it is the kind of Americanised non-place you'd
flee to if you were pretending to be dead, part-transit zone and part-central American
wilderness—making it a compact place to visit for an all-in-one experience."*
—Darius Sanai, freelance writer.

The first thing one notices, even long before the skyscrapers of Panamá come
into view, is the amount of shipping streaming in and out. Annually, between
13000 and 14000 ships pass through the Panamá Canal, which averages out
to approximately 40 or so per day. If this isn't intimidating enough, consider this:
Approximately every 36 minutes, we had an island-size vessel either charge up to us
from behind or come straight for us, and at times, we had ships pass us in both
directions, at the same time, one on either side. Although the rules of the road give
sail the right-of-way, these commercial giants chose not remember that part of the
test, requiring us to stay out of their way. Still, we weren't sailing, but motoring with
sails up, which gave use even less right to be where we were.

I tuned the VHF radio to the traffic control where I could hear all the comings
and goings of ships and the pilots guiding them. From the sounds of it, everyone was
on a tight schedule and dodging around an errant sailboat wasn't part of the program.
All in all, I found it nerve-wracking, but I attempted to conceal my anxiety from the
crew. No sense worrying them as well.

"Ashley, can you keep a lookout behind me and let me know if that ship behind
us changes his course? He should miss us, but if he alters even a little bit, he will be
too close," I said

"Yeah sure, Andy," she replied as she swung her legs onto the bench seat so that
she could face backwards and watch.

There were so many ships now they were hard for one person to keep track of.
The radar was running and set to the 7.4-kilometre (4-nautical mile) range, but like
flies on a rancid corpse, there were far too many to count. The black dots on the
screen, half of which appeared to be moving, rendered the radar functionally useless.
Aside from all the ships headed into or out of the canal zone and the nearly 150 ships

anchored out waiting, we saw tug boats, fuel barges and pilot boats zipping about, along with a pair of larger river dredges heading out to sea to dump a fresh load of sediment they had recently sucked up from the bottom of the canal. It was organized chaos on a grand scale, and like a leashed shiatsu at the Calgary Stampede, I hoped little *Maiatla* was not about to get crushed underfoot.

Figure 104. Large ships would pass uncomfortably close to *Maiatla.*

The Isthmus of Panamá, along with its canal, is the connection between two great oceans, the Pacific and Atlantic, which shortens the passage for shipping between San Francisco and New York by over 16,668 kilometres (9,000 nautical miles). Until the opening of the Panamá Canal in 1914, the only way around North American was through the Northwest Passage, over the top of Canada and the Arctic Ocean, which for most of the time was impassable due to ice, and the only way around South American was to sail down around the bottom end and its infamous Cape Horn.

The opening of the canal was a boon to shipping, saving time, money and lives of mariners; however, it took the lives of almost 6000 construction workers. Panamá is the crossroads of the world's commerce and has been so for over 500 years, initially with the plundered riches of the Aztec, then the Inca empires. On its long journey to Spain, the riches of these two great civilizations were loaded onto mule trains to traverse across the isthmus. A flow of wealth that continues today in the form of containerships packed full of Ikea furniture, Asian-made automobiles and Wal-Mart junk.

For the past four months, I had not seen a building greater than three stories tall, and here we were approaching the third largest and the tallest city in Central America, with over 1.5 million people. Even from several miles offshore, the immensity of Panamá City was evident with its towering stoical concrete mountains, which included the distinctive 70-story Trump International Hotel. The massive eye-catching edifice dominated the waterfront, the shape of which reminds me of a Sea Pen.

Four and a half years after departing Vancouver, British Columbia, bound for the Panamá Canal and a shocking 50 years after my first visit, we were finally arriving at Panamá City. We set a course for Isla Flamenco, located at the head of the 2.8-kilometre (1.5-nautical mile) long Amador Causeway, which is the eastern bank of the Panamá Canal. The Amador Causeway was constructed in 1913 with rock excavated from the Culebra Cut during the construction of the canal. The causeway joins Panamá City with four offshore islands: Naos, Perico, Culebra and Flamenco.

Flamenco, the outermost island, supports an airport-like control tower where, using VHF radios, controllers choreograph the shipping, as well as radar station for tracking all the vessels.

Erick, our Panamá agent, had informed vessel control of our pending arrival, so as instructed, I hailed the control tower when we closed to within a couple of miles and gave them my ship identification number, which Erick had already arranged for us. After several tries, I finally contacted a controller and we were given permission to find a place to anchor at La Playita, on the west side of Isla Flamenco. I had heard a great deal about this particular anchorage, most of which was not good. It was exposed to the wakes of passing ships and had a soft mud bottom, which apparently didn't like to hold onto anchors, that was also littered with debris. To make matters worse, thieves patrolled the waterfront, looking for rich tourists or unattended boats to target. Nevertheless, we had little choice at this point.

The tiny bay, approximately a third of a nautical mile wide, already contained 30 or 40 other private yachts and charter boats of all descriptions and flags. And like us, they were waiting for a transit date or were resting after already having made the crossing from the Caribbean side. I moved *Maiatla* in as close to the outside of the cluster of boats as I could before dropping the hook. Satisfied the holding was good, I had a look around. I was farther out than I had liked and we were dammed close to the shipping channel. Whenever a vessel passed by, which was about every 20 minutes or so for a large ship and nearly constant for tugs and pilot vessels, their wakes kept us rolling around. I vowed to find a way to move in closer to a more protected spot, but it would have to wait until morning, as it was growing dark and the crew was hungry.

"Andy, it's pretty rolly here, with all that boat traffic. Is it going to keep up all night, you think?" Janet asked after I set the anchor snubber and return to the cockpit.

"Yes, I think so, hun, but we will try and move in over there tomorrow," I said as I pointed to what looked like a bit of an opening between a pair of trawlers and some small sailboats close to shore.

"I will also see about maybe getting a dock at the marina if they have space," I added.

The La Playita marina had a reputation of being expensive and, at times, not too accommodating to the cruising crowd, but they did permit people from the anchorage to use their dinghy dock, for a fee of course. We could tie to a dock for $35 USD per week for three people and $5 for each additional crew member. One day or seven, it was $40 for us to land and leave the dink, but the dock came with a steely-eyed security guard, who scrutinized everyone coming and going while making sure the fee had been paid. The dinghy dock was cheap compared to the marina costs for *Maiatla,* as I would later learn, which were $150 USD for the first night and $130 USD per day after that. We decided to stay on the hook and take our chances out in the anchorage.

Kara was looking much better, and she was starting to move around without so much groaning. Her abdomen still appeared as if she had an alien ready to burst forth, or perhaps as if she was wearing an extremely bad tie dye shirt, but she was otherwise healing nicely. I asked if she wanted to go to the hospital for a checkup, but she declined.

"I'll see how I feel in the morning," she said as she sat propped up in the corner of the cockpit while taking in all the sights. "I don't think I'm bruising anymore, and now it's just a dull ache," she added with a forced smile.

The sun was setting fiery red to the west as a blanket of clouds formed over the city. A slight breeze filled in from the east, carrying with it a pungent mixture of jungle and civilization laced with steamy humidity. The concrete jungle absorbed the day's heat, only to belch it out in the evening, as if the city had held its breath during the day, just waiting for the sun to desert the sky before exhaling. The evening breeze was like the hot breath of a giant, searing your brow or the nape of your neck. With all the hatches open and the wind socks in place, the wind did little to cool the boat; nevertheless, we were thankful for the air movement. What didn't help the matter was the engine had been running most of the day, adding its own broiling breath to the atmosphere down below.

Silently, Janet stood on the deck next to the cockpit, watching boats cruise by. Off in the distance we could see the lights of the great city grow in intensity with the fading sun. I came up behind Janet, wrapped my arms around her, then kissed her cheek.

"Welcome to Panamá, hun," I said while giving her a bit of a squeeze.

Janet remained silent while awestruck by the sight before us. After a few moments of contemplation, she finally replied, "This place looks crazy busy, and it's way too fucking hot!"

Our night on the outside of the anchorage wasn't as bad as I had anticipated. The changing tide permitted us to swing to take the waves on the bow instead of the beam of the boat, but we were still determined to move at the first opportunity. Both Janet and Kara slept surprisingly well thanks to the breeze, which did eventually cool down the night, and a healthy dose of sleeping or pain pills. I had a bit of a talk with Captain Morgan before turning in, so I too had little trouble sleeping.

By mid-Friday morning the following day, I was ashore at the marina office to pay our fees. Then it was a taxi ride to customs and immigration to check in, along with a quick trip to the phone store to buy a chip for my cell phone after which I called Erick. I was pleased to hear we had a date for measuring *Maiatla,* which was in three days, first thing Monday morning. Days before, I had received an email from Erick explaining the cost and the procedures of our canal transit, the email read as follows:


```
Dear Capt. Andy,
```

360

I here to anticipate proforma and scenario for your sailing boat.

Transit tolls $800.00 (under 50ft length) or $1300.00 (50 ft. and under 80 ft.)

Transit inspection 54.00

Transit Security fee 130.00

Bank/tax/cc per cent 60.00

Fenders and lines rental 60.00

Buffer Fee (return after transit) $890.00 Cash

Agent service Fee $350.00

Scenario:

Once the above information is submitted to the canal authorities a Ship Identification Number is assigned, I will provide you the number by email.

Upon arrival contact flamenco signal station and report. With an arrival time register, I may order the Canal Admeasurement inspector to measure your boat at anchorage between Isla Culebra and Isla Flamenco West towards the channel way, (08.9088-079.5265). Inspections are done Monday through Friday and they are not done daily due to other commitments with merchant vessel. However, I will be pushing to obtain an inspection as soon as possible. Therefore, could be two to three days for an inspection or, if we are lucky, the following day of your arrival, if it's Monday-Friday and in some cases on Saturdays as well.

Upon completion of admeasurement inspection, a transit can be obtained for between two to three days after or a fix date with anticipation.

Once a transit is lined up, I will then collect funds, transit tolls and agent fee in credit card, three to four business days before, in order to guarantee your transit. Buffer fee $890.00 in cash to be refunded in cash at Shelter after transit if not used.

Important to state your real speed on admeasurement form, view transit will be scheduled based the information given. Five to 8 kts are acceptable but subject to:

If they program the transit to start early with a completing time in the afternoon, then you have to meet the schedule. (Otherwise the buffer fee $890.00 will be applicable if you do not meet the times.)

Or

Program starting a transit in the morning without completing time, means that you will be anchored at the lake on canal convenience, and resuming the following day (no charges will be applicable).

Then I will provide eight round fenders and four set of lines 125 ft. long 7/8. Transit pilots are assigned from 0600 to 09:00 a.m. daily and you will transit the first day all the way or partially, depends on canal scheduling program. You will have to meet the last locks on about 1400-1500hrs and finishing transit about 1700hrs. Otherwise, if you do not meet the schedule because of an under speed of 5-8 knots, then Buffer fee will cover Pilot delay, mooring at Gatún, launch service $890.00.

You will need four persons as hand-liners for canal transit + the Captain steering. If need hand-liners, I will provide at a cost of $100.00 each.

Immigration and check in declaration will be done at Flamenco Port authorities offices and costs involved are Cruising permit $193.00 + $20.00.

Clearance/check out $35.00

Immigration visa $105.00 each + ($40.00 one time)

Please be guided.

Best regards,

Erick Galvez

Centenario & Co.S.A.

In total, we would pay $1,454.00 USD for the canal, not including the Panamá cruising permit and immigration fees for the crew—a hefty assortment of fees but necessary if we wanted to see the Caribbean and avoid the four to six month journey around the Horn. I was still short one line handler, but I was hoping to pick someone up from another boat for a day or two. I found it funny that when I first proposed transiting the canal to family and friends the year previous, I had a slew of volunteers to help us along the way, too many in fact. I had intended to give family members, sibling's, first crack at *Maiatla's* limited bunk space, and I wasn't looking forward to having to tell anyone there wasn't any more room, but I needn't have worried.

As often happens, other people's netherworld shackles are far too restraining, and when the time finally arrived and I put out the call, no one who had originally said they would come, came. I could use the line handlers Erick was prepared to provide for a fee, and I was reasonably sure he would provide qualified people. However, I had heard some horror stories from other cruisers who used locals for the transit, stories of people not following directions, being drunk, or raiding the refrigerator in the middle of the night to outright theft of monies and gear. Better to find my own people if I could.

Before the Canal Authority would assign a transit date, the boat had to be measured for length and displacement, and it's these figures on which the transit fee is based.

There was nothing I could do about *Maiatla's* displacement, but her length was another matter.

The fees were $800 for boats under 50 feet in length or $1300 for boats 50 feet and over and up to 80 feet. From the tip of our bowsprit to the end of my dinghy davits, *Maiatla* was a solid 54 feet, which I already knew, so I had decided that I would put our inflatable dinghy on the foredeck and unbolt the dinghy davits and store them on deck, shortening our overall all length to 49 feet 6 inches and saving us $500 USD. If our cost seems a bit harsh, a containership can pay upwards of $200,000 USD. But since the opening of the new section of the Panamá Canal in 2017 which can handle even larger vessels, the transit fees have now climbed to well over $800,000 USD for the Panamax container ships, which can carry up to 19000 shipping containers.

Passenger cruise ships are charged in part by how many cabins they have aboard: $110 for an empty cabin and $150 for an occupied one. With the latest cruise ships capable of accommodating up to 6000 passengers, their canal transit fees are now pushing the half-a-million dollar mark. With money like this to be raked in by the canal board, it's miraculous they even make room for small private yachts, like *Maiatla*. However, new pilot trainees cut their teeth on the yachties until they become experienced enough to move up the line to the bigger commercial vessels.

Interesting enough, the lowest fee ever paid for a transit was made by an American adventurer Richard Halliburton, who swam the full 77-kilometre (48-mile) length of the Panamá Canal in 1928. As fees were primarily based on displacement, the weight of water displaced when an object is set in the water, Halliburton was only charged 36 cents to swim through the locks and the adjoining Gatún Lake. Followed by a photography boat that had a crew member armed with a rifle, as the lake is infested with crocodiles, Halliburton completed the swim in only 50 hours, with stops at night to rest. Halliburton was a travel writer and lecturer and had a flair for the dramatic, which would distinguish his life from others in his day. A vocation that ultimately lead to his death.

Halliburton was what we now might call an adrenaline junkie, a publicity seeker and a professional celebrity, but he was also an accomplished writer, whose bestselling books introduced international travel to thousands of Americans. He was arguably the most successful celebrity travel writer and adventurer of his generation. Nevertheless, at the age of 39, his life would come to a tragic end. His last great adventure commenced when Haliburton commissioned the construction of a 23-metre (75.4-feet) Chinese junk, with the intent of sailing it from Asia on a 14,816-kilometre (8000-nautical mile) journey across the Pacific Ocean in time to be displayed at the International Exposition in San Francisco. On March 3, 1939, Halliburton left on a gaudily painted vessel, described by one writer "as looking more like a movie prop than an ocean going ship." The *Sea Dragon* departed Hong Kong only to be greeted by a storm. The boat's crew, which included a professional captain, was last heard from via a radio message approximately 1609 kilometres (1000 miles) west of Midway Island, in the central Pacific Ocean. The message, sent to a passenger steamer by the captain of the *Sea Dragon,* reported: "Southerly gales. Rain squalls. Lee rail under water, wet bunks. Hard tack. Bully beef. Having wonderful time. Wish you were here instead of me."

Later in the day, the storm developed into a full-blown cyclone. The *Sea Dragon,* Richard Halliburton and his crew of 14 were never seen again. I found it interesting that only two years earlier in 1937, the famed female flyer Amelia Earhart disappeared on the same line of longitude in the Pacific as the *Sea Dragon*, albeit Earhart was lost some 3148 kilometers (1700 nautical miles) further south, right on the equator. Like Halliburton, she was only 39 years old.

With all of our business conducted ashore, we returned to *Maiatla*, but not before scouting out the anchorage for a better spot. We found one close in shore, between a pair of American trawler yachts and a sad-looking 15-metre (49.4 feet) ketch, which, caked in city grime and with an anchor laden with a heavy encrustation of muscles and barnacles, appeared to have been there for some time.

"It looks a bit tight, hun, but if we keep the scope short, I think there is enough room. What ya think?" I asked as I slowed the dink to circle around in the spot.

"I guess so, if you think we will fit," Janet said as she gauged the anchorage. "It does look calmer in here, and I guess having all those other boats between us and the channel would act like a bit of a breakwater. Let's give it a try.

The anchorage was a busy one, with boats coming or going on a daily basis or just shifting about as we were attempting to do, so spots opened up, to be quickly filled again. We needed to move fast.

An hour later, under the gaze of our new neighbours and no more than three boat lengths away from the closest boats, we set the hook while giving it a good pull to make sure we were tight and not likely to drag if the wind were to build. Our new home next to the shore was a comfortable one, and I wasted no time in removing the solar panels mounted atop of the davits, then the davits themselves. It was a bit of a tricky operation, as I had to lean way out over top of the water to reach the bolts securing the davits. I felt a bit like the fellow who was sawing off a tree limb while sitting on the wrong side of the branch.

The task could have been best accomplished from the dinghy, but the girls had taken it ashore to do a bit of exploring, so unless I wanted to wait, as the admiral rightly suggested, I would have to just make do. In the end, the davits came off at a the cost of some skinned knuckles, two bolts, three washers, one nut and my best crescent wrench, which, save for the knuckles, were added to the junk pile I suspected already lined the bottom of the bay. Under normal circumstances, I would have stripped off and gone searching for my tool, but considering the stiff current and amount of oil and apparent sewage floating by (not to mention crocs), I thought better of it.

We had three days before our inspection and had much to do, including finding some fuel, as I wanted to enter the locks with full tanks. To run out of diesel after we entered the locks would cause us to forfeit our $890 buffer fee, not to mention putting us in danger of being run down in the narrow waterways.

It was also Ashley's 28th birthday, so we had cause for celebration. A dinner was planned ashore, but Janet felt ill. The girls went without us to find a restaurant and perhaps some of Panamá's legendary night life. Panamá was a city in heat, in more ways than one. Ashley thought to maybe connect with Joshua, the fellow the girls had met on the plane on their way down. Joshua and his car would later prove themselves useful, as the girls convinced him to help with a laundry run. While the girls played tourist over the weekend, Janet rested while I kept myself busy preparing for the transit.

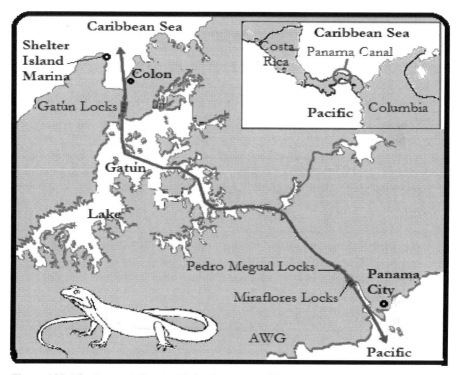

Figure 105. The Panamá Canal with its three sets of locks and connecting Gatún Lake.

On one of my many dinghy runs ashore, I met a middle-aged couple on *Sea-Nettle*, a Tayana 37 cutter. David and Nancy were from Seattle, Washington, and had been cruising Central American for the past two years. They had intended to transit the canal this month, put the boat in a marina, then fly home to their jobs, both working in a cannery in Alaska. However, as plans go, they had to reconsider their strategy because, as often happens to most cruisers, money was the issue.

The cost of transiting the canal and putting the boat up for six months in Shelter Marina was hefty, so they opted for Plan B, which was to sail to the nearby Island of Taboga and leave the boat on a mooring ball with a Panamánian by the name of Chuy (pronounced Chew-wee). I had heard of Chuy's mooring field many years ago, and other cruising friends had used him to babysit their boat when they flew home for a visit or to work long term. A mooring ball was half the cost of a marina, and most I had talked to had nothing but good things to report about Chuy.

It was a spot I had considered for *Maiatla,* but I did not like the idea of not having a dehumidifier running on the boat while we were gone. After going back to Marina Chiapas and finding the boat full of mould this year, I was determined to have her better cared for. No! *Maiatla* needed to be on a dock and plugged in, with a dehumidifier's fans circulating the air and an attentive watch keeper to keep things running while we were gone.

The crew of *Sea Nettle* jumped at the chance to crew through the canal, just for the experience, so we made plans to pick them up the morning of our transit, which, if Erick was correct, should be sometime in the middle of the following week.

On Sunday, the girls hit the town on another whirlwind tour while Janet and I settled on a Duck ride around the harbour. At the marina office, a tour booth advertised Duck tours, a tour of the old city streets and waterfront in an amphibious truck. It turned out to be surprisingly fun and far less energetic than the tour Kara and Ashley had planned.

As scheduled, on Monday morning, we pulled the hook to move to the outside of the anchorage and re-anchor to wait for the pilot boat, which would bring the officials to measure *Maiatla.* On time, the pilot boat dropped off a pair of fellows to do the honours, and I must say they were professional and polite when accepting an offer of bottled water. In less than 30 minutes, they were off. Since we were on the move anyway, I decided to head around the island to the Flamenco marina to use its fuel dock to top up our tanks.

Where we were, Marina La Playita, also had fuel, but it was a bit more expensive. I wasn't concerned with the cost, the problem was they required a minimum sale of 100 gallons, and I wasn't sure we could take that much, so it was off around the corner. I was required to call the harbour master to request permission to approach the fuel dock. At first we were told to stand off and wait, so we cruised the other small boat anchorage, which was located on the east side of Isla Flamenco. The municipal anchorage, Las Brisas de Amador, near the Flamenco Yacht Club, was packed with boats that, judging from the amount of growth on their bottoms, had not moved in years.

Our tour of the anchorage was cut short, as the call came and we were given permission to enter the marina and take on fuel—which went smoothly. While I pumped diesel, Kara and Ashley filled the water tanks and gave the boat a good freshwater bath, which she sorely needed. It was the first since leaving México a good four months earlier, and at least a month since getting doused in a solid rain squall. It's remarkable how much salt will build up on a boat. In places on *Maiatla's* foredeck, you could strip the salt off in thin sheets and feel the gritty grains of salt when walking barefoot on deck. We still kept a pan of fresh water next to the cockpit to rinse our feet before entering the cockpit, in an effort to keep as much salt out of the boat as possible.

As I was paying for our fuel, Erick called to inform us we had a transit time of 7 a.m., Wednesday morning. It was now still well before noon. We had a full day and a half to kill before our pilot would arrive to commence our transit. Not wanting to waste a moment, I called the crew together to propose that we not return to the anchorage today, but instead sail to the nearby tourist island of Taboga and its uninhabited sister island, Uravá, for a little sightseeing and perhaps some snorkelling.

Chapter 43

Isla Taboga or Bust!

"You can't do anything about the length of your life, but you
can do something about its width and depth."
—Evan Esar

It was only a short 11-kilometre (7-mile) sail over to Isla Taboga, little time for hoisting all the sails. We settled for unfurling the headsail, which whipped us along at a good 6 knots into the 15 knots of wind filling in from the northeast, bringing with it some welcomed cloud cover. If I had remembered how crazy busy it was sailing through this area when we first arrived, I may have given Taboga a pass, but we were committed, so we were now engaged, for a second time, in a high stakes game of dodge ball with all the commercial shipping.

As we approached the island, the wind continued to build until we were propelled by over 25 knots, whistling through the rigging, making for a fast sail. I suspected, though, the north-easterly would be wrapping around the tip of Isla Taboga, driving right into the anchorage. The seas were likewise building, setting up an ugly chop with breaking whitecaps. Looking back over my shoulder, I suddenly realized if these conditions held into the next day, we would have one hell of a beat upwind to reach our anchorage. So much for a nice leisurely sail to and from the islands. I cut close into shore of Isla Morro de Taboga, the tiny island protecting the anchorage from the summertime northerlies. Janet was the first to state the obvious.

"Andy, it looks awfully rough in there. Are we going to find a calm place to anchor?"

From a quarter mile out, we could see the colourful beachfront community, with possibly dozens of restaurants and bars, and offshore were a dozen mooring buoys holding what looked to be cruising boats. I assumed this was Chuy's mooring field, but what had me concerned was how the boats were bouncing all over the place.

"Not sure, hun. Let's just head in and have a look," I said, not sounding too hopeful. "Kara and Ashley, can you furl the headsail please?"

Under power, we toured the anchorage, but the only open and calm spots remaining were too close inshore where I could see the bottom. We could stay, but unless the wind died, it would be a rough night on the hook, and I didn't want Janet to get tired again. We needed to find somewhere else to go or head back to the anchorage at La Playita.

"Ashley, you want to take the helm while I have a look at the charts to see where else we can go?"

"Okay, Andy, but where do you want me to go?"

"Oh, just pull some tight donuts, but don't hit anything and stay off the beach, okay?" The sarcastic remark was all in good fun. Both the girls had become competent helmsmen (helmswomen?) over the past month, and I had every confidence in their abilities to keep us out of trouble.

Back in my commercial diving days, I had graduated from getting wet on every dive to becoming the co-pilot for a manned submersible, a tethered diving bell with propulsion. *"The Arms Bell"* was tiny two-man submarine, with mechanical arms and CCTV cameras and diving capabilities to 914 metres (3000 feet). My job was to man the life support and TV systems, but the best part was that the sub was dry. Right next to my station on the wall was a plaque my partner and pilot had placed. The plague read:

It is a superior pilot who uses his superior knowledge and superior judgment to avoid situations that requires his superior piloting skills!

An obvious truism I believe can equally be applied to cruising and situations like this.

Considering how many boats were either anchored out or like us, trying to find a place to anchor, it may have been a tall order, requiring a careful assessment. It took me a while to figure out what to do, but we weren't rushed. With Ashley on the helm and Kara keeping watch while giving instructions, I wasn't worried for *Maiatla* at the moment.

Janet and I looked at the chart, and it soon became obvious, we had little choice.

"Hun, if we follow the shore and head between the two islands, I think we can get out of the wind in this tiny bay here," I said as I pointed at the computer screen. There was a narrow gap between Isla Toboga and Isla Uravá that lead to the west side of both islands, which should offer protection from the wind and waves.

"If we go over there and find it too rough as well, can we get back to Panamá before dark? I don't think I want to cross the shipping lanes at night. It was bad enough in the daylight," Janet confessed.

She was right. We did have time to get back if we left right now, but it would be a hard and wet slog back. Foolishly, I had not checked the weather reports before deciding to sail over here, so I had no idea if the wind would remain or die out at sunset.

"Let's give the bay a try. It may calm down by morning, then we will run back. In the meantime, let's head through the pass and see if we can find a place to drop the hook," I suggested. "Worst case scenario: We can come back here and anchor out in front of the town and tough it out."

Neither Janet nor I were happy, and the girls less so for having a glimpse of what could have been a great little resort town full of fun and adventure, but we could not stay. I took back the helm while the girls reset the headsail. It was a pleasant downwind sail along a few miles of the shore. Isla Toboga is often referred to as "The Island of Flowers" for the hibiscus, bougainvillea, jasmine and the Tobago rose that bloom in riotous abundance in its "Mediterranean climate," as described in our tour books. It was indeed a beautiful island, and I was sorry we were going to miss it, as I was looking forward to dinner and a few beers at one of the colourful palapas.

The pass between the islands was wider than what I read on the chart, and as predicted, once we popped out on the far side, the blustery wind ceased. On a nearly flat smooth sea, we manoeuvred close into shore, the girls furled the sail, then we dropped the hook.

"Well, hun, what ya think? This will do, eh?" This was more a statement than a question. It was a beautifully quiet spot in the lee of a rocky, jungle clad island, with flocks of sea birds swirling above. From our deck, we felt as far from civilization as one could possibly get, despite having a million and a half people living just beyond the island's ridge top. To celebrate, we had beers, then a swim off of the boat. I barbequed some steaks, and we all ate in the cockpit, enjoying the solitude while we talked of the transit to come. Kara had been receiving updates on Travis, and he appeared to be doing better. For the first time since his diagnosis of stomach cancer, there was reason for some optimism, though guarded.

Somewhere around 10 p.m., I thought I saw the lights of Panamá City, but it turned out to be the loom of the moon as it broached the ridge top. The evening was beautiful, with just enough breeze reaching us to cool the boat, but just a little.

First thing in the morning, I attempted some fishing from the back deck, but aside for a small pufferfish, I struck out. Flustered, I decided to go straight to the source and hauled out my diving gear, spear gun, then called below.

"I'm going diving on the point. Anyone want to come for a ride?"

Janet opted to stay in bed to read for a while, but Kara and Ashley were up for a little outing. So after a quick breakfast of French toast and bacon, the girls help me load the dink.

"You girls can drive the dinghy and follow me around and come pick me up when I'm done," I said.

The girls gave each other a sideways glance, Kara asked, "How are we going to do that if you are underwater?"

"I will be towing a buoy along behind me. Just follow the float, and after say 45 minutes and I haven't surfaced or haven't moved for a while, just pull me up, okay?"

Figure 106. A lone and inflated pufferfish was all that would take my bait.

I have been sports diving this way for many years, and more often than not, it was just Janet and I out in some isolated spot. Towing the float behind gave Janet a method of following and, if the need be, retrieving me. The truth be known, the tether was more of a "body recovering technique" than a lifesaving tool. For over 30 years, Janet has tended to me this way until, at age 50, while in Cancun México, she took her first diving course and finally discovered what she had been missing all these years.

Out on the point, armed with my spear gun and down at 22 metres (72.1 feet), I concluded it would have been better to have stayed in bed with Janet, snuggled up with her and a good book. The water was brown and murky, which reduced the visibility to only a couple of metres (6.5 feet) at best, and the strong current that was absent on the surface when I entered forced me to cling to the rocks to keep from being swept away.

The rock wall I was diving was devoid of most life, as if all had been scoured off, and what few fish I saw were insufficient in size to even bait a hook, never mind warrant lighting the barbeque. I was hopeful to at least find a couple of lobster to invite for dinner, but all the best little holes bugs normally like to inhabit were as empty as my goodie bag. After pulling myself along the cliff for over half an hour, I had had enough. On the whole, as a hunting trip, the dive was a bust, but at least I received my morning exercise.

After sandwiches for lunch, we pulled anchor and motored towards the pass with the intent of heading back to the canal. As we cleared the point, we were slammed on the nose by the same wind we had so neatly ducked the day before. If nothing else, I was thankful the conditions had not worsened overnight. The mileage it took us to cover in an hour and a half the previous day was now a 7-hour up wind bash to get us back to La Playita. In an effort to hasten our trip, the girls raised the main and mizzen sails to aid the engine as we motored sailed into the steep 2-metre (6.5-feet) waves.

In an effort to avoid as many ships as possible, we had inadvertently sailed a course that took us to the far west side of the channel where a shallow and massive mud bank stretches for miles. A couple of times while tacking back and forth, trying to get the best angle on the wind while dodging ships, we had closed on the bank and had nearly run aground. If it were not for the sharp eyes of the girls, constantly checking the depth sounder, we could have struck bottom more than once.

It was getting dark by the time we set the hook back in our tight little spot next to shore. Settled in, I called our new friends on *Sea-Nettle* to let them know we were back and to make sure they had not changed their minds or pulled a vanishing act. It could have been a real problem if they had bailed, as it would have forced us to reschedule the transit while losing my buffer fee deposit. David and Nancy were still onboard for the transit and eager to get on with it. We decided on an early night for all, as it had been a tiring day, with the next couple promising to be busy and adventurous as well.

Chapter 44

The "Order of the Ditch" for Maiatla

"We can't be afraid of change. You may feel secure in the pond that you are in, but if you never venture out of it, you will never know that there is such a thing as an ocean, a sea. Holding onto something that is good for you now, may be the reason why you don't have something better."
—C. JoyBell C., writer.

In the morning, while Janet and I moved *Maiatla* to the outside of the anchorage to wait for our pilot, the girls in the dinghy were off to fetch our two new line handlers. Out and re-anchored near the channel, we started to worry as the girls had not caught up to us and our appointed time was fast approaching. The concern centred on my decision to send the dink to pick up David and Nancy.

The dinghy engine had been acting up, and I was now fearful the engine had died on Kara and Ashley and now the four of them were drifting aimless though the anchorage while frantically trying to restart the engine. The wind was still strong, which would have negated the possibility of them rowing the dink back home. I had visions of having to up-anchor and go search for them while the pilot boat circled around searching for us. My fears were coming true when I spotted the pilot boat round the bend, then alter course straight for us.

However, when I turned to check the anchorage, thankfully, there was our dink. It appeared between two anchored boats, loaded to the gunnels with crew and baggage. The crew boarded just minutes before the pilot boat pulled alongside.

Emanuel, our pilot, spoke broken English, but we had little difficulty understanding each other, and he wasted no time in telling us to up-anchor and get underway. It was approximately 9.6 kilometres (6 miles) from our anchorage to the first of the canal locks, and our journey upstream was an exciting and pleasant one, as we had the still cool morning breeze in our faces and lots to see along the shore.

Along the way, Emanuel instructed me to stay tight against the starboard side of the channel, which permitted a large containership heading upstream to pass, and then a river dredge heading down. Emanuel briefed us on lock procedures and what was required of the line handlers. Kara and Ashley would handle the two stern dock lines, while David and Nancy would take the pair of bow lines. Since the angle of the dock lines changes drastically as the boat rises or falls, we needed to remove the life lines at the bow. Not removing the lines, we ran the risk of having the lifelines and supporting staunches ripped from the deck, but now there was a new hazard—the crew could more easily fall overboard.

The canal narrowed slightly as we approached the Bridge of the Americas and Highway 1, which connects north, central and South America, making it truly the bridge of the Americas. The bridge was completed in 1962, but the designers never envisioned the size of ships to come. With a clearance from the water of 61.3 metres (201 feet), it is still not high enough to accommodate some of the largest cruise ships. *Maiatla's* main mast was only 17 metres (55.7 feet) tall, so we would not have a problem with the clearance. As we passed under the bridge, all went well, and with Janet at my side, it was a grand milestone moment until it wasn't.

Figure 107. Nancy and Ashley inspect the Balboa Yacht club located on the east shore of the canal, and off in the distance is the Bridge of the Americas. Our transit of the famous Panamá Canal has begun.

I was sitting in the helm seat, looking at the bridge pass overhead, one hand on the helm, the other holding Janet's hand, when I heard it. Instantly my heart sank into my stomach. The engine faltered, revving up, then slowing back down, as if suddenly starved for fuel. In a near panic, I said to Janet, "Here drive!" And I jumped from my seat to dash below to the engine room. Throwing open the doors, I quickly placed my hands on the pair of fuel valves, throwing one open while shutting the other off. The engine hiccupped a couple of more times, then settled out. The old Perkins continued to rattle and hum as she usually does. I listened carefully for any sounds out of the ordinary, but there were none, other than the calls from Janet asking what was going on. After several minutes, with my ear tuned to *Maiatla's* heart, I closed the doors and went back topside to be greeted by a pair of worried looking faces, Janet's and Emanuel's. The rest of the crew was sitting up forward on the cabin top, sightseeing and total oblivious to what had just transpired.

"What's the matter, *Capitán*? Is you running out of fuel?" Emanuel had also heard the engine stumble, and he too was concerned.

"No, I have lots of fuel. I just needed to change tanks that's all. It's all good," I insisted as I swapped seats with Janet. I sat there soaked in sweat from the heat of the engine room and from nearly having a heart attack. I could not explain why the engine did what it did, nor could I guarantee it wouldn't do it again or, worse, just die while we were in the middle of the lock.

"Is it okay to continue, Andy?" Janet quietly asked. She has known me long enough to see I was troubled despite attempts to appear casual.

I turned my ear back to the engine before answering. "Yes, I think we are okay, babe," I said, with a forced smile.

As if transiting the locks wasn't stressful enough, the engine skipping a beat wasn't the only hiccup in *Maiatla's* transit of the canal that would come to stress me out.

Just beyond the bridge, the first of the canal locks slowly came into view. Miraflores is the name of one of the three locks forming the Pacific side of the Panamá Canal. In the Miraflores Locks, vessels are lifted (or lowered) 16.5 metres (54 feet) in two stages, allowing them to transit to or from Miraflores Lake.

It was exciting to see the locks come into view. Just ahead of us were two other small vessels heading in the same direction, while a bit farther ahead was the butt end of a massive freighter passing through the steel lock doors. Apparently, these three vessels would be our lockmates for this part of the transit. The plan according to Emanuel was for us to raft to the other sailboat before reaching the locks and we would enter, as one, in line behind the freighter. The sail boat was a Panamánian registered 12-metre (39.3-feet) racing sloop, with a captain and crew of 10, which included four local, rented line handlers and two women. The women, I assumed, were the owner's wife and adult daughter. We sent greeting waves across the water, but it soon became evident our lockmates didn't speak English, which might be a bit of a problem.

Kara asked, "Where are they going to sleep all those people on that boat when we get to the lake?" It was a good question. Emanuel said the line handlers would sleep on deck.

While still motoring at 5 knots, with all available bumpers from each boat over the side, we brought the two sailboats together. The lines were tossed and the line handles attempted to draw the boats together, but it was as if we were trying to leash together a pair of alpha male dogs—the boats didn't want anything to do with each other. However, the fault lay with the line handlers, as they attempted to pull the boats together instead of letting me and the other captain drive the boats together. As the line handler pulled on *Maiatla's* bow line, I lost steerage, causing us to turn sharply away from the other boat. After much arm waving and cursing in two languages, we managed to get the boats securely tied together. By judicially using both boat's throttles and helms, we finally managed to learn to drive together and none too soon, because by the time we figured it out, we were already entering the first lock. Aside from the massive freighter in front of us, we would have to share the remaining space with the other yacht—a beautiful Nordhavn 52, a luxurious trawler named Vesper, registered in Georgetown, Bahamas. The Nordhavn was instructed to tie along the wall on the east side while we were instructed to secure along the west wall, which would prove easier said than done.

Figure 108. Securing to our lockmates as Ashley supervises before entering our first set of locks.

We did a pretty good job of entering the lock in the centre of the canal and bringing the boats to a stop before acting like a suppository for the ship ahead of us. However, when the lines were tossed from the line handlers on the canal wall to our buddy boat the fellow who was supposed to be catching the bow line missed. The line was quickly pulled back out of the water and readied to be tossed again, but in the meantime, the current caught hold of us and had nearly spun us sideways in the lock. At this rate, it was looking like we were about to be unceremoniously spit back out the doors. After some more frantic line tossing, arm waving and a human against boat tug-o-war going on, we were finally tied securely to the canal wall.

"Shit, I hope it isn't going to be like this every time!" I said to Janet as I slumped wearily into my chair. The canal workers wasted no time. As soon as we were secured, the doors were closed behind us and the water rushed into the canal commencing our lift. As it was, the crew of the *Maiatla* didn't have anything to do on the lift but relax. It was our buddy boat that had to take in their lines as the pair of boats rose on the artificial tide.

"That went well," I said sarcastically to everyone, but to no one in particular. "If nothing else, we provided good entertainment for all of the spectators." I chuckled a bit. Aside from perhaps several canal workers on the wall and the four crew and two owners standing on the aft deck of the Nordhavn watching the show, the crowd on the public viewing platform located high above the lock got an eyeful.

Using our cell phone, we also got in touch with our daughter, Melissa, back home and sent pictures to her of our transit as it happened. She in turn emailed back to us snap shots taken from the live web video cameras lining the canal. In a shot she sent us, there we were, for the entire world to see, sideways in the lock. Once the flooding of the lock was complete, the far set of doors opened up and out went the freighter, followed by the Nordhavn, then us, still rafted together, bound for the next set of locks, which lay just ahead. Our manoeuvring into the second set of locks went far better than the first and, for the most part, without incident. I was pleased to see the last gate open up, and once the ship had moved on, a small lake now stretched out before us.

The canal workers tossed us our lines, so we throttled up and commenced to move out. Clear of the rugged concrete walls of the canal, I was finally able to breathe a sigh of relief while receiving some measure of comfort knowing we were not the only ones to have had some difficulty within the lock. It was the Nordhavn's turn to pay a price. Not a big price, but it did take some of the sting out of my wounded pride.

As the Nordhavn cast her lines off to leave, the owner's wife came on deck to watch, and when she did, a sudden gust of wind snatched her expensive Panamá hat from her head, launching it off of the boat to land in the foaming, swirling water. Irretrievable to them, they were forced to leave it behind. As we cast off, Ashley ran aft where she grabbed up the fishing net, and with one fell swoop, she snatched up the hat right out of the rabid jaws of the canal. Ashley was so pleased with herself, and after trying it on for size, she smiled and said, "It's mine now!"

Ashley spent part of the following week swooning over that elegant hat and made special arrangements within her bags to take it home, but she would be sorely disappointed. Three days after arriving at the Fort Sherman Marina, the hat's rightful owner, the Madame of the Nordhavn, paid us a visit to ask for the hat's return. Apparently, she had seen Ashley rescue it and wanted it back. With some hesitation, I instructed Ashley to fetch the hat from her cabin, but before she disappeared below to do as I instructed, I saw the daggers in Ashley's eyes, which, I believe, were more directed at me than the lady. Thankfully, Ashley's pout-on only lasted an hour or two. Our motor over the mile of lake to the next lock gave the crews of both boats time to relax a little and afforded Kara and Ashley time to start flirting with a couple of the young Panamánian line handlers, who didn't mind the attention they were drawing from a pair of pretty *gringas*.

Figure 109. *Maiatla's* two stern line handlers in action as the lock doors close behind us.

Figure 110. The water floods in on *Maiatla* and her lockmates. Along the wall is the Nordhavn 52. *Vesper.*

"So what happens when we get to the other side of Pedro Miguel Locks? Do we have to stay rafted together all the way through the cut and Gatún Lake?" I asked Emanuel as he sat on the cockpit combing next to me.

No, *Capitán*, we breakaway, but must arrive together when we get to the other side," he said. "The other boat *capitán* says he can motor at 10 knots. Can you keep up?" He looked at me, waiting for an answer.

No, not at 10 knots. I can push up to 8 knots, but only if I have too," I replied.

Emanuel frowned, then said, "That might be a problem."

Like old pros, we managed to get through the next set of locks without a hitch or fanfare. The next stretch of the canal was to be done through what is known as the Culebra Cut, a 12.6-kilometre (7.8-mile) artificial valley cutting through the Continental Divide, linking Gatún Lake to the system. Much of the cut is less than 300 metres (984 feet) wide, not much room left over when you have to share it with a mountain-size Panamax freighter. In the cut, the Nordhavn, as expected, left us in its wake, and even though we had some difficulty keeping pace with our sleek boat buddy, we managed. With the first set of lock successfully behind us, we now faced the cut and the flooded jungle and croc-infested Gatún Lake before reaching the Atlantic side and the locks that would release us into the Caribbean Sea—thus, crossing the continental divide and completing our "Order of the Ditch."

Chapter 45

Swimming with the Crocs and a New Ocean for Maiatla

"The cure for anything is salt water: sweat, tears or the sea."
—Isak Dinesen

I have a vague recollection of the Culebra Cut from when I was a child of eight, standing at the railing of the cruise ship SS. *Australis,* way back in 1968. My family was returning from our failed attempt at immigrating to Australia, and the Panamá Canal was on our way home, back to Canada. I have little memory of the locks themselves, just the mule trains pulling us through and the blast of dirty diesel engine smoke I received in the face as I leaned over the side in an effort to get a better look at the tugboat shoving us along. I remember standing at the rail alongside my brothers, Steven and Greg, and older sister, Jackie, looking upward at the terraced rock wall known as "Contractor's Hill" and its monument, a bronzed plaque depicting workers shouldering shovels. I recall thinking: "How could they dig such a big hole with just shovels?"

My father had informed us of the thousands of men who had died while digging the canal, mainly from disease caused by mosquito bites, and that this plaque memorialized them. Profound thoughts for a child, this child anyway.

As *Maiatla* approached Contractor's Hill, I was eager to see if the plaque was still there. I knew the plaque had been removed and returned, as the canal has been widened several times. But as my only solid memory of the transit with my family so long ago, perhaps that was why I felt I needed to see the plaque again. In truth, as a child, I probably found the trip through the canal boring, missing most of the sites while swimming in the pool or playing in the arcade with my siblings.

Emanuel's hand held radio squawked in Spanish. He snapped a reply before turning to me.

"*Capitán* Andy, there is a big ship coming around the corner. You need to move as far as you can to starboard, okay?"

I did as directed while coming uncomfortably close to the rocky shore. But according to the depth sounder, I still had 5 metres (16.4 feet) under the keel, so I suspected we would hit the rock wall before striking the bottom.

Figure 111. The steep sides of Contractor's Hill and the Cut were chiseled out of solid rock.

As Emanuel had predicted, a ship nosed its way around the corner and it was one of the biggest cargo ships I had ever seen, but perhaps that was because we were so close to it. Nevertheless, I had no time to gawk, as the water the ship pushed before it created a surge and swirl, challenging my steering. At one point, I found *Maiatla* pointing towards shore, but I managed to spin the wheel and counter steer, as if in a car coming out of a slide. When the ship had passed, the water settled. It was a bit of a tense moment, but nothing unmanageable; however, the disheartening part of the encounter was that because I had been so busy driving, I forgot to look for the monument on the hill. Looking back and to the retreating ship's starboard, was Contractor's Hill, but I could not see the monument.

"Shit," I said out loud, my words drawing everyone's attention.

"What's the matter, Andy?" Janet asked.

"I wanted to get a picture, but missed it." I said.

Looking a bit confused at first, Janet then said, with a smile, "Don't worry. There will be other ships coming along."

By the time we reached the end of the 12.6-kilometre (7.8-mile) long cut, the wind had filled into a solid 12 knots, with gusts up to 20 knots, and of course, it was right on the nose. The Nordhavn had long since disappeared around the bend, and I suspected she was already halfway cross Gatún Lake. Our rafting buddy was still ahead, but barely. I had been keeping an eye on them and noticed when the wind started to build, they slowed down. Apparently motoring into a wind and seaway was the slick racing yacht's Achilles heel.

By the time we reach Gatún Lake, it was blowing a steady 20 knots while kicking up a 1-metre (3.2-feet) wind chop, which *Maiatla* promptly ignored. Without any difficulty, we maintained our 6 knots; however, our buddy boat was not so fortunate. As we made our way across the lake, we passed them, gave a wave and kept going, and it wasn't long before we nearly lost sight of them.

Figure 112. Looking aft back, leaving Contractor's Hill behind. Another *Maiatla* milestone surpassed.

Gatún Lake, or Lago Gatún in Spanish, is an incredible place. It is large artificial lake complete with inlets and jungle islands. Our route would take us on an awe-inspiring, 33-kilometre (21-miles) passage across the Isthmus of Panamá. On the lake's perimeter banks and island shores stand the skeletal remains of great trees, old mahogany giants rising from the water. Sunken stumps and submerged snags also form a hazard for any small vessels wandering off the marked channels or foolish enough to attempt to anchor. I was relying on Emanuel to keep us on course and out of trouble.

The lake was created in 1913 by the building of the Gatún Dam across the Chagres River, which flowed into the Caribbean Sea near Colon. At the time, it was the largest man-made lake in the world. The geography of the area was ideal for the creation of a large lake here, as the hills bordering the valley of the Chagres open up widely around the area of the lake, but come together to form a gap just over 2 kilometres (1.2 miles) wide at the location of the dam.

Gatún Lake has an impressive area of 425 square kilometres (164 square miles), and at its normal water level, it is 26 metres (85 feet) above sea level, storing 5.2 cubic kilometres (183 billion cubic feet) of water. With the creation of the lake, many hilltops became islands, the biggest of which is Barro Colorado Island, home of the world-famous Smithsonian Tropical Research Institute (STRI).

The canal follows a clearly marked route around the lake's islands, following the deeper water south from Gatún Locks, and then east. A small "shortcut" channel, the "Banana Cut" as it is called, runs between the islands, providing a slightly shorter route through the lake. This is used by canal launches and yachts to cut a little time off the crossing and to avoid the heavy ship traffic. This would be *Maiatla's* route.

"Andy, I can't see the other boat anymore," Kara said as she peered out from under the shade of the dodger, with the binoculars pressed to her face. "Think that they may be just behind that island back there," she added as she slipped back inside the cockpit. Hearing Kara's claim, Emanuel had a look for himself, then turned to me at the helm.

"*Capitán*, you better slow down now, as we need to arrive on the other side all together."

Doing as instructed, I throttled down to slow us to 4 knots. "There ya go. That should give that 10-knot boat a chance to catch up," I said just a little sarcastically.

As the afternoon progressed, the clouds thickened, filtering the intense sun nicely, but with them came more wind and waves. *Maiatla* was now nose diving into some steep waves, launching some spray across the foredeck. Because he could still not see our buddy boat, Emanuel became ever more irritated, so much so he had me throttle down two more times in hopes of our companions overtaking us. Despite having us crawling along at less than 3 knots, we never did see them again on the lake.

Emanuel wasn't the only one getting irritated. *Maiatla* had so little headway that every sixth or seventh wave, which was bigger than the rest, slammed into the boat bringing us to almost a complete stop. After lunch, I slipped below to check the engine and our progress on the chart plotter. Janet came in behind me; she can always sense when I'm frustrated.

"So how we doing? Are we going to make it across the lake before dark, Andy?"

"At this rate, not a chance, and I don't like it," I said. "It doesn't make sense why we have to arrive together. If Emanuel needed that, he should have told us to stay together and not let that other boat fall behind in the first place. If I get back up to 6 knots, we should make it before nightfall, and I don't want to arrive at the other locks in the dark with all those ships converging on us."

Fortunately, our route across the lake separated us from all the big ships, but we would all come back together, just a mile or so before the locks.

"Oh, to hell with this. I'm taking us back up to speed, and I'm not going to ask for permission!" Now determined, I dashed topside, sat behind the helm and throttled up to 6 knots, then waited for Emanuel, who was sitting beside me to say something, but he never did. Happy now we were making good progress, I was able to relax. The wind held true from the north, and when we rounded a small island and found our new course, I was pleased to see we were now on a broad reach, with 20 knots of wind on the beam—*Maiatla's* favourite and fastest point of sail.

"Hey, Emanuel, is it okay we just unfurl the headsail? In this wind, I will be able to maintain the speed without the engine."

A stern look shot across our pilot's face. "Oh no, *Capitán*. It is forbidden to sail on the lake. We must motor."

I knew sailing is forbidden here from readings, but it was at least worth a try. An hour before sunset, the Gatún Locks came into view, just off of the starboard bow. We were instructed to head over to the east bank and anchor, just off of the lock's administration building. The anchorage was defined by a set of markers in a triangular pattern. It was small and the holding was questionable, as we had to make three attempts before the CQR anchor grabbed hold. The water was deep, 23 metres (75.4 feet), and from the way the chain was rattling over the bottom, I suspected it was mostly rock. By the time we were settled in, it was dark, but at least we were there. For the previous hour, Emanuel had been on his radio confirming the arrangements for our lock-down, which would happen sometime in the morning. When, he did not know, but he instructed me to have the radio on. The pilot would contact us during the day to let us know when he was coming.

So for now, all we could do was wait and fire up the barbeque for some hamburgers and beers. Approximately two hours after our arrival and amidst a sudden rain shower, our buddy boat pulled in and anchored. Once settled, their pilot radioed to arrange a pickup for himself and our pilot, Emanuel. We bid each other farewell. With Emanuel gone, all we had to do now was wait.

"You know," I said to Janet as we waved goodbye, "here I thought that there was some important reason that we had to arrive all together, but now it is apparent that the only reason Emanuel had us slowdown was because he could not leave our boat until the other boat arrived." Then I added, "That sucks. Forcing us slug it out on the lake, longer than necessary, just so the two pilots could share a ride. So what if Emanuel had gotten here first? It just gave him a chance to relax and eat before getting picked up."

It didn't make sense to me, but I guess that was just the way it was.

With the setting sun, the wind died to a gentle breeze, taking the cloud cover with it. It was a pleasantly calm night, with oodles of stars to admire, which we did between watching both freighters and cruise ships enter or exit the locks less than a mile away. Fortunately, all the ships passed at dead slow, so there were no irritating wakes to rock our boat.

The morning arrived bright and beautiful, and the first thing I did was switch on the radio to wait for the call. After breakfast, we performed a few boat chores, then the crew sat topside to either sun themselves or, like Nancy and David, lounge in the shade of the cockpit reading. We were anchored directly off a building that looked to be part of a country club, as we could see gardens, manicured lawns with picnic tables, and flanked by a shaded patio where events were most likely held. Next to the water is a set of skookum docks where some idle pilot boats sat obediently waiting for their masters' return. Surprisingly, the place looked well kept, and aside from some caretakers cutting grass and hedges, the place was all but deserted. I had asked Emanuel the day before if we could go ashore, but it is not permitted. "You must stay on the boats," he emphatically declared.

It was a shame because from the smell of it, somewhere beyond the tall palms, a kitchen was preparing brunch. We didn't have to wait long to find out who the food was for.

Earlier in the morning, a large cruise ship exited the Gatún Locks after being raised from the Caribbean. The ship entered the lake, then promptly anchored, not far from us. The ship was so close we could hear the onboard public address system announcing the life boats were being lowered on the starboard side to commence ferrying passengers ashore. For the next hour, a steady stream of half a dozen lifeboats shot past *Maiatla* on their way to the nearby dock to unload. The wakes of the boats were sharp and irritating, as they kept us rolling, still we waved back at the mostly elderly passengers, many of whom became excited when spotting *Maiatla's* Canadian flag, hanging limp from the backstay. Fellow Canucks, I would assume. No sooner had the last passenger been set ashore than the boats returned home and the cruise ship up-anchored and headed to the Gatún Locks and back to the Caribbean. Apparently, this is how many "do" the Panamá Canal. While the ship was headed back out the locks, the passengers were treated to a shore side buffet, followed by a jungle tour before rejoining the ship down in Colon. With no invites to join anyone ashore for lunch, there was not much else to do.

"Anyone up to a swim?" I asked as I made my way aft to grab the boarding ladder. The girls were still sunning on the cabin top when I posed the question.

"Aren't there crocodiles in this lake?" Ashley asked as she shot questioning glances between Kara and me.

"Yep, big ones, I hear. Every year, from what I have read, villagers up at the top end of the lake get eaten, like at a rate of two or four people a year," I said as I locked the boarding ladder in place. "But they ain't here! They are over in the jungle there." I pointed to the greenery a couple of miles away.

"How do you know that?" Kara asked.

Again I pointed, but this time towards shore. "See that there? That floating raft with the water slide? I don't think the Panamánians would have a swimming deck and water slide if there were any danger of crocs eating them."

I did not wait for my explanation to sink in; I just pulled my shirts and shorts off and dived in. I guess my logic was sufficient because, a few moments later, Kara was naked and diving, followed by Ashley who, perhaps feeling a little self-conscious around David and Nancy, left her shorts and shirt on.

"How's the water?" Nancy queried from behind her book.

"It's warm and great!" the girls said in unison.

"But it feels weird swimming in fresh water after swimming in the ocean," Kara noted. "The water feels slick, and it's harder to float."

I assume Nancy received the reply she was hoping for. Without much fuss or reluctance, Nancy put her book down and moved to the cabin top, stripped drown to her panties and bra, then dived headlong into the croc-infested waters of Gatún Lake. David decided a swim was not in his best interest, so he remained in the shade. Janet likewise declined my invitation and retreated to the cool of our cabin to read. The rest of us had a great time splashing and diving about the boat. It was a glorious way to idle the day away in paradise. Sometime later, I realized we should have tried fishing, as the lake, to the great delight of the crocs no doubt, had been stocked with bass for local anglers to pursue. The well-stocked lake created a fishery for native tribes that were still living a hunter–gatherer lifestyle on the lake's jungle shores and inlets. On Gatún Lake, it is possible to see a nearly naked Indian spearing fish from a dugout canoe, a scene juxtaposed against the backdrop of the high rises of Panamá City.

By 2 p.m., we still had not heard from the Canal Board or from our next pilot. I was a bit worried. It was getting late and I did not want to pass through the locks just in time for dark, as we still had a ways to go to our marina dock. Anxious for information, I phoned my agent, Erick, who said he knew nothing, but would make a call and get back to us. Sure enough, he phoned back 20 minutes later with news. Our pilot was on his way with a scheduled a 3 p.m. transit time for entering the locks. By the time the boarding ladder was brought back aboard and secured, our new pilot had arrived.

We quickly up-anchored, then set a course for the lock. Our new pilot was much younger than Emanuel, by at least 20 years. Still, Ernesto was confident and pleasant.

"Can you speed up, *Capitán*? We need to get to the lock before that ship there," Ernesto said as he pointed over his shoulder and out into the lake. Behind us was going to become our other lock buddy, a sizable ship heavily laden with cargo. On the way to the locks, we rafted once again to our racer buddy boat and made for the open lock doors. The rejoining of the two boats gave Kara and Ashley another opportunity to flirt with the Panamanian line handlers, who responded by engaging in some male puffery. I suspected, before this transit was over, perhaps some phone numbers would exchange hands. As we approached, it was surprising to see the locks were empty. That was when I realized we were going to be first in and the ship following would come in behind.

We had little difficulty getting into the locks or making our way to the end. Ernesto instructed both captains to stop our boats, and the four lines were tossed and secured. With our nose just 10 metres (32.8 feet) or so from the giant steel doors, I looked back with some concern, as the ship behind filled all the remaining space in the lock while leaving just a couple of boat lengths between us.

Everyone was watching, and I said, "I sure hope they have good breaks, because if he doesn't, we are going to get shoved right out this end."

I moved to the aft deck for a better view and to take some photographs. On the bow of the ship, there were a few Asian-looking crew members glaring down at us as they approached. In good fun, I frantically waved my arms to warn them away, directing them to pass, then placed my hands over my eyes, as if to not to want to see the impending crash.

Figure 113. With just two locks remaining, we got our first view of the Caribbean Sea and a new ocean for *Maiatla* and her crew.

My action was well received. The crew waved back laughing. As they were closing the rear doors, I moved forward and had my first good look of what lay ahead. We were about to commence locking down, taking the first of three steps that would bring us level with the Caribbean Sea.

The water was high in our lock, leaving barely a metre (3.2 feet) of the doors in front of us visible above the water. A strange and disturbing image flashed through my mind when I pictured what it would be like if all of a sudden the doors failed and they abruptly opened. It may have been a real possibility if the ship behind us could not stop in time. Quickly, I shook the notion out of my head, permitting myself to take in the incredible view.

Before us was the grand image of the Bahía Limón, the harbour basin, with the city of Colon to the right and a dense jungle and mud flats to the left. And there, way off in the distance, was the shimmering teal waters of the Caribbean Sea. Just like on the Pacific side, we could see hundreds of ships anchored or coming and going. Gazing outward, it suddenly dawned on me that we, and *Maiatla*, were on the verge of entering an entirely new ocean, as the gateway to the Atlantic was about to part and spew us forth. While snapping photographs of the moment, I noticed something ominous on the distant horizon in the form of heavy and dense clouds, thick bulbous mountains. The upper portion of the mass appeared fibrous and was flattened in the shape of an anvil, with a black, ragged base.

Figure 114. First in and secured, *Maiatla* waits for the ship behind to fill the remaining of the lock.

The thunderstorm would arrive at around the same time as we exited the last locks and, I suspected, bring with it ponderous rain and wind. The sight instilled in me an anxious tremor. I realized that, although the great Pacific Ocean had relinquished its grip upon us, the indomitable Atlantic had decided to take hold of us and greet us in a blusterous fashion, testing our resolve.

Chapter 46

Tide and Tempest and Finally, Safe in Port

"No one would have crossed the ocean if he could have gotten off the ship in the storm."
—Charles Kettering

Our transit of the Gatún Locks went well, with no hang-ups, and we even had a fun moment upon reaching the second step. The locks come in sets, they twin, so as one is lowering down a vessel, as in our case, just metres away the other is lifting up a vessel. Next to us and on the rise was a freighter and a pair of other cruising sailboats headed into the lake, then ultimately down into the Pacific.

When the crews of all the sailboats spotted each other, a chorus of cheers and whistles erupted, along with blaring of horns and fervent hand waving. The moment was joyous, almost euphoric, and we followed it by shouts of fair winds and voyages back and forth. It was a brief but intense moment of camaraderie among cruisers who were in the midst of their latest adventure—the proverbial "ships passing in the night," except it was still daylight.

As I had feared, by the time we exited the last lock, the sun was setting. The sky had already clouded over, and as we powered up, the first of the storm's rain drops fell, followed by the raising wind. A pair of enormous ocean-going tugs, with great white bones in their teeth, rounded the bend, racing our way. Apparently, the tugs were intent on guiding our freighter lockmate down the narrow channel. The tugs pushed before them a mountain of water, a wave I was sure would find its way aboard if I was not careful to take them on the nose.

"Kara and Ashley, close the deck hatches, and Dave and Nancy, can you zip the dodger up, please?" I commanded. "I think it's going to start to rain hard in a few minutes." The oncoming waves were obvious, and anyone of *Maiatla's* ports or hatches left open could invite a deluge to invade the boat. Likewise, the pending rain was not just a guess on my part. I had been watching with great interest the storm's approach on the radar, and from the black mass just a mile or so away, I knew the rain was thick and coming.

Bahía Limón is a massive bay. From the locks to our dock at Marina Fort Sherman, it was 14.8 meandering kilometres (8 nautical miles). Both boats had to head along the east arm to drop our pilots off at the town of Colon, then cut back across the bay to the mouth of the inlet where Marina Sherman was located. The detour meant crossing an unfamiliar harbour and busy shipping channel at night with a gale building. We had almost a 3-nautical mile (4.8-kilometre) slog upwind to get the channel leading us into Colon, and from our vantage point, all I could see ahead was rain clutter, effectively masking all but the closest ships, as well as the canal-marker navigation lights. As I gazed off in the distance, I spotted the black silhouette of a large freighter off our port. Surprisingly, the ship had no lights on at all and didn't appear to be moving either. I pointed out the ship to Ernesto.

"Why is that ship blacked out? Wouldn't think that would be permitted here," I said.

Ernesto didn't even have to look at the ship I was referring too; he just kept his forward gaze when he replied, "That ship dragged anchor during a storm many years ago and was washed up on the mud flats. It's been abandoned."

As a diver, I have always been a wreck hound, so I made a mental note to perhaps pay the ship a visit by dinghy while we were here in Panamá. However, it would have to wait. At this point, I needed to focus on *Maiatla*, or we could also find ourselves in trouble, as it happens all too easily with a moment of carelessness.

"Kara, can you jump down below and turn on the running lights, please?" With darkness settling in, it was well past the time to light up the boat so that others could see us. Ever since leaving the lock, we had been following our buddy boat, maintaining four or five boat lengths away, but they were getting harder to see in the fading light.

"Ernesto, can you call our buddy boat and tell them to switch on their running lights? If they slow down any, I may just run up their ass. I can't see them well."

The boat was clearly visible on radar, but that would do little to warn me if they were to stop suddenly. Ernesto radioed his counterpart and nearly instantly a bright white stern light appeared. Moments later, Ernesto answered a radio call, then he turned back to me and said, "They want you to turn your lights on as well?" A request I found odd because our lights should have been on.

"Kara, do you want to check the breaker for the running lights again? You flipped the wrong switch."

"Don't think so, Andy, but I will check." Kara shot back down below to the electrical panel. Several moments later, she returned. "Andy, when I turn the switch on, it flips itself back off a few seconds later. It won't stay on," she said.

The running lights had a short circuit, which meant we did not have any running navigation lights. We needed to illuminate the boat so that others could see us.

"Okay, Kara, turn on the masthead anchor light and spreader lights, will you, please?" The spreader lights would destroy my night vision, preventing me from spotting the lights of ships passing nearby, but with the rain being so heavy now, my ability to see any lights was almost gone. I would just stay close to our buddy boat, with eyes glued to the radar screen. It took us a good 45 minutes to cover the 5 kilometres (3 miles) to Colon's anchoring basin and to the spot where we were to rendezvous with our pilots' water taxi.

We idled down to maintain our station, which, from the look of all the passing ships, was located right on the edge of the shipping channel. There were several tense moments, as some of the ships appeared to be heading directly for us until, just before running into us, they would make a slight turn. Ernesto knew exactly where we were and was not the least bit concerned. While I stood watch with Ernesto, waiting for the taxi to appear, everyone else was below helping to prepare dinner or just sitting at the galley table talking. We drifted about for a good hour before the taxi arrived. We gave our thanks to Ernesto, then waved him off. It was time for the final leg of our journey, which would take us across the harbour, bringing us uncomfortably close to the mud flats and its, now invisible, ghost ship. Fortunately, our buddy boat had been here before, so I decided to stay close on his tail and let him guide us in, or at the least he would run aground first, giving us a bit of a warning.

After timing the passage of the latest ship, we made a dash across the channel, reaching the far side without incident. We altered course to a more easterly direction, and out of the rain and night appeared a line of ships, stacked up bow to stern, each vessel lit up with every available deck light to make them easier to see. I had been watching the parade of ships on radar for some time, and it quickly became obvious they were all at anchor and motionless. I was reluctant to approach, but when our buddy boat cut between the stern of one ship and the bow of another, I decided to follow suit.

With less than two *Maiatla* boat lengths of clearance on either side, we cut between the ships. As we passed close under the fantail of a ship registered in Columbia, a single soul dressed in the dirty whites of galley staff stood bent over the rail, smoking. The man did not wait to see us pass; instead, with a shower of sparks, he flicked his cigarette into the wind, then retreated inside. We emerged safely on the far side where directly ahead was the rock breakwater, defining the harbours outermost boundary, and on the far side, I assumed was the open Caribbean. We had nearly made it. All we had to do now was parallel the wall, and it would lead us straight into Fort Sherman Marina. Still hot on our buddy boat's tail, I continued to let him take the lead as he knew the way. However, as would soon become evident, he didn't, not on this dark night anyway.

Studying the chart plotter closely, and from what I could determine, our friend was too far to the south side of the channel and dangerously close to shallow water. I decided to trust my own navigation and to stay in, what I believed to be, the centre of the channel. After another quarter mile, my suspicions were confirmed. Our buddy boat, which was now a couple hundred metres ahead of us, came to a complete stop, then circled around in an effort to avoid hitting bottom. To give him room, I throttled down. On the radar, I could see him spin around several times, then settle on a heading that would bring them back towards us.

"What's up, Andy? Why are we stopping?" Janet asked as her head popped out of the companion hatch. Janet knew we still had a ways to go, and slowing down was an indication of possible trouble.

"Think our buddy boat is lost. He can't find the channel, and from the speed at which he stopped, he may have hit the bottom," I said.

I waited for our friends to re-orientate themselves and get back underway, which they did, but less sure of themselves, they were now moving at a snail's pace. Knowing we were within half a mile from our dock and confident in my own position, I throttled up and took the lead, which our friend was more than happy to give up, as evident by the smile on the captain's face and his friendly wave as we passed them by. The channel narrowed while growing shallower, but just when I started to get nervous, from around a slight bend, a cluster of yachts appeared, all tied neatly to a set of concrete docks. At the head of the first dock was a security guard waving his hands, directing us to a vacant berth.

It was just after 10 p.m. by the time we were all secured and plugged into shore power. The wind died and with it, the rain. Even before all of our spring lines had been run, David and Nancy passed their bags to Kara on the dock in preparation for leaving. The couple were in a hurry to catch a taxi into town to find a hotel for the night and then catch the train back to the Pacific coast in the morning. It was great having them along, so I gave them both a hug, then waved them off. For better or worse, Fort Sherman would become *Maiatla's* new home for the rest of the season, at least. This year's voyage from México to the Galápagos Islands and through Panamá had been an incredible adventure, but little did we know the drama was not over yet. Instead, it would stalk all of us right to the bitter end.

Chapter 47

Maiatla *and the Cocaine Duo, the Panamá to Vancouver Connection!*

"Trust him not with your secrets, who, when left alone
in your room, turns over your papers."
—Johann Kaspar Lavater

Marina Shelter Island at Fort Sherman proved to be the perfect place to leave the boat. The marina staff was very professional and attentive. The facility boasts a nice air-conditioned restaurant and bar, outdoor patios, showers and laundry service. Soon to become a favourite spot of Janet and mine during the heat of the day was the waterfront pool and deck. To pamper *Maiatla,* there is a full-service boat yard, a marine chandlery, convenience store and a secure storage yard, not to mention an onsite sail loft for canvas repairs, which we desperately needed.

The bulk of the marina tenants were mostly transients, coming from or going to the canal, a group that would prove to be a friendly bunch, eager to share their knowledge and experiences over a sundowner or while out for an evening stroll upon the dock.

The marina is surrounded by dense jungle and nature preserve. Fort Sherman was formally a U.S. Army infantry base, with construction beginning in 1912. The fort's intent was to protect the Caribbean side of the Panamá Canal from invasion by hostile powers that wanted to choke off the West's commerce. The old fort, and now reserve, consists of 93 square kilometres (22980 acres) of land, approximately half of which is covered by wild tropical forests, which was used to train jungle fighters. The developed areas of the base included personal housing and barracks for over 300 servicemen, all supported by a small airstrip, various recreational areas and churches. The base was decommissioned and the U.S. Military moved out in 1999 when the canal zone was turned over to the Panamánians, as required by the Panamá Treaty of 1977.

On a pleasant evening walk from the marina, down the now overgrown paved roads, we discovered much of the old fortifications are still intact and free to explore. A large portion of the base's buildings have been reclaimed by the jungle, requiring some "bush-whacking" if you want to discover the entrances of many of the underground bunkers and interconnecting tunnels. Janet and I spent several evenings hiking the jungle and exploring the ruins and bunkers. The overgrowth of many of the battlements and the free-roaming two-toed sloths, marmosets and troops of howler monkeys, screaming at you from the treetops, give the impression that you have walked into a real-life version of Kipling's children's classic, *The Jungle book*. Our time here would be short but memorable.

We have always tried to be friendly travellers—greeting customs and immigration officials with a smile and a pleasant thank you for riffling through our bags full of underwear—and not just to the officialdom, but to people in general who greet us with welcoming smirks as we travel about their country and overcharge us for items just because we are foreigners. All sarcasm aside, in all of Janet and my travels aboard *Maiatla* through Central and South America as well as my work travels, which have taken me to Europe and the Middle East, we had almost never had any kind of problem with either officials or the people of the host land (Costa Rica, the only exception).

We have never felt fear when travelling, but we are not naïve. We trust as much as necessary while guarding ourselves, making sure not to leave ourselves open to exploitation or harm. Someone once said, "Locks only keep honest people honest." We never tempt otherwise honest people by leaving ourselves exposed, leave valuables about or flaunt what may be deemed as affluence. Hiding even meagre wealth can be difficult at times, as some may see you travelling on a vessel worth more money than they could possibly earn in 10 lifetimes—a lesson some of our crew members would learn the hard way.

We had only been at the dock in Fort Sherman for three days, bedding the boat down in preparation for leaving her for another season when, after washing the dodger, Kara and Ashley cornered me in the cockpit. It was obvious the girls had something on their minds, and I had also heard them talking between themselves and making plans. I was beginning to wonder when they would get around to discussing them with me.

"Andy, we have a flight booked to go home to Abbotsford in four days, and we would like to leave a bit early and travel back to Panamá City to do a bit of sightseeing before heading home. What do you think?" Kara asked as Ashley sat in the corner of the cockpit, rolling up the newly washed windows.

I wasn't surprised by the question, as I had pieced together the gist of their plans from the fragments of their conversation I had overheard the past few days. Not only didn't I mind that they wanted to leave early, but I was hoping they would do just that. I appreciated all their hard work in cleaning up *Maiatla* and helping me bed her down, but in reality, Janet and I hadn't been alone on the boat for close to a month. We loved the girls, but not being more than a score of feet away from them was getting in the way of our husband and wife snuggle time. Janet and I had a flight home booked for the following week as well, and we both desired a few days alone here in Panamá before we had to leave. If the girls hadn't asked to leave, I may have just booted them off the boat anyway.

The girls happily packed their bags, and the marina office arranged a taxi to take them to their Panamá City hotel, which proved to be a two-hour ride. There was a cab driver who regularly worked out of the marina and was often used by boaters to either head into Colon or Panamá City and the international airport.

The driver, Javier, was waiting for the girls at the head of the dock at the designated time of 10 a.m. I helped to load the bags into the car, and then Janet and I gave the girls one last great hug before taking their departure photos. I also took a shot of the driver, the car and licence plate just in case. It was my way of saying to the Javier, "I know who you are and how to find you!" Guess my protective fatherly instinct was peaking. In hindsight, perhaps I had sensed something may go wrong, but what, I had no idea. Janet and I were both saddened and elated to see the girls drive off, but despite our mixed emotions, we now had *Maiatla* all to ourselves.

Having the often giddy pair of adult adolescents aboard, with their constant playful banter between them, was at times tiresome, and they were often too exhausting during daylight hours to keep up too. For Janet and I, it was like sending our children off to college; we were glad to see them go, but would miss them, nonetheless.

With the girls gone, I carried on removing gear and hardware to prepare *Maiatla* before she was hauled out of the water while Janet kept up her scrubbing chores down below. Janet was still complaining about the heat, mainly in the late afternoon, as it was the hottest part of the day, so I offered to turn on the boat's central air conditioner. It would only have taken half an hour to do, as I had to open and prime the saltwater feed lines, but surprisingly, Janet said I had enough to do, so she told me not to bother. Having Janet discouraging me from starting the AC was unexpected, and I took it as a sign she may be finally acclimatized to the heat, an assertion she would hotly deny when I brought it up. From my perspective, I found the east coast of Panamá slightly cooler, and perhaps more pleasant, than the weather we had left behind on the Pacific side and in the Galápagos. Perhaps it was just the effects of the nearly constant trade winds blowing in off the Caribbean Sea, but whatever it was, it didn't matter—Janet was more comfortable, and that's all that mattered to me.

The following two days were pleasant, as we took turns working on the boat and taking advantage of the marina's restaurant and pool, especially during the early afternoon when it was hottest. We even took long walks into the jungle so that I could show Janet the deserted ruins of the old Army base and we could look for howler and capuchin monkeys in the treetops. It was a relief to be just us once again.

One night as we walked past tall coconut trees on the deserted beach, Janet said, "You know, aside for the five days after Mark and Teri left and the kids arrived and the few days we waited for Kara and Ashley in the Galápagos, this is the first time we have been alone in four months."

Janet was right. It was now almost April, and we have had a boat full of people since the beginning of December. Janet hugged me and I could see tears welling up in her eyes. Having crew aboard has always been the exception, not the rule. We have always spent most of our time aboard *Maiatla* all on our own, revelling in our solitude, as well as each other. The previous year while sailing down the coast of México from Mazatlán to Chiapas, México, for over five months, we had Marina aboard for four weeks, then our daughter, Melissa, for another two. That was it. It was Janet and I, *Maiatla* and the sea, the rest of the time, which had been typical for the past four years as we ventured along the coast. We enjoy other company; however, I believe we enjoy each other even more.

The moon rose over the trade wind tossed Caribbean Sea as I promised next year would be different. It would just be us, Janet and I, taking our time and in a big hurry to go nowhere. As far as I was concerned, we had arrived. We will cease to be voyagers, traversers of oceans, and revert to "gunkholing cruisers," with no place to be and no desire to go anywhere that doesn't present our backs to the wind. We would spend each day lounging in the sun, spear fishing on a reef and then, at night, swing on the hook in the lee of a palm fringed tropical isle and read to one another until we fall asleep. Janet deserved nothing less after all she endured to get here, and at this time, I desired nothing else.

The third morning after the girls departed, I sat at the galley table waiting for Janet to finish making breakfast. It was still early, before 6 a.m., and I was flipping through my cell phone, looking for any new emails, when I noticed I had missed a phone call from Kara at 1 a.m. this morning.

"Looks like Kara called me last night," I said to Janet as she poured the pancake batter into the pan.

"Why would they call that late?" Janet asked, without turning from her chore at the stove.

"Don't know. Maybe they accidentally pocket dialed me while dancing at some club last night," I offered with a chuckle.

"Aren't they flying back today?" Janet asked as she scraped the last of the batter into the pan.

"Yes, I think so, at 10 or 11, so they must be about ready to head to the airport now," I replied. Not giving it much more consideration, I texted Kara back:

> Hey got your call at 1 a.m. Guess you pocket dialed me.

Moments later, Kara responded:

> It wasn't a mistake. Can you call me now?

"Wow that's strange," I said aloud.

"What is it" Janet asked. The pancakes were ready.

"Kara called me on purpose last night. Guess there must be a problem."

"What kind of problem?" Janet sounded concerned now.

"Don't know, babe, but I will call and find out."

Kara answered on the second ring.

"Hi, Kara, so what's up?" I asked.

In a frantic tone, she told me their tale. Before the girls left the boat, Janet and I had given the girls one of our suitcases full of our clothes to take home with them, as we had a load of boat stuff to go back and didn't have room for everything. When Kara and Ashley arrived at the hotel, they placed our bag in the closet, and it stayed there until the girls decided to repack their bags two days later. She was not sure why, but Kara decided to check the contents of the bag we had given her, perhaps just so she would know what it contained if asked by border officials, or then again, she may have sensed something was wrong.

Kara removed the bag from the closet and opened it, and when she did she was stunned to see, in plain view, a large Ziploc bag containing what looked to be raw sugar. Not sure what to make of it, she called me right away, but of course, at that time of the night, I did not answer. Neither Kara nor Ashley had any previous experience with drugs, but their suspicion was strong. After a Google search and comparing online photos of various narcotics, they came to the conclusion that what they were now holding was a bag of uncut cocaine—over 453 grams (a pound) of it.

When Kara informed me of this, I was just as stunned as the girls and at a bit of a loss as what to do. When they couldn't get a hold of me, they called a fellow Kara had met after arriving in Panamá City and had a few drinks with, a musician from Argentina by the name of Lautaro. Kara texted him pictures of the suspected drugs. His reply was: "Yep, that's cocaine," and he estimated the U.S. street value at $20,000 dollars. Later, I did a bit of checking and learned the street value of cocaine in Houston, Texas, was around $50 per gram, which translates into just over $22,000 USD. Kara's new musician friend obviously had some knowledge on the subject. I wanted to question why their new friend would know such things, but that would not be helpful at the moment.

"What do we do, Andy?"

"I'm not sure," I said. The gravity of the situation was not lost on me. If the girls had been caught with these drugs entering the United States, I knew just saying "They weren't mine" was not going to cut it. And what of the drug smugglers who planted the drugs in my bag? Were they watching? Were they going to follow the girls to the States, then rob them once they arrived, steal the bags and drugs, or worse? Members of drug cartels could be ruthless, but by comparison, this was a small amount.

In the state of Texas, smuggling over 400 grams of cocaine can earn you a life sentence, unless you can prove you had no knowledge of what you were carrying, but, good luck with that. On one hand, the girls had the drug dealers to worry about, and on the other, there was law enforcement, both Panamánian and U.S. police and customs officials. The girls' lives and freedom were in danger.

Of course, I had no idea how the drugs found their way into our bag. Later, I asked Kara if, when she first found the drugs, she thought I may have set her up to be a drug mule. She didn't hesitate to respond. "Well, ya, for an instant, but when I thought it through, I knew you would not do that to us. No way!"

I didn't blame Kara for considering it, as in reality, it could have been possible, no matter how unlikely. Likewise, I wondered if one of chaps they had met down there had talked the girls into packing this stuff and they were now getting cold feet. Again possible, but I have known Kara since her mid-teens, so the notion of her smuggling coke vanished from my head as quickly as her thought of me planting it on them. No, we both knew this was done by outsiders.

"Hey, Kara, tell you what I'm going to do. I'll call my brother Greg, who is a police officer back home in Port Moody, and ask him what to do, and I will call you back in a few minutes, okay."

"Okay, but hurry. We need to leave for the airport soon!"

I called my brother, but received no answer at first, so Janet and I sent off a flurry of Facebook messages to my sister-in-law, Ela, Greg's wife, and to all of our kids and nieces, asking them to find Greg and have him call or text me. Within a few minutes, the 911 pleas got through and my brother texted me back. After explaining what was going on, he suggested I instruct the girls to dump all of the coke into the toilet and clean the bags as best they could. They need to try and disguise the bags by wrapping them or putting them into a duffel bag or another suitcase. Kara's duffel bag was distinctive as it was bright yellow.

Greg went on to say they are not to tell any local authorities about the coke, not the cops or customs officials in Panamá—no telling who may be involved. They were to get on their flight as normal. The girl's flight would take them to Houston, their first U.S. stop, where they were to overnight before returning to Canada the following day. Greg suspected the bag was likely to be intercepted by airport ground crews when it arrived in Houston, and the drugs removed from the bag before it reached customs inspections.

"Andy," Greg went on to say, "Tell the girls that as soon as they get to Houston, they need to go directly to customs. Don't collect their bags, but tell the customs agent what had happened. They will advise them what they should do. That way if the bags get tagged by the drug dogs before they pick them up, they would have already reported it, so they should be in the clear, or at least we hope so!"

I thanked Greg and called Kara back to relay the message. Kara flushed the drugs and got busy washing out their bag. Thankfully, both Kara and Ashley were keeping cool heads, well sort of. Kara later admitted to me that they were almost crapping their pants over this.

As the drugs were disposed of, Ashley remarked that Kara now had her finger prints all over the empty bag of coke. An excited discussion ensued about wiping the bag clean and disposing of it somewhere not connected to them. A dumpster outside the hotel fit the bill.

Satisfied they had done all they could do, while looking hard over their shoulders, they left the room to meet the hotel airport shuttle bus down by the lobby. For now, it would remain a mystery as to how the drugs got into the girl's possession. They needed to start their travels home while fearing the worst.

The bus trip was uneventful, but Kara said it was unbelievable how many suspicious-looking people they encountered along the way. Kara wanted nothing more than to get rid of their bags, check them in, but they were early for their flight and the airline booth was not open. Nervously they sat in the unsecured waiting area expecting the worst, still battling to control their bodily functions. It was with great relief they finally managed to check the troublesome baggage and get behind secured doors.

With the airport's guards and closed-circuit TV cameras nearby, the sense of relief continued, and Kara decided to unwind, which involved the lining up and murdering of three tequila shots at the airport bar. Despite assurances and encouragement from Kara, Ashley, still vibrating with anxiety and fear, decided at least one of them needed to keep her wits about them and watch for killer drug dealers. She declined to join her friend in partaking in the liquid courage. It proved to be a long, but thankfully, uneventful flight to Houston. They were relieved to be back in a First World country, but they also knew this was where the smugglers were most likely to come after the drugs or, worse, them.

As soon as they were off the plane, they went searching for a U.S. customs agent. Houston is an ultra-modern international airport, and in keeping with technology, most of the customs process is automated, so finding a live person to tell their story proved a bit difficult. Finally, after being herded through a series of cattle gates and corrals, they saw a live face with a badge. It would take repeated telling of their story, up the customs agent's hierarchy, before they were taken seriously. Kara suspected some of the agents thought they were trying to pull a fast one, maybe creating a diversion for unknown accomplices lurking in the shadows.

"They were definitely suspicious of us at first," Kara later told me. "When I told the agent about the cocaine, he asked, 'How would you know what cocaine looks like? And how do you know it weighed a pound?'"

It took some time, but eventually the customs agent decided to take the girls down to the carousel to retrieve their bags, but none of their baggage could be located, all of their suitcases had mysteriously vanished after departing the aircraft. At this time, Kara felt the agents now believed them. The girls were escorted to a secure interrogation room and told to wait. Thankfully, a sympathetic female agent told them they weren't in trouble, but had to wait here so that they could conduct a search for their missing luggage.

It took some time, but the bags were finally located in the far back section of a warehouse, in a section with bags due to be loaded onto another aircraft bound for Canada. The agent went on to explain that this should not have happened. They were obviously intercepted and rerouted, as my brother Greg has suspected.

After a thorough search and finding nothing, Kara and Ashley were told they could take their bags and go to their hotel. Hearing this, Kara exclaimed, "There is no way we are taking these bags out of the airport and taking them to our hotel!" Kara was livid.

"What if someone is waiting outside to follow us to the hotel? What if they want to know what happened to the drugs? The bags make us a target!" It wasn't an unrealistic fear and a good possibility.

Kara was adamant, and despite assurances from the customs agent that her fears were unfounded, she would not budge. Conceding to the girl's uncertainties, they were permitted to recheck their bags and leave them at the airport overnight, a concession which was normally against airport policy. I can only assume the agents sensed the girls' genuine fear and decided to bend a rule or two.

It was a nerve-wracking night at their Houston hotel, and it took some time for Kara to convince Ashley to venture out of the room to go next door for dinner and beer. Neither girl breathed a deep sigh of relief until Kara's mother picked them both up from the airport in Vancouver the following day.

The thought of what could have happened left me with the chills. I had visions of visiting Kara and Ashley in a Houston, or worse, a Panamánian jail while they waited to face drug trafficking charges. After the girls were safely at home, I asked them if they had come to any conclusions as to who might have planted the drugs.

I asked if Kara's musician friend, Lautaro, had any opportunity to access my bag. Could he have planted the drugs? Kara was adamant he and no other friend had an opportunity, as no one was ever in their room, so unless one of their friends had a connection at the hotel or burgled their room, they could not have done it.

We then talked of the taxi driver, Javier, who had taken the girls on an extensive sightseeing tour of Colon on their way to the airport. Kara said he seemed thrilled about showing them his city before they went home. "He drove us all over town for no extra charge," Kara told me.

They made a stop at the old Hotel Washington where the girls went inside to view the architecture, leaving all the bags unattended in the trunk of the cab. There was an opportunity for someone to plant the drugs, but the driver would have had to have known Kara's and Ashley's flight itinerary, which they claim was not discussed with the driver. Still, both Kara and Ashley are relatively new to third world travel, and I have seen them eagerly share tales of their travels on the boat to total strangers.

"So, Kara, if it wasn't the cabby or one of yours and Ashley's new Panamá acquaintances, who was it?" I asked.

"You know, we have given it a lot of thought, and we have come to the conclusion that it was the hotel staff in Panamá," Kara said on the phone to me some weeks later. "I didn't think much about it at the time, but there were some strange things at the hotel."

"Like what kind of strange things?" I queried.

"The hotel's manager arranged for us to take the hotel shuttle to the mountain to see some monkeys. Once there, the driver walked with us, but he didn't appear to be too interested in playing tour guide. Instead, he spent a lot of time on his phone messaging someone. When we got back to the hotel, the manager at the desk was surprise we were back so early," Kara said, with little hesitation. "The manager stopped us to ask a bunch of questions. While this was happening, I noticed a hotel maid moving quickly out of the corridor containing our room. As there were only two rooms down there, I assumed she had just finished cleaning one or the other. The questioning by the manager stopped, so we headed to our room, but when we got there, we found an electronic card key in the door slot. The key appeared old and worn, so we assumed it belonged to the maid and that she would return to get it." Kara paused to reimaging the encounter, then concluded, "Upon entering the room, all appeared as we had left it in the morning, messy with the bed still unmade and wet towels lying around. It was obvious the maid had not been in there to clean. We didn't give it much more thought, just complained to each other about the poor room service."

Kara and Ashley concluded the hotel staff was likely responsible. However, proving it was not possible, so lacking any more insight, it would remain a mystery.

Figure 115. *Maiatla* hauled out of the water, shrink wrapped and bedded down to wait for our return.

There is never a dull moment for cruisers in paradise. Now, when asked if we have ever run into pirates, I still say no, but my crew, Kara and Ashley most assuredly have and were fortunate enough to realize it before it became too late.

After Janet and I finished cleaning up *Maiatla*, we had her hauled out of the water and placed in a secure storage compound and she was bed down and shrink-wrapped and to keep her insides free from mould, a dehumidifier was installed.

It broke our hearts to leave our girl all alone for another summer. However, we were taking home with us some great memories and experiences. *Maiatla* would be patiently waiting for our return the following season. The best part was that there was a great new cruising ground waiting for us to claim as our own—the Caribbean Sea.

About the Boat

SV *Maiatla II* is a Voyager 44 designed by Hardin International and built by the Kaohsiung Shipyard of Taiwan in 1980. The boats were sold until 1982 through a U.S. Distributor, East West Yachts of Marina Del Rey, California. The first production Hardin 45's came with large salon windows, which in hindsight proved to be a liability offshore in big seas. Redesigned, the boats transformed into the Hardin Voyager 44, which came with a slightly lower profile and much smaller windows, creating more pleasing lines and a fine offshore cruiser—as *Maiatla* would prove herself to be. However, after intensive investigation, I discovered *Maiatla* incorporated the traits of at least three different Hardin designs, making her a unique one-off design.

Maiatla is 13.7 metres (45 feet) on the deck and 16.5 meters (52 feet) overall, but 54 by my harbour manager's tape measure. She has a beam of 4 metres (13 feet 4 inches) and a water line of 9.8 metres (32 feet 3 inches). She has a fully modified keel, with a cutaway forefoot, and a draft of 1.8 metres (6 feet), or at least she had until we moved all of our worldly possessions aboard. Now she rides a full two inches lower in the water. *Maiatla* is the two-cabin model, with a large V-berth forward and a great master cabin with a queen size bed aft. The master cabin is accessible from both sides of the vessel: through the head on the starboard side or through the navigation station on the port. The galley is amidships port, with a large salon table to starboard. The main salon is forward and sunken, with a sofa on the starboard and a pilot berth above against the hull. Opposite the sofa is the diesel heater, flanked by a pair of upholstered armchairs, and a second pilot berth above.

Shortly after taking possession of *Maiatla,* I commenced the first of a long list of modifications and upgrades. A chore spanning many years as *Maiatla* evolved from a family cruising boat to one destined to be occupied by empty nesters. The port side cabin, formally Thomas's room, remains as he had left it. Plans to revert it back to a navigation station has not yet been undertaken and most likely never will.

The galley boasts a top loading, 4-cubic foot fridge, with a laminated oak butcher-block lid adjacent to the gimballed, four-burner propane range with oven. On deck *Maiatla* is equipped with a Furlex roller reefing system to manage the big headsail. On the foredeck, an 18-to 24-foot telescoping whisker pole is stored and ready for use to improve *Maiatla's* stability on downwind runs when sailing wing and wing with the main sail.

And of course the item no sailor ever hopes to use: A Viking, four-man offshore life raft is mounted just behind the cockpit over the aft cabin. The boat came with a 45-pound CQR anchor, along with 350 feet of 0.5-inch chain and a Lofrans power windlass. I purchased an additional 350 feet of 1-inch gold braid anchor rode and shackled it to 40 feet of 0.5-inch chain and swivel. I also purchased a 65-pound CQR to complete what I would call my "Hail Mary" rig, better known as my hurricane ground tackle. Later, the 65-pound CQR found its way onto the all chain rode and became part of our everyday tackle. We never had the misfortune to drag, even in the foulest of weather. For a kedging anchor, I have a 35-pound Danforth, with 40 feet of chain attached to 200 feet of 0.5-inch, braided nylon rode.

Maiatla's electronics consist of a Furuno 1623, 24-mile radar, with the display, in the cockpit next to the helm, and Simrad apparent wind, speed and depth instruments. For long distance communication and for downloading weather GRIBs to the computer, satellite photos and high-seas weather reports, there is a HAM/SSB high frequency radio interfaced with a Pactor 4 modem. The ham radio base station is an ICOM 700 pro, a 130-automatic tuner, with 14 metres (45.9 feet) of backstay for an antenna.

Interfaced with a Garmin 48 Global Positioning System is my laptop computer equipped with Nobeltec charting software, our primary navigation system, with electronic charts for over half the world. However, in case of disaster, we carry a complete set of full-size paper charts.

Our passive electrical system has changed over the years, and now consists of a 100-watt Siemens solar panel mounted on the dinghy davits and a pair of 45-watt panels capable of swing outboard, hanging on the life lines, port and starboard aft of the cockpit. If all that solar energy is not enough, the 400-watt Air Marine wind generator at the top of the mizzenmast nicely tops up the 750 amp-hour battery bank.

Just to ensure we have ample power for all of our electrical devices whenever the sun does not shine or the wind doesn't blow, we carry a 2000-watt gas generator for good measure. As it turns out, the generator has come in handy over the years.

Maiatla is equipped with hydraulic steering and a Raymarine Automatic Pilot. This has proven itself a dependable system. And the heart of *Maiatla's* luxury systems is the Village Marine "Little Wonder," a $200 USD gallon-per-day watermaker neatly installed in the engine room. The boat is equipped with a pressure water system that has a Bosch hot water on demand system. *Maiatla* has two 75-gallon water tanks, as well as identical tanks for fuel. With 150 gallons of onboard water and the watermaker to keep them topped up, water has never been a problem. *Maiatla's* power plant and propulsion system consists of a fuel efficient, 68-horse power Perkins 4-154 diesel engine.

With 150 gallons of diesel in the main tanks and a 30-gallon reserve tank, primarily used for the diesel heater, we have almost 2092 kilometres (1300 miles) of cruising range under power—as long as we keep her at 6 knots and don't use the cabin heater. In the many years we have owned her, *Maiatla* has proven herself time after time to be a capable offshore boat equipped in a manner that not only provides us with a comfortable and safe home, but also affords her crew the self-sufficiency that we cherish so much as we sail about the world.

About the Author

Figure 116. Andrew and new friend. This photo was taken in 2016 at the banana plantation where the crew had lunch after visiting Playa Chino on San Cristóbal Island, Galápagos Islands, Ecuador.

Andrew Gunson is a storyteller with the heart of an adventurer. He has the ability to infect others with his zeal for life and his love of the sea. Andrew grew up in and around boats on the Great Lakes and always dreamed of following the paths of such intrepid sailors as Joshua Slocum and Eric and Susan Hiscock. A Canadian National sailing champion at the age of 14, he grew up racing and competing at the world championship level. At the age of 18, he moved to Canada's West Coast and discovered a new world of sailing. Leaving the hi-tech racing yachts behind, he commenced to follow his dream of becoming a "cruiser." Together with his father, he purchased his first cruising sailboat, a Columbia 36, and never looked back.

Although a fourth-generation mason and bricklayer, Andrew's adventurous spirit led him to attend the College of Oceaneering in Wilmington, California. By age 21, he was a commercial bell diver working on oil-drilling ships in the Beaufort Sea in the high Canadian Arctic.

He eventually became a co-pilot in the submersible program aboard a Norwegian drill ship and worked beneath the frigid waters of the Davis Strait, off the coast of Labrador. Before his 30th birthday, he retired from commercial diving to focus on raising his young family. With his wife Janet, they purchased and operated a convenience store in Vernon, British Columbia. After selling the business, Andrew and Janet earned their securities licenses and became a personal financial analyst and small business tax consultants.

Andrew's love affair with the sea endured. He continued to dream, just waiting for his own chance to sail off. After a series of life-altering events, including a brush with a deadly skin cancer and a pair of automobile accidents that almost claimed Andrew's life, not to mention being accidentally shot while bear hunting, the couple decided it was time to stop dreaming. The Gunsons commenced planning their escape before it was too late. Hence the saga of the sailing vessel *Maiatla II* and the Naked Canadian began.

The Gunsons would go on to become full-time liveaboards on SV *Maiatla* on the rugged West Coast of British Columbia where they raised their two young children as they chased their cruising dreams. At the time of this publication and 20 years and 12 countries later, with over 48280 Bluewater kilometres (30,000 Bluewater miles) under their keel, they are still at it. Book four in the Naked Canadian Cruising Series is a saga, taking the Gunson's into uncharted waters (for them anyway) through central America, then on to South America and the jewels of Ecuador, the primeval archipelago, the Galápagos Islands and finally the Panamá Canal.

The Gunson's preceding voyages have inspired the author to write, *The Voyage of the* Maiatla *with the Naked Canadian, One Family's Mexican Odyssey,* followed by the second book of the series, *The Tahiti Syndrome, Hawaiian Style.* Book three of the series is the *Slow Boat to Panamá: Vancouver, B.C., to Costa Rica* and now this, the fourth book in *Maiatla's* ongoing saga.

The *Maiatla* collection is available in hardcover, paperback and e-book format from Amazon and Smashwords.

Maiatla's Articles

Please read the following Ship's Articles carefully. Once signed, they are part of a binding agreement between you and **SV *Maiatla*** and her owners.

As is the custom aboard any vessel that sails upon the sea, the ship's rules and operating procedures are set down and enforced by the vessel's captain for the safety of both the crew and the vessel. These rules must be strictly adhered too.

Sailing offshore can be a potentially dangerous endeavour; environmental conditions, weather and even marine life can threaten a vessel the size of *Maiatla,* and when help, if there is any available, may be days or even weeks away, it is imperative the crew be as self-sufficient and as professional as is practically possible.

A ship is not a democracy, it is a dictatorship, and the ship's captain has the ultimate authority over the vessel and the crew that sail her. The captain alone bares the responsibility for the vessel and all aboard.

Below is a list of ships rules and what is required of anyone who sails aboard *Maiatla.* By signing these ships' articles, you agree to abide by these rules and to follow the direction of the ship's captain or his appointed representative without question or argument. It is also understood that the captain retains the right to change the sailing schedule (start and finish dates, ports of call and destinations) of a particular voyage, if in his opinion, the safety of the vessel or crew may be in danger.

Articles

There are no passengers aboard *Maiatla;* all who sign aboard her will agree to participate actively as crew. General duties may include **one or all** of the following:

- Sailing of the vessel, sail handling on deck during whatever the weather.

- Standing watch at the helm during designated watch, duration of four or six hours (usually with a partner). **Note:** Watch will be kept 24 hours per day for the duration of the voyage. At the discretion of the captain, watches may also be kept while at anchor or even dockside if he deems it necessary.

- Cooking, cleaning and general ship's maintenance will be required.

- The captain will attempt to run a happy and safe ship and divide watches, duties and responsibilities equitably between all crewmembers. An attempt will be made to make the voyage interesting, challenging and enjoyable, but keep in mind, this is an open sea voyage and there are likely to be times when crew members encounter rough, heavy weather or physically frightening situations, which must be dealt with on an individual basis.

General House Rules

- While standing watch at the helm, the crewman will wear a life harness and be secured to the vessel at all times, day or night.

- Crew who must leave the cockpit to work on deck shall also be required to wear a harness and be secured to the "jack lines," which run fore and aft.

- No crew member will leave the cockpit to work on deck unless a second crew member is in the cockpit and watching.

- No crewmember will alter the ships heading or sail plan without first consulting the captain.

- If a ship is sighted, either visually or on the radar, the captain is to be immediately notified.

- The use or possession of illegal drugs, contraband or substances while on board or ashore is strictly forbidden and any violation of this article will result in the immediate removal of the offender, who may be turned over to local authorities and/or left to their own resources to find their own way home. Illegal activities within a foreign country by members of the crew put the vessel in danger of being impounded and the captain of being arrested.

- Each crewmember agrees to abide and respect all local laws, ordinances and customs.

- The captain reserves the right to expel any crew member from the vessel for whatever reason he deems fit. If a crew member exhibits socially unacceptable, physically violent behaviour or is uncooperative in regard to the agreed common goals of the ship, they will be put ashore at the nearest port to be repatriated to a place of their choosing, at their own expense. If asked to leave under the above circumstances, you agree by signing this agreement not to seek redress or sue for any real or imagined damages.

- The crewmember will assume all financial responsibility for their personal expenses and as well as the cost of their return flights and expenses and post their own personal bonds if a country requires them. (Bonds usually amount the cost of a one-way plane fare home and are refundable if unused.)

- At his discretion, the captain has the right to search all areas of the vessel for contraband, which includes any personal belongs brought aboard *Maiatla*.

- Due to the limited space aboard, it is paramount that all the crew respect each other's personal space and belongings. This consideration includes limiting noise, music which may disturb off watch crewmembers that may be sleeping after a night watch.

- Prior to departure or joining the vessel in transit, the crewmember will provide proof of financial solvency, in the form of cash, travellers cheques and or return plane tickets. The captain may request to hold the funds or tickets in the ship's strong box for safe keeping. Proof of health travel insurances and vaccinations will also be required.

- Each crewmember must produce a valid passport and other identification, which will not expire within six months of departure.

- The crewmember also agrees that the owners of *Maiatla* may take and use any photographs or video to be used in any manner the owners deem fit. This use may include magazine articles or in published books, displayed in a cruising blog or Facebook page. The crewmember also understands as a member of the crew, he/she may be depicted or characterized in literature in any books or magazine articles that may be written and published by the owners related to this voyage.

It is the crewmembers responsibility to inform the captain prior to departure of any medical condition or prescription medication they are on or conditions that may limit the crewmembers ability to perform his or her tasks. It is also the crewmembers responsibility to carry original doctor's prescriptions for all medications in possession of any crewmember that can be presented to foreign immigration officials.

(Don't assume just because a prescription drug is legal in Canada it is legal in other countries!)

I have read and agree to carry out the above Ship's Articles.

Signed: _____ Date: _____

Additional information for Crew

Use of the Head

The vessel's head (toilet) is connected directly to the ocean and improper use can result in the flooding of the vessel. Each crew member will be instructed in its use prior to its use. Printed instructions are also placed upon the bulkhead as a reminder. Only the provided toilet paper shall be placed in the bowl, along with what comes naturally. No foreign object, such as Q tips, paper towels or feminine hygiene products, shall be flushed. **Anyone** who plugs the toilet will be required to dismantle the unit to clear any obstruction. The captain will be happy to coach you through the operation as he has done it far too many times.

Recommend Personal Gear

- PFD c/w "pea-less" whistle and strobe light
- Best available/affordable high seas jacket and bib-pants (Helly Hansen, etc.), sea-boots, gloves, cowl
- Several peaked caps (ball caps, you'll lose one)
- Sunglasses, two pairs (same reason as above)
- Synthetic fleece vest/shirt/jacket/pants
- "Tilley"-type, quick wash/dry underwear
- Sleeping bag (knowing it will get foul and wet)
- Large Ziploc bags to keep underwear, socks, etc., dry
- Waterproof bag for valuables (wallet, passport, etc.) and your own "ditch bag"
- MP3 player/phone, reading material and journal
- A small day pack or belly pouch for shore excursions
- All should fit in one soft, sea bag. No rigid frame bags with wheels!

Self Quartermastery

- Individual packages of instant oatmeal, hot chocolate, soups and juice crystals (if desired)
- S/S thermos bottle and coffee mug (avoid glass or porcelain)
- Ginger snap cookies & ginger candies (known for anti-seasickness qualities)

Personal Medic Kit

- Seasick pills/potion
- Good medi-scissors, tweezers and magnifying glass
- Hot/cold compress, butterfly bandages, Elastoplast rolls
- Lip balm, skin lotion, after-shower talcum mixture
- Topical anesthetic pads

Other "Stuff"

- Binoculars, a cheap watch (Timex, leave any good ones at home) and a camera, alarm clock, flashlight & extra batteries
- Antiseptic hand soap & nail brush,
- Perhaps a few "trading goods" (use your imagination)

Upon Arrival at the Vessel

– Aside from the usual safety familiarization and with the skipper's permission, check all the rigging possible to familiarize yourself, check all pad eyes, shackles, shackle pins, winches, blocks, sail tracks and reefing gear—even fresh from the shipyard, pins & bolts can be the wrong size/material, lose or missing. Insist on practicing reefing and head-sail changes. A "shake-down" cruise in home waters is essential if possible.

– Make a diagram of all thru-hull fittings (where they are) and go find them—also rudder shaft fitting and propeller shaft fitting/stuffing box. FIND AND KNOW WHERE ALL THE HOLES IN THE BOAT ARE.

– Find and examine all hand-holds (and other fittings/fixtures that you may grab), especially around the galley and in the head, to ensure they will take your weight when being tossed about.

– Report ANYTHING to the skipper that doesn't "feel" right and GET RESOLUTION with him to allay any future doubts or determine a course of action, in advance, for those feelings.

Weird Stuff

– Do not present yourself or your abilities with any exaggeration but do emphasize any particular abilities or talents you have confidence in.

– Needless to say, privacy on any yacht is at a premium and in the tropics, nudity is not uncommon—this applies to both sexes and can be troublesome if not fully confronted. If you've got any "hang-ups" about either, ask and clear the air.

Additional Feedback

– Never have a rigid time schedule—the ways of the sea are not timely as weather, a great anchorage (or beach bar), breakdowns/repairs, etc., can eat into schedules. And trying to keep a schedule usually coincides with s#*t happening.

– You'll never have too much money or enough credit resources—just don't flaunt the amount or how to access your private stash. Yep, I've seldom met a sailor who cruised "under budget" or purposely missed the bargain of the century in some foreign port.

– Get fit and keep fit—the vessel will be constantly moving and so will muscles you never thought you had. Legs, arms, upper body and, believe it or not, some internal organs (your intestines are muscles, too). Therefore, bowel movements (or lack of them) aren't necessarily only affected by anxiety, diet and the sea's motion if you're trying to diagnose an uncomfortable feeling—usually tummies settle down after three or four days.

– Hydration—drinking water is something often overlooked when you're surrounded by the stuff. Make sure you drink enough, at least 3 litres/day, ideally 4+ litres. Aboard *Maiatla*, we have a 200 gallon a day watermaker, but the rule is to conserve water at all times. You will need the captain's permission to take a shower. At times he may insist!

– Attitude is EVERYTHING. Your new shipmates may include strangers with their own "baggage," ambitions and skills. Always look for the best in everyone and be prepared for the sharing of deepest secrets—and hearing the most outrageous lies/life stories—when huddled in the cockpit or under starry skies.

– Above all, especially for neophytes (and sailors with notoriously short memories), remember as romanticized as sailing is, you WILL find discomfort, fear and a hankering for terra firma at times. This will be offset by finding personal strength in challenging your surroundings, overcoming fears and, perhaps, falling hopelessly in love with the sea, its shores and our fragile, beautiful world.

– Finally, remember, the boat represents a large investment to the owners—as crew, treat it with respect.

Andrew & Janet Gunson, owners and masters of SV *Maiatla II*

"The lovely thing about cruising is that planning usually turns out to be of little use."
—Dom Degnon

Index

Made in the USA
Columbia, SC
03 June 2022

61281498R00230